Classroom Assessment and Educational Measurement

Classroom Assessment and Educational Measurement explores the ways in which the theory and practice of both educational measurement and the assessment of student learning in classroom settings mutually inform one another. Chapters by assessment and measurement experts consider the nature of classroom assessment information, from student achievement to affective and socio-emotional attributes; how teachers interpret and work with assessment results; and emerging issues in assessment such as digital technologies and diversity/inclusion.

This book uniquely considers the limitations of applying large-scale educational measurement theory to classroom assessment and the adaptations necessary to make this transfer useful. Researchers, graduate students, industry professionals, and policymakers will come away with an essential understanding of how the classroom assessment context is essential to broadening contemporary educational measurement perspectives.

Susan M. Brookhart is Professor Emerita in the School of Education at Duquesne University, USA, and an independent educational consultant.

James H. McMillan is Professor in the Department of Foundations of Education in the School of Education at Virginia Commonwealth University, USA.

The NCME Applications of Educational Measurement and Assessment Book Series

Editorial Board:

Technology and Testing: Improving Educational and Psychological Measurement
Edited by Fritz Drasgow

Meeting the Challenges to Measurement in an Era of Accountability
Edited by Henry Braun

Fairness in Educational Assessment and Measurement
Edited by Neil J. Dorans and Linda L. Cook

Testing in the Professions: Credentialing Policies and Practice
Edited by Susan Davis-Becker and Chad W. Buckendahl

Validation of Score Meaning for the Next Generation of Assessments: The Use of Response Processes
Edited by Kadriye Ercikan and James W. Pellegrino

Preparing Students for College and Careers: Theory, Measurement, and Educational Practice
Edited by Katie Larsen McClarty, Krista D. Mattern, and Matthew N. Gaertner

Score Reporting Research and Applications
Edited by Diego Zapata-Rivera

Classroom Assessment and Educational Measurement
Edited by Susan M. Brookhart and James H. McMillan

For more information about this series, please visit: www.routledge.com/NCME-APPLICATIONS-OF-EDUCATIONAL-MEASUREMENT-AND-ASSESSMENT/book-series/NCME

Classroom Assessment and Educational Measurement

Edited by Susan M. Brookhart and James H. McMillan

Routledge
Taylor & Francis Group

NEW YORK AND LONDON

First published 2020
by Routledge
52 Vanderbilt Avenue, New York, NY 10017

and by Routledge
2 Park Square, Milton Park, Abingdon, Oxon, OX14 4RN

Routledge is an imprint of the Taylor & Francis Group, an informa business

© 2020 Taylor & Francis

Library of Congress Cataloging-in-Publication Data
A catalog record for this title has been requested

ISBN: 978-1-138-58004-6 (hbk)
ISBN: 978-1-138-58005-3 (pbk)
ISBN: 978-0-429-50753-3 (ebk)

Typeset in Minion Pro
by Swales & Willis Ltd, Exeter Devon, UK

Contents

Contributors   vii

Introduction   1
SUSAN M. BROOKHART AND JAMES H. MCMILLAN

PART I: CLASSROOM ASSESSMENT INFORMATION   9

1. Perspectives on the Validity of Classroom
   Assessments   11
   MICHAEL T. KANE AND SASKIA WOOLS

2. Cognitive Diagnosis Is Not Enough: The Challenge
   of Measuring Learning with Classroom Assessments   27
   JACQUELINE P. LEIGHTON

3. Language in Practice: A Mediator of Valid Interpretations
   of Information Generated by Classroom Assessments
   among Linguistically and Culturally Diverse Students   46
   ALISON L. BAILEY AND RICHARD DURÁN

4. Feedback and Measurement   63
   SUSAN M. BROOKHART

5. Discussion of Part I: Assessment Information
   in Context   79
   JAMES H. MCMILLAN

PART II: THE USE OF CLASSROOM ASSESSMENT INFORMATION TO ENHANCE LEARNING ... 95

6. Guidance in the *Standards* for Classroom Assessment: Useful or Irrelevant? ... 97

    STEVE FERRARA, KRISTEN MAXEY-MOORE, AND SUSAN M. BROOKHART

7. Defining Trustworthiness for Teachers' Multiple Uses of Classroom Assessment Results ... 120

    ALICIA C. ALONZO

8. Learning Progressions and Embedded Assessment ... 146

    DEREK C. BRIGGS AND ERIN MARIE FURTAK

9. The Role of Technology-Enhanced Self- and Peer Assessment in Formative Assessment ... 170

    E. CAROLINE WYLIE AND CHRISTINE J. LYON

10. Discussion of Part II: Should "Measurement" Have a Role in Teacher Learning about Classroom Assessment? ... 192

    LORRIE A. SHEPARD

PART III: EMERGING ISSUES IN CLASSROOM ASSESSMENT ... 207

11. Towards Measures of Different and Useful Aspects of Schooling: Why Schools Need Both Teacher-Assigned Grades and Standardized Assessments ... 209

    ALEX J. BOWERS

12. Digital Technologies: Supporting and Advancing Assessment Practices in the Classroom ... 224

    MICHAEL RUSSELL

13. Fairness in Classroom Assessment ... 243

    JOAN HERMAN AND LINDA COOK

14. Discussion of Part III: Emerging Issues in Classroom Assessment ... 265

    MARK WILSON

Index ... 276

Contributors

Alicia C. Alonzo is associate professor in the Department of Teacher Education at Michigan State University. Much of her work concerns how assessment—broadly construed—may influence the teaching and learning that occurs in science classrooms. She received a 2014 Presidential Early Career Award for Scientists and Engineers and was selected as a Kavli Fellow of the National Academy of Sciences in 2018.

Alison L. Bailey is Professor in the Department of Education, University of California, Los Angeles. She is a developmental psycholinguist working on issues germane to children's linguistic, social, and educational development. Dr. Bailey is a member of the National Assessment of Educational Progress (NAEP) Standing Committee on Reading, the National Council on Measurement in Education (NCME) President's Task Force on Classroom Assessment, and the National Academy of Sciences' Consensus Committee on English Learners in the STEM Disciplines.

Alex J. Bowers is an associate professor of Education Leadership at Teachers College, Columbia University. His research interests include organizational-level data analytics, organizational behavior, school and district leadership, data-driven decision-making, high school dropouts and completion, educational assessment and accountability, education technology, and school facilities financing.

Derek C. Briggs is a professor of quantitative methods and policy analysis and chair of the Research and Evaluation Methodology program at the University of Colorado Boulder. He is also the director of the Center for Assessment Design Research and Evaluation (CADRE). Dr. Briggs's research agenda focuses upon building sound methodological approaches for the measurement and evaluation of growth in student learning.

Susan M. Brookhart is Professor Emerita in the School of Education at Duquesne University. Her interests include the role of both formative and summative classroom assessment in student motivation and achievement, the connection between classroom assessment and large-scale assessment, and grading. Recent publications and current projects focus on feedback, assessment and the co-regulation of learning, and assessment to inform teaching and learning.

Linda Cook is retired from Educational Testing Service as Vice President of Assessment. She remains professionally active and is currently chair of the Management Committee for the Standards for Educational and Psychological Tests. Her research interests include fairness in testing and comparability of assessment scores.

Richard Durán is Professor in the Gevirtz Graduate School of Education, University of California, Santa Barbara. He conducts research on literacy, learning, and assessment in classroom and community settings from learning science and sociocultural perspectives with special attention to multilingual youths. He is a member of the NAEP Validity Studies Panel and a recent National Academy of Science, Engineering, and Medicine consensus committee issuing the 2017 report *Promoting the Educational Success of Children and Youth Learning English: Promising Futures*.

Steve Ferrara is a Senior Advisor for Measurement Solutions at Measured Progress. His focus areas include classroom assessment practices and design, analysis, standard setting, and validation for formative, summative, alternate, and language proficiency assessments.

Erin Marie Furtak is Associate Dean of Faculty and Professor of STEM Education in the School of Education at the University of Colorado Boulder. Her research investigates the ways that secondary science teachers design and enact formative assessments, how this process informs teachers' learning, and in turn how improvements in teachers' formative assessment practice over time relates to student achievement. She currently directs a long-term research–practice partnership, funded by the National Science Foundation and the Spencer Foundation, with a large, economically, culturally, linguistically, and ethnically diverse school district focused on supporting high school teachers' classroom assessment practices.

Joan Herman is Director Emerita at UCLA's National Center for Research on Evaluation, Standards, and Student Testing (CRESST). Her research has explored the design and use of assessment to support accountability and improvement, and has recently focused on teachers' formative assessment practices, the assessment of deeper learning, and validity and fairness applications of the *Standards for Educational and Psychological Testing*.

Michael T. Kane is the Messick Chair at the Educational Testing Service. His main areas of research are validity theory, generalizability theory, and standard setting.

Jacqueline P. Leighton is Professor of School and Clinical Child Psychology at the University of Alberta. Dr. Leighton's research focuses on the assessment of learning, academic achievement, and emotional well-being.

Christine J. Lyon is a lead research project manager at Educational Testing Service. She focuses her research on supporting and evaluating formative assessment in K-12 classrooms with the goal of improving learning and teaching. She is currently co-PI of an IES-funded project that is examining peer-to-peer classroom observations focused on formative assessment and the relationship between observations, feedback, and changes to practice.

James H. McMillan is professor in the Department of Foundations of Education at Virginia Commonwealth University. Dr. McMillan has taught educational psychology, research methods, and assessment for over 30 years, and has published widely in classroom assessment. His current research is focused on student perceptions of assessment.

Kristen Maxey-Moore is Section Chief of Test Development at the North Carolina Department of Public Instruction. She oversees the development of all statewide assessments for evaluative and interim purposes and focuses on building assessment literacy across the state.

Michael Russell is Professor in the Department of Measurement, Evaluation, Statistics, and Assessment, Lynch School of Education, Boston College. Michael's research focuses on technology-based assessment, accessible assessment, large-scale test development, validity theory, and the intersection of race and quantitative methodology.

Lorrie A. Shepard is University Distinguished Professor in the School of Education at the University of Colorado Boulder. Her research focuses on psychometrics and the use and misuse of tests in education settings. Most cited are her contributions to validity theory, standard setting, bias detection, the effects of high-stakes accountability testing, and the integration of learning theory with classroom formative assessment.

Mark Wilson is a professor of education at the University of California, Berkeley, and also at the University of Melbourne. He teaches courses on measurement in the social sciences, multidimensional measurement, and applied statistics. His research focuses on the development of sound frameworks for measurement, new statistical models, instruments to measure new constructs, and on the philosophy of measurement.

Saskia Wools is manager of CitoLab at Cito. At this Dutch institute for educational measurement, she is responsible for research and innovation in the area of educational assessments. Her research focuses specifically on validity and validation within this field.

E. Caroline Wylie is a Research Director at Educational Testing Service. Her current research centers on issues around balanced assessment systems, with a focus on the use of formative assessment to improve classroom teaching and learning. She is currently PI of an IES-funded project that is examining peer-to-peer classroom observations focused on formative assessment and the relationship between observations, feedback, and changes to practice.

Introduction

Susan M. Brookhart and James H. McMillan

The mission of the National Council on Measurement in Education (NCME) is "To advance the science and practice of measurement in education." This mission has been met primarily through the development and use of large-scale summative assessment. With some notable exceptions (e.g., Ebel, 1965; Stiggins, 2014), classroom assessment has received much less attention. The core *purpose* of educational measurement is to support student learning. In a series of recent articles, papers, and other initiatives, NCME has emphasized that this purpose may be best met with effective classroom assessment that provides essential information teachers and students can use to improve learning, as well as other educational outcomes. As Wilson (2018) has recommended, NCME needs to "rebalance their focus so that classroom assessments are seen as being at least as important as large-scale assessments" (p. 5). Since the most important agents in learning are the student, the teacher, and other school-based professionals, the position is that classroom assessment is the type of measurement activity closest to student learning, with the best opportunities to improve student proficiency.

Purpose and Organization of This Volume

As exemplified by the creation of the NCME Classroom Assessment Task Force, NCME has recognized the need to better understand how classroom assessment perspectives can inform educational measurement, and how educational measurement perspectives can inform classroom assessment. The purpose of this volume is to explore this two-way influence. The volume examines how educational measurement concepts, both theoretical and practical, function in classroom assessment of student learning, and also explores how the classroom assessment context informs and enriches educational measurement science and practice. For a long time, the nature and quality of classroom assessment has been evaluated through the lens of measurement theory. Recently, however, scholars have observed that measurement theory developed for large-scale assessment, with its underlying focus on test-takers as examinees, may not always apply straightforwardly to classroom assessment, with its underlying focus on students as learners (Brookhart, 2003; McMillan, 2013; Shepard, 2006).

Organization of the Volume

The chapters in this volume are divided into three parts. Within each part, some chapters primarily look at classroom assessment through the lens of measurement; others examine measurement through the lens of classroom assessment. Each part ends with a discussion that pulls chapter themes together in light of the purpose of the volume—expanding understanding of the connections between classroom assessment and educational measurement.

The first part explores and describes the nature of classroom assessment information, using the term "information" to encompass both measures (e.g., classroom test scores) and qualitative interpretations of classroom learning evidence (e.g., judgments of students' thinking processes as they answer questions). Part I addresses classroom assessment information with questions such as: What constructs underlie the information students and teachers gather in classroom assessment? What does the information itself look like? How is the information used for providing feedback? How should validity be evaluated? To what extent should classroom assessment include social and emotional measures? How does language diversity affect the accuracy and validity of assessment information?

The second part explores the use of classroom information to support learning, arguably the most important purpose of classroom assessment information. Part II deals with issues such as how teachers understand the meaning and quality of the assessment evidence to make educational decisions, how educators can reclaim the concept of assessment as something that is embedded within the curricular activities of teachers and students, and how students and teachers participate together in noticing and interpreting evidence of learning.

The third part explores selected emerging issues in the field of classroom assessment, including how grades help define and describe what "school learning" means, how digital technologies are changing the kind of information available in the classroom, and how issues of diversity, equity, and inclusion affect classroom assessment information and its use for learning.

Selection of Chapters and Authors

The editors selected chapter authors who are doing new work in the space between classroom assessment and educational measurement, so that the book becomes a contribution toward accomplishing the goals of the Classroom Assessment Task Force charter and a scholarly source of information and ideas for NCME members and others to advance classroom assessment and educational measurement. Authors were given the theme and purpose of the volume—the mutual influence of classroom assessment and educational measurement science and practice—and framed their work as a contribution to this theme.

The editors were aided by a group of very capable reviewers, selected for their scholarship in the respective areas each chapter addressed. The editors wish to express sincere gratitude to them: Elaine Allensworth, University of Chicago Consortium on School Research; Heidi Andrade, SUNY Albany; Randy Bennett, Educational Testing Service; Sarah Bonner, Hunter College CUNY; Neil Dorans, Educational Testing Service; Amelia Gotwals, Michigan State University; Margaret Heritage, UCLA; Leslie Keng, Center for Assessment; Anthony Nitko, University of Pittsburgh; Barbara Plake, University of Nebraska-Lincoln; Maria Araceli Ruiz-Primo, Stanford University; Lorrie Shepard, University of Colorado Boulder; Stephanie Smith Budhai, Neumann University; Guillermo Solano-Flores, Stanford University; and Robin Tierney, Research-for-Learning.

As the chapters came together, the editors realized that in addition to the two official purposes of the volume concerning how classroom assessment science and practice enriches measurement science and practice, and vice versa, a third issue arose, namely the identity of classroom assessment. Unlike some related terms that have generally accepted definitions (e.g., measurement, formative assessment, feedback), the domain of classroom assessment does not have a generally agreed upon definition. Indeed, the authors of chapters in this book do not agree on what constitutes classroom assessment. Accordingly, the next three sections of this introduction describe how this book helps readers begin to think about three questions, not just two: What is classroom assessment? What is the role of the measurement community in classroom practice? How does the study of classroom assessment broaden and enrich measurement theory and practice?

What Is Classroom Assessment?

The editors began this book project using McMillan's (2013) definition of classroom assessment. This definition is often the one that is cited when a definition of classroom assessment is needed, as opposed to, for example, specific definitions of formative assessment or feedback:

> CA [classroom assessment] is a broad and evolving conceptualization of a process that teachers and students use in collecting, evaluating, and using evidence of student learning for a variety of purposes, including diagnosing student strengths and weaknesses, monitoring student progress toward meeting desired levels of proficiency, assigning grades, and providing feedback to parents. That is, CA is a tool teachers use to gather relevant data and information to make well-supported inferences about what students know, understand, and can do (Shavelson & Towne, 2002), as well as a vehicle through which student learning and motivation are enhanced. CA enhances teachers' judgments about student competence by providing reasoned evidence in a variety of forms gathered at different times. It is distinguished from large-scale or standardized, whether standards-based, personality, aptitude, or benchmark- or interim-type tests. It is locally controlled and consists of a broad range of measures, including both structured techniques such as tests, papers, student self-assessment, reports, and portfolios, as well as informal ways of collecting evidence, including anecdotal observation and spontaneous questioning of students. It is more than mere measurement or quantification of student performance. CA connects learning targets to effective assessment practices teachers use in their classrooms to monitor and improve student learning. When CA is integrated with and related to learning, motivation, and curriculum it both educates students and improves their learning.
>
> (McMillan, 2013, p. 4)

The editors believed that this definition was specific enough to serve as a guiding conceptualization for the chapters in this volume and for the field more broadly. However, chapter authors draw the line between classroom assessment and large-scale assessment in different places. The issues seem to center around McMillan's concept of "locally controlled."

One approach sees local control in teachers' *use* of assessment for classroom learning. The argument is that if teachers use assessment in the classroom, for purposes of student learning, then it's classroom assessment. By this reasoning, assessments developed with large-scale methods but packaged for teachers to use count as classroom assessment, even though they share some characteristics with large-scale assessment (e.g., reliability over forms and occasions, score meaning that is generalizable across classroom contexts, the use of item response theory or other large-sample modeling or scaling algorithms). Authors whose chapters are consistent with this approach include Alonzo, Briggs and Furtak, Russell, and Wilson. The author team of Ferrara, Maxey-Moore, and Brookhart disagree among themselves, with at least one taking this view and one taking the next view.

Another approach sees local control in teachers' creation or selection of the assessment method as well as its use. By this reasoning, there are two main types of classroom assessment: (1) formative assessment during learning, which is a process and function more than a set of methods or tools (Wiliam, 2010), is classroom assessment; and (2) grading or classroom summative assessment (Brookhart, 2013), both the act of assigning grades to individual assessments and the act of combining them into composite report card grades, is classroom assessment. Anything beyond these two types of assessment, even if carried out by teachers in classrooms, is not classroom assessment. For example, teachers usually administer the annual state accountability test to their students, as well as benchmark and common assessments. These would not be considered classroom assessment. Authors whose chapters are consistent with this approach include Bailey and Durán, Bowers, Herman and Cook, Kane and Wools, Leighton, McMillan, Shepard, Wylie and Lyon, and at least one of the Ferrara, Maxey-Moore, and Brookhart team.

One source of tension in the definition of classroom assessment is the use of technology. Technology allows assessment tasks intended to be used in classroom lessons to be designed, developed, and piloted at research centers, and made available for classroom use via computer. These assessments are developed using traditional large-scale psychometrics because they need to be useful across classroom contexts. Thus, they have a bit of a "neither fish nor fowl" aspect: the development and validation uses large-scale methods, but the use is classroom-focused.

Another source of tension seems to be what Ferrara, Maxey-Moore, and Brookhart (this volume) call "accountability creep." The current accountability climate, at least in the United States, has brought large-scale interim and benchmark tests into teachers' classrooms whether they want them there or not. District policies and administrator direction require that teachers use the results for instructional decisions, again whether they want to do this or not. In fact, some research suggests that teachers use these tests most for grouping or for procedural instructional responses, not for understanding and teaching for students' conceptual understanding (Oláh, Lawrence, & Riggan, 2010). For many teachers, decision-making about their classroom assessments reflects tension between what teachers need to do to improve learning and the influence and pressure of high-stakes accountability testing. Accountability pressures also explain the recent rise in the use of the SLO process in schools, although unlike interim and benchmark tests the main object of inference here is teacher competence.

The editors view these recent sources of tension in defining classroom assessment as distinctly different. Technology will only continue to be more and more prevalent for all types of assessment. Educators would do well to harness it, as educators harnessed previous new technologies such as the printing press and the ballpoint pen, to use for student learning. The rise of accountability measures is a sociocultural phenomenon, one that is influenced by political and educational policy changes, as, for example, the "minimum competency tests" of the 1970s rose in prominence and then declined. Thus, unlike technology, accountability pressure may not continue unabated, but may be amenable to change.

Since 2013, much literature and attention to classroom assessment suggests that a revision in how classroom assessment is defined is appropriate. Here is our revised definition:

> Classroom assessment is a process that teachers and students use in collecting, evaluating, and using evidence of student learning for a variety of purposes, including diagnosing student strengths and weaknesses, monitoring student progress toward meeting desired levels of proficiency, assigning grades, providing feedback to students and parents, and enhancing student learning and motivation. Classroom assessment includes both qualitative understandings and expressions of student thinking and quantitative measures of student learning, as long as these are collected, interpreted, and used in the context of individual classroom learning communities. Classroom assessment instruments may be designed by the teacher or may be externally designed and selected by the teacher for

a particular purpose (e.g., a unit test in a textbook, or a set of embedded questions in a computer-based learning program). However, they must be locally controlled by the teacher who sets the purpose, and not an external agent, as is the case for interim/benchmark assessments.

What Is the Role of the Measurement Community in Classroom Practice?

Given this definition of classroom assessment, a collaborative model that combines measurement with what is needed to improve student learning in specific contexts seems reasonable. Measurement experts are very proficient at operationalizing some but not all aspects of the classroom assessment enterprise as defined above. More specifically, measurement expertise provides technical knowledge about such critical constructs as validity, reliability, and fairness, and has much to offer concerning the design, collection, and interpretation of assessment information so that student proficiency is accurately measured and reported. Classroom teachers and building and district administrators are experts in understanding the local context, especially the learning environments in a district, the taught curriculum (as differentiated from the written curriculum), and the local policy context. At the most important level, individual classrooms, teachers are experts about the nature of their students, content knowledge, and what is needed to move students forward in learning and other outcomes (e.g., motivation, social skills, self-efficacy).

Next Steps for Measurement Professionals

Some examples of collaboration between measurement experts and local educators are contained in several chapters in this volume. For example, Wylie and Lyon describe the GENIUs project, where external developers produced a technology-based feedback system. In another example, Briggs and Furtak describe the Aspire project, a research–practice partnership between a university and a district. Careful reading of both of these examples shows that neither project uses a traditional research/practice model, where the researchers as measurement specialists provide materials and practitioners implement them. Rather, in both cases, the line is blurred. Researchers' project development is informed by local educators, and local educators' understanding of results is informed by research partners.

Next Steps for Measurement Theory

This book also contains examples that support potential shifts or expansions in measurement theory. Here, contemplating the nature of classroom assessment that improves student learning suggests that some level of refinement of measurement theory may contribute to an increased impact of measurement on classroom practices and student outcomes. Three of the chapters (Alonzo, Kane & Wools, McMillan) describe changes in thinking about validity as applied to classroom assessment. These chapters illustrate this book's theme of mutual influence. Kane and Wools review validation in measurement theory and practice, and argue for a different application of validation principles in the classroom. Alonzo begins with the assessment purposes classroom teachers must accomplish, and reasons from there to the trustworthiness principles that will best serve them. Both are informed by the authors' understanding of validity as the measurement community thinks about it as well as an understanding of classroom assessment purposes as currently practiced. All three of the chapters (Alonzo, Kane & Wools, McMillan) lift up the contextualized nature of information about learning in the classroom and the importance of assessment information's consequences for learning as defining features of information quality.

More broadly, these three chapters show that validity theory as currently espoused in the measurement field has room for growth. Expansion may not only lead to development in validity theory for classroom assessment, but also to a need for consideration of validity theory in other contexts (e.g., with digital tools, with other unstandardized assessment applications).

Two chapters (Ferrara, Maxey-Moore, & Brookhart; Herman & Cook) show that the *Standards for Educational and Psychological Testing* may have broader applications than originally intended. Again, appropriate next steps for measurement theory are seen as expansion from a one-size-fits-all theory that privileges standardization to a multilayered theory that adapts to a broad array of contexts.

How Does the Study of Classroom Assessment Enrich Measurement Theory and Practice?

Following the argument that the influence between measurement and classroom assessment should be mutual—and doing so will enhance and expand both fields—the final question for this volume is: How does the study of classroom assessment enrich measurement theory and practice? The editors believe that broadened thinking about validity, showing mutual influences from the measurement community and from classroom assessment, as discussed above, are the most profound examples this volume contributes to answering that question. In addition, several of the chapters bring conceptualizations of classroom assessment to bear on measurement theory and practice.

Next Steps for Classroom Assessment Theory

Three of the chapters address the general question: What is learning? An underlying assumption in each is that learning that is assessed with current, conventional measures that focus on student proficiency needs to be broadened, both because of student and contextual differences as well as the connections between cognitive proficiency and dispositions such as self-regulation, belonging, self-efficacy, and identity (Shepard, Penuel, & Pellegrino, 2018). This assumption is contrary to the more conventional measurement approach that promotes invariance of achievement measures over forms, occasions, and contexts. Bailey and Durán (this volume) describe how classroom performance assessments, embedded in students' language and learning context, may provide more valid assessments of learning, especially for culturally diverse learners. Leighton (this volume) suggests that current measures of learning typically ignore the social-emotional context of learning, and that emotional and social factors need to be included in a comprehensive conceptualization of classroom assessment. Bowers (this volume) suggests that grades communicate a multidimensional assessment of school learning. He contends that this may be more useful than a report of subject matter proficiency largely redundant to standardized achievement because they reflect contextual factors as well as other important schooling outcomes.

Next Steps for Classroom Assessment Professionals

Taken together, chapter authors suggest that classroom assessment practitioners need to be partners with measurement specialists in the development of assessment theory that promotes student learning, as well as in applying and expanding well-researched measurement principles to classroom contexts. This is particularly relevant for validity, reliability/precision, and fairness. The realities of classroom assessment, especially the focus on context and the purpose of improving learning, can help conventional measurement theorists and practitioners provide more useful measures. Likewise, measurement theory can benefit those who work in classroom assessment. Much excellent work in test bias, for example, is instructive for developing classroom assessments that take account of students' cultural and linguistic differences. Sources of error inherent in theoretical descriptions of reliability/precision offer much guidance to teachers to know how to appropriately determine accuracy. Classroom assessment practitioners also have a role in helping to develop the classroom assessment literacy of their counterparts in the large-scale measurement community.

Conclusion

This book begins what the editors hope will be a journey of mutual influence between the two fields of measurement and classroom assessment. The book shows that these are closely related fields of study and practice, especially in their major goal of yielding theoretically sound and practically actionable information about student learning and motivation. To this end, the science and practice of each field has the potential to improve the science and practice of the other.

References

Brookhart, S. M. (2003). Developing measurement theory for classroom assessment purposes and uses. *Educational Measurement: Issues and Practice, 22*(4), 5–12.

Brookhart, S. M. (2013). Grading. In J. H. McMillan (Ed.), *SAGE handbook of research on classroom assessment* (pp. 257–271). Los Angeles, CA: SAGE.

Ebel, R. L. (1965). *Measuring educational achievement.* Englewood Cliffs, NJ: Prentice Hall.

McMillan, J. H. (2013). Why we need research on classroom assessment. In J. H. McMillan (Ed.), *SAGE handbook of research on classroom assessment* (pp. 3–16). Los Angeles, CA: SAGE.

Oláh, L. N., Lawrence, N. R., & Riggan, M. (2010). Learning to learn from benchmark assessment data: How teachers analyze results. *Peabody Journal of Education, 85*, 226–245.

Shavelson, R. J., & Towne, L. (Eds.). (2002). *Scientific research in education.* Washington, DC: National Academy Press.

Shepard, L. A. (2006). Classroom assessment. In R. L. Brennan (Ed.), *Educational measurement* (4th ed., pp. 623–646). Westport, CT: Praeger.

Shepard, L. A., Penuel, W. R., & Pellegrino, J. W. (2018). Using learning and motivation theories to coherently link formative assessment, grading practices, and large-scale assessment. *Educational Measurement: Issues and Practice, 37*(1), 21–34.

Stiggins, R. (2014). *Revolutionize assessment.* Thousand Oaks, CA: Corwin.

Wiliam, D. (2010). An integrative summary of the research literature and implications for a new theory of formative assessment. In H. L. Andrade & G. J. Cizek (Eds.), *Handbook of formative assessment* (pp. 18–40). New York: Routledge.

Wilson, M. (2018). Making measurement important for education: The crucial role of classroom assessment. *Educational Measurement: Issues and Practice, 37*(1), 5–20.

Part I
Classroom Assessment Information

Perspectives on the Validity of Classroom Assessments

Michael T. Kane and Saskia Wools

This chapter examines how some general principles of validity theory might apply to classroom assessment. In particular, we consider two perspectives on the evaluation of classroom assessments, a functional perspective and a measurement perspective, and we consider how these two perspectives play out in classroom assessments. We suggest that the functional perspective does and should play a larger role in classroom assessment than the measurement perspective.

For all assessments, validity is an important concern (American Educational Research Association [AERA], American Psychological Association [APA], & National Council on Measurement in Education [NCME], 2014). The concept of validity has been developed mainly in the context of summative high-stakes testing, but we will discuss validity for classroom assessment and emphasize the evidence needed for the validation of assessments in this context.

We define validity in terms of the plausibility and appropriateness of the interpretations and uses of assessment results, and therefore validity depends on the requirements inherent in these interpretations and uses. A systematic and effective approach to validation involves three activities: the development of a clear sense of the proposed interpretation and uses of the assessment results; the development (or identification) of an assessment that would be expected to support the intended interpretation and uses; and an evaluation of how well the assessment supports the interpretation and uses.

Cronbach (1988) described two perspectives on the validity of assessments, a measurement perspective and a functional perspective, and we make use of both of these perspectives in evaluating the validity of classroom assessments. The *measurement perspective* focuses on the accuracy and precision of scores as measures of some construct, and the *functional perspective* focuses on how well the assessment serves its intended purposes. The measurement perspective and the functional perspective are both relevant to the validation of all assessments, but they focus on different evaluative criteria. We will argue that for classroom assessment, the functional perspective is of central concern, and the measurement perspective plays a supporting role.

We define classroom assessment broadly as involving the collection of information from a variety of sources, with the intention of promoting effective teaching and learning. Classroom assessments take a variety of forms, such as teacher observations of the students in various contexts, interactions with students, quizzes, tests, assignments, and projects. This variety causes classroom assessments to be quite varied in their levels of standardization and formality, but it provides very rich sources of information on student performance, skills, and achievement. Classroom assessments also serve a variety of purposes (e.g., monitoring student progress, diagnosing gaps and problems in learning, motivating students, and informing parents and others about student performance and progress). The main users of these assessments are teachers and students.

The validity of classroom assessments will depend mainly on how well they support the intended uses of the assessment results by teachers and students. Although all potential uses of classroom assessments might be informative to discuss, in this chapter we will focus on the use of the results by teachers for providing feedback to students, evaluating student competencies on particular tasks and over content domains, and diagnosing students' strengths and weaknesses.

When validity is studied in the context of large-scale high-stakes tests, the technical, or psychometric, characteristics of the tests play a central role. In these high-stakes contexts, those characteristics include, for example, standardization, consistency, and fairness (Cronbach, 1988). Since the results from these standardized tests are used for high-stakes decisions that extend well beyond the context in which the assessment took place, standardization and empirical evidence for consistency over contexts serve an important function in supporting trust in the processes being employed and in the trustworthiness of the results (Porter, 2003).

In a classroom, assessment-based decisions generally involve less far-reaching inferences. Rather, the results are interpreted and used locally. The results need to be practical and useful in fulfilling the main goal of classroom assessment: promoting effective teaching and learning. These decisions are generally less high-stakes than those based on standardized test results, but this does not imply that technical characteristics become irrelevant. An inaccurate conclusion about a student's ability might not be catastrophic, but it is not likely to be helpful in planning future instruction, and therefore in supporting learning. For classroom assessments, a functional perspective that focuses on how well the assessment promotes learning by improving the quality of instruction is the central concern, and measurement characteristics are of concern mainly in terms of their impact on the effectiveness of the assessment in supporting teaching and learning.

The bottom line in validating classroom assessments (as in all assessments) is to identify the qualities that the assessment results need to have, given their particular interpretations and uses in the context at hand, and then to examine whether the assessment results meet these requirements.

The next section outlines an argument-based approach to validation, and the following section describes the functional and measurement perspectives on validation. The two perspectives are complementary in that each focuses on characteristics that are necessary for an effective assessment, but the relative importance of the two perspectives in evaluating an assessment will vary depending on the goals and contexts of the assessment. In the third section, we describe some uses of classroom assessments and examine how these assessments might be evaluated in terms of interpretations and uses and the two perspectives. We conclude that the functional perspective should be primary in classroom assessment, with the measurement perspective playing a supporting role in this context.

Argument-Based Approach to Validation

As indicated earlier, the validity of assessment interpretations and uses depends on the plausibility of the interpretation and the appropriateness of the uses. A natural approach to validation is to specify the interpretation and use, develop (or identify) an assessment program that would be expected to meet the specified requirements, and then evaluate how well the interpretations and uses are justified. Validation is most often associated with the last of these three steps, but in fact it depends critically on all three steps.

The argument-based approach to validation (Cronbach, 1988; Crooks, Kane, & Cohen, 1996; House, 1980; Kane, 2006, 2013; Shepard, 1993) provides a general framework for specifying and validating interpretations and uses of assessment results. If we are going to make claims and base decisions on assessment results, these claims and decisions should be well founded (AERA et al., 2014; Messick, 1989).

A relatively simple and effective way to specify proposed interpretation and uses of the assessment results is to develop an *interpretation/use argument* (*IUA*) that lays out the reasoning leading from observed assessment performances to the claims being made. The general idea is to identify the inferences and assumptions inherent in the interpretations and uses of the assessment results.

The argument-based approach is contingent in the sense that the structure of the validity argument and the conclusions reached about validity depend on the structure and content of the IUA. For modest interpretations that do not go much beyond the observed performances, the IUA will be modest, including few inferences and assumptions; for ambitious interpretations (involving broad generalizations, constructs, or predictions), the IUA will require strong inferences and supporting assumptions. If the IUA is found wanting, because it lacks coherence and completeness or because the evidence does not support some of its inferences and assumptions, the interpretation and use would not be accepted as valid. If the IUA is coherent and complete, and its inferences and assumptions are adequately supported, the proposed interpretation and uses can be considered valid. The inferences based on classroom assessments tend to be local and limited, and therefore do not require strong assumptions.

Interpretation/Use Arguments (IUAs)

The IUA is to provide an explicit statement of the sequence or network of inferences and supporting assumption that gets us from the observed performances to the claims based on these performances. The inferences are supported by *warrants*, which are general rules for making claims of a certain kind based on certain kinds of data. Warrants are based on assumptions and generally require *backing*, or support. For example, in drawing conclusions about a student's level of competence in a domain on the basis of a sample of performances, we rely on a warrant that says that such generalizations are reasonable, and this warrant can be backed by evidence indicating that the sample is large enough and representative enough to support the generalization. The IUA would consist of a sequence or network of such inferences leading from the assessment results to the conclusions and decisions based on these performances.

The IUA provides a general framework for drawing inferences based on assessment results, and thereby for interpreting and using the assessment results for individual students. Although they may not be explicitly mentioned in discussing the results, the warrants for various inferences are integral parts of the IUA. Assuming that the warrants employed in the IUA are supported by appropriate evidence, the IUA provides justification for claims and decisions based on assessment results.

Validity Arguments

The *validity argument* provides an overall appraisal of the IUA, and thereby of the proposed interpretation and uses of the assessment results. It depends on the scope and content of the IUA, which specifies the inferences and assumptions that need to be evaluated. A simple interpretation in terms of skill in performing a particular kind of task (e.g., solving two-digit addition problems presented horizontally, such as "23 + 46 = . . .") would focus on the adequacy of sampling of this type of task as a basis for deciding whether students can solve this kind of problem. Assessments of more broadly defined domains of skill would typically require more evidence and more kinds of evidence.

The validity argument starts with a critical review of the IUA, with particular attention given to identifying the most questionable inferences and assumptions. Many assumptions may be accepted without much discussion. Some assumptions may be evaluated in terms of the appropriateness of the procedures used (e.g., the relevance of observed performances to the skill of interest, the size of the sample of observations). Some assumptions (e.g., that the students were motivated to perform well) may be based on experience and/or observations made during the assessment.

In order to make a strong case for an interpretation or use of assessment results, the validity argument has to provide backing for the IUA as a whole, and particularly for its most questionable inferences and assumptions. Serious doubts about any inference or assumption can raise questions about the IUA as a whole. Therefore, the IUA needs to be understood in enough detail so that the inferences and assumptions on which it depends can be identified and evaluated. A validity argument is never definitive because we cannot exhaustively evaluate all of the IUA, and therefore the most doubtful parts of the argument should get the most attention. As Cronbach (1980) suggested, "The job of validation is not to support an interpretation, but to find out what might be wrong with it. A proposition deserves some degree of trust only when it has survived serious attempts to falsify it" (p. 103). The question is whether the interpretation and use of the assessment results makes sense, given all of the evidence.

Note that it is not necessary to be concerned about assumptions that are not included in the IUA. For example, if the proposed interpretation and use assumes that the attribute being assessed would not vary much over extended periods of time, we would be concerned about the extent to which the performances are stable over time. But if the characteristics being assessed are expected to vary (e.g., due to learning), stability would not be required, and it might even constitute evidence against the validity (the instructional sensitivity) of the assessment.

The basic ideas guiding the argument-based approach is that we should be clear about the reasoning that is to take us from observed student performances to conclusions about the student, and that we should critically evaluate this reasoning and its embedded assumptions.

Perspectives on Assessment

Assessments can be evaluated from multiple perspectives, and it is generally helpful to consider the evaluative criteria associated with different perspectives (Cronbach, 1988: Dorans, 2012; Holland, 1994). Different perspectives focus on different aspects of interpretation and use, and therefore on different criteria for evaluating validity. The perspectives are not mutually exclusive, and any that are relevant in a particular case deserve attention.

Addressing concerns about the assessments' interpretation and use from multiple perspectives may seem like a major burden, but it is not particularly burdensome if the evaluation is approached reasonably; in fact, it may facilitate the process of validation. It has long been recognized that validation requires that the assessment results be evaluated by identifying potential challenges (e.g., sources of bias, construct-irrelevant variance, construct underrepresentation) and evaluating their impact (Cronbach, 1988), and the different perspectives can be a fruitful source of legitimate challenges to proposed interpretations and uses.

We will consider two perspectives on classroom assessment, the functional perspective and the measurement perspective. As noted earlier, the functional perspective focuses on how well the assessments support the attainment of various goals in some contexts, while a measurement perspective focuses on the assessment as a measurement instrument (i.e., in terms of precision and accuracy of the results). Assessment uses need to achieve the purpose for which they are intended, and they need to be defensible as measurements. Both perspectives can be accommodated in an argument-based approach to validation that supports the claims inherent in the intended interpretations and uses of assessment results, and that addresses challenges to these interpretations or uses.

The Functional and Measurement Perspectives

The *functional perspective* (Cronbach, 1988) views assessments primarily as tools that can be helpful in realizing desired outcomes, and therefore it focuses on how well the intended outcomes are achieved and on the extent to which undesirable outcomes are avoided. From a functional perspective, an assessment is evaluated mainly in terms of its consequences, intended and unintended.

Cronbach (1988) begins his discussion of the functional perspective by contrasting it with more descriptive concerns about the accuracy of interpretations:

> The literature on validation has concentrated on the truthfulness of test interpretations, but the functionalist is more concerned with worth than truth. In the very earliest discussions of test validity, some writers said that a test is valid if it measures "what it purports to measure." That raised in a primitive form, a question about truth. Other early writers, saying that a test is valid if it serves the purpose for which it is used, raised a question about worth. Truthfulness is an element in worth, but the two are not tightly linked.
>
> (p. 5)

The functional perspective is concerned with the functional worth, or utility, of the assessment in achieving the goals that it is intended to help achieve. An assessment is implemented to achieve some purpose, and it is evaluated in terms of its functional worth in achieving this purpose.

The *measurement perspective* views assessments primarily as measurement instruments, and as a result it focuses on certain technical criteria, particularly the generalizability (or reliability) of scores and their accuracy as estimates of the attribute of interest. It emphasizes standardization and objectivity (Porter, 2003) and generally relies on statistical models to generate interpretations in terms of traits or latent variables (Dorans, 2012; Holland, 1994), but the basic principles associated with generalizability and accuracy can be applied without adopting specific statistical models.

The measurement perspective emphasizes several kinds of analyses, particularly generalizability (or reliability) and accuracy (or freedom from bias of any kind). The generalizability of assessment results refers to how broadly the interpretation of the results can be generalized. For example, if we observe a student successfully solving a particular mathematics problem, we can pretty safely say that the student solved the problem. Once we go beyond that basic claim, more doubt tends to arise. If the goal is to determine whether the student can solve that kind of problem, we might want more evidence (e.g., performance on several exemplars of this kind of problem). If the goal is to estimate the student's *level of competence* in some larger domain (e.g., algebra), we would want even more evidence (e.g., performance on a representative sample of tasks from the domain). To the extent that we are concerned about generalizing over occasions and contexts, we would want to include observation made on different occasions and in different contexts. As the breadth of generalization of our inferences increases, the need for supporting evidence increases.

Reliability and generalizability analyses play similar roles in evaluating assessments from a measurement perspective; they both address the question of whether the results would be more or less the same for each student if the measurement were repeated (or replicated) on each student, under conditions for which the attribute being measured is not expected to change (Brennan, 2001; Haertel, 2006; Kane, 1996). We will use the term "generalizability" to refer to the issue of expected consistency over repeated observations, rather than the term "reliability," but for purposes of this discussion the two terms have essentially the same meaning.

Applying Both Perspectives

In measurement theory, it is generally assumed that the variable being measured has a definite value for each individual, and the goal is to estimate this value as accurately as possible. Random errors of measurement of various kinds (i.e., sources of variability that add "noise" or random variability to estimates of the attribute of interest) need to be controlled. The magnitudes of random errors are traditionally estimated by generalizability or reliability coefficients, or standard errors, and a core goal of the measurement perspective is to make these random errors as small as possible (e.g., by averaging over repeated observations, by standardizing assessment procedures, by statistical adjustments). So, for example, if we have a test with a number of items, and we want to generalize over items, we can estimate a coefficient, such as coefficient alpha, that indicates the correlation that would be expected between the test scores and scores on a similar test with a different sample of items of the same kind (Haertel, 2006). Quantitative indices for generalizability are especially useful in contexts where the results are to be used by individuals who are not directly involved in the local educational context, because the indices are objective in the sense that they are not influenced by subjective judgment or local norms. In most textbooks on educational measurement and in the context of standardized testing, generalizability (or reliability) is usually analyzed quantitatively.

The second major concern for the measurement perspective is the need for estimates that are accurate in the sense that they are not unduly influenced by systematic errors (effects that tend to distort or "bias" the outcomes of an assessment in some way). These errors are systematic in the sense that they tend to recur over repeated instances of the assessment. For example, students are likely to be more comfortable reading passages on some topics (those that they are interested in and familiar with) and be less comfortable reading passages on other topics (those that they are less interested in and less familiar with), and passages may differ in their difficulty for these and other reasons, some of which may not be so obvious. So, in assessing a student's reading level, one might want to use several passages on different topics, or pick a topic that is likely to be of interest to the student, in order to avoid a negative bias associated with the student's lack of interest. Any particular characteristic of an assessment (e.g., context, timing, format) that tends to interfere with a student's performance can constitute a source of systematic error (or bias).

In contexts where the goal is to get objective estimates of some attribute, rather than in using assessment results to achieve some immediate purpose, the measurement perspective tends to be dominant. More generally, in contexts where assessments are intended to promote valued outcomes, a broader range of perspectives is called for, and the measurement perspective may play a less central role, but even in these cases some level of generalizability and accuracy is needed in order to achieve valued outcomes.

The distinction between the functional and measurement perspectives can be useful in thinking about the level of attention to give to different issues in evaluating assessments, but both perspectives are generally necessary for an effective assessment. The idea is not to choose one or the other, but to examine the assessments through both lenses. We want the use of the assessment to be justified in terms of its appropriateness and its success in achieving certain goals (e.g., student learning), and the assessment results have to be accurate and generalizable enough to provide confidence in the conclusions drawn and the decisions made.

Classroom Assessment

In the remainder of this chapter, we will consider the functional perspective and the measurement perspective as frameworks for evaluating classroom assessments, which are mainly used to promote student learning (e.g., by providing feedback to students, for planning individual and class instruction). The functional perspective emphasizes an assessment's effectiveness in promoting these efforts. The measurement perspective emphasizes the generalizability and accuracy of the assessment results. To the extent that assessments are to be effective in promoting any goal, they have to be sufficiently accurate and generalizable to satisfy the assumptions inherent in their use.

Teachers have a daily stream of observational data that can help them to understand their students (Brookhart, 2003; James, 2017; Moss, 2003; Stiggins, 2005). They observe their students' performance on a variety of tasks in a variety of contexts (e.g., one-on-one interactions, classroom discussions, quizzes and projects) over the school year. They get information from parents, other teachers, and other school staff. They also have access to scores on standardized tests and in school records.

The functional perspective views classroom assessments as tools that teachers use to accomplish several goals, and the evidence required by the measurement perspective to support the generalizability and accuracy of the claims based on assessments depends on the intended uses of the results. We will consider five common functions for classroom assessments:

1. Evaluating a particular student's performance with the aim of providing helpful feedback to the student on the quality of the performance (and how it might be improved).
2. Evaluating a student's general level of performance on this kind of task.
3. Evaluating a student's strengths and weaknesses in performing this kind of task.
4. Evaluating a student's current level of achievement in some performance domain.
5. Evaluating the achievement level of the class as a whole.

As we proceed from the first function to the fifth, the generality of the inferences based on the observed performances tends to increase from an evaluation of a particular performance to an evaluation of the student's level of competence based on a long sequence of performances, and in combination with other students' performances, to class-level performance.

The first function or goal would be to provide a student with feedback on a particular performance, with the aim of helping students to improve their future performances. Assessments of this kind could be based on a student's performance on an assignment, performance on a quiz, or one-on-one interactions with the student. In terms of the functional perspective, the effectiveness of this kind of assessment would be evaluated in terms of whether the feedback does or does not seem to lead to improvement in student performance; such evaluations are likely to be subjective, qualitative, and tentative. In providing such feedback, teachers do not need to generalize their conclusions beyond the specific performances being evaluated, and they do not need to generalize over occasions or contexts. Each evaluation applies to a specific student performance or product.

A second possible goal would be to determine whether a student can perform a particular kind of task (e.g., solving a quadratic equation, using a particular irregular verb correctly). Such inferences are also qualitative, leading to a conclusion about whether the student can perform the task or not, and do not require a quantitative scale. There can be uncertainty in drawing such conclusions based on a single observation, so the teacher might want to base it on a number of observations, perhaps in different contexts and employing different instances of the task.

The third goal would be to understand the student's performance in more detail (e.g., in terms of strengths and weaknesses), and would also be qualitative. In drawing conclusions about the student's strengths and weaknesses, based on their conceptual frameworks and their observations of student performance, the teacher can be thought of as employing inference patterns that are basic to science (Popper, 1962), to construct validity (Cronbach & Meehl, 1955), and to much of everyday reasoning. Given the conceptual frameworks and the observations, we can draw inferences about some aspect of the world (e.g., a pattern of strengths and weaknesses for a student). The claim about the student's strengths and weaknesses constitutes a conjecture or hypothesis that can be used with the frameworks to generate predictions about future observations. If the predictions turn out to be accurate most of the time, we have evidence that supports both frameworks and the claims about student strengths and weaknesses. If the predictions are often inaccurate, the evidence suggests that either the frameworks or the claims about student strengths and weaknesses are inaccurate.

The fourth goal would be to evaluate the student's current level of achievement in some domain. Evidence relevant to this goal could also be obtained from one-on-one interactions with the student, from assignments, and from quizzes. For example, if one wanted to get a sense of how well a student is reading, it would probably be highly informative to observe the student reading passages from various sources and at various difficulty levels. As part of this process, the teacher would probably start with reading materials at a level that the student would be expected to be able to handle and move on to more demanding texts if the student is successful or less demanding texts if the student has trouble (using an adaptive strategy). The estimate of the student's level of performance is likely to involve a rough ordering in terms of a limited number of ordered levels (e.g., akin to a learning progression), and the teacher's confidence in the estimate will depend on the number and range of observations on which they are based and on the student's consistency in performance across texts. Getting a good indication of the student's reading level would generally require several observations.

A fifth possible goal would be to evaluate overall achievement for the class. The teacher can get a pretty good indication of overall class performance by aggregating the evidence gathered for the second and third purposes over the individual students' levels of performance in the class. If most of the students have achieved some level or better, the teacher could conclude that the class has, in general, achieved that level. In addition, particularly for this purpose, the teacher might want to use a more formal assessment, or test administration, for the class as a whole; the test would assess achievement on the content and skills being taught in the class, and therefore would preferably be locally developed. In addition, the teacher might get some information on class performance from state-mandated, standardized tests. There is no need to generalize over classes in evaluating the class because the interpretation applies to this one fixed class.

In addition, the teacher may use assessments to help direct student efforts toward particular goals by indicating topics and kinds of performance that the teacher wants to emphasize and by motivating students to pursue these goals; in any case, the teacher would not want to focus student attention in undesirable directions. Assessments can shape the students' perceptions of the goals being pursued by the teacher in this class, and thereby support the goals of instruction by communicating and reinforcing these goals. For example, if one of the main goals of the social studies curriculum is to develop the ability to analyze historical events in terms of social, political, and economic trends, then both instruction per se and the assessment tasks should involve these kinds of analyses rather than the recitation of facts, dates, and textbook explanations of events. Even if the teacher does not have this as an explicit goal for the assessments, it is likely that the assessments will play a role in shaping these perceptions (Crooks, 1988).

In using assessments to achieve any of these goals, the teacher makes use of their content knowledge, their familiarity with the enacted curriculum in their class, and their current understanding of each student's level of achievement, and of the students' strengths and weaknesses. The teacher's pedagogical content knowledge and their familiarity with the students will shape the kinds of information that they seek in their assessments and how they interpret and use this information. The intersection of the different components of the teacher's expertise provide the framework for their assessment activities, and the teachers are experts about what is going on in their classrooms. This framework can be thought of as an elaborate IUA for analyzing information on student performances of various kinds and drawing conclusions about their students and making instructional decisions.

A teacher's understanding of the competencies and interests of new students is likely to be limited and general, but it can be gradually refined as the teacher interacts with the students. The teacher's view of each student is never complete nor completely accurate, but it can get more complete and better supported over time:

> Teachers use their evolving views of the students to guide their interactions with students in various contexts. These views generate expectations about student performances on various tasks in various contexts. The teacher does not generally predict future events, but does anticipate them . . . in the sense that, for a particular student and situation, some kinds of events are seen as more likely than others. If these expectations are confirmed, the teacher's confidence in his or her current views increases. To the extent that the expectations are not confirmed, the teacher may modify assumptions about the student, the tasks, or the context. The teacher's view of each student develops over an extended period and can be self-correcting . . .
>
> (Kane, 2006, p. 47)

If a teacher's working hypotheses are not working well for a student, the teacher may need to rethink his or her view of that student. For example, if a student struggles in reading an essay that the teacher expected the student to be able to read easily, the teacher may conclude that the student is not as strong a reader as the teacher had thought, that the essay is more difficult than the teacher thought, that the student is not interested in the topic, or that some extraneous feature in the environment interfered with the student's performance.

Given a conclusion about a student's general level of reading ability, a teacher would be likely to use this information (and perhaps information about the student's interests) to select texts for the student to read. From a functional perspective, the accuracy of the teacher's estimate of the student's reading level would be evaluated in terms of the accuracy of the predictions based on the teacher's sense of the student's reading level and on the student's progress in learning to read. If the student struggles with a text that the teacher expected to be easy for the student, the teacher would need to reconsider the estimate of the student's reading level; on the other hand, if the teacher's predictions based on their estimate of the student's reading level yields the expected outcome, the teacher's confidence in the estimate is likely to increase; the teacher's general framework for characterizing student competence would be supported. For this purpose, we would want to generalize over samples of performance, and perhaps over different types of text. Over time, the students' achievement levels are expected to improve as they gain skill and confidence in reading more and more demanding texts.

Evaluating Classroom Assessments from a Functional Perspective

As indicated above, classroom assessments are intended to serve a number of related functions and employ a number of assessment-based inferences to support the intended uses. Teachers make extensive use of their subject matter and pedagogical expertise in conducting assessments and in interpreting the results. Teachers generally have expectations about how students are likely to perform on various tasks (e.g., solving a particular kind of math problem), and therefore can choose tasks at appropriate levels of difficulty for their students. The teacher is also well acquainted with what has been taught in the class and how it has been taught, and with the goals of instruction.

The teacher's conceptual frameworks serve as the warrants for their interpretive evaluations, and the backing for these frameworks as appropriate for the interpretation of classroom observations rely on the training and experience of the teacher. Peer or external review can provide additional confirmation of the teacher's inferences. Moss (1994) emphasizes the role of dialogue within a "critical community" of individuals with expertise and shared values.

These interpretations and uses are, at least roughly, nested, with the simplest interpretation/ use involving a formative evaluation of a specific performance. The inference is qualitative, with judgments about what was done well and what could have been done better. The teacher's evaluation of the performance is not necessarily generalized to performance on any other tasks; it is specific to this performance on this task in this context on this occasion. The effectiveness of the feedback can be evaluated (or validated) by observing whether the student seems to understand the feedback and whether the student's performance seems to improve in response to the feedback that is provided.

A second and somewhat more general inference goes from different performances to a judgment about a student's ability to perform a kind of task. This inference is also qualitative and addresses the question of whether or not the student can perform this kind of task. This interpretation in terms of ability to perform some kind of task involves generalization over instances of the kind of task, and perhaps over contexts, but does not involve generalization over kinds of tasks. The expectation is that a student judged able to perform this kind of task can in fact perform this kind of task, and can therefore move on to more advanced tasks. If this conclusion proves to be true, the conclusion is useful to the teacher in planning instruction, and if not the results lack functional worth.

In some cases, classroom assessments can yield convincing conclusions about student competencies, even if they involve relatively few observations. For example, if a student solves an algebra problem correctly using a standard technique (e.g., factoring a quadratic equation) and says that that is what they did, the conclusion that the student knows when and how to use that technique is well supported. As Frederiksen (2003) pointed out, this kind of performance "may reveal that a student has used problem-solving approaches and forms of knowledge that are highly generalizable to other task situations, thus backing a student-model claim about generality of skill" (p. 71). That is, the teacher may be able to draw a general conclusion about student competencies from a very small sample of observations, even a single performance.

Such inferences tend to be less compelling in the opposite direction, in that a student who knows how to solve the problem may make an arithmetic mistake or "slip," or may be distracted or unmotivated, but the inference can be quite strong in the negative direction as well. If the teacher is observing the performance directly, they can tell the difference between a careless error and a lack of understanding, and in the one-on-one context the teacher can prompt the student by suggesting possible approaches (i.e., by providing some scaffolding); if the student still flounders, the teacher can be quite confident that the student lacks certain skills. In addition, the teacher's familiarity with the student can help to detect and control threats to the accuracy of the conclusions.

A third inference would go beyond task performance to conclusions about the student's specific strengths and weaknesses. This inference involves an inference to a profile of specific skills required for overall competency and is also qualitative. The teacher's content knowledge and familiarity with common student misconceptions provide the basis for the teacher's conclusions, and these conclusions could be evaluated primarily in terms of their coherence and their consistency. The evaluation of student competencies could then be used to plan remedial instruction for the student, if necessary, and the effectiveness of the assessment instruction combination could be evaluated in terms of the student's progress. The conclusions drawn about the student's skill can also be used to make predictions about the student's performance on various tasks requiring different combinations of skills, and these predictions can be evaluated against subsequent observation of performance on these tasks.

The evidence needed for this kind of explanatory interpretation could be derived from many sources (e.g., quizzes, assignments), but in a classroom one-on-one interactions with students are feasible and would probably be especially informative, and the teacher can collect such information on a regular basis. For this purpose, the tasks presented to the student would probably need to be at a level that the student finds somewhat difficult, and the teacher's sense of the student's level of competence could provide a basis for choosing the tasks to be employed; optimally, the tasks would be chosen to indicate the student's strengths and weaknesses (e.g., tasks that require a particular set of competencies). The focus is on a profile of specific competencies in an area of instruction, and the goal is to characterize each student in terms of what they can and cannot do so that this information can be used to guide ongoing instruction for the student. As part of this ongoing process of instruction and evaluation, the teacher could use their insights about the student's profile of competencies to select the tasks for the student to work on; for example, if the student does not "carry" correctly in multi-column addition, the teacher might present the student with examples of problems with and without carries and help the student to work through these examples. Again, the conclusions to be drawn about the student's strengths and weaknesses are qualitative, involving descriptions or profiles of student competencies rather than a scaled score.

A fourth interpretation goes from different performances and other sources of evidence (e.g., quizzes, assignments, in-class performance) to a judgment about a student's overall level of achievement in some content domain. This evaluation does involve generalization over tasks, possible performances, and contexts; the teacher is drawing a somewhat general conclusion based on a sample of performances. This inference is also qualitative but would generally involve an ordinal scale referenced to a hierarchical set of categories, forming a learning progression of sorts. The teacher knows the goals of ongoing instruction in the classroom and has a sense of how students progress through the curriculum. The teacher also has a sense of the different kinds of performance associated with different levels of achievement. Their overall framework for instruction and assessment provides a basis for choosing what to assess and how to assess, and how to interpret the results. The conclusions drawn about the student's overall competence can also be evaluated in terms of predictions about the student's performance on tasks at different levels of difficulty (i.e., different levels of the learning progression) against subsequent observation of performance on these tasks.

Fifth, once the teacher has a sense of the performance levels of the students in a class (through quizzes and the teacher's individual and group-level interactions with students), drawing inferences about them can involve some sort of aggregation over the individual performance levels. This inference can be justified mainly in terms of the justification for the judgments about the individual students and the reasonableness of the aggregation. For this purpose, conclusions about the class flow directly from conclusions about the students in the class.

To a large extent, the validity of classroom assessments is evaluated in terms of how well the assessments help to achieve instructional goals (i.e., in terms of the extent to which the use of the assessment results has the intended positive consequences and avoids any potential negative consequences). The effectiveness will depend on the generalizability and accuracy of the assessment results, but it will also depend on other factors, including how well the assessment procedures fit the daily educational practice of the classroom and on the extent to which teachers are able to work with the results.

Teacher assessments employ continuously evolving IUAs, in which the conclusions being drawn, the evidence supporting these conclusions, and the teacher's confidence in their conclusions all evolve over time. Teachers start the year with general conceptual frameworks but relatively little information about individual students. The frameworks tend to focus the teacher's evaluations of student performance and help the teacher to anticipate environmental factors and student characteristics that might have impacts on learning for the class and for individual students. The teacher's conceptual frameworks tend to generate expectations about student performance, which provide working guidelines for instruction and assessment, and to the extent that the expectations are in agreement with subsequent performance on new tasks, the conceptual frameworks tend to be supported.

Toward the end of the school year, the teacher may be called upon to provide a general evaluation of each student's achievement during the year, and such assessments may be used as the basis for high-stakes decisions (e.g., promotion, placement).

Evaluating Classroom Assessments from a Measurement Perspective

From a measurement (or psychometric) perspective, classroom assessment is quite a complicated enterprise. As noted above, it serves multiple purposes, and corresponding to these purposes it yields multiple interpretations. It also makes use of many sources of data (quizzes, projects and assignments, one-on-one interactions), most of which are not standardized, with each of the data sources providing evidence that is relevant to different interpretations. For example, a one-on-one interaction in which a teacher helps a student to work through a math problem helps the student to understand how to solve the problem and any missteps the student had made, but it also provides the teacher with information about the student's strengths and weaknesses in solving this kind of problem and some information about the student's level of achievement in a larger domain of mathematical competencies, as well as a little evidence on class performance.

Within the measurement perspective, on assessment several key concepts are addressed, particularly generalizability (or reliability) and accuracy. In classroom assessments, the statistical methodologies based on measurement theory are less salient than they are in standardized testing, but concerns about generalizability and accuracy are still relevant:

> No commentator on evaluation devalues excellence with respect to experimental design, reproducibility, statistical rigor, etc. But we do say that these virtues are purchased at too high a price, when they restrict an inquiry to what can be assessed with greatest certainty.
>
> (Cronbach, 1988, p. 7)

It is not that measurement criteria are irrelevant, but for classroom assessment they are less salient than the functional criteria.

Basically, the measurement perspective focuses on the generalizability and accuracy of assessment results. Generalizability is concerned with whether we have a large enough and representative enough sample of performance to support the breadth of our conclusions. Accuracy is concerned with the interpretability of the claims and is concerned with whether they are reasonable and relatively free of potential sources of systematic error.

As noted earlier, the claims based on classroom assessments can be considered nested. A first interpretation/use consists of feedback on a specific student performance on a particular task. The results are not generalized or interpreted in terms of any scale, and therefore generalizability and scaling are not concerns. However, there are aspects of assessment design that can enhance the accuracy and effectiveness of the feedback. Is the task at an appropriate difficulty level and clear enough to the student, and was the student able to demonstrate their ability in a fair way? There might be motivational problems or other issues that prevent a student from performing as well as they might; any concerns about the accuracy of the interpretation need to be considered in interpreting student performances.

Second, the teacher may use assessments to draw conclusions about whether students can perform a certain kind of task by observing their performance on this kind of task. As noted earlier, the conclusion here is an answer to a binary, qualitative question about whether the student can perform that kind of task, and therefore traditional scaling issues do not arise. Concerns about generalizability do arise because a single observation or a small sample of observations may not provide a dependable answer to the question. If we ask a student to perform a task of the specified kind and the student fails to do so, the failure may result from a lack of motivation or from confusion about what is expected in the assessment context. On the other hand, a student may arrive at a correct answer using a flawed algorithm. So, it is always desirable to base conclusions on a sample of observations involving different instances of the task, different contexts, and different occasions. Larger, more diverse samples tend to provide more generalizable conclusions.

If the inference is based on performance on a sample of instances of the task type on a single occasion, indices of reliability could be useful in evaluating generalizability over instances of the task type, but generally the use of quantitative indices is not likely to be feasible for classroom assessments. However, if the teacher has observed the student performing many instances of the task type over a period of time, conclusions about the student's ability to perform the task could be drawn with considerable confidence. The accuracy of such conclusions is also supported by the fact that teachers are in a good position to detect potential threats to the accuracy of assessment-based inferences because of their experience with the students in their class.

Third, the teacher would want to understand the student's performance in more detail (e.g., in terms of strengths and weaknesses). As noted earlier, one-on-one interactions with students would probably be especially informative for this purpose. The conclusions to be drawn about the student's strengths and weaknesses are qualitative, involving descriptions or profiles of student competencies rather than a scaled score, and the uncertainty in the conclusions drawn can be reduced by basing them on a sample of observations.

Based on the teacher's conception of the student's strengths, weaknesses, and possibly misconceptions, the teacher can predict tasks that the student will be able to do easily and tasks that the student is likely to find difficult. To the extent that these predictions turn out to be wrong, the teacher would need to reconsider their mental model for the student; if the teacher's predictions are generally correct, their confidence in their interpretations of the assessment results is likely to increase. There is no intent to generalize the results across curricula, contexts, or extended time periods, and therefore traditional models for reliability/generalizability play a relatively limited role, but more general concerns about the adequacy of the evidence for various inferences play a major role. This process of making predictions based on a model of performance and a characterization of a student's capabilities in terms of that model, and then checking the predictions against new observations, provides a nice example of construct-related validity evidence.

Note that in classroom assessments, these inferences and the evaluations of these inferences do not usually involve statistical models and formal inferential reasoning, but rather less formal, qualitative reasoning about the more specific competencies required by various kinds of performance and how these competencies come into play. Teachers' reasoning about specific student competencies tend to be similar to the patterns of inference that have been built into more formal mathematical models. This similarity derives, in part, from the modelers' attempts to capture in their models what good teachers have always done. For example, in teaching mathematics, effective teachers have attended to the patterns of student mistakes as a source of information about misconceptions and gaps in understanding, and this approach has been built into a number of diagnostic assessment models (Rupp, Templin, & Henson 2010; Tatsuoka, 1983).

Fourth, a more general claim involves an inference from some observed performances to an estimate of a student's level of achievement in some performance domain, thus generalizing over tasks, and over occasions and contexts. In classroom assessment, this inference is referenced to a hierarchical set of categories, or a learning progression of sorts. In drawing this inference, the teacher would need to rely on adequate evidence about overall performance in the domain. Such inferences would generally require that the teacher collect performance data on a representative sample of performances from the domain, and these observations might occur over an extended period and involve different kinds of assessments. If the inference is based on performance on a sample of tasks on a single occasion, indices of reliability could be useful in evaluating generalizability over tasks, but more generally the use of quantitative estimates of reliability are not likely to be feasible. However, if the teacher has observed the student responding to a representative sample of tasks from the domain on a number of occasions, the student's level of achievement could be evaluated with considerable confidence.

In drawing conclusions about the level of achievement for the class as a whole, the teacher can simply summarize the results over the students in the class. In some contexts (e.g., program evaluation), it would make sense to generalize over classes, but for classroom assessment claims about class performance are derived by aggregating over the students in the class.

Standard psychometric analyses would be hard to apply to classroom assessment (because of small sample sizes and variability in the formats of the assessments), and it is not clear that they would shed much light on the enterprise if they could be applied, in part because of its complexity, but more basically because of the immediacy and context-dependency of the inferences being drawn. For most classroom assessments, there is no intention of generalizing over occasion, over contexts or curricula, or over teachers. The teacher is generally interested in how well each student is doing in this class with this curriculum and teacher and at this time.

The assessments need to be accurate enough to support the decisions being made in the classroom. The interpretation of the assessment results and the decisions based on these results tend to be made in the context of the teacher's understanding of their students' current levels of achievement and their profiles of strengths and weaknesses, and in terms of the teacher's goals. The interpretations are likely to be accurate to the extent that the teacher's interpretive framework is accurate and the assessment results are relatively free of systematic error.

To the extent that the classroom teacher employs tests as such (e.g., standardized assessments involving a number of tasks and a limited range of formats), generalization over tasks would generally be relevant, and generalization over occasions might be relevant in some cases, but for day-to-day classroom assessments, where there is no intent to generalize conclusions over samples of tasks or occasions, indices that evaluate such generalizations would be irrelevant and unnecessary. There is an expectation that the skills being acquired by students will be useful in the future and in other contexts, but those projections are not directly evaluated.

Concluding Remarks

As is the case for most assessments, classroom assessments can be analyzed from multiple perspectives, and of these the functional perspective and the measurement perspective are particularly relevant. The more quantitative aspects of the measurement perspective (reliability, generalizability, and scaling analyses) are generally not feasible in the classroom, but the basic principles of the measurement model (i.e., generalizability, accuracy) are applicable and necessary.

Teachers use classroom assessments for a number of purposes that rely on evaluations of student performance at a particular time and with reference to a particular curriculum. Various sources of information about student performances are combined to provide feedback to students and to draw conclusions about students' skill in performing certain kinds of tasks, about each student's strengths and weaknesses (e.g., missing skills or, worse, misconceptions), about the students' overall levels of competence in some domain, and about the overall achievement of the class. Using their conceptual frameworks, teachers interpret student performances and plan instruction on an ongoing basis. The teacher's conclusions are developed, checked, refined, and extended over time. The process is quite dynamic. The teachers seek to construct a coherent interpretation of performance by "continually revising initial interpretations until they account for all of the available evidence" (Moss, 1994, p. 8).

From a functional perspective, the accuracy of the teacher's sense of the student's level of achievement and their strengths and weaknesses would be evaluated in terms of the usefulness of the assessment results in promoting teaching and learning. For example, to the extent that teachers can use their assessment results to remediate student weaknesses and to correct misconceptions, the effectiveness of the assessments in achieving the teacher's goals is supported. If the efforts are not generally successful, the teacher may need to revise their sense of student competencies and/or modify their instructional approaches. As Cronbach (1988) suggested, "The bottom line is that validators have an obligation to review whether a practice has appropriate consequences for individuals and institutions, and especially to guard against adverse consequences" (p. 6). The focus is on the outcomes of the instructional decisions suggested by the assessment results.

From a measurement perspective, the plausibility of the teacher's interpretation of the assessment results can be evaluated in terms of whether the assessment-based conclusions are based on a larger enough and representative enough sample of observations to support the generalizations being made, and on whether the interpretation of the results is plausible, given all of the available evidence. In doing so, teachers rely on general notions of generalizability and of Cronbach and Meehl's (1955) conception of construct validity, but do not give much if any attention to the more formal, statistical models that have been developed in support of large-scale, standardized testing. Statistical estimates of generalizability coefficients are used to check on the tenability of invariance assumptions that are not particularly relevant to most classroom assessments (Baird, Andrich, Hopfenbeck, & Stobart, 2017; Kane, 2017), but the teacher needs to replicate their observations often enough to justify their inferences about student performance and progress. We would also expect that two equally well-informed teachers would arrive at similar conclusions about the students (Bennett, 2011).

There are two contexts in which the traditional concerns about reliability play a significant role in classroom assessments. First, to the extent that the teacher relies on tests that involve a sample of tasks from some domain and interprets the test scores in terms of expected performance over the domain, we want the sample to be large enough and representative enough to provide a sound basis for generalizing to the domain as a whole. Traditional indices of internal consistency (e.g., coefficient alpha) can provide useful evidence for generalizability over the domain.

Second, in drawing conclusions about overall student achievement (e.g., in generating end-of-year grades), concerns about the statistical properties of the component assessments and about how they are to be combined (e.g., the weights to be used) can raise issues that have been analyzed in some depth in the measurement literature (Haertel, 2006), but in the classroom these concerns are likely to be evaluated qualitatively and far less formally.

References

American Educational Research Association (AERA), American Psychological Association (APA), & National Council on Measurement in Education (NCME). (2014). *Standards for educational and psychological testing.* Washington, DC: American Educational Research Association, American Psychological Association, & National Council on Measurement in Education.

Baird, J., Andrich, D., Hopfenbeck, T., & Stobart, C. (2017). Assessment and learning: Fields apart? *Assessment in Education: Principles, Policy & Practice, 24*, 317–350.

Bennett, R. E. (2011). Formative assessment: A critical review. *Assessment in Education: Principles, Policy & Practice*, *18*, 5–25.

Brennan, R. (2001). An essay on the history and future of reliability from the perspective of replications. *Journal of Educational Measurement*, *36*, 295–317.

Brookhart, S. (2003). Developing measurement theory for classroom assessment purposes and uses. *Educational Measurement: Issues and Practice*, *22*(4), 5–12.

Cronbach, L. J. (1980). Validity on parole: How can we go straight? *New Directions for Testing and Measurement: Measuring Achievement over a Decade*, *5*, 99–108.

Cronbach, L. J. (1988). Five perspectives on validity argument. In H. Wainer & H. Braun (Eds.), *Test validity* (pp. 3–17). Hillsdale, NJ: Erlbaum.

Cronbach, L. J., & Meehl, P. E. (1955). Construct validity in psychological tests. *Psychological Bulletin*, *52*, 281–302.

Crooks, T. J. (1988). The impact of classroom evaluation practices on students. *Review of Educational Research*, *58*, 438–481.

Crooks, T., Kane, M., & Cohen, A. (1996). Threats to the valid use of assessments. *Assessment in Education*, *3*, 265–285.

Dorans, N. (2012). The contestant perspective on taking tests: Emanations from the statue within. *Educational Measurement: Issues and Practice*, *31*(4), 20–37.

Frederiksen, J. (2003). Issues for the design of educational assessment systems. *Measurement: Interdisciplinary Research and Perspectives*, *1*, 69–73.

Haertel, E. H. (2006). Reliability. In R. Brennan (Ed.), *Educational measurement* (4th ed., pp. 65–110). Westport, CT: American Council on Education and Praeger.

Holland, P. W. (1994). Measurements or contests? Comment on Zwick, Bond, and Allen/Donogue. In *Proceedings of the Social Statistics Section of the American Statistical Association, 27–29*. Alexandia, VA: American Statistical Association.

House, E. R. (1980). *Evaluating with validity*. Beverly Hills, CA: SAGE.

James, M. (2017). (Re)viewing assessment: Changing lenses to refocus on learning. *Assessment in Education: Principles, Policy & Practice*, *24*(3), 404–414.

Kane, M. (1996). The precision of measurements. *Applied Measurement in Education*, *9*(4), 355–379.

Kane, M. (2006). Validation. In R. L. Brennan (Ed.), *Educational measurement* (4th ed., pp. 17–64). Westport, CT: American Council on Education/Praeger.

Kane, M. (2013). Validating the interpretations and uses of test scores. *Journal of Educational Measurement*, *50*(1), 1–73.

Kane, M. (2017). Loosening psychometric constraints on educational assessments. *Assessment in Education: Principles, Policy & Practice*, *24*, 447–453.

Messick, S. (1989). Validity. In R. L. Linn (Ed.), *Educational measurement* (3rd ed., pp. 13–103). New York: American Council on Education and Macmillan.

Moss, P. (1994). Can there be validity without reliability? *Educational Researcher*, *23*, 5–12.

Moss, P. (2003). Reconceptualizing validity for classroom assessment. *Educational Measurement: Issues and Practice*, *22*(4), 13–25.

Popper, K. (1962). *Conjecture and refutation: The growth of scientific knowledge*. New York: Basic Books.

Porter, T. (2003). Measurement, objectivity, and trust. *Measurement: Interdisciplinary Research and Perspectives*, *1*, 241–255.

Rupp, A., Templin, J., & Henson, R. (2010). *Diagnostic measurement: Theory, methods, and applications*. New York: Guilford Press.

Shepard, L. (1993). Evaluating test validity. In L. Darling-Hammond (Ed.), *Review of research in education* (pp. 405–450). Washington, DC: American Educational Research Association.

Stiggins, R. (2005). *Student-involved assessment for learning* (4th ed.). Upper Saddle River, NJ: Pearson/Merrill Prentice Hall.

Tatsuoka, K. K. (1983). Rule space: An approach for dealing with misconceptions based on item response theory. *Journal of Educational Measurement*, *20*, 345–354.

2

Cognitive Diagnosis Is Not Enough
The Challenge of Measuring Learning with Classroom Assessments

Jacqueline P. Leighton

Preparation of this chapter was supported by a grant to the author from the Social Sciences and Humanities Research Council of Canada (SSHRC Grant No. 435-2016-0114). Grantees undertaking such projects are encouraged to express freely their professional judgment. This chapter, therefore, does not necessarily represent the positions or the policies of the Canadian government, and no official endorsement should be inferred. Jacqueline P. Leighton (jacqueline. leighton@ualberta.ca) can be contacted via airmail at 6-119D Education North, Dept. of Educational Psychology, Faculty of Education, University of Alberta, Edmonton, Alberta, Canada T6G 2G5.

All learning has an emotional base.

—Plato

Classrooms are complex social environments. Economic, language, cultural, and mental health issues are just some of the key variables that need to be considered in relation to students. For example, the National Center for Children in Poverty indicates that 21% of U.S. children currently live in families that are considered officially poor. According to the Child Trends DataBank, the proportion of children in the U.S. population who are first- or second-generation immigrants increased by 51% between 1994 and 2014. In 2011–2012, the National Survey of Children's Health indicated that just under 50% of U.S. children experienced one or more adverse experiences such as physical or emotional or sexual abuse. A single adverse experience usually signals a child is dealing with some form of chronic stress, which carries an increased risk for smoking, alcoholism, mental illness, and chronic health problems into adolescence and adulthood. Therefore, many children walk into classrooms on the first day of school not as blank slates or even ideally as little scientists, but rather as learners with a host of social and emotional vulnerabilities. Because students will spend as much as eight hours in school on any given day, the teacher often functions as a surrogate parent in the classroom (Pianta, 2016).

In this complex social environment, a teacher is expected to facilitate and support all students in their learning. However, learning involves not only enhancing students' cognitive skills, but also creating an environment of social and emotional support for students to learn. Thus, a challenge exists when classroom instructors and teachers approach the measurement of student learning from a purely cognitive perspective. On the one hand, teachers, policymakers, scholars and even scientists have become increasingly adept at discussing human learning in light of the latest neuroscientific, psychological, and sociocultural findings showing that states of emotion and states of connectedness or relatedness go hand in hand with states of knowing (e.g., Leighton, Guo, Chu, & Tang, 2018a; Pekrun, Goetz, Titz, & Perry, 2002; Pianta, 2016; Ryan & Deci, 2000; Tyng, Amin, Saad, & Malik, 2017; Wiliam, 2018). For example, Pekrun et al. (2002) articulate the importance of emotions: "emotions affect students' achievement, [and] feedback of achievement and related experiences of success and failure can in turn influence students' emotions and may in fact be a major source of human affective development today" (p. 102). Likewise, Pianta (2016) underscores the criticality of connection: "Interactions with peers and teachers—with curricula and media—are in large part the pathways through which education is most directly linked to student learning and development" (p. 98). Yet, on the other hand, despite this understanding, public education policy and classroom practice continues to primarily focus on the assessment of states of knowing—knowledge and skills—without sufficient focus on measuring and integrating students' states of emotion or connectedness. For example, educators might talk about student motivation for being engaged in numbers and student–teacher relationships as essential elements for learners to persevere and learn higher-level mathematical concepts, but when administrators and policymakers get down to directing the assessment of student outcomes, only the mathematical concepts get measured.

Testing specialists have an important role to play in recognizing the complexity of student learning so as to advise and support teachers on best practices for reliable and valid student claims based on classroom assessment results. For example, testing specialists can advise on ways to address linguistic and cultural diversity in assessment practice so that items are aptly formulated and performance properly interpreted for all test-takers (Stecher & Hamilton, 2014). However, linguistic and cultural diversity reflect only some of the individual differences that need to be considered. Learners' states of emotions and connectedness must also be considered. Messick (1984) alerted us to this situation decades ago:

> It is a truism that for most educational purposes, achievement measures should not be interpreted in isolation but rather in relation to specific conditions of instruction and learning. But this cliché is rarely adequately transformed into action because of the complexity of the contextual information needed.
>
> (p. 216)

Messick goes on to describe the complexity of the information required, including students' personality structures, differences in sociocultural backgrounds, and learning histories.

The complexity of this information compels an ecological systems view of student learning and achievement (Bronfenbrenner, 1979) that recognizes that students are active agents imbedded within distinct systems (e.g., home and school), and that understanding student learning involves integrating information from component parts of these systems. Thus, although cognition may be what gets measured in the classroom, it is only one part of the information required to understand and support student learning (Ysseldyke, Lekwa, Klingbeil, & Cormier, 2012). Other parts include students' states of emotion and relatedness within the environments in which learning and assessment activities are embedded.

The variables that need to be considered in designing and interpreting student assessments are indeed complex. However, the accurate and fair assessment of student classroom learning depends on it. The stakes for how testing specialists respond to this challenge is high. Educational measurement experts should have a strong voice in advising teachers and administrators on practical, policy-driven questions about: (1) how to accurately measure relevant aspects of student learning in the classroom, including constructs involving states of emotion and relatedness; and (2) how to integrate socio-emotional data with classroom assessment results to diagnose student learning impasses, design feedback interventions, and make student decisions. Although both questions touch upon reliability and validity issues, the second has the added component of what to do with the results for actionable teaching—assessment, diagnosis, feedback intervention, and response to intervention.

The purpose of this chapter is to explore the challenge of measuring supplementary variables for the purpose of contextualizing classroom assessment results. Given space limitations, the chapter focuses exclusively on variables reflecting students' states of emotion and relatedness. Although variables reflecting linguistic and cultural diversity are clearly important and should be considered in the design and interpretation of classroom assessments (Bailey and Durán, this volume; del Rosario Basterra, Trumbull, & Solano-Flores, 2011), a brief consideration of too many variables would shortchange the suitable discussion of any variable. The balance of this chapter begins with the goals of classroom assessments and their relationship to learning. Second, the psychometric challenge of measuring students' states of emotions and relatedness alongside states of knowing is outlined given the variability of available tools. Third, a learning and assessment model is presented in an effort to show one way to begin to consider the kinds of socio-emotional data to measure in contextualizing classroom assessment results for diagnosis, design of feedback interventions, implementation, and response to intervention. Finally, contextualized concepts for reliability and validity are presented given the nature of learning constructs measured in classrooms.

Terms such as *state of emotion* and *state of connectedness or relatedness* are used interchangeably with *socio-emotional*. These terms are used broadly to encompass the range of emotions and social relations that are essential to human learning and its assessment (Pekrun et al., 2002; Pianta, 2016; Ryan & Deci, 2000; Weissberg, Durlak, Domitrovich, & Gullotta, 2015). For example, states of emotion, including joy, pride, anger, and anxiety, influence not only the learning process, but also how learning is manifested in assessment results and in responses to feedback. Likewise, states of relatedness include trustworthy teacher–student relationships, empathic peer-to-peer interactions, and a sense of belonging to a group. In considering the scope of these terms, it is useful to consider a description by Järvelä (2012), who indicates, "the basic assumption involved in the focus on socio-emotional aspects of learning is that learning situations are not purely cognitive situations but are also emotionally and motivationally loaded and situated within a social context" (p. 3139). *Socio-emotional* is therefore used to refer to any type of non-cognitive state involving affective and/or socially shared states as opposed to strictly isolated intellectual states. Moreover, the social context considered is the classroom environment, including the relationships formed by students with peers and teachers.

Basic Goal of Classroom Assessments: Supporting Student Learning

Articles, book chapters, and even entire volumes have been devoted to the many facets of classroom assessment theory and practice, including but not limited to its history, forms (e.g., formative and summative), rubrics, learning models, assessment design, associated student feedback, inclusive practices, and corresponding teacher development to name a few (e.g., Brookhart, 2003; McMillan, 2013; Shepard, 2006). It is beyond the scope of this chapter to review this literature, but attention is drawn to a specific aspect of classroom assessments, namely its basic goal or guiding objective: What is the basic reason for instructors administering assessments in the classroom?

Perhaps the most straightforward response is that classroom assessments, whatever their form, are designed to yield data that will inform teachers about how to help students learn. The data are expected to inform specific diagnoses, feedback interventions, and/or decisions about student promotion (Lipnevich, Berg, & Smith, 2016). For example, formative assessments can be used to generate diagnostic-type data about whether the student comprehends the subject matter being taught, shows any misconceptions, and requires specific feedback to rectify any misunderstanding. Summative assessments also yield data to support student learning such as whether the student has achieved the learning objectives of a particular unit and is therefore ready for the next unit. Although a hard formative/summative distinction is somewhat superficial as both forms of assessment are designed to yield data in support of student learning and can be used in a variety of ways, it is worth noting that these forms generally provide a different lens with which to view student progress (Black, 2013; Brookhart, 2003; Cizek, 2010). However, classroom assessment data provide only one source of information about student learning.

Other sources of information about student learning involve emotions and social connections. For example, the investigators associated with the Collaborative for Academic, Social, and Emotional Learning (CASEL; www.casel.org) focus on student social and emotional learning as a specific instructional goal. According to CASEL, socio-emotional learning (SEL) is described as being fostered "through explicit instruction and through student-centered learning approaches that help students engage in the learning process and develop analytical, communication and collaborative skills" (Weissberg et al., 2015, p. 6). Thus, states of emotion and relatedness are measured not only as supplements in the contextualization of academic assessment results, but rather as a means to foster and evaluate the explicit instruction of non-cognitive learning goals. This is an objective that goes further than just using socio-emotional data to better understand or contextualize cognitive outcomes from classroom assessments. In the present chapter, the proposed objective for socio-emotional data is circumscribed as it is suggested that these data should be used primarily to contextualize classroom assessment results.

Collecting socio-emotional data to make sense of students' classroom assessment performance provides a supplementary source of evidence for understanding how to help students learn. For example, Pekrun and colleagues have spent decades studying college students' achievement-related emotions and how these emotions have a significant influence on assessment outcomes (e.g., Pekrun & Frese, 1992; Pekrun et al., 2002; Pekrun, Elliot, & Maier, 2009). Pekrun and colleagues' research suggests that achievement goal orientations (e.g., mastery, performance) are predictive of emotions, which in turn are predictive of assessment results. Although the limitation with much of this work is that it focuses largely on adult learners, college and university students, it should not be ignored for its potential to generalize to younger student populations. For example, Pianta (2016) and his associates (e.g., Sabol & Pianta, 2012) have studied and tracked empirical trends outlining the significant effects of teacher–student relationships, and the significant emotional overtones associated with these relationships for student learning and achievement. The collective of this research indicates that states of emotion and states of relatedness are not only pertinent, but consequential, in student learning.

A review of the literature on cognitive development indicates little attention on children's emotions (Meadows, 2006). Within the field of cognitive science, Gardner (2016) comments that states of emotion and relatedness were, only until recently, largely neglected. Given accumulating neuroscientific evidence, however, the neglect of these states is now impossible (Immordino-Yang & Damasio, 2007). For example, as early as the 1980s, neurological evidence indicated that emotions were necessary in guiding thinking and decision-making. Patients with sustained damage to a section of the frontal lobes, the ventromedial prefrontal cortex, were found to show post-injury deficits in carrying out job-related cognitive tasks, making business decisions, and communicating with others. When tested for logical abilities, declarative content knowledge, and knowledge of social conventions, patients' information processing was found to be intact. However, what was found to be compromised was not a deficit in their cognitive processing, but a problem in their emotional processing, namely an inability to use emotional memories to narrow down the set of logically possible cognitive responses. For example, patients could no longer remember or apply social emotions such as embarrassment or compassion to help them make an appropriate work decision or in communicating a response to a friend (Immordino-Yang & Damasio, 2007). In studies of children who sustained similar injuries and showed similar patterns of intact cognitive but disrupted emotional processing, compensation of brain function as they aged was not found.

Although states of emotion and connectedness are not typically measured formally by teachers to better understand student learning (Pekrun et al., 2002), student motivation, self-regulation, and metacognition are now increasingly considered (see reviews by Andrade, 2013; Black, 2013; Brookhart, 2013; McMillan, 2018; Pellegrino, Chudowsky, & Glaser, 2001). However, these states still reflect forms of cognition, albeit higher-level forms. For example, metacognition is normally defined as thinking about thinking, and self-regulation is often defined in relation to monitoring and regulating progress toward desired cognitive goals via feedback (see Butler & Winne, 1995; Nicol & Macfarlane-Dick, 2006). To be sure, motivation reflects more than cognition as it involves the reasons students engage in classroom activities. However, the steadfast focus on motivation and other higher-order cognitive states such as metacognition and self-regulation distracts attention from basic socio-emotional variables such as trust or empathy arising from student–teacher and student–peer relationships (Pianta, 2016). For example, Pekrun et al. (2002) indicate that emotions such as enjoyment, hope, anger, anxiety, and boredom are differentially related to components of self-regulation, including motivation (e.g., study interest and effort), learning strategies (e.g., elaboration), cognitive resources (e.g., irrelevant thinking), and regulation (e.g., external and self-regulation). Furthermore, Pianta (2016) describes the robust body of evidence showing how trusting teacher–student interactions is key for supporting student learning, but also the significant gaps in our knowledge of how these interactions are measured and incorporated into teacher practice for working with students. There is still surprisingly little research on students' basic states of emotion (e.g., Meadows, 2006; Pekrun et al., 2002) and relatedness with teachers and peers in the classroom (Pianta, 2016). One challenge is the variability in evidence for psychometric tools with which to measure students' states of emotion and relatedness (Duckworth & Yeager, 2015). Thus, aside from informal indicators of students' states based on observations and conversations, there are few guidelines for deciding which tools to use and in which situations to measure these states for contextualizing assessment results.

The Challenge of Integrating Students' Personality Traits with Classroom Assessment Results

The influence of non-cognitive factors on student learning, classroom assessment, and academic achievement has been slowly but increasingly considered in the last 50 years (for a recent meta-analysis, see Poropat, 2009; see also Chamorro-Premuzic & Furnham, 2006; Eysenck & Cookson, 1969). Although non-cognitive *states* of emotion and relatedness were mentioned earlier, traits may eventually also need to be considered. For example, according to Chamorro-Premuzic and Furnham (2006), differences in intellectual competence, including classroom learning and academic performance, rely not only on the traditional cognitive state or "capacity to acquire and consolidate knowledge throughout the life span, [but also on] . . . self-assessed abilities and personality traits" (p. 259). From a definitional perspective, Chamorro-Premuzic and Furnham (2006) explain that personality is inclusive of individual differences in patterns of cognition, emotions, and behavior, and thus should be better incorporated in how learning and academic performance are understood; this includes classroom assessment results.

Conceptualizing patterns of cognition as falling under the larger construct of personality has implications for student classroom assessment. It suggests that interpreting students' cognitive skills on classroom assessments in isolation from their trait-based patterns of emotions and behavior in social environments could systematically bias the diagnostic claims teachers make about student performance, its underlying causes, and the nature of feedback interventions that might work to help students learn. For example, persons who score above average on the personality trait of openness to experience have been shown to exhibit strong academic performance relative to those persons who score below average (Ackerman & Heggestad, 1997). One explanation for this relationship is that individuals who are open to experience tend to seek out interactions and activities that allow them to expand and deepen their knowledge, personal development, and confidence (Chamorro-Premuzic & Furnham, 2006). For example, students open to experience may engage more often with assessment feedback than those who are not, wishing to discuss their mistakes with teachers, exploring what they missed, why they missed it, how to fix these errors, discussing possible alternative strategies, and following through on a variety of approaches for consolidating their knowledge. In contrast, students less open to experience may wish to avoid feedback interactions and activities altogether where specific errors are discussed.

Students less open to experience may feel threatened about what the content of these feedback interactions may reveal about their effort or capabilities, and thus avoid these interactions. Teachers may infer that students who do not seek out or implement feedback may do so because they are uninterested or unable. However, in the absence of data to support such an inference, it is also possible and likely that students, even high-achieving learners, may be avoiding feedback interactions because they wish to avoid the emotional discomfort that comes from discussing mistakes that could lead to negative attributions about the self (e.g., lack of ability). For example, Leighton, Tang, and Guo (2018b) developed an inventory to measure students' attitudes toward mistakes on typical classroom types of assessments and activities. Although not designed to be a trait-based measure, Leighton et al. (2018b) found that undergraduate students who possessed negative emotional attitudes toward their mistakes were less open to discussing their mistakes with instructors, which lowered their positive perceptions of the utility of teacher feedback. Thus, knowing students' states of emotion in relation to their mistakes may be a critical measure to use for understanding how to prepare students for assessments and feedback interactions.

Although personality assessments are well established psychometrically, their administration and interpretation must be conducted by trained psychologists. This requirement makes it difficult for teachers to use and integrate trait-based data with classroom assessment results unless it is done in collaboration with a psychologist. For this reason, trait-based measures are not discussed further. However, in the next section, state-based measures are discussed. These may be more straightforward for teachers to administer in comparison to trait-based measures; however, cautions nonetheless exist for how this is done in contextualizing classroom assessment results.

The Challenge of Measuring Students' States of Emotion and Relatedness

The *Standards* (American Educational Research Association [AERA], American Psychological Association [APA], & National Council on Measurement in Education [NCME], 2014) emphasize that one of the most important steps in measurement is to define what it is one is trying to measure. The range of terms that have surfaced for referring to socio-emotional states—non-cognitive, soft skills, twenty-first-century competencies, personal attitudes—renders discussion of the construct ambiguous as it is unclear whether all these terms involve similar features. One of the terms, "non-cognitive," which is not currently favored, appears to have originated unintentionally with the work of Messick (1979), who wrote: "Once the term *cognitive* is appropriated to refer to intellective abilities and subject-matter achievement in conventional school areas . . . the term *noncognitive* comes to the fore by default to describe everything else" (p. 282, emphasis in original) (cited in Duckworth & Yeager, 2015). However, Messick (1979) underscores the drawback with this term as it suggests that non-cognitive constructs are devoid of thought, which is not the case. Using other terms such as *personality* or other trait-based terms is also not recommended as these suggest an impenetrability to change (Duckworth & Yeager, 2015). Although agreement on a single definition is unlikely, clarity and specificity in construct definition is necessary for an accurate interpretation of socio-emotional data in light of using these data to contextualize classroom assessment results.

Feasibility

There is variability in the administrative feasibility of instruments designed to measure states of emotion and relatedness in students. For example, McKown's (2015) review of the state of the art in direct assessments of children's socio-emotional knowledge included assessments to measure students' self-awareness of feelings (e.g., *Berkeley Puppet Interview*), social awareness of others' feelings (e.g., *Diagnostic Assessment of Nonverbal Accuracy*, or DANVA), relationship skills or the ability to deal with conflict (e.g., *Developmental NEuroPSYchological Assessment*, or NEPSY-II), responsible decision-making (e.g., *Social Information Processing*, or SIP), and self-management (e.g., *Mayer-Salovey-Caruso Emotional Intelligence Test*). These assessments have evidence of reliability, validity, and normative data. However, McKown (2015) notes significant barriers for many teachers to use these assessments in the classroom. For example, most of these direct assessments are not designed for universal or mass student administration in the classroom, but rather individual administration in the context of a clinical evaluation. Moreover, clinical training is required to administer, score, and interpret assessments in standardized form, which makes them as impractical for teachers to use as the personality trait-based measures described earlier. Finally, each assessment requires significant time to administer, leading McKown (2015) to conclude that what is needed "are practical, usable, feasible, scientifically sound assessments that are suitable for mass administration" (p. 330).

Although research-based measures designed for mass administration are available, their reliability, validity, and normative evidence are limited. For example, there are a multitude of experimental self-report surveys found in the published literature (e.g., self-efficacy, achievement goal orientation, motivation, self-control) that can be mass administered to students, do not require clinical training to score, exhibit adequate internal consistencies in some cases, and are often interpreted by describing the extracted constructs from a factor analysis of survey items (Duckworth & Yeager, 2015; Kyllonen, 2016; Lipnevich, MacCann, & Roberts, 2013; McKown, 2015; Stecher & Hamilton, 2014; West, 2016). A case in point is the extensive research conducted by Pekrun and his colleagues on university students' emotions (e.g., test anxiety, distress, joy) using self-report surveys and correlated responses to achievement (e.g., Pekrun & Frese, 1992; Pekrun et al., 2002). This research has led to development of the *Achievement-Emotions Questionnaire* (AEQ; Pekrun, Goetz, & Perry, 2005). However, the cautionary note with many experimental surveys, including the AEQ, is that they are often designed for a particular population of learners, such as university students. The reliability and validity of using these instruments with other populations is less certain because psychometric evidence is limited. Thus, even surveys that have been vetted by scholarly review present limitations.

Generally, there is also reason to be cautious about the reliability and validity of the claims based exclusively upon self-reports. Specifically, Duckworth and Yeager (2015) and West (2016) outline the following limitations with self-report surveys and questionnaires: (1) misinterpretation of items by students or teachers; (2) inaccurate reports of feelings or behaviors due to lack of insight by students or teachers; (3) lack of sensitivity of questionnaire items to short-term changes in what is being measured; (4) differences in the frame of reference used by students or teachers in responses; and (5) faking or social desirable responses. Although self-report surveys are typically validated by using exploratory or confirmatory factor analysis to identify internal structure (constructs), as well as by using structural equation modeling to show relationships with other, external self-report measures, there is usually little additional evidence gathered from student observations, parent and/or teacher interviews, contextual information, and/or academic follow-up. In this regard, exploring other survey methods such as anchoring vignettes may be necessary to control for idiosyncrasies in students' scale interpretation and social desirability in their response sets (King & Wand, 2007; Kyllonen, 2016). Moreover, even performance tasks designed to elicit specific socio-emotional behaviors present limitations: (1) misinterpretation by teachers of the underlying reasons for engaging in behavior; (2) insensitivity to typical behavior; (3) measure of irrelevant competencies; (4) artificiality of the task and situation; (5) practice effects; and (6) extraneous situational influences (Duckworth & Yeager, 2015). However, if socio-emotional measures are used mainly to provide data for contextualizing classroom assessment results *instead* of making strong claims about students' socio-emotional learning, using these experimental tools may be warranted; the data are being used to provide additional evidence in support claims about student learning and in the design of feedback interventions.

Contextualization of classroom assessment results means that teachers place student performance within the socio-emotional environment in which the assessment performance is embedded. From an ecological systems perspective, the context involves not just instructional opportunities, whether the teacher covered the material, but also students' socio-emotional readiness for learning such as their interest, motivation, well-being in the classroom and in the home, and trust in the teacher for helping them through the process (Leighton et al., 2018a). Although McKown (2015) indicates a shortage of frameworks for guiding integration of socio-emotional data with classroom assessment results (see also West, 2016), socio-emotional data may still be collected and used to contextualize the interpretation of classroom assessment results. This is because these data are being collected not to make categorical, report card decisions about students' socio-emotional learning, but rather to have a broader base of information about why students may be performing as they are on classroom assessments. For example, by engaging in individual discussion with students, administering self-report surveys, observing student behavior, and requesting parent–teacher conferences, teachers can systematically collect evidence to place a student's performance in perspective and plan accordingly. For example, a teacher might observe a student experiencing persistent difficulty with peers in the classroom and carefully broach the issue when talking to the student about his or her poor assessment results. The student may need the teacher's assistance integrating socially into the class, which the teacher might be able to facilitate. Alternatively, the student may be potentially suffering from debilitating effects of social anxiety, and though the teacher may not be able to help directly, the teacher can recommend and arrange a consultation with the school psychologist for assessment.

A Model for Contextualizing Classroom Assessment

To gain a richer understanding of how learning evolves and is demonstrated by students on classroom assessments, it is necessary to consider theories of learning and human development. Cognitive constructivism (Piaget, 1968), social constructivism (Vygotsky, 1978), attachment (Bowlby, 1969; Pianta, 2016), and ecological developmental systems (Lerner, 1996, 2006) indicate that meaningful student learning and the assessment of that learning are influenced by many factors aside from students' memory and understanding of knowledge and skills. Furthermore, theory and research in formative assessment and feedback suggest that successful shaping of knowledge and skills in students requires clear goals, appropriately designed tasks, and actionable feedback (e.g., Black & Wiliam, 2009; Shute, 2008). However, there are surprisingly few models that integrate learning and assessment explicitly (e.g., Durlak, Weissberg, Dymnicki, Taylor, & Schellinger, 2011; McKown, 2015) so as to generate directional hypotheses about how changes in social or contextual practices in the classroom might affect students' emotional well-being and perception of learning and their performance on classroom assessments. In an effort to generate a framework for helping teachers understand the directional relationships between social, emotional, and cognitive student inputs and outputs, the Learning Errors and Formative Feedback (LEAFF) model was developed (Leighton, Chu & Seitz, 2013; Leighton et al., 2018a). As shown in Figure 2.1, the LEAFF model reflects three basic interrelated components: the classroom social environment (including teacher and peer relations), students' working mental models, and academic performance (formative and summative classroom assessments). Due to space limitations, only a brief description of the

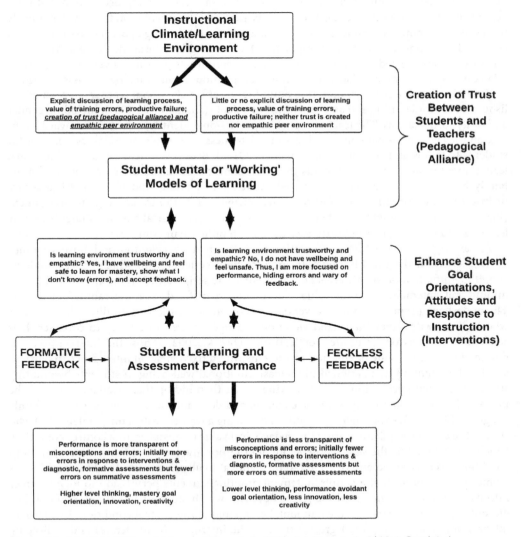

Figure 2.1 Adapted LEAFF model (see Leighton et al., 2013; Leighton et al., 2018a). Reprinted with permission.

model is provided in the following paragraphs. The reader is referred to Leighton et al. (2013) and Leighton et al. (2018a) for a full description of the original and revised model.

Classroom Environment: Teacher and Peer Relations

The first component of the LEAFF model involves the classroom environment, including the student–teacher relationship, as well as the relationship the student has with classmates. In this social context, the teacher communicates using words and/or actions the goals of learning and assessment to students. For example, the teacher might explicitly convey to students a preferred orientation toward learning by emphasizing mastery, collaboration, depth, and exploration of knowledge. Alternatively, the teacher might express a focus on performance, competition, breadth of knowledge, and certainty in responses. Although teacher communication may be explicit, implicit messages are also conveyed to students (Sadker, Sadker, & Zittleman, 2009). For example, teachers might verbally communicate a mastery learning orientation, but non-verbally behave in ways that reveal a competitive performance orientation that involves mostly worksheet assignments, simple questions, and a binary right/wrong approach to dealing with student discussions and assessment responses. Over the length of the academic year, these messages would be expected to shape students' states of emotion (e.g., comfort versus anxiety) and relatedness (e.g., trusting collaboration versus competition) about learning and assessment.

There is extensive research literature outlining the effect classroom teachers have in establishing a tone for learning and assessment with students (Sadker et al., 2009), including gender and other forms of bias. The teacher's sense of professional identity, orientation toward learning, and level of personal connectedness or relatedness with students becomes a model for students to follow and emulate (Leighton et al., 2018a). Because the teacher is the educational leader, mentor, and for most students the most significant adult in their lives outside of the family home, the teacher has an outsized influence in helping students establish a secure or insecure base for emotional and social well-being in relation to learning and assessment (Pianta, 2016). How might a teacher establish a secure psychological base for students to view learning and assessment as opportunities for growth rather than punishment?

An example of a teaching intervention was designed by Leighton and Bustos Gomez (2018), based on the LEAFF model, to increase the frequency with which college students would identify their academic errors on handouts. The scripted intervention involved a two-minute oral statement about the value of academic errors for deep and meaningful learning. The underlying premise for the intervention was based on well-known findings that students who have growth rather than fixed views on intelligence are more likely to consider their academic errors as opportunities for learning (Dweck, 2002). Thus, the intervention was designed to alter the state of emotion of students with a fixed view on intelligence in particular. The intervention was designed to increase emotional well-being in students by granting students "explicit permission" for identifying rather than hiding their academic errors. The intervention was tested using a simple experimental design: college students were randomly assigned either to an experimental condition involving a trained instructor (confederate) who started the class by explicitly stating the pedagogical value of mistakes, or a control condition, which was also led by the same confederate but did not involve this explicit statement. Both conditions were scripted and observed to be identical in all other ways. Leighton and Bustos Gomez (2018) found that a simple statement granting students permission to identify their mistakes significantly increased the frequency with which students identified material they did not understand (errors on the handouts) compared to the control condition. In addition, intervention students reported greater trust in the instructor (confederate) and well-being throughout the learning session compared to control students (for replication of results, see also Chu & Leighton, 2016).

There are three reasons for having teachers use interventions focused on underscoring the value of academic errors with students. First, teacher statements about the value of student errors in class discussions and in private conversations create opportunities for teachers to understand sources of emotional distress for students and begin an explicit process of destigmatizing errors for students who possess fixed views on intelligence. It is for these students especially that assessment errors are most threatening, because for these students errors reveal innate intellectual deficiencies that cannot be modified. Thus, assessment feedback for these students may often be interpreted at the metalevel of "the self" unless there is an explicit attempt by the teacher to change the level at which these students tend to interpret the feedback (Kluger & DeNisi, 1996; Hattie & Timperley, 2007). The teacher, as educational leader and mentor, can explicitly set a tone of security and classroom well-being by addressing students' emotional misconceptions about academic errors, intelligence, learning, and assessment objectives. Second, student assessment errors are obvious opportunities for teachers to build trust with students because they can use the handling of student errors to overtly "walk the talk" of how errors are to be treated in the classroom. For example, teachers who verbally claim errors are tools for learning but then do not devote time to exploring the root of student errors during feedback conversations miss a critical chance to show themselves as truthful or honest agents for guiding student learning. Third, student assessment errors present implicit opportunities for teachers to model strategies for thinking and feeling about assessment errors. For example, many good teachers would know not to begin the feedback conversation with an immediate discussion of the errors made on an assessment. Rather, a teacher who recognizes the sensitivity a student might have about mistakes begins the conversation by asking the student about how she or he feels about the performance, concerns, and then carefully alleviates these concerns by reviewing the performance, offering mastery-focused encouragement, and importantly a clear and actionable feedback plan for addressing the errors or concerns.

Students' Working Models and Assessment Performance

The second component of the LEAFF model involves students' working models of the classroom learning environment. Based on the intervention described earlier (Leighton & Bustos Gomez, 2018), one of the predictions derived from the model is that students' working models about intelligence, effort, learning success, and assessment failure may be constructively shaped when teachers are constantly verbalizing and acting in ways that reinforce specific ways of responding to learning and assessment. For example, when teachers are actively attending, measuring, and responding to the implicit beliefs and emotions students harbor about their own learning, which can often extend to anxieties related to classroom assessments and engagement with feedback, teachers can shape students' emotional and belief systems (Dweck, 2002; Kluger & DeNisi, 1996; Sadker et al., 2009). Thus, using surveys and other available tools, teachers can gain insight and contextualize student performance so that feedback interventions to address academic errors are designed to help alleviate students' emotional distress, and with social supports to increase the chances of a good student response to intervention.

The third component involves the anticipated effects of the classroom environment (e.g., teacher interventions) and students' working models on formative and summative assessment performance. According to the LEAFF model, the first desired result is to increase students' trust in the teacher and emotional well-being in the classroom to encourage exploration and discussion of assessment errors. The second desired result is to use these discussions as vehicles for strengthening student learning and, by extension, performance on formative and summative assessments. Both these desired effects would be expected from having teachers engage in specific practices or actions that increase their relatedness to students by: (a) talking explicitly to students about the value of errors; (b) taking time to explore the nature of mistakes with students; (c) using experimental tools to measure students' implicit beliefs and feelings about learning and assessment; (d) synthesizing the socio-emotional information to gain insight about students' perspectives; and (e) delivering feedback to students that explicitly shifts the focus away from the self and onto the task.

Although initially these instructional practices may not lead to a surge in student summative performance, this performance should improve with repeated discussion about how to address errors and misconceptions over the course of the academic year. For example, in a longitudinal study of 250 elementary students, Leighton et al. (2018a) found that students who reported strong states of relatedness with their teachers also indicated strong emotional well-being, engagement, empathy toward their peers, and academic performance on classroom summative assessments. However, there is currently little training, direction, or clarity about how specifically teachers should establish better relations with students to guide students in their learning. For example, large-scale studies of elementary student experiences such as the NICHD Study of Early Child Care and Youth Development indicate that even in basic instruction "across grades, the likelihood of a student being exposed to an interactively skilled teacher—rated in the top third for emotional and instructional features of teacher behavior—was less than 10%" (Pianta, 2016, p. 100). Although students' socio-emotional states need to be considered to obtain a fuller understanding of learning, how this is done proficiently by teachers in the classroom is still an open question.

The structure of the LEAFF model is premised on two basic principles. First, classroom assessment results are not actionable until teachers establish relatedness with students and understand their socio-emotional states. Although classroom assessment results may lead to inferences about whether a student has acquired a given knowledge or skill, these inferences do not provide diagnostic information about why students might have underperformed or provide much context for how a feedback intervention might be designed to address an existing knowledge gap. This is because classroom assessment results only narrowly inform teachers about acquisition of cognitive skills but do not shed light on the foundation for learning—students' states of emotion and relatedness. Therefore, measures of socio-emotional learning should be incorporated to contextualize students' classroom assessment results. This can be done in several ways that exist along a continuum of formality. For example, teachers can identify struggling students and collaborate with school psychologists to formally screen students for learning disabilities, but also for their socio-emotional status on variables such as anxiety, self-management, self-awareness of feelings, relationship skills or the ability to deal with conflict, and responsible decision-making (McKown, 2015). Some of these socio-emotional measures involve established methods such as conducting clinical interviews with students that only a licensed psychologist is trained to do and interpret (McKown, 2015). In these cases, teachers can collaborate with psychologists to initiate formal measures and work with findings. However, teachers can also use many informal research-based surveys to gain insights into students' motivation, learning orientation, mindset, anxieties, and overall emotional and social well-being. The experimental status of these tools needs to be recognized but the goal is to use the tools flexibly to acquire more information from students. The information can be used to guide teachers in conversations with students and in discussions with parents to help the student learn.

Second, socio-emotional data should be collected with enough frequency to measure students' baseline states as well as gauge changes in these states in response to feedback interventions. Without a gauge of students' social and emotional readiness to learn, be assessed, and receive feedback, teachers may not be able to formulate appropriate feedback intervention plans. For example, an elementary teacher might organize a reading circle with a new class of third grade students where a character in a story experiences a series of academic setbacks. The story is used as a springboard to begin to ask students questions about learning, intelligence, and mistakes prior to describing assessments, their interpretation, and purposes. Teachers might follow up individually with students who stay unusually quiet or indicate concerns. If students are older, administering short-form question-and-answer surveys about their beliefs and feelings about learning can also provide information about students' socio-emotional states. For example, an adolescent who is being bullied at school, highly anxious about meeting parental expectations, or feeling unsupported in the classroom may require special support or formal intervention of some kind depending on the issue. These data should be used to bolster what is already known academically about the student to better understand the emotional and social context in which students' assessment results are embedded and how to deliver feedback that is supportive but actionable. In short, collecting data about students' socio-emotional standing begins an important pedagogical process of: (a) identifying non-cognitive variables that are likely to be associated with classroom assessment results; (b) initiating a conversation with the student and/or parents about what may be happening to the student and hindering their academic work; and (c) collaborating with students, parents, and/or psychologists depending on the severity of the issue to determine appropriate interventions in support of the student.

Empirical work on the LEAFF model continues and several areas for strengthening the model remain. First, the model currently lacks a stronger developmental systems approach in describing students' socio-emotional and cognitive states. Although the model includes the classroom environment, other systems such as the home environment are not included and students' working models are significantly shaped by parental influences (Lerner, 2006; Ysseldyke et al., 2012). Second, the reciprocal effects of students on teachers need to be taken into account. Third, the model does not currently provide a prescribed framework for integrating data from distinct sources (e.g., survey responses, individual conversations) and potentially multiple environments so as to yield the most contextualized inferences about student learning from classroom assessments.

The LEAFF model was proposed as a reaction to what is considered to be an extraordinarily narrow, albeit traditional, view on student learning and assessment. In the LEAFF model, classroom assessment is placed in the service of student learning, and not the other way around. However, implicit in the model is the idea that technical concepts of reliability and validity, designed for large-scale assessments, are necessary, but they must be revised to serve the objective of assessing student learning, with all its complexity, in the classroom (Brookhart, 2003). Failure to do so undermines the student learning objective that classroom assessments are designed to satisfy. In the next section, it is argued that reliability and validity concepts need to be rethought for classroom assessments given the constructs measured. In particular, the construct of classroom learning is framed as *fluid and fine-grained*. Consequently, the assessment of such a construct must be *frequent* and *flexible*; both these attributes necessitate different conceptions of reliability and validity not just for assessments of cognition, but also emotion and relatedness.

Psychometric Perspectives for Measuring Student Learning with Classroom Assessments

Traditionally defined psychometric principles of reliability and validity (see AERA et al., 2014), developed for large-scale assessments of achievement and other constructs, are often used inappropriately when evaluating the quality of classroom assessments (Brookhart, 2003; Shepard, 2006). Brookhart (2003) explains that many teacher-made classroom assessments do not satisfy typical requirements of reliability, normally defined as involving precision and consistency of scores under similar conditions. Likewise, many teacher-made classroom assessments do not satisfy requirements of validity, which require particular design decisions such as sampling from a universe of items and collecting evidence that items or tasks measure the underlying constructs of interest. However, applying these traditionally defined concepts to classroom assessments may be problematic for several reasons. Aside from the fact that teachers are not trained in classical or modern test score theory, Brookhart (2003) explains that several elements of the classroom—including: (a) the psychosocial environment; (b) the use of assessment data to inform teacher practices; and (c) the use of assessment data to inform student learning—make these assessments different in objectives from large-scale assessments to render traditionally defined reliability and validity concepts unsuitable.

All three points made by Brookhart (2003) suggest that a contextualized, ecological systems view of reliability and validity, one that incorporates socio-emotional elements, may be required. In particular, Brookhart's (2003) latter two points underscore the need for classroom assessment to be *frequent* and *flexible* to accomplish the objectives of informing and updating teacher practices given the nature of the construct, namely a *fluid* and *fine-grained* process of student learning. The evidence for the fluid and fine-grained process of the measured construct comes in part from systematic research on children's learning. In his micro-genetic empirical research of children's learning, Siegler (2006) elaborates on the character of this fluidity and fine granularity:

> Cognitive changes involve regressions as well as progressions, odd transitional states that are present only briefly but that are crucial for the changes to occur, generalization along some dimensions from the beginning of learning but lack of generalization along other dimensions for years thereafter, and many other surprising features. Simply put, the only way to find out how children learn is to study them closely while they are learning.
>
> (p. 469)

The fluidity and granularity of learning does not originate solely from the developmental process of acquiring knowledge and skills, but also from the variability injected by states of emotion and relatedness. For example, anxiety is the most studied achievement emotion known to interfere with academic performance (Pekrun et al., 2002).

The variability of the measured construct in classroom learning naturally gives psychometricians reason for pause. Moving targets are hard to measure. Fluid and fine-grained processes may not follow linear trajectories and would be expected to change with feedback interactions and interventions. Thus, it is unsurprising that traditional psychometric concepts of reliability and validity would fail to apply as intended. Furthermore, these concepts fail to apply not only to formative classroom assessments that are expected to be frequent and flexible, but also to summative classroom assessments. Even summative classroom assessments should be frequent and flexible if the goal is to measure fine-grained learning outcomes associated with multiple units of instruction to determine whether the student is prepared for the next level of study. Thus, the frequency and flexibility of formative and summative classroom assessments make them appropriate and useful measures of fluid and fine-grained learning processes. However, the characteristics that make these assessments useful in the classroom are the very characteristics that make them poor candidates for satisfying traditionally defined concepts of reliability and validity.

New notions of reliability and validity are therefore needed. Contextualized notions of reliability and validity may be developed without necessarily generating new measurement theory (Bonner, 2013). For example, as outlined by Brookhart (2003, p. 9, Table 1), reliability as applied to classroom assessment may be better regarded as supplying "sufficiency of information" about the nature of the gap between where the student is at and desired performance. Reliable classroom assessments, then, are those that provide some satisfactory level of evidence about the relative location of a student's fluid and fine-grained performance in light of the learning objectives. However, understanding the nature of the gap is informed not only with frequent and flexible classroom assessments, but also with frequent and flexible measures

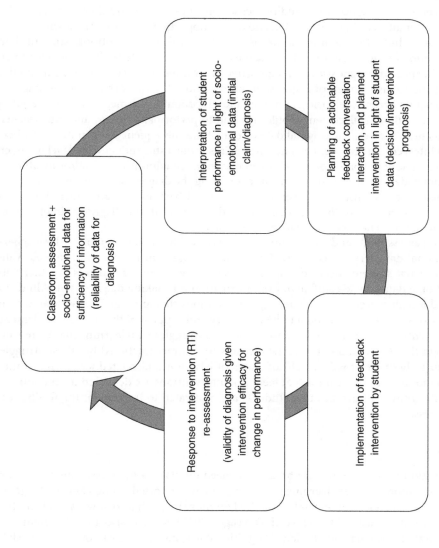

Figure 2.2 Contextualized notions of reliability and validity for the frequent and flexible measurement of fluid and fine-grained learning construct.

of socio-emotional data to contextualize student performance and plan appropriate feedback interventions. What is the evidence that sufficiency of information has been achieved? One source of evidence is students' response to intervention (performance) based on the feedback intervention provided to them. If sufficient information was collected in pursuit of an accurate original diagnosis, including classroom assessment results and also data about socio-emotional states, a student's response to intervention should show learning gains.

Likewise, unlike the traditional concept of validity that requires five sources of supportive evidence and typically involves claims about static constructs (AERA et al., 2014), a contextualized classroom-based concept of validity focuses on fine-grained and fluid constructs that require five different steps in the collection and use of supporting evidence. As shown in Figure 2.2, the steps include: (a) the integration of cognitive and socio-emotional student data; (b) interpretation of these data to make a diagnosis; (c) an actionable feedback plan for intervention and expected prognosis; (d) a supportive environment for student implementation of the plan; and (e) assessment of response to intervention. If an incorrect student diagnosis has been generated from the socio-emotional and classroom assessment data, the resulting feedback intervention or placement should not lead to performance gains, and thus teachers and students must reassess the original data or one of the subsequent steps in the cycle. Poor response to intervention provides evidence that claims about a student's current level of understanding were inaccurate based on the classroom assessment administered and/or insufficient socio-emotional data were considered in contextualizing the diagnosis and feedback intervention designed. The response to intervention must be fed back into a reconsideration of the classroom assessments used, the socio-emotional data collected, the diagnosis, intervention, and implementation. The process is naturally recursive.

Classroom assessments and socio-emotional measures should be used jointly by teachers. Socio-emotional data serve to contextualize student assessment results so as to yield valid claims about what students need to help them learn. Classroom assessments together with socio-emotional data provide sufficiency of information for making diagnoses of a fluid and fine-grained learning process, and planning interventions that are more likely to succeed in the presence of socio-emotional data to help delivery and support of the student implementing the intervention. The reason is because a student's struggles with learning may stem from states of cognition (e.g., failing to understand how to subtract fractions) but these struggles always need to be understood in light of states of emotion and relatedness. It is within a context of emotion and relatedness that feedback interventions are delivered to students and it is also within this background that students are motivated to implement the feedback to achieve success.

Conclusion

The introduction to this chapter emphasized the need for classroom assessments to measure more than cognition if student learning is to be genuinely supported. Significant challenges lie ahead in how this is done. Not only is there a need for more research into how states of emotion and relatedness are measured (Duckworth & Yeager, 2015); there is also a need to figure out how to integrate these data with students' cognitive states, namely their knowledge and skills (McKown, 2015). It is particularly important that testing specialists lead in this development and integration as the ethics and fairness of what is measured and how it is interpreted are considered. Policymakers and practitioners need guidance from testing specialists for ensuring quality in the broader array of assessments that are incorporated in the classroom. This is especially relevant to avoid misinterpretation of socio-emotional data and assessment results. Devoting expert attention to developing models and frameworks of classroom learning and assessment, including refining measures that encompass a wider spectrum of constructs and states, is intended to help produce the sufficiency of information required for properly diagnosing students in their learning. These data reflect the different systems in which the learner is embedded. These data can help facilitate: (1) the validity of student diagnoses; (2) resulting interventions; and (3) evaluations of student responses to intervention to meet the basic goal of classroom assessments—student learning.

It is easy enough to call attention to the need for including basic states of emotion and relatedness for contextualizing classroom assessment results. However, significant gaps and limitations in available tools exist, as well as teacher preparation and knowledge for how to integrate these types of data into instruction and specific feedback conversations with students (Schonert-Reichl, Hanson-Peterson, & Hymel, 2015). In addition, it is also essential to recognize that psychological understanding of how students' states of emotion and relatedness influence learning is extraordinarily limited and requires more study (Meadows, 2006). Thus, one of the primary tasks for testing specialists may be to devote more attention to constructs associated with states of emotion and relatedness as they pertain to the fluidity and granularity of student classroom learning. A secondary task for testing specialists is to advance frameworks, models, and guidelines for implementing and interpreting classroom assessments that reflect contextualized concepts of reliability and validity. For example, the LEAFF model outlines the socio-emotional components that should be included in aiming for sufficiency of information in understanding student learning in light of assessment results. Validity of diagnoses, interventions, and decisions can be systematically tracked and observed in the success of student outcomes. Based on comprehensive frameworks, guidelines for the frequency and flexibility of classroom assessments can be advanced so that students' knowledge and skills are captured in light of the socio-emotional context in which they occur and change.

References

Ackerman, P. L., & Heggestad, E. D. (1997). Intelligence, personality, and interests: Evidence for overlapping traits. *Psychological Bulletin, 121*(2), 219–245.

American Educational Research Association (AERA), American Psychological Association (APA), & National Council on Measurement in Education (NCME). (2014). *Standards for educational and psychological testing.* Washington, DC: American Educational Research Association, American Psychological Association, & National Council on Measurement in Education.

Andrade, H. L. (2013). Classroom assessment in the context of learning theory and research. In J. H. McMillan (Ed.), *SAGE handbook of research on classroom assessment* (pp. 17–34). Thousand Oaks, CA: SAGE.

Black, P. (2013). Formative and summative aspects of assessment: Theoretical and research foundations in the context of pedagogy. In J. H. McMillan (Ed.), *SAGE handbook of research on classroom assessment* (pp. 167–178). Thousand Oaks, CA: SAGE.

Black, P., & Wiliam, D. (2009). Developing the theory of formative assessment. *Educational Assessment, Evaluation, and Accountability, 21*, 5–31.

Bonner, S. M. (2013). Validity in classroom assessment: Purposes, properties, and principles. In J. H. McMillan (Ed.), *SAGE handbook of research on classroom assessment* (pp. 87–106). Thousand Oaks, CA: SAGE.

Bowlby, J. (1969). *Attachment and loss: Vol. 1. Attachment.* London: Hogarth Press and the Institute of Psycho-Analysis.

Bronfenbrenner, U. (1979). *The ecology of human development: Experiments by nature and design.* Cambridge, MA: Harvard University Press.

Brookhart, S. (2003). Developing measurement theory for classroom assessment purposes and uses. *Educational Measurement: Issues and Practice, 22*(4), 5–12.

Brookhart, S. (2013). Classroom assessment in the context of motivation theory and research. In J. H. McMillan (Ed.), *SAGE handbook of research on classroom assessment* (pp. 35–54). Thousand Oaks, CA: SAGE.

Butler, D. L., & Winne, P. H. (1995). Feedback and self-regulated learning: A theoretical synthesis. *Review of Educational Research, 65*, 245–281.

Chamorro-Premuzic, T., & Furnham, A. (2006). Intellectual competence and the intelligent personality: A third way in differential psychology. *Review of General Psychology, 10*, 251–267.

Chu, M.-W., & Leighton, J. P. (2016). Using errors to enhance learning and feedback in computer programming. In S. Tettegah & M. McCreery (Eds)., *Emotions and technology: Communication of feelings for, with and through digital media. Volume I: Emotions, learning, and technology* (pp. 89–117). New York: Academic Press.

Cizek, G. J. (2010). An introduction to formative assessment: History, characteristics, and challenges. In H. L. Andrade & G. J. Cizek (Eds.), *Handbook of formative assessment* (pp. 3–17). New York: Routledge.

del Rosario Basterra, M., Trumbull, E., & Solano-Flores, G. (Eds.). (2011). *Cultural validity in assessment: Addressing linguistic and cultural diversity.* New York: Routledge.

Duckworth, A. L., & Yeager, D. S. (2015). Measurement matters: Assessing personal qualities other than cognitive ability for educational purposes. *Educational Researcher, 44*(4), 237–251.

Durlak, J. A., Weissberg, R. P., Dymnicki, A. B., Taylor, R. D., & Schellinger, K. B. (2011). The impact of enhancing students' social and emotional learning: A meta-analysis of school-based universal interventions. *Child Development, 82*(1), 405–432.

Dweck, C. S. (2002). Messages that motivate: How praise molds students' beliefs, motivation, and performance (in surprising ways). In J. Aronson (Ed.), *Improving academic achievement* (pp. 37–60). New York: Academic Press.

Eysenck, H. J., & Cookson, D. (1969). Personality in primary school children: 1. Ability and achievement. *British Journal of Educational Psychology, 39*, 109–122.

Gardner, H. (2016). Foreword. In M. H. Immordino-Yang, *Emotions, learning and the brain: Exploring the educational implications of affective neuroscience* (pp. 7–10). New York: W. W. Norton & Company.

Hattie, J., & Timperley, H. (2007). The power of feedback. *Review of Educational Research, 77*(1), 81–113.

Immordino-Yang, M. H., & Damasio, A. (2007). We feel, therefore we learn: The relevance of affective and social neuroscience to education. *Mind, Brain and Education, 1*(1), 3–10.

Järvelä, S. (2012). Socio-emotional aspects of learning. In N. M. Seel (Ed.), *Encyclopedia of the sciences of learning* (pp. 3139–3140). Boston, MA: Springer.

King, G., & Wand, J. (2007). Comparing incomparable survey responses: Evaluating and selecting anchoring vignettes. *Political Analysis, 15*, 46–66.

Kluger, A. N., & DeNisi, A. (1996). The effects of feedback interventions on performance: Historical review, a meta-analysis and a preliminary feedback intervention theory. *Psychological Bulletin, 119*, 254–284.

Kyllonen, P. C. (2016). Socio-emotional and self-management variables in learning and assessment. In A. A. Rupp & J. P. Leighton, *Handbook of cognition and assessment* (pp. 174–197). New York: Wiley.

Leighton, J. P., & Bustos Gomez, M. C. (2018). A pedagogical alliance for trust, wellbeing and the identification of errors for learning and formative assessment. *Educational Psychology: An International Journal of Experimental Educational Psychology, 38*(3), 381–406.

Leighton, J. P., Chu, M.-W., & Seitz, P. (2013). Cognitive diagnostic assessment and the Learning Errors and Formative Feedback (LEAFF) model. In R. Lissitz (Ed.), *Informing the practice of teaching using formative and interim assessment: A systems approach* (pp. 183–207). Charlotte, NC: Information Age.

Leighton, J. P., Guo, Q., Chu, M.-W., & Tang, W. (2018a). A pedagogical alliance for academic achievement: Socio-emotional effects on assessment outcomes. *Educational Assessment, 23*(1), 1–23.

Leighton, J. P., Tang, W., & Guo, Q. (2018b). Undergraduate students' attitudes towards mistakes in learning and academic achievement. *Assessment and Evaluation in Higher Education, 43*(4), 612–628.

Lerner, R. M. (1996). Relative plasticity, integration, temporality, and diversity in human development: A developmental, contextual perspective about theory, process, and method. *Developmental Psychology, 32*, 781–786.

Lerner, R. M. (2006). Developmental science, developmental systems, and contemporary theories of human development. In W. Damon & R. M. Lerner (Eds.), *The handbook of child psychology. Vol. 1: Theoretical models of human development* (6th ed., pp. 1–17). Hoboken, NJ: Wiley.

Lipnevich, A. A., Berg, D. A. G., & Smith, J. K. (2016). Toward a model of student response to feedback. In G. T. L. Brown & L. R. Harris (Eds.), *Handbook of human and social conditions in assessment* (pp. 169–185). London: Routledge.

Lipnevich, A. A., MacCann, C., & Roberts, R. D. (2013). Assessing non-cognitive constructs in education: A review of traditional and innovative approaches. In D. H. Saklofske, C. R. Reynolds, & V. Schwean (Eds.), *The Oxford handbook of child psychological assessment* (pp. 750–772). Cambridge, MA: Oxford University Press.

McKown, C. (2015). Challenges and opportunities in the direct assessment of children's social and emotional comprehension. In J. A. Durlak, C. E. Domitrovich, R. P. Weissberg, & T. P. Gullotta (Eds.), *Handbook of social and emotional learning: Research and practice* (pp. 320–335). New York: Guilford Press.

McMillan, J. H. (Ed.). (2013). *SAGE handbook of research on classroom assessment.* Thousand Oaks, CA: SAGE.

McMillan, J. H. (2018). *Using students' assessment mistakes and learning deficits to enhance motivation and learning.* New York: Routledge.

Meadows, S. (2006). *The child as thinker: The development and acquisition of cognition in childhood.* London: Routledge.

Messick, S. (1979). Potential uses of noncognitive measurement in education. *Journal of Educational Psychology, 71*(3), 281–292.

Messick, S. (1984). The psychology of educational measurement. *Journal of Educational Measurement, 21*(3), 215–237.

Nicol, D., & Macfarlane-Dick, D. (2006). Formative assessment and self-regulated learning: A model and seven principles of good feedback practice. *Studies in Higher Education, 31*(2), 199–218.

Pekrun, R., Elliot, A. J., & Maier, M. A. (2009). Achievement goals and achievement emotions: Testing a model of their joint relations with academic performance. *Journal of Educational Psychology, 101*, 115–135.

Pekrun, R., & Frese, M. (1992). Emotions in work and achievement. In C. L. Cooper & I. T. Robertson (Eds.), *International review of industrial and organizational psychology* (vol. 7, pp. 153–200). Chichester: Wiley.

Pekrun, R., Goetz, T., & Perry, R. P. (2005). *Achievement Emotions Questionnaire (AEQ): User's manual.* Munich: Department of Psychology, University of Munich.

Pekrun, R., Goetz, T., Titz, W., & Perry, R. P. (2002). Academic emotions in students' self-regulated learning and achievement: A program of qualitative and quantitative research. *Educational Psychologist, 37*(2), 91–105.

Pellegrino, J. W., Chudowsky, N., & Glaser, R. (Eds.). (2001). *Knowing what students know: The science and design of educational assessment.* Washington, DC: National Academy Press.

Piaget, J. (1968). *Six Psychological Studies*, Anita Tenzer (Trans.). New York: Vintage Books.

Pianta, R. C. (2016). Teacher–student interactions: Measurement, impacts, improvement and policy. *Policy Insights from the Behavioral and Brain Sciences, 3*(1), 98–105.

Poropat, A. E. (2009). A Meta-analysis of the five-factor model of personality and academic performance. *Psychological Bulletin, 135*(2), 322–338.

Ryan, R. M., & Deci, E. L. (2000). Self-determination theory and the facilitation of intrinsic motivation, social development, and well-being. *American Psychologist, 55*, 68–78.

Sabol, T. J., & Pianta, R. C. (2012). Recent trends in research on teacher–child relationships. *Attachment & Human Development, 14*(3), 213–231.

Sadker, D., Sadker, M., & Zittleman, K. R. (2009). *Still failing at fairness: How gender bias cheats girls and boys in school and what we can do about it.* New York City: Scribner.

Schonert-Reichl, K. A., Hanson-Peterson, J. L., & Hymel, S. (2015). SEL and preservice teacher education. In J. A. Durlak, C. E. Domitrovich, R. P. Weissberg, & T. P. Gullotta (Eds.), *Handbook of social and emotional learning: Research and practice* (pp. 406–421). New York: Guilford Press.

Siegler, R. S. (2006). The microgenetic analyses of learning. In W. Damon & R. M. Lerner (Eds.), *The handbook of child psychology. Vol. 2: Cognition, perception and language* (6th ed., pp. 464–510). New York: Wiley.

Shepard, L. A. (2006). Classroom assessment. In R. L. Brennan (Ed.), *Educational measurement* (4th ed., pp. 623–646). Washington, DC: American Council on Education.

Shute, V. (2008). Focus on formative assessment. *Review of Educational Research, 78*, 153–189.

Stecher, B. M., & Hamilton, L. S. (2014). *Measuring hard-to-measure student competencies: A research and development plan.* Santa Monica, CA: RAND Corporation.

Tyng, C. M., Amin, H. U., Saad, M. N. M., & Malik, A. S. (2017). The influences of emotion on learning and memory. *Frontiers in Psychology, 8*, Article 1454. doi:10.3389/fpsyg.2017.01454

Weissberg, R. P., Durlak, J. A., Domitrovich, C. E., & Gullotta, T. P. (2015). Social and emotional learning: Past, present and future. In J. A. Durlak, C. E. Domitrovich, R. P. Weissberg, & T. P. Gullotta (Eds.), *Handbook of social and emotional learning: Research and practice* (pp. 3–19). New York: Guilford Press.

West, M. R. (2016, March 17). Should non-cognitive skills be included in school accountability systems? Preliminary evidence from California's CORE districts. *Economic Studies at Brookings. Evidence Speaks Reports, 1*(13). Retrieved from www.brookings.edu

Vygotsky, L. (1978). *Mind in society.* London: Harvard University Press.

Wiliam, D. (2018). *Embedded formative assessment* (2nd ed.). Bloomington, IN: Solution Tress Press.

Ysseldyke, J., Lekwa, A. J., Klingbeil, D. A., & Cormier, D. C. (2012). Assessment of ecological factors as an integral part of academic and mental health consultation. *Journal of Educational and Psychological Consultation, 22*(1–2), 21–43.

3

Language in Practice

A Mediator of Valid Interpretations of Information Generated by Classroom Assessments among Linguistically and Culturally Diverse Students

Alison L. Bailey and Richard Durán

Current U.S. college and career-ready standards expect students to learn in collaborative contexts requiring communication with each other. This emphasis requires educators and researchers to be aware of appropriate language practices that can support learning through such collaborative interactions during their design of assessments of academic content. For example, in the area of mathematics learning at the primary grade level, students are expected to "understand and explain why the procedures [for multiplying whole numbers] work" and "apply their under-standing of models for division, place value, properties of operations, and the relationship of division to multiplication as they develop, discuss, and use efficient, accurate, and generalizable procedures to find quotients" by fourth grade (National Governors Association Center for Best Practices, Council of Chief State School Officers [CCSSO], 2010a, p. 27). To succeed, students will need opportunities for developing situated (i.e., during classroom interaction with peers and teachers) and integrated (i.e., the oral and written language learned during the course of a mathematics lesson) language competencies. These language competencies support the deeper mathematical thinking and student discussion as a process of skill acquisition, refinement, and extension and as ongoing resources for students' learning repertoires.

More generally, integrated language and content demands have gained attention since the adoption of standards for deeper content learning in English language arts, mathematics, and science (e.g., *Common Core State Standards in English Language Arts and Literacy in History/ Social Studies, Science, and Technical Subjects*, CCSSO, 2010b; *Common Core State Standards in Mathematics*, CCSSO, 2010a; *Next Generation Science Standards*, NGSS Lead States, 2013). Integration of language and content learning may place challenging linguistic demands on all students, but may be particularly demanding for students acquiring English as an additional language at the same time they are also learning new mathematics, science, and ELA content (e.g., Bailey & Wolf, 2012; Heritage, Walqui, & Linquanti, 2015; Lee, Quinn, & Valdés, 2013).

In this chapter, we argue that large-scale summative testing cannot in isolation reveal much about an individual student's linguistic and content responses to situated instruction or achievement of classroom-embedded learning outcomes called for in the content stand-ards, and will require a classroom-level assessment solution. We first claim that large-scale testing cannot adequately measure the more contextualized and process-oriented aspects of language and content learning, and thus presents a problem for the valid assessment of academic achievement of linguistically and culturally diverse learners, who perhaps more so than their English-speaking or English-proficient peers may rely on their understandings of situated and integrated classroom settings as an effective pedagogical resource to facilitate their simultaneous language and content learning (Lee et al., 2013; National Academies of Sciences, Engineering, and Medicine [NASEM], 2018). In this sense, language practices of the classroom can mediate (i.e., influence or play an intervening role in) both a student's experience of classroom assessment as direct engagement in learning and a teacher's grounded diagnostic interpretation of information generated empirically by his or her use of classroom assessments.

We also claim that formative assessment that focuses on understanding a student's learning process during the course of instruction with its emphasis on providing student feedback on learning (e.g., Black & Wiliam, 2009) helps with the need to situate performance in social and learning interactions, and to closely observe student performances over time. Paying close attention to language in practice is therefore also a "mediator" in the sociocultural theory sense of a mediator being a tool for attaining ends (Pryor & Crossouard, 2008)—in this case, teachers using classroom interactions to generate evidence of student content learning.

We therefore propose that research on classroom assessment investigate how this assessment approach might be best conducted with English learner (EL) students, who, as a culturally and linguistically diverse group, are among the most vulnerable academically and may be less familiar with linguistic conventions expected of English speakers in the classroom context. The chapter begins by reviewing literature that supports these claims. We also take the opportunity to contrast the kinds of test items that students often encounter in large-scale academic achievement tests with the integrated language and content knowledge and skills emphasized by the college- and career-ready standards. We then move to illustrations of classroom interaction involving EL students during content learning and a discussion of the assessment and measurement challenges and possible advantages afforded by classroom assessment involving socially and culturally sensitive interactions among EL students and with a teacher.

Limitations of Large-Scale Testing of Situated Language Practices during Instruction

Three main limitations of large-scale testing in the context of linguistically and culturally diverse learners include concerns with the appropriateness of trait versus growth models of learning, meeting the assumptions necessary for drawing valid inferences from large-scale assessment results, and adequately measuring the communicative language constructs demanded by the current college- and career-ready standards. We review each below.

Appropriateness of Trait versus Growth Models of Learning

More broadly, both researchers and educators, as well as policymakers, have questioned whether large-scale assessment can meaningfully measure student knowledge and skills given that knowledge and skills are dynamic and subject to the specificity of local conditions (Koretz, 2018). For example, Mosher and Heritage (2017) warn:

> For purposes either of informing instruction or targeting accountability, it is unwise to try to develop large-scale assessments that are intended to be administered to widespread student populations during some common time period of necessarily limited duration, in the hopes of producing "scores" that will be both comparable across jurisdictions and useful for guiding instructional decisions.
>
> (p. 61)[1]

We need to keep in mind that the most pervasive large-scale achievement assessments serve accountability purposes and are constructed to make accurate inferences about how well aggregate groups of students have mastered a broad and diffuse set of content areas and practices reflected in the specifications for an assessment. As Durán (2008) has pointed out, there are:

> inherent limits of large-scale assessments as accountability tools for ELLs as a means for directly informing a deep understanding of individual students' learning capabilities and performance that can be related to instructions and other kinds of intervention strategies supporting ELL schooling outcomes.
>
> (p. 294)

The advantage of assessment closely tied to contemporaneous classroom instruction over large-scale assessment as a census of knowledge amassed over a longer interval is that classroom assessment can be tied to instruction designed to integrate standards into authentic day-to-day meaning-making tied to the life and culture of a classroom. Indeed, Bailey (2017a) has referred to formative assessment as "day-to-day" stakes with teachers having the opportunity to always review their instructional decisions on an ongoing basis. This advantage is also likely true of interim summative assessments such as those being developed by assessment consortia (e.g., Smarter Balanced Assessment Consortium). While this chapter focuses on formative assessment, it is pertinent to point out that interim assessments can also be aligned closely and in real time with classroom instruction, given that the results of an interim assessment can be returned to teachers quickly, if not scored by teachers themselves, so the information they yield about student learning may also be actionable for meaningful instruction.

Large-Scale Assessment Assumptions Not Met with EL Students

The need to understand specific and more complex performances of both language and content learning as microdevelopmental outcomes (i.e., capturing incremental growth), as well as their integration into the ongoing learning repertoires of students, is most certainly critical in the case of linguistically and culturally diverse groups of students, especially those who are still acquiring English while they are learning new academic content. Large-scale assessments assume homogeneity of the test-takers' experiences and backgrounds in order to make valid inferences about performance based on a test's score. This assumption is not met with EL students who vary tremendously in their language proficiency, opportunities to learn content and communicate content to others, and so forth. A key challenge, therefore, of assessing the content knowledge of EL students stems from the fact that we cannot assume students share the same language practices or have comparable opportunities for exposure and learning of scholastic language practices; indeed, students will inevitably have differential familiarity with school tasks as genres for thought and action (Mislevy & Durán, 2014). The role of students' language styles and variation (both in English and a first language) may also affect the design of valid classroom assessments of academic content learning.

Young EL students especially may perform differently on large-scale assessments not because of differences in their knowledge and skill in what is being assessed, but because of extraneous factors such as anxiety, lack of familiarity with assessment formats and directions, testing fatigue, and other student-level factors such as exposure to differing curricula that make them an extremely heterogeneous group (Bailey, 2016, 2017b; Bailey, Heritage, & Butler, 2014).

Classroom assessments can, of course, benefit from the many traditional education measurement considerations of large-scale assessment of student learning. Many of these considerations have guided the fair and unbiased assessment of student content learning and are set out in the *Standards for Educational and Psychological Testing* (American Educational Research

Association [AERA], American Psychological Association [APA], & National Council on Measurement in Education [NCME], 2014). Classroom assessment can learn from the large-scale assessment arena by overtly addressing content and construct relevance (and guarding against construct irrelevance), strength of validity arguments and interpretations, and issues of bias and fairness during assessment design and implementation (Bailey & Heritage, 2019; Heritage, 2018). In the case of classroom assessment and formative assessment in particular, these measurement ideas can guide teachers to ensuring that the construct they intend to gather evidence about is fully represented, includes all the important dimensions of the construct, and is sufficient for drawing fair and unbiased inferences about a student's performance.

During classroom assessment, teachers will need to learn to closely observe social interaction and extract useful evidence of learning. While student language is highly varied and can differ stylistically, it can still be functional in the classroom context. For example, a student may casually exclaim to another student, "No way!" rather than more formally state, "Your claim is not defensible" in evaluating a conclusion drawn by a student in dyadic interaction. Both utterances are equally comprehensible in a classroom collaborative learning context. This presents a challenge not only to large-scale assessment of student performance, of course, but to teachers who are assessing formatively in the classroom and who may miss the contribution of students who do not initially know and use the more formal statement. In this sense, fairness to students of all backgrounds is a key measurement concern of both assessment approaches.

Communicative Language Constructs Best Measured by Classroom Assessment

Recognizing the limitations of large-scale assessment with EL students, Durán (2008) called for the need to have:

> assessments do a better job of pinpointing skill needs of students developmentally across time, better connect assessments to learning activities across time and instructional units, and better represent the social and cultural dimensions of classrooms that are related to opportunities to learn for ELL students.
>
> (p. 294)

Thus, the language practices that might best be defined and measured within authentic classroom learning contexts and academic tasks include interactions among students and between students and teachers, and academic discourse practices of a genre nature important to classroom learning such as co-constructing oral explanations and arguments (e.g., Gibbons, 2009).

These genre-like practices provide the constructs that can be systematically observed and be targets of instruction and learning during formative assessment, as we illustrate later in this chapter. Specifically, interactions among students and between students and teachers require language and discourse skills necessary to participate in conversational exchanges (e.g., question formulation, turn-taking abilities). The language of oral explanations and arguments and genres such as personal narrative and storytelling require students to organize the content they wish to convey linguistically and conceptually over an extended stretch of discourse (e.g., several consecutive sentences), both solo and in collaboration with others.

These constructs contrast with a narrower vision of the English language construct assessed in the United States and elsewhere that has used direct, large-scale, standardized language tests. Such assessments have been designed to measure a unitary trait-construct (i.e., general English proficiency), or at best additional separate interrelated subcomponents of general English proficiency tied to speaking, listening, reading, and writing that can be readily assessed by the discrete items of large-scale summative language proficiency assessments (NASEM, 2017). Even though recent standards for English language development or proficiency (ELD/P) have taken account of how language and content are integrated in disciplinary practices (Lee et al., 2013) and contrast with the shortcomings of older English language development standards that may not have been a close reflection of the language used in school (Bailey & Huang, 2011), assessments of English proficiency continue to report assessment outcomes using static trait models of student performance. These have no doubt been influenced by federal mandates for such reporting, and they do not capture the broad interactive contexts of learners' lived experiences during classroom instruction and interaction that would be best described as the processes of learning.[2]

Examining the publicly released practice speaking test items on a large-scale summative assessment of English language development for a sixth to eighth grade span test form, for example, shows students are asked to respond to items that require them to produce multi-word utterances that describe a drawn image or scene; to produce an appropriate response to an elicited speech function (e.g., asking for information); to support their opinion (i.e., having been given alternative positions that they can take on a topic); to present and discuss information (e.g., responding to a question that can be answered based on details in a graphic); and summarize information just heard in a presentation (e.g., summarizing steps in a scientific procedure or process) (California Department of Education, 2017). The subsection requiring students to present and discuss given information particularly would seem to elicit interactive uses of language, but a response to an item on a large-scale speaking assessment cannot induce the conditions under which students realistically "discuss" their ideas and thoughts on a topic. Oral discussions take place between individuals (not with self on paper as in a written discussion) and include building on the ideas of others. More specifically, an oral discussion would presuppose certain language forms and functions such as linguistically marking (referencing) each speaker's prior remarks, using nonverbal communication such as gesture, explaining one's standpoint, having one's ideas challenged or supported, and making a (counter)argument or acknowledgment to other people's input in real time. In sum, oral discussion requires students to have command of pragmatic skills. These are the abilities needed to understand intentions, negotiate meaning-making, and read the linguistic and non-linguistic cues associated with communication during face-to-face interaction (Bailey & Heritage, 2018).

Similarly, the large-scale summative assessment of the academic content areas is unlikely to capture the learning that results from collaborative interactions between students, even though the assessments designed to be aligned with the college- and career-ready standards make claims about the communicative and collaborative emphasis of the standards. For example, the following is the final part of a three-part item assessing knowledge of fractions in a released test item of the Smarter Balanced Assessment Consortium (n.d.):

Part C: Benito's bag has a total of 10 pencils inside, and James' bag has a total of 5 pencils inside. How can the fraction of sharpened pencils in James' bag be the same as the fraction of sharpened pencils in Benito's bag, even though they have a different number of pencils? Explain your answer using both numbers and words.

The test developers make two claims about the overall item. The primary claim in the category of communicating reasoning reads: "Students can clearly and precisely construct viable arguments to support their own reasoning and to critique the reasoning of others." A secondary claim in the category of concepts and procedures reads: "Students can explain and apply mathematical concepts and carry out mathematical procedures with precision and fluency." These claims, we argue, are underspecified from linguistic and cultural points of view, and moreover the released item, as written, may not generate the opportunity for students to demonstrate the skills described in the claims. It is difficult to see how test scorers will make any inferences about a student's abilities to critique the reasoning of others from the explanations they are required to write. Another's reasoning has to be offered for a critique to be made.

More subtly, there are discourse-level differences between arguments and explanations. Osborne and Patterson (2011), for example, have made the critical distinction between explanation and argument as discursive practices: "arguments are essential to the process of justifying the validity of any explanation as there are often multiple explanations for any given phenomenon" (p. 629). The released item asks students to explain their answers, perhaps eliciting responses that can meet claim 2, but this item does not overtly signal construction of viable arguments that would take the form of justification of the students' explanations. From both discourse and cultural perspectives, Kuhn's (1991) work has suggested that children's ability to construct arguments may be related to their participation in formal schooling, specifically the "'academic' discourse mode may encompass the attitude that assertions must be justified and that alternatives should be considered" (p. 290). Given the construction of clear, precise, and "viable arguments" may be a school-based genre, this will impact English learners who many have different, culturally proscribed practices for argumentation that may go unrecognized by test developers and scorers (and indeed by teachers in classroom assessment settings, no less).

In contrast with this large-scale test release item, the next section illustrates the authenticity of the communicative and collaborative meaning-making demands placed on students in the context of classroom assessments that directly serve learning and academic performance.

Classroom Assessment: Capturing Situated EL Student Performance in Interaction

Classroom assessment approaches such as formative assessment, as well as performance assessment (e.g., students applying newly acquired knowledge and skills to a task) and dynamic assessment (e.g., students' potential for targeted learning evaluated in a three-step unitary process involving use of an initial assessment that guides diagnostically relevant instruction or intervention, followed by a post-assessment), are advantageous for linguistically and culturally diverse students because students can demonstrate their content knowledge through authentic language practices that they have exercised during content learning. These practices may conform to expected formal language usage associated with learning tasks and success criteria (i.e., academic language pertinent to a discipline) and, as suggested earlier, may also alternatively involve additional communicative conventions and practices adapted for academic task completion but that have been socialized outside of the classroom in everyday community settings shared among peers (Bunch, 2014).

Broad sociocultural approaches such as cultural historical activity theory (CHAT) (Cole & Engeström, 1993) and more narrowly focused sociocognitive approaches to assessing student classroom learning are important to consider and suggest the potential importance of drawing teachers' attention to interaction in classrooms that can capture how learning performance is related to the variety of sociolinguistic means exercised by students to conduct the cognitive business at hand (Mislevy & Durán, 2014; Shepard, Penuel, & Pellegrino, 2018). Regarding sociocultural perspectives, Shepard et al. (2018) remark: "Participation in sociocultural activity necessarily involves more than simply acquiring knowledge; it involves processes of identification that in turn, present opportunities for participants to become certain kinds of people in activity (Lave, 1993a; Lave & Wenger, 1991)" (p. 23). This is a very prescient remark akin to the theoretical work of Van Lier (2004), who called attention to L2 learners as socio-emotional beings making sense of who they are as they learn the range of cultural and social etiquettes expected of them in new immigrant/migrant communities of settlement—albeit made much more complex given the readiness of existing community members to be accepting and supportive of new settlers.

Sociocognitive assessment theory (Mislevy, 2018; Mislevy & Durán, 2014) introduces a more focused complementary theory resonating with sociocultural approaches that can guide classroom assessment. Sociocognitive assessment theory places a strong focus on assessment as a tool to guide understanding of what students know and can do in a content domain given the conceptual organization of a domain, and very importantly can introduce notions of learning progressions hypothesized to capture students' mastery of content and operations with content. In introducing their distinction between broader sociocultural theory and sociocognitive theory as applied to assessment, Shepard et al. (2018) state:

> Learning progressions are the most prevalent example of the more detailed models that Penuel and Shepard (2016a, 2016b) identified as sociocognitive models of learning . . . Sociocognitive models attend to the social nature of learning and to discipline-specific ways that core ideas and practices are developed over time. The general "social" theory underlying sociocognitive development efforts is consistent with sociocultural theory in that it posits "that individual cognition develops through social interaction, as individuals solve problems, complete tasks, and devise strategies to pursue particular goals" (Penuel & Shepard, 2016b, p. 147).
>
> (p. 24)

We view these contrasts in perspectives as valuable, though suggest they must be joined together in formulating effective classroom assessments. Student participation in authentic everyday classroom discussions and tasks gives educators a unique opportunity as never before to evaluate how much their students know about the disciplines they are teaching—and with appropriately designed activities and success criteria, provide evidence of students' self-awareness of their competencies and responsiveness to learning interventions, and movement along a hypothesized learning progression (e.g., see Pryor & Crossouard, 2008; Wilson & Toyama, 2018).

How educators go about designing innovative classroom assessments drawing on students' linguistic repertoires should capitalize on that very participation of students in their classrooms enabled by these repertoires, rather than solely relying on the traditional methods of assessment that adopt trait models that are decontextualized and far removed from how students convey their knowledge and learning as social beings when interacting with others. Traditional models of measurement are better suited as group status measures regarding performance of an entire classroom when one wishes to compare classrooms against attainment of standards.

In contrast, formative classroom assessment can offer the advantages of being "proximal" to learners in terms of their learning needs (e.g., Erickson, 2007), and, in the case of English learners, in terms of having opportunities to clarify task demands and for matching the language of assessment tasks to students' own language complexity levels (e.g., Bailey, 2017a; Trumbull & Solano-Flores, 2011).

While large-scale assessment may obviously be a blunt instrument to use with a group of students with such varied and nuanced learning experiences (i.e., possibly missing the knowledge and skills they have and are able to display in the everyday contexts of learning and instruction), assessing linguistically and culturally diverse students in the classroom setting will also present its own unique challenges unless one adopts a combined sociocultural/sociocognitive view of student learning and assessment.

Both approaches are needed to guide effective and innovative classroom assessment. Concepts from the two theoretical approaches allow us to map out types of aspects of learning and assessment that are relevant to assessing learning among culturally and linguistically diverse students. From a sociocognitive perspective, learning tasks and criteria for success nested within broader learning activities need to be designed so that their observation and evaluation of products generated by students can provide linguistic and cognitive evidence of what students know and can do tied to a cognitive theory of learning in a content domain. Additionally, sociocultural interpretation of students' competence in enacting the role of "student," including sociolinguistic competence, in the contexts of learning activities needs to be folded in. The latter not only includes evidence of competence from the students' perspective; it also needs to include attention to teachers' and other students' mutual recognition of being participants in a learning community that involves recognition of the rights and responsibilities of participants working together to achieve mastery of subject matter—and most importantly, an appreciation that what is being learned is valuable beyond the immediate completion of learning tasks (e.g., Yeager et al., 2014). Moreover, students benefit when their teachers begin the classroom assessment process by considering the positive consequences of their assessment practices (e.g., improve instruction and student learning), and only then moving on to determining what to assess and how to assess it to bring about the desired consequences (Bachman & Dambӧck, 2018).

Relatedly, teacher preparation in classroom interpretive assessments should address teacher bias (Solano-Flores, 2016) to forestall the focus on what students cannot do rather than a focus on what they can do and what assets, including linguistic and cultural assets, students bring to their content learning. Teachers may inadvertently only focus on correctness and linguistic conventions rather than on how students can make meaning with their developing language skills and use of an informal register. Teachers will need to build familiarity with and come to recognize different cultural ways of making meaning in assessment contexts.

Language Practices as Assessment Mediator

We can concretize concepts of the sociocultural and sociocognitive theoretical approaches by attempting to categorize key aspects of interaction during assessment episodes. Specifically, attention to the instructional unit structure, participation social structure, task goal structure, task-supporting artifacts, process/procedure demands, and evaluative criteria may reveal how the following examples of interaction can be understood as classroom assessment. Paramount to the process is that student and teacher action and interaction show evidence of consciousness of these aspects in ways that constitute their ongoing and evolving social, cultural, and linguistic identities as learners and school and extended community participants. With a sociocultural and sociocognitive understanding of language practices, we are now in a position to argue that language practices as social action (Van Lier & Walqui, 2012) mediate both the student experience of classroom assessment and educators' abilities to draw valid inferences from assessments.

While classroom assessment based on close observation of interactions through discourse analytic techniques and analysis of problem-solving holds the promise of being a fairer and more valid indicator of the language and content learning of linguistically and culturally diverse students, how well students are familiar with the disciplinary discourse practices of their classrooms will impact how well they can demonstrate their content knowledge and skills during classroom tasks. As Gee (2014) argues, the language of schooling is a variety of social language in that it is a style of language used for a specific social purpose and "acquiring any social language (including originally our vernacular dialect) requires one to learn how to recognize certain patterns of lexical and grammatical resources and how to match them to certain communicative tasks or social practices" (p. 5).

In the case of EL students, they may be positioned on the "periphery" of classroom discussions and group interactions not by their own choice, but because native-speaking or more proficient English students may overlook them and their attempted contributions (Hawkins, 2004). This (dis)placement may afford them with very little opportunity to participate in and gain knowledge of the "patterns of lexical and grammatical resources," as well as acquire the pragmatics governing such school-bound social interaction. The pragmatics specifically implicate the speech acts involved in how to negotiate or manage the actions of others, nominate actions and topics, or summarize a prior speaker's contributions to show comprehension of the content and move the discussion forward. For example, Bailey and Heritage (2018) analyzed the following exchange between two Spanish-speaking fourth grade students participating in a collaborative task about probability (predicting whether a tack shaken in a cup will land flat side up or down) reported by Barajas-Lopez, Enyedy, and Bailey (2005). These students are each able to successfully participate in this paired interaction because they had the relevant conversational moves associated with inquiry learning practices in mathematics. Angelika first negotiates the next action by saying, "Okay, the prediction for the next one. Hmm." Elena responds with a nomination for action: "Call it again now." Angelika eventually summarizes their joint understanding to this point with: "Porque mira [because look]. Like right now (pauses), up (pauses). I doesn't land like all the time . . . It always lands like . . . most of the time end up." The teacher who uses this task to observe and rate students' performances is able to notice both their language used in support of learning as well as their nascent conceptual understanding that the tack has a bias to one orientation.

Similarly, as mentioned earlier, students may not be familiar with specific genres for thought and action tied intimately to discipline-specific language practices (e.g., arguing from evidence in science discourse). Students who have less familiarity with both the language to participate in interactions and the specific genre and discourse practices of the disciplines may not be able to demonstrate their content knowledge, and in turn educators may be unable to draw valid inferences from the tasks they create to assess students in their classrooms. However, as discussed in the next section, when fourth grade students are introduced to a complex language arts activity involving generating and assessing critical opinion statements, classroom teachers are able to collect evidence of students' capacity to master what is expected of them through their independent and collaborative work utilizing both academic language and informal peer talk.

Effects of Students' Language Variation on the Design of Valid Classroom Assessments

Complex learning activities aligned and sensitive to English language arts standards tied to well-specified learning goals provide rich grist for exemplifying implementation of new forms of moment-to-moment formative assessment informed by sociocultural and sociocognitive approaches to formative assessment. Relevant high-level learning genres of this sort that recur throughout the grades, with increasing importance, and that connect with preparation for higher education, include activities such as describing, summarizing, explaining, opining, and argumentation.

Akin to Wilson and Toyama's (2018) idealized model for formative assessment, a key to developing and implementing formative assessments of such genres can start by examining: (1) a clear specification of learning goals and their interconnections expected of students as they perform a well-specified set of complex targeted learning activities; (2) how a teacher instructs and scaffolds students' conduct of requisite learning tasks to attain goals, including use of learning materials that support students' conduct of tasks and generation of learning products; and (3) guidance and strategies that a teacher or affiliate assessor can follow to observe, record, and qualitatively analyze the interaction and action of students showing their degree of mastery of intended instructional goals. More unique to sociocultural and sociocognitive approaches to formative assessment (see Erickson, 2007; Heritage & Heritage, 2013), in carrying out step 3 a teacher or assessor needs to consider patterned ways that students are expected to interact with each other and with a teacher, and with materials as they pursue tasks as social action (Van Lier & Walqui, 2012).

Below, we illustrate how such an approach to formative assessment might be implemented. We overview qualitative analysis of a segment of interaction by a pair of fourth grade students working on an editing task that was part of a language arts genre-like activity teaching students how to generate and constructively critique written opinion pieces. This example illustrates how guiding and scaffolding students' interactional goals during a peer conversation can yield rich *in situ* proximal formative assessment evidence of student pairs' reasoning and mastery of language arts goals evaluated against standards for performance and mastery set by the teacher. In the activity at hand, students are allowed to mix informal ways of peer talk with use of formal academic language. Of particular importance is how informal expressive ways of talk with socio-emotional yet analytic overtones serve a metapragmatic function (Verschueren, 2000)— helping a pair of students negotiate or manage each other's actions and verbal contributions as they discuss editing suggestions for another pair of students' draft opinion piece—all the while practicing, questioning, refining, and applying understanding of concepts and terms related to the academic genre being learned based on explicit standards set by the teacher. These latter standards pertain to the intended conceptual meanings, occurrence, and use of analytic terms such as "dialog," "opinion," "thesis statement," "topic sentence," "evidence," "explanation," and "support" as descriptors of deep linguistic and cognitive components of meaning-making enabled through written texts, and are established as explicit instructional goals with criteria for successful student performances.

The opinion activity asked students to read a text passage regarding the global migration to California that occurred during the gold rush of 1849 as part of a combined English language arts and social science/history unit. Pairs of students were asked to discuss a draft outline of an opinion piece corresponding to the prompt: *In your opinion, what was the best route for forty-niners to migrate to California during the gold rush of 1849?* Prior to responding to the prompt, the classroom teacher introduced students to one model for opinion pieces as a genre that involved starting with a concise thesis statement answering the prompt question. The opening statement was then to be followed by up to three paragraph outlines that each served as a separate justification for the overall thesis statement. Preceding the activity in question, the teacher introduced students to the explicit set of standards for effective opinion pieces and ways to evaluate the adequacy and appropriateness of opinion pieces from a writing process point of view where feedback on an initial draft was intended to guide students in improving their opinion pieces against their judged degree of attainment of standards for effective opinion pieces. Each paragraph outline was expected to start with a topic sentence supporting the main thesis, followed by mention of evidence in the original text supporting or not supporting the claim made in a corresponding topic sentence, followed by an explanatory statement arguing connections between the topic sentence and the evidence. Pairs of students were given a structured worksheet to fill out in generating their outline based on their pair discussion.

Subsequently, pairs of students exchanged their worksheets with other pairs of students who were conducting the same assignment. The next phase of the activity involved each pair discussing and generating feedback to another pair on the adequacy of their outline given the standards criteria set by the instructor for a strong opinion piece. Each pair of students was given a worksheet to fill out that summarized their feedback to the recipients. The intent of the instructor was also to support students' understanding of dialogic reasoning among pairs of students (O'Connor & Michaels, 2007) as a deep form of meaning-making prominent and valued in the classroom learning community. Regarding assessment standards, the entries on the peer feedback worksheet asked a pair of students to discuss yes/no and open-ended feedback to the other pair addressing prompts applied to each sub-outline such as: *Does the (provided) evidence support an opinion statement? Is the evidence (statement) included in their thesis statement? Can you find their (cited) evidence in the (source) informational text? Do you think the (cited) evidence is important (and) why? Do they have a good topic sentence, suggestions (including grammar and spelling errors)? Do you have suggestions to improve evidence? Does their explanation support their opinion?* Subsequently, each pair discussed the critique of the editing pair and went on to re-edit their outline.

Overall, we found that students' discourse and joint actions in carrying out the activity revealed a rich set of outcomes reflective of both their mastery of the teachers' learning objectives in the sociocognitive sense against the standards set by the teacher, and just as importantly how the sociocultural affordances of peer interaction style and communicative resources served the underlying process of formative assessment and learning. Importantly, this included the students actively assessing both their peers and themselves against their interpretation of the teacher's criteria for an effective opinion piece.

Consider the interactional segment shown below illustrating some of the key phenomena we observed:

Student 1: [Reads peer pair's main thesis statement at start of their outline] "Miners traveled to California to go to the gold rush they had to survive on resources. Cape Horn is a better way because other ones you can get diseases and you always don't survive." So let's read their opinion and see if it supports their . . .

Student 2: Yah. [Latches, overlaps S1 as he replies, signaling he is following S1; Such interruption would probably be considered pragmatically inappropriate by most teachers, but is acceptable in informal peer interaction and serves to signal he is synched with S1.]

Student 1: [. . .]thesis statement.

Student 1: [reading text] "In the shortcut of Panama I know that it is not safer than Cape Horn" so that would be a good reason, but they didn't mention Panama in their thesis statement, so now they have to mention . . . now they have to support this to this. [pointing to work sheet] [Note S1's assessment of the adequacy of the evidence and explanation for the thesis statement.]

Student 1: So they . . . [S1 starts to add more, but is interrupted by S2]

Student 2: But did they, it say in the text? [S2 interrupts by raising a further assessment concern given the guidance on the evaluation worksheet. The interruption is on topic and shows an understanding of what could be taken up next.]

Student 1: It didn't- yes it did say in the text but they didn't put it in their opinion thesis statement so . . . and this and this supports their topic sentence [pointing at outline] and- but see- read their explanation see if it supports their evidence and opinion. [referring to worksheet guideline for a critique of an effective opinion piece] [Usage of "but see- read" suggests S1 is thinking critically about intent of the authors of the outline, possibly to consider feedback that would allow the authors to complete their argument more adequately.]

Student 2: I think they're talking about the the wha- the best of about the Panama shortcut. [S2 expands on this possibility]

Student 1: I think this- their explanation should be their topic- topic sentence and then their explana- their topic sentence right now should be their explanation. That'd be a good idea and then its gonna be better, cuz like right here it says "Panama short cut is not the safest route to take" that would be a good opinion and then they say "in the shortcut of Panama I know it is not safer than Cape Horn."

In this short interaction, a teacher is in a position to observe how student 1 generates potential advice responsive to the teacher's intent to use dialogic reasoning involving feedback to support learning among peers (both the recipients of the critique and the two students we witness here working together to conduct their review of the peer pair's writing). Student 2 questions if there is an omission in the text-based argument being attempted by the peer pair whose writing they are critiquing and encourages student 1 to confirm. Student 1's comments show an understanding of the intent of student 2 and adds advice for their peer pair to reorder the information in their outline that is consistent with it.

Linguistically, the two students demonstrate that they can effectively build coherence during discussions by making referential ties to the written text they are critiquing and to each other's contributions. For example, there are a series of "it" pronouns used by student 1 in his response to student 2's query about what was in the text ("it did say in the text but they didn't put it") that are used to refer to the statement in the peer pair's text that the shortcut through Panama was not safer than Cape Horn. Notice the student's use of demonstrative pronouns (e.g., *this* and *that*) to refer to sections of the text he wants to draw his partner's attention to. In a "here and now" setting such as classroom interaction, such context-dependent references are readily understood and are linguistically appropriate.

Beyond such language forms that are specific to the face-to-face interaction, the boys display pragmatic abilities to maintain the conversation. The boys effectively manage each other's verbal contributions (as mentioned, the interruptions are tolerated, and this may be because they are intended as extensions of one another's thoughts and not as bids to take over the floor for another purpose), they are able to nominate next actions to further their intellectual inquiry (e.g., when student 1 suggests, "but see- read their explanation see if it supports their evidence and opinion"), and summarize contributions by a partner to show comprehension and perhaps move the discussion of feedback for their peers' writing forward. In this instance, student 2 raised the issue of whether the text supports the peer pair's opinion and student 1 called for the strategy of rereading the outline to uncover the inconstancy, which he then voices more concretely ("their explanation should be their topic- topic sentence and then their explana- their topic sentence right now should be their explanation. That'd be a good idea"). Student 1 goes beyond the queried concern of student 2 when he suggests the reordering that seems necessary in the outline.

The social regulation of interaction via pragmatic and metapragmatic means (especially assessing the target language meaning and attaining intended "force" in, for example, a written persuasive piece) requires a teacher's keen attention to the connection between conventionalized academic language form/usage and how it guides recipients' access to the intended meaning. Acquiring such deep language competence (proficiency) builds on worrying closely about how language works (Wong Fillmore & Fillmore, 2012), and how such worrying and learning is enabled by the fuller sociolinguistic repertoires of students that can be exercised through dialogic interaction, whether in spoken or written form.

Leveraging the Effects of Students' Language Variation for Improved Assessment

The variation in students' language can have an impact on the design of valid classroom assessments of academic content learning. Unknown (i.e., unmeasured) student language competencies are tied to student linguistic and cultural background, and are not viewed as conforming structurally or referentially to expected academic usage, and have been traditionally positioned as a threat to test validity much in the same way that the English language proficiency of English learners itself has been treated as a measurement issue in large-scale assessment of academic achievement (e.g., Abedi & Lord, 2001). Classroom assessment provides an opportunity to transform this measurement validity concern into a strategy for supporting linguistically and culturally diverse students' learning performances, and for building teacher awareness of how academic language conventions are functional in classroom contexts yet connected to student stylistic competencies.

In a recent study, Rodriguez-Mojica (2018) asked what emergent bilinguals[3] can do in English as they engaged in classroom interactions during ELA tasks. She found that they could produce a wide range of academic speech acts (language functions) in English that were aligned with state academic expectations, and "even emergent bilinguals considered 'struggling' by conventional standards used in schools showed evidence of using English to accomplish academic tasks in ways aligned to state academic expectations" (p. 31).

Only by taking account of interaction in a classroom context was Rodriguez-Mojica (2018) able to show how students are meeting the current college- and career-ready standards for ELA. For example, she reports the following short exchange between two students who are reading and reviewing the writing of one of the students (Tommy):

(4) Student: This doesn't make sense
Tommy: What?
Student: A lot of parts of Yosemite is wonderful

(p. 55)

Rodriguez-Mojica (2018) explains that:

Some might argue that simply asking "what?" is a nonspecific question because the question omits information about what specifically needs clarification. I argue that in the context of Excerpt 4 "what?" is a specific question that uses the common conversation device ellipsis. Within the context, "what doesn't make sense?" would be redundant because it was clear that Tommy sought clarification about what didn't make sense and not about something completely unrelated like what his peer had for breakfast.

(p. 55)

This kind of elliptical response in everyday conversation (i.e., omission of words from an expression under the assumption they are taken as given) is possible because of the nature of oral interaction where a response of one speaker to what has just been uttered by another speaker commonly takes into consideration the situated meaning and intent of the just prior utterance (Halliday & Hasan, 1976). Such elliptical usage by any student (not only EL students) is not seen as ambiguous or void of meaning. It does not lead a teacher to surmise that Tommy does not know how to accurately ask for clarification in English. However, in the context of large-scale assessment of English proficiency or other academic disciplines including ELA, student elliptical responses are not as functional. The context-reduced nature of large-scale assessment does not allow for meaning-making in this fashion; rather, responses most frequently need to be in full sentence forms because ambiguities cannot be queried by a test scorer.

This example also serves to show another advantage of classroom assessment over large-scale summative assessment; the reader of Tommy's writing is able to stop and orally prompt Tommy for further clarification when the concepts expressed or the wording of his writing do not make sense. For EL students, this provides flexibly exercised opportunities to learn and to modify their understanding as judged necessary by clarifying and bridging meaning in real time through feedback during authentic interaction. This kind of interaction may prove to be vital to EL student language growth and eventual academic success, and its efficacy for improved assessment and learning with EL students needs to be further researched.

Concluding Remarks

In this chapter, we have attempted to explain how student participation in authentic classroom discussions around appropriately designed activities creates the context in which teachers can assess their students' language and discipline knowledge and generate evidence of students' self-awareness of their competencies and responsiveness to learning interventions. By using teacher real-time cues and feedback sensitive to students' level of comprehension, assessment of academic content in the classroom setting can be made more suited to language-learning students.

The requisite language practices for deeper learning, we argue, are better defined and measured by understanding how and how well students take up and engage in academic tasks in authentic classroom learning contexts through language as action (e.g., via conversational exchanges, and co-constructing written explanations and arguments) rather than assessed solely as constructs targeting discrete skills in a decontextualized manner using direct, large-scale, standardized language tests. A wide variety of integrated language practices under the umbrella of sociocultural and sociocognitive functioning mediate successful classroom learning experiences, and accordingly assessment experiences of students and inferences made by teachers must be carefully considered so as to reflect the agency and response processes of students as learners and mutual (i.e., peer) assessors in a classroom community and its learning activities.

Contemporary assessment validity theory calls attention to warranting claims about what students know and can do in target assessment contexts based on conceptual and empirical models of students' capabilities (e.g., Kane, 2006). Traditional trait-oriented accounts of capabilities cannot provide direct evidence of response processes underlying competencies exercised in authentic classroom learning contexts where students' meaning-making and language usage are tied to sociocultural and sociocognitive functioning. Shepard et al. (2018) remind us that "sociocultural approaches make it possible to design for equity in educational settings by attending both to who learners are when they join a community and who they might become" (p. 24). Future ethnographic and close-in discourse analytic study of diverse students' actions and authentic language usage represented by several of the studies describe here (e.g., Rodriguez-Mojica, 2018) based on close-in observational analysis of classroom interaction can reveal much about how students learn and their metacognitive and metalinguistic processes that are not captured through large-scale assessments (Bailey & Heritage, 2018; Shepard et al., 2018).

The continued research of the limitations and complementary nature of large-scale and classroom assessment are critical for teacher pedagogical practices, including assessment literacy. Classroom assessment has a distinct advantage in that it can play both a formative and summative role in educational decision-making where large-scale assessment cannot contribute to the formative purpose of quotidian decision-making with the individual student. Furthermore, we hope to have shown here how only in authentic classroom interaction are students' conceptual understandings of academic content successfully observed in the face of often quite marked language constraints and/or differences in style. Taking account of content learning and language development in classroom settings may be valuable for all students (native English speakers also come from backgrounds that have wide variety in use and style within English), but is particularly important for linguistically and culturally diverse students, as we have shown with our selection of examples in this chapter.

Teachers will need tailored preparation to acquire the know-how to discern language and conceptual learning during interaction that includes conversational and discourse analytic skills. For students to acquire deep language competencies requires that both students and teachers know how language works. Student sociolinguistic repertoires that reflect this kind of language learning can be supported by teachers through pedagogies that design opportunities for students to practice and acquire fluency in dialogic interaction (Michaels & O'Connor, 2012). Moreover, assessment literacy that focuses on teachers recognizing where all students are on their paths to learning irrespective of how they express their knowledge should be no less important than assessment literacy that focuses on interpretation of test scores to summarize student learning after a period of learning.

Although Wilson and Toyama (2018) were speaking specifically about their developmental approach to assessment of learning progressions based on construct maps of domains used as a common frame of reference for connecting curriculum, instruction, and assessment, their comments are pertinent to our claims when they state that "for EL students, teachers should attend to local and cultural variations in how EL students access, engage and respond to assessment tasks" (p. 254), and we add to this *during moment-to-moment instructional task implementation*. This emphasis on the local and proximal processes underlying meaningful learning by EL students (in terms of both their language development and their academic content learning) could be the test case that helps to:

> turn the direction of influence of summative standardized assessment on formative assessment (and hence to instruction and learning) around to the opposite—where instruction and learning, in hand with formative assessment, give the direction to summative assessments and hence to accountability.
>
> (Wilson & Toyama, 2018, p. 255)

Finally, it is important to note that we have intentionally not addressed formal measurement model approaches to sociocognitive assessment design of classroom assessments also serving formative and diagnostic assessment of EL students. Such approaches are possible and are described by Kopriva and Wright (2017), Mislevy and Durán (2014), Solano-Flores (2016), and Wilson and Toyama (2018). These approaches deserve a separate and detailed treatment, keeping in mind that their quantitative modeling of student performance faces limits in adequately representing the responsiveness of EL students to opportunities for learning *in situ* in actual learning settings.

Notes

1 Mosher and Heritage (2017) go on to claim that "the purpose of instruction is to change knowledge and skill, so using measures that tend to be weighted toward relatively unchanging attributes to assess the outcomes of instruction is inappropriate. Assessing whether particular things that are instruction's goals have in fact been learned, especially if those goals are complex and ambitious, requires looking at specific, often complex and extended, performances, which can take more, and more varying, time than large-scale testing is likely to afford" (p. 61).
2 This is a significant oversight or lack of alignment between ELD/P assessment and language constructs, because ELD/P assessments are meant to inform educators of when EL students no longer need to receive language support services to access the content of the academic disciplines (*Every Student Succeeds Act*, 2015).
3 Emergent bilingual is becoming increasingly common as the term to refer to English learners because it acknowledges the linguistic capital or assets students have and their potential to become bilingual in both their first language and English as an additional language (e.g., García, 2009).

References

Abedi, J., & Lord, C. (2001). The language factor in mathematics tests. *Applied Measurement in Education*, *14*(3), 219–234.

American Educational Research Association (AERA), American Psychological Association (APA), & National Council on Measurement in Education (NCME). (2014). *Standards for educational and psychological testing*. Washington, DC: American Educational Research Association, American Psychological Association, & National Council on Measurement in Education.

Bachman, L., & Damböck, B. (2018). *Language assessment for classroom teachers*. Oxford: Oxford University Press.

Bailey, A. L. (2016). Assessing the language of young learners. In E. Shohamy & I. Or (Eds.), *Encyclopedia of language and education. Vol. 7: Language testing and assessment* (3rd ed., pp. 1–20). Berlin: Springer.

Bailey, A. L. (2017a). Progressions of a new language: Characterizing explanation development for assessment with young language learners. *Annual Review of Applied Linguistics*, *37*, 241–263.

Bailey, A. L. (2017b). Theoretical and developmental issues to consider in the assessment of young students' English language proficiency. In M. K. Wolf & Y. G. Butler (Eds.), *English language proficiency assessments for young learners* (pp. 25–40). New York: Routledge.

Bailey, A. L., & Heritage, M. (2018). *Self-regulation in learning: The role of language and formative assessment*. Cambridge, MA: Harvard Education Press.

Bailey, A. L., & Heritage, M. (2019). *Progressing students' language day by day*. Thousand Oaks, CA: Corwin Press.

Bailey, A. L., Heritage, M., & Butler, F. A. (2014). Developmental considerations and curricular contexts in the assessment of young language learners. In A. J. Kunnan (Ed.), *The companion to language assessment* (pp. 423–439). Boston, MA: Wiley.

Bailey, A. L., & Huang, B. H. (2011). Do current English language development/proficiency standards reflect the English needed for success in school? *Language Testing, 28*(3), 343–365.

Bailey, A. L., & Wolf, M. K. (2012). *The challenge of assessing language proficiency aligned to the Common Core State Standards and some possible solutions*. Understanding Language Initiative, Commissioned Paper, Stanford University, CA. Retrieved from www.ell.stanford.edu

Barajas-Lopez, F., Enyedy, N., & Bailey, A. L. (2005, April). *Language disconnects between small group problem solving and whole class discussions*. Paper presented at the annual meeting of the American Educational Research Association, Montréal, Québec, Canada.

Black, P., & Wiliam, D. (2009). Developing the theory of formative assessment. *Educational Assessment, Evaluation and Accountability, 21*(1), 5–31.

Bunch, G. C. (2014). The language of ideas and the language of display: Reconceptualizing "academic language" in linguistically diverse classrooms. *International Multilingual Research Journal, 8*, 70–86.

California Department of Education. (2017). *English language proficiency assessments for California, grades 6–8 speaking practice test*. Sacramento, CA: California Department of Education. Retrieved from www.elpac.org/s/pdf/ELPAC_Grades_6-8_Practice_Test_2018.pdf

Cole, M., & Engeström, Y. (1993). A cultural-historical approach to distributed cognition. In G. Salomon (Ed.), *Distributed cognitions: Psychological and educational considerations* (pp. 1–46). New York: Cambridge University Press.

Durán, R. P. (2008). Assessing English-language learners' achievement. *Review of Research in Education, 32*(1), 292–327.

Erickson, F. (2007). Some thoughts on "proximal" formative assessment of student learning. In P. Moss (Ed.), *Evidence in decision making: Yearbook of the National Society for the Study of Education* (vol. *106*, pp. 186–216). Malden, MA: Blackwell.

Every Student Succeeds Act of 2015, Pub. L. No. 114-95 § 114 Stat. 1177 (2015–2016).

García, O. (2009). Emergent bilinguals and TESOL: What's in a name? *TESOL Quarterly, 43*(2), 322–326.

Gee, J. P. (2014). Decontextualized language: A problem, not a solution. *International Multilingual Research Journal, 8*(1), 9–23.

Gibbons, P. (2009). *English learners, academic literacy, and thinking*. Portsmouth, NH: Heinemann.

Halliday, M. A. K., & Hasan, R. (1976). *Cohesion in English*. London: Longman.

Hawkins, M. R. (2004). Researching English language and literacy development in schools. *Educational Researcher, 33*(3), 14–25.

Heritage, M. (2018). Making assessment work for teachers. *Educational Measurement: Issues and Practice, 37*(1), 39–41.

Heritage, M., & Heritage, J. (2013). Teacher questioning: The epicenter of instruction and assessment. *Applied Measurement in Education, 26*(3), 176–190.

Heritage, M., Walqui, A., & Linquanti, R. (2015). *English language learners and the new standards: Developing language, content knowledge, and analytical practices in the classroom*. Cambridge, MA: Harvard Education Press.

Kane, M. T. (2006). Validation. In R. L. Brennan (Ed.), *Educational measurement* (4th ed., pp. 17–64). Westport, CT: American Council on Education/Praeger.

Kopriva, R. J., & Wright, L. (2017). Score processes in assessing academic content of non-native speakers. In K. Ercikan & J. W. Pellegrino (Eds.), *Validation of score meaning for the next generation of assessments: The use of response processes*. New York: Routledge.

Koretz, D. (2018). *The testing charade: Pretending to make schools better*. Chicago, IL: University of Chicago Press.

Kuhn, D. (1991). *The skills of argument*. Cambridge: Cambridge University Press.

Lee, O., Quinn, H., & Valdés, G. (2013). Science and language for English language learners in relation to Next Generation Science Standards and with implications for Common Core State Standards for English language arts and mathematics. *Educational Researcher, 42*(4), 223–233.

Michaels, S., & O'Connor, C. (2012). *Talk science primer*. Cambridge, MA: TERC.

Mislevy, R. J. (2018). *Sociocognitive foundations of educational measurement*. New York: Routledge.

Mislevy, R. J., & Durán, R. P. (2014). A sociocognitive perspective on assessing EL students in the age of Common Core and Next Generation Science Standards. *TESOL Quarterly, 48*(3), 560–585.

Mosher, F., & Heritage, M. (2017). *A hitchhiker's guide to thinking about literacy, learning progressions, and instruction*. CPRE Research Reports. Retrieved from http://repository.upenn.edu/cpre_researchreports/97

National Academies of Sciences, Engineering, and Medicine (NASEM). (2017). *Promoting the educational success of children and youth learning English: Promising futures*. Washington, DC: National Academies Press. https://doi.org/10.17226/24677

National Academies of Sciences, Engineering, and Medicine (NASEM). (2018). *English learners in STEM subjects: Transforming classrooms, schools, and lives*. Washington, DC: National Academies Press.

National Governors Association Center for Best Practices, Council of Chief State School Officers (CCSSO). (2010a). *Common Core State Standards for mathematics.* Washington, DC: National Governors Association Center for Best Practices, Council of Chief State School Officers. Retrieved from www.ccsso.org/sites/default/files/2017-10/MathStandards50805232017.pdf

National Governors Association Center for Best Practices, Council of Chief State School Officers (CCSSO). (2010b). *Common Core State Standards for English language arts & literacy in history/social studies, science, and technical subjects.* Washington, DC: National Governors Association Center for Best Practices, Council of Chief State School Officers. Retrieved from www.corestandards.org/assets/CCSSI_ELA%20Standards.pdf

NGSS Lead States. (2013). *Next Generation Science Standards: For states, by states.* Washington, DC: National Academies Press.

O'Connor, C., & Michaels, S. (2007). When is dialogue "dialogic"? *Human Development, 50,* 275–285.

Osborne, J. F., & Patterson, A. (2011). Scientific argument and explanation: A necessary distinction? *Science Education, 95*(4), 627–638.

Pryor, J., & Crossouard, B. (2008). A socio-cultural theorisation of formative assessment. *Oxford Review of Education, 34*(1), 1–20.

Rodriguez-Mojica, C. (2018). From test scores to language use: Emergent bilinguals using English to accomplish academic tasks. *International Multilingual Research Journal, 12*(1), 31–61.

Shepard, L. A., Penuel, W. R., & Pellegrino, J. W. (2018). Using learning and motivation theories to coherently link formative assessment, grading practices, and large-scale assessment. *Educational Measurement: Issues and Practice, 37*(1), 21–34.

Smarter Balanced Assessment Consortium. (n.d.). *Grade 4 mathematics sample items.* Retrieved from www.rcoe.us/educational-services/files/2013/11/asmt-sbac-math-gr4-sample-items.pdf

Solano-Flores, G. (2016). *Assessing English language learners: Theory and practice.* New York: Routledge.

Trumbull, E., & Solano-Flores, G. (2011). The role of language in assessment. In M. R. Basterra, E. Trumbull, & G. Solano-Flores (Eds.), *Cultural validity in assessment: Addressing linguistic and cultural diversity* (pp. 22–46). New York: Routledge.

Van Lier, L. (2004). The semiotics and ecology of language learning: Perception, voice, identity and democracy. *Utbildning & Demokrati, 13*(3), 79–103.

Van Lier, L., & Walqui, A. (2012). Language and the Common Core Standards. In K. Hakuta & M. Santos (Eds.), *Understanding language: Language, literacy, and learning in the content areas* (pp. 44–51). Palo Alto, CA: Understanding Language, Stanford University. Retrieved from http://ell.stanford.edu/publication/language-and-common-core-state-standards

Verschueren, J. (2000). Notes on the role of metapragmatic awareness in language use. *Pragmatics: Quarterly Publication of the International Pragmatics Association (IPrA), 10*(4), 439–456.

Wilson., M., & Toyama, Y. (2018). Formative and summative assessments in science and literacy integrated curricula: A suggested alternative approach. In A. L. Bailey, C. A. Maher, & L. C. Wilkinson (Eds.), *Language, literacy and learning in the STEM disciplines: How language counts for English learners* (pp. 231–260). New York: Routledge.

Wong Fillmore, L. W., & Fillmore, C. J. (2012). What does text complexity mean for English learners and language minority students? In K. Hakuta & M. Santos (Eds.), *Understanding language: Language, literacy, and learning in the content areas* (pp. 64–74). Palo Alto, CA: Understanding Language, Stanford University. Retrieved from http://ell.stanford.edu/publication/what-does-text-complexity-mean-english-learners-and-language-minority-students

Yeager, D. S., Henderson, M. D., Paunesku, D., Walton, G. M., D'Mello, S., Spitzer, B. J., & Duckworth, A. L. (2014). Boring but important: A self-transcendent purpose for learning fosters academic self-regulation. *Journal of Personality and Social Psychology, 107*(4), 559–580.

4

Feedback and Measurement

Susan M. Brookhart

The purpose of this chapter is to explore the relationship between feedback and measurement, with a focus on the meaning of feedback and measurement information in the context of classroom learning. Both feedback and measurement are means of conveying information to learners and to the educators who are responsible for their learning. Feedback and measurement are, as the chapter will argue, the only vehicles whose central purpose in the classroom context is to convey information about learning. Therefore, understanding the relationship between meaning conveyed through feedback and meaning conveyed through measurement is important for both research and theory-building, not only in the areas of feedback and measurement, but also in the areas of learning, motivation for learning, and instruction.

The National Council on Measurement in Education (NCME, 2018) has affirmed the importance of classroom assessment to its mission and its position as more central to learning than standardized, large-scale assessments. The NCME statement explained and supported the affirmation in this way (see also Wilson, 2018):

> The National Council on Measurement in Education (NCME) believes that the science and practice of classroom assessment are essential because they can improve student learning in a way that other forms of assessment cannot. Classroom assessment's core purpose is to facilitate learning for all students. Those most directly involved in that effort are students, teachers, and other school-based professionals. From this perspective, the most salient moments in student learning are orchestrated by teachers and students in the classroom—the place where the most immediate decisions about student learning are made, and where the greatest impact can occur.

Not all classroom assessment, however, fits the definition of measurement. Classroom assessment information is derived from both measurement and other sources. If classroom assessment is central to the mission of NCME, the question arises: What is the relationship between classroom assessment and measurement? This chapter focuses on one important part of that question, namely: What is the relationship between the meaning of the information communicated by classroom feedback and the meaning of information communicated by measurement in the classroom?

Because of its basis in classroom assessment, this chapter will focus on feedback for learning and measurement of learning (as opposed, for example, to feedback and measurement about behavior or effort) in the context of schooling.

Before discussing how the two are related, it is important to specify what is meant by feedback and what is meant by measurement. Therefore, the first section of this chapter describes current understandings of feedback and measurement. The next section describes the different kinds of meanings conveyed by different types of feedback and measurement, identifying areas of overlap and relationships between them, and discusses views of learning compatible with each type. This analysis forms the core of the chapter and is summarized in Table 4.1. The third section shows that feedback, both quantitative and qualitative, has an important role in the validation process, and may itself be subject to validation. A concluding section summarizes the argument in this chapter and suggests next steps for research and theory-building.

Definitions and Key Concepts

Both "feedback" and "measure" have many meanings in common parlance. For example, "feedback" can mean the squeal of speakers when a microphone gets too close, and "measure" can mean a quality ("the measure of a man") or a quantity ("the table measures 45 inches"). This section focuses on more specific definitions of the terms "feedback" and "measurement" as they are used in the respective research literatures on classroom assessment and measurement, because these are the concepts upon which the argument in this chapter will rest. It is worth noting that both definitions have changed over the last century as learning theory has changed.

Feedback

Feedback is arguably the most important source of assessment information that supports learning (Hattie, 2009; Ruiz-Primo & Brookhart, 2018) or formative assessment information. Formative feedback has a large impact on school performance (Hattie, 2009) and is also, as this chapter will show, an area of classroom assessment that clearly includes both measurement and non-measurement information. Summative classroom assessment can be used formatively as well to support further learning (Brookhart, 2001; Wiliam, Lee, Harrison, & Black, 2004). In this chapter, then, "feedback" is understood to serve a formative purpose, but as the definitions below show, classroom feedback can come from assessment originally intended to be formative or summative.

The definition of feedback has evolved with changes in learning theory (Brookhart, 2018). In the early and middle twentieth century, learning was understood from a behaviorist point of view as acquiring a command of facts and concepts. From this point of view, assessment meant checking to see how many facts and concepts had become established in students' brains and was primarily summative (Shepard, 2000). Assessments consisted of rather simple tasks requiring recall or basic comprehension of these facts and concepts, with clear correct answers, and feedback was information to students about which of their answers were right and which were wrong. Feedback was interpreted in light of Thorndike's (1913) law of effect, namely that reinforcement increases the likelihood of a behavior and punishment decreases it. Positive feedback was seen as reinforcement and negative feedback as punishment (Skinner, 1958). However, the results of early studies of feedback did not bear out this theory. Kluger and DeNisi (1996, pp. 255–257) presented a historical perspective on early feedback research. They reported that feedback consisting of simple knowledge of results had been found, in research dating back 100 years, to have very small effects on performance.

With the advent of cognitive and constructivist views of learning in the mid to late twentieth century, the understanding of learning expanded from command of a set of facts and concepts to include applying those facts and concepts to new situations, solving problems, and other complex learning outcomes. The underlying view of learning is that students construct their own meaning by taking in new information and making connections with prior knowledge. The understanding of feedback changed accordingly, from primarily summative information about correct answers to primarily formative information describing students' current understandings and suggesting next steps to deepen understanding. Feedback is information students can use to move that learning process forward. Hattie and Timperley (2007) defined feedback as "information provided by an agent (e.g., teacher, peer, book, parent, self, experience) regarding aspects of one's performance or understanding" (p. 81), and this widely accepted definition is the one adopted in this chapter. Shute (2008) defined formative feedback specifically as "information communicated to the learner that is intended to modify his or her thinking or behavior to improve learning" (p. 153). Further, she asserted that feedback that has negative effects on learning is not formative (p. 156). Studies of feedback interpreted in this way have found large effects on learning. Hattie and Timperley (2007, p. 83) estimated the average effect size of feedback across many meta-analyses at 0.79, among the most powerful effects on learning reported.

The current definition of feedback is broader than the behaviorist view, and encompasses both quantitative information (e.g., right/wrong, number correct) and qualitative information (e.g., a description of the work's strengths and suggestions for improvement). As might be expected, effect sizes in individual studies are therefore variable (Hattie & Timperley, 2007; Kluger & DeNisi, 1996). Current reviews of the feedback literature identify the most effective feedback as descriptive information that helps students understand the current quality level of their work and suggests steps they can take to improve (Hattie & Timperley, 2007; Kluger & DeNisi, 1996; Shute, 2008; Van der Kleij, Feskens, & Eggen, 2015). The section "Synthesis: Relationships between Types of Feedback and Types of Measurement" below expands on these ideas.

In short, then, the objective of feedback is to move learning forward. Feedback is information, in various forms and from various sources, that is useful for accomplishing this goal. Feedback is effective if it supports learning and ineffective if it does not. Feedback therefore derives its value from the learning it enables. Feedback that is not used, or is misapplied and does not enable learning, is ineffective.

Measurement

Lorge (1951) presented an extended definition and explanation of measurement in his canonical chapter "The Fundamental Nature of Measurement." He wrote:

> In general, measurement involves the assignment of a class of numerals to a class of objects. Measurement, therefore, must consider three factors: first, it must deal with the classes of objects; second, it must deal with the classes of numerals; and third, it must deal with the rules for assigning numerals to objects.
>
> (p. 534)

In his discussion of the first factor, he wrote, "The concept of a *property* or *characteristic* of an object or of a person is crucial in measurement" (p. 536, emphasis in original). The numeral is assigned to the property, not the object itself. Further, the property must be something a person can conceive of, because one cannot observe what one cannot define. In measurement, observations are made (by an observer or instrument, p. 538), and then numerals are assigned using a variety of kinds of scales.

For purposes of this chapter, two elements of Lorge's explanation are especially worth noting. First, he emphasized the conception of the property being measured. All else depends on how the property is conceived by the scientists behind the measures. Late in the chapter, he used the term "construct" (p. 557) for the property observed. Second, he emphasized that meaning and understanding is the goal of measurement. In a section called "Explanation as the End of Measurement," he wrote:

> The conventions of test construction all too frequently confuse the understanding of social and psychological properties and traits by attempting to make the field conform to the standards of mathematics. Insofar as mathematical models correspond to the realities of a given field, there is a justification for their use. The primary concern of measurement, however, should be *for* an understanding of the entire field of knowledge rather than *with* statistical or mathematical manipulations upon observations.
>
> (pp. 556–557, emphasis in original)

He continued by pointing out that statistical operations (e.g., factor analysis) can help clarify constructs, but that ultimately factors, or any other statistical results, are not the properties themselves. Rather, scientists' shared understanding of the meaning of the measured properties, including other properties and qualities to which they are related, is the construct.

As learning theory developed toward more cognitive and constructivist views, discussions of the specific properties underlying measures of learning became more nuanced. The nature of the measures themselves changed accordingly. While early tests and measures added up discrete bits of information, mostly calling for recall and simple comprehension, current measurement instruments require alignment with both the content and cognitive levels of intended learning outcomes, and where appropriate include tasks that produce evidence of student thinking.

Haertel (1985) explored the idea that items and tasks on achievement tests, as well as anticipated responses, should be sampled from a well-defined achievement domain derived from the learning goal[1] to be measured. The achievement domain is derived from the construct the test measures. Haertel (1985) wrote:

> The recognition that educational outcomes are constructs should bring no revolution in CRT design and use . . . Rather, the perspective of construct validation can focus and orient the tasks of test design, construction, use, and interpretation, leading to more informed and systematic applications of existing methods.
>
> (p. 33)

He applied his approach by discussing construct validation of a test of functional literacy. Similarly, Glaser and Baxter (2002) gave an example of how they defined a science content and process space that was useful for specifying science tasks and anticipated effects on student performance for the construction of assessments in science.

Glaser and Baxter (2002) and Haertel (1985) wrote about large-scale assessment. However, with the move to acknowledge that achievement domains are based on intended learning outcomes derived from constructs, the stage is set for application to classroom assessment. Most classroom assessment seeks to indicate student achievement of an intended learning outcome, whether for formative or summative purposes.

A major difference between the intended learning outcomes referenced by large-scale and classroom assessment of learning is the grain size of the achievement construct (Pellegrino, Chudowsky, & Glaser, 2001). Large-scale assessment often samples broad achievement domains (e.g., "mathematics"), while classroom assessment is usually concerned with lesson-sized or unit-sized achievement domains (e.g., "distinguishing the ones from the tens place"). The learning goal is still derived from a construct, albeit one of smaller size. Smaller-size classroom learning goals typically refer to aspects of the larger achievement goals (e.g., curricular or state mathematics standards) derived from yet larger constructs (e.g., "mathematics"). The assessment items or tasks are still a sample that must be carefully selected to represent both the mathematical content and intended cognitive level and/or mathematical process skills. When quantification is needed, anticipated student responses must still be assigned numerals that facilitate sound interpretations of learning and uses that improve and/or audit learning. For example, quantification is helpful, and even necessary, to produce information that can be aggregated or to support more equivalent comparisons between groups.

In short, then, the objective of measurement is to convey meaning. Differing perspectives on measurement still hold to the centrality of meaning in measurement. For example, Wright and Stone's (2004) approach to observation is more inductive (noticing sameness) than deductive (looking for a rigorously defined property, Lorge, 1951). However, they still ground their observations, and hence their measures, in meaningful distinctions made by observers. And for measures of learning, the objective is to convey meaning about a domain of learning.

The Centrality of Meaning in Feedback and Measurement

The discussion in the preceding section suggests that the learning goal or intended learning outcome is the central focus of feedback from which its meaning derives. Theorists of formative classroom assessment make this clear. In most contemporary discussions of formative assessment, learning is envisioned as a process in which the student engages:

> Stated explicitly, therefore, the learner has to (a) possess a concept of the standard (or goal, or reference level) being aimed for, (b) compare the actual (or current) level of performance with the standard, and (c) engage in appropriate action which leads to some closure of the gap.
>
> (Sadler, 1989, p. 121)

Sadler thinks of these as simultaneous processes, not sequential steps, because each informs the other and must be in mind simultaneously in order for learning to improve. Hattie and Timperley (2007) describe this same process:

> Effective feedback must answer three major questions asked by a teacher and/or by a student: Where am I going? (What are the goals?), How am I going? (What progress is being made toward the goal?), and Where to next? (What activities need to be undertaken to make better progress?)
>
> (p. 86)

In many classrooms, the three questions that constitute the formative learning cycle are used with students as: Where am I going? Where am I now? Where to next? (or something similar).

Feedback is a message conveying information that feeds all three parts of the formative learning cycle. Effective feedback helps clarify the student's concept of what learning looks like (Where am I going?), provides critical information about current performance (Where am I now?) and suggestions for improvement (Where to next?). In summary, feedback derives its meaning from the learning goal, whether that goal is small ("Can you find the sentence that needs a period?") or larger ("How could you more effectively persuade readers who do not already agree with you?"). Ultimately, feedback is only effective if it helps students move closer to the learning goal.

The description in the previous section suggests that meaning is the ultimate goal of measurement as well. That meaning inheres in the construct that is measured by a particular instrument. For measures of learning and achievement, learning goals are the constructs of interest, just as they are for classroom assessment of learning and for feedback.

Thus, it follows that the same learning goals that give meaning to measures of achievement also give meaning to feedback. This deduction is central to a discussion of the relationship between feedback and measurement and is the backbone of the argument that, in fact, feedback and measurement are related. This does not mean that all feedback is measurement, or all measurement is feedback, but it does mean that the same sources of meaning, namely the learning goals, stand behind both, and therefore they *are* related.

Suppose a specific learning goal is the construct behind both a quantitative measure (say, a classroom quiz) and some written feedback on a piece of student work (maybe that same quiz, or maybe another work sample). That learning goal is related to other learning goals, which may also have measures and feedback associated with them in a classroom unit of instruction. In a well-functioning classroom, the learning goals add up to larger (e.g., curricular goals) and larger (e.g., state standards) learning goals that are also constructs that may be measured (e.g., with a benchmark or state accountability test).

Many things besides feedback and measurement are related to learning goals. For example, classroom instruction is based on learning goals, but also on principles of pedagogy, students' prior background and experience in the content area, and available resources to name a few. Or, for another example, educational materials, such as textbooks and videos, are based on learning goals and other things as well.

However, for instruction, materials, and all other aspects of schooling that are based on learning goals, the purposes are broader than communicating messages about how students are doing with their learning. *Feedback and measurement are the only two things that are based on learning goals and also intend to directly communicate a message that describes student learning relative to learning goals.* Feedback and measurement are information *about* learning that are intended to be used to *interpret* learning. They are, metaphorically, two different languages that one can use to appraise and send messages about student learning, although in fact there is some overlap between the two.

To push the language metaphor, some kinds of information translate better than others. The next section seeks to analyze this translation, and in so doing to analyze the relationship between feedback and measurement. The section explores the types of messages or information communicated by feedback, whether quantitative or qualitative in nature, and the types of messages or information communicated by quantitative measurement.

Types of Feedback, Types of Measurement, and Their Relationship

In this section, "type" refers to the nature of the *message or information communicated*, whether by feedback or measurement. It does not refer to a data collection method or assessment strategy. The focus here is on the nature of the information or message teachers and students, and potentially others, receive from feedback and measurement—which affects how they interpret it and what they can do with it.

Types of Feedback

Different types of feedback send different messages. Why are some types of feedback more powerful than others? The answer to that question can be found in theories of learning. Some feedback messages are more central to current understandings of how students learn than others. Current understandings of learning, as pointed out above, are cognitive and constructivist in nature. As cognitive psychology gained prominence in learning theory, interest in student self-regulation of learning grew. The self-regulation of learning refers to "self-generated thoughts, feelings, and actions that are planned and cyclically adapted to the attainment of personal goals" (Zimmerman, 2000, p. 14). If it is not quite true that all learning is to some extent self-regulated—although it might be—at the least, "the most effective learners are self-regulating" (Butler & Winne, 1995, p. 245).

Butler and Winne (1995) synthesized a model of self-regulated learning that included an explicit feedback component. They then used their model to analyze research on feedback. In fact, many subsequent reviews of the formative assessment literature have drawn on Butler and Winne's model (Panadero, Andrade, & Brookhart, 2018). Butler and Winne identified two main types of feedback, characterized by the kind of messages they conveyed: *outcome feedback* and *cognitive feedback*. Similarly, Shute (2008), citing Kulhavy and Stock's (1989) earlier review, described two general types of feedback, depending on whether the purpose of the feedback information was *verification* or *elaboration*.

Outcome Feedback

Butler and Winne (1995) wrote that the simplest and most common type of feedback is outcome feedback, sometimes called knowledge of results. This is feedback about the correctness of answers, typically in right/wrong terms. Traditional feedback research typically studied the effects of this kind of feedback on achievement in some defined domain of learning. Butler and Winne pointed out that this feedback does not give the student any information to help them self-regulate: to select new goals, decide on further learning strategies, or monitor the results. Shute (2008) called this type of feedback verification, which she described as information about the correctness of student work.

Feedback in computer-based instruction often conveys a message of simple verification or outcome feedback. It can, however, be more elaborated. Mason and Bruning (2001, pp. 5–6) reviewed studies of feedback in the context of computer-based instruction and identified eight levels of feedback:

- *No feedback*—proportion of correct responses on a whole test.
- *Knowledge-of-response*—verification of the correctness (or not) of individual answers.
- *Answer-until-correct*—individual item verification, and the learner must stay on the same item until it is correct.
- *Knowledge-of-correct-response*—individual item verification plus supplying the correct answer.
- *Topic-contingent*—individual item verification plus general elaborative information about the topic.
- *Response-contingent*—individual item verification and elaboration (e.g., explaining why an incorrect answer was wrong).
- *Bug-related*—individual item verification plus identifying procedural errors.
- *Attribute-isolation*—individual item verification plus information about key aspects of the concept to be learned.

Notice that these levels of feedback are arranged in a general order from simple verification through more elaborated feedback. Mason and Bruning (2001) found that in general, the more elaborated feedback was more effective, with some exceptions for low achievers and low-level tasks. Van der Kleij et al. (2015), also reviewing studies of feedback in the context of computer-based instruction, found that elaborated feedback produced a higher effect size (mean weighted effect size 0.49) than either of the verification strategies: knowledge of results (0.05) or knowledge of correct answer (0.32).

Notice, however, that none of these eight types of feedback in the computer-based instruction context are highly elaborated. By contrast, studies of written and oral teacher feedback in classrooms have produced typologies that move from evaluative knowledge of results to highly elaborated descriptive statements about work and suggestions for next steps or even feedback conversations in which the teacher and learner co-create ideas for next steps.

Cognitive Feedback

Citing Balzer, Doherty, and O'Connor (1989), Butler and Winne (1995) called the kind of feedback that does contain information that students can use to self-regulate further learning cognitive feedback. Cognitive feedback gives students information that connects the conditions set out in the task and their achievement. The task conditions, or cues, that students attend to are filtered by their prior knowledge and beliefs. Feedback that helps students interpret the task and connect it with their understandings and performance gives students information they can use to set new goals and self-regulate. While this explanation uses the language of self-regulation, it is the same reasoning described earlier in this chapter as the formative learning cycle. Further, Butler and Winne (1995, pp. 251–252) identified three types of cognitive feedback, which they named task validity feedback, cognitive validity feedback, and functional validity feedback. Task feedback alerts the learner to aspects of the task that are useful for guiding performance. Cognitive feedback alerts the learner to notice or reflect on aspects of the task she used in her work. Functional feedback helps learners improve the accuracy of their self-monitoring. Any of these three may be expected to help students engage in more effective self-regulation of learning after they have received the feedback and begin the process of using it.

Similarly, Shute (2008) used the term elaboration for feedback that helps interpret students' performance for them. Elaboration can: "(a) address the topic, (b) address the response, (c) discuss the particular error(s), (d) provide worked examples, or (e) give gentle guidance" (Shute, 2008, p. 158). Overall, she reported that elaborative feedback has shown to be more effective for learning, with verification feedback sometimes being useful for low-level tasks and for lower achievers.

Other typologies of feedback have also focused on whether feedback evaluates correctness or describes student thinking. Tunstall and Gipps (1996) observed Year 1 and Year 2 (roughly equivalent to U.S. first and second grade) teachers and categorized their feedback according to whether it was primarily evaluative (right/wrong) or descriptive. Evaluative feedback serves a verification purpose, and descriptive feedback serves a more elaborated purpose. Tunstall and Gipps's (1996, p. 394) typology for feedback on learning included four types, moving from two primarily evaluative types through two primarily descriptive types of feedback: Type A, rewarding or punishing; Type B, approving or disapproving; Type C, specifying attainment or specifying improvement; and Type D, constructing achievement and constructing the way forward (with the student). As feedback moves from Type A to Type D, the positive and negative poles are replaced with descriptions of achievement and suggestions for improvement. Research on student perceptions of feedback suggests that students do, in fact, see suggestions for improvement as positive and not as criticism, as long as they have the chance to act on those suggestions (Brookhart, 2018; Gamlem & Smith, 2013).

Even though Tunstall and Gipps's (1996) typology was constructed from observations of primary students, Types C and D feedback push beyond the attribute-isolation feedback described in studies of computer-based learning. The use of criteria and models features prominently in Tunstall and Gipps's descriptions of Types C and D feedback, and in Type D the child has a role in articulating learning and deciding what to do next. In other words, self-regulation is explicitly built into these conceptions of feedback. Ruiz-Primo and Brookhart (2018, pp. 66–67) extended Tunstall and Gipps's typology by explicitly adding student participation and teacher instructional moves as part of the feedback enterprise.

Hattie and Timperley (2007) also explicitly built self-regulation into their consideration of types of feedback. Their model of feedback is based on the notion that the three formative questions (Where am I going? How am I going? Where to next?) can be answered at each of four levels (p. 87). *Task-level feedback* describes how the student understood and performed the task. *Process-level feedback* describes the processes the student used to do the work. *Self-regulation-level feedback* describes the student's self-direction and self-monitoring. These three levels are reminiscent of Balzer et al.'s (1989, p. 410) task information, cognitive information, and functional validity information, respectively. Hattie and Timperley (2007) add a fourth level. *Self-level feedback* (the only "level" that does not follow in order) provides personal evaluations (e.g., "Good boy").

Personal Feedback

Self-level feedback works in a similar manner to an ad hominem argument. The person, rather than the qualities of the work or evidence of learning, is made the focus of the feedback, receiving personal praise for high-quality work and blame for poor-quality work. Tunstall and Gipps's (1996) Type A (rewarding/punishing) and Type B (approving/disapproving) feedback are of this type.

Hattie and Timperley's (2007) review of the feedback literature demonstrated that task, process, and self-regulation feedback are useful for learning, and self-level feedback is not. Shepard (2008) summarized research literature on motivation and learning that supports this conclusion as well. Hattie (2009) wrote:

> Some types of feedback are more powerful than others. The most effective forms of feedback provide cues or reinforcement to the learner, are in the form of video, audio, or computer-assisted instruction feedback, or relate feedback to learning goals. . .the key is feedback that is received and acted upon by students . . . Programmed instruction, praise, punishment, and extrinsic rewards were the least effective forms of feedback for enhancing achievement.
>
> (p. 174)

Both Hattie and Timperley (2007) and Tunstall and Gipps (1996) pointed out that personal feedback was not recommended, but that they included it in their typologies of feedback because this kind of feedback was common. For the same reason, this chapter considers personal feedback alongside outcome feedback and cognitive feedback and analyzes the kind of message it sends to students—but notes that personal feedback has not been found to support learning.

Information from Feedback and Measurement in Light of Theories of Learning

One's view of learning has implications for the kind of information that should be needed to learn. If learning means adding facts to one's mental files, then a count of correct facts is relevant information for learning. If learning means expanding one's mental schema in the direction of more complete and nuanced understandings of a concept, then a description of current thinking and suggestions for what to think about next is relevant information for learning. This section discusses the kinds of information available from different kinds of feedback and measurement and evaluates them according to how they support learning.

Information from Feedback

Cognitive feedback (Butler & Winne, 1995) or elaboration (Shute, 2008; Van der Kleij et al., 2015) produces verbal information, typically oral or written feedback on student work. Sometimes verbal feedback is accompanied by knowledge of results as well, as when a problem set is marked for correctness but also contains written feedback, or when a rubric score is assigned but also includes descriptions of performance at both current and aspirational levels.

There is a classification system for the type of information words are intended to convey. Text can be classified as narrative, descriptive, expository, or argumentative (sometimes called persuasive). Narrative text communicates a story. Descriptive text depicts something in terms of what the writer observes. Expository text explains or informs the reader about something. Argumentative text takes a position and tries to convince the reader of its soundness. The type of verbal information in feedback helps determine the message the feedback carries.

For written feedback to be cognitive (i.e., to support further student learning), it should be descriptive and/or expository. That is, feedback should describe the student's work against criteria and make at least one suggestion for a next step (Ruiz-Primo & Brookhart, 2018). In some instances, cognitive feedback can take the form of argumentative text, if it states an evaluative position (e.g., "This paper doesn't grab readers' interest") and then explains why ("You used examples most of your readers wouldn't care about"). However, such argumentative text should swiftly turn to exposition, explaining and suggesting what the student might do about the issue.

Cognitive or elaborated feedback has been shown to support learning (Balzer et al., 1989; Hattie & Timperley, 2007; Shute, 2008; Van der Kleij et al., 2015). Butler and Winne (1995) address the probable mechanism by which this happens. Cognitive feedback gives students information they can use in the self-regulation of learning. A description of current work status helps students clarify what they are trying to learn, adjust their learning or studying strategies, and modify goals if needed. Suggestions for next steps help students decide on the actions they will take to get closer to their goal. Hattie and Timperley (2007) discussed this same process using the language of the formative learning cycle.

Cognitive feedback is more effective if the tasks themselves are designed in such a way as to allow student thinking to show (Shepard, 2000). Low-level tasks do not lend themselves to providing rich feedback about student thinking because the tasks do not elicit much evidence of student thinking. Earlier, the point was made that measurement science, informed by advances in learning theory, increasingly calls for rich tasks in order to better reference complex learning goals.

Situative views of learning are concerned with the social and contextual aspects of learning, which they think of as participating in a community of practice (Pellegrino et al., 2001; Shepard, Penuel, & Pellegrino, 2018). Situative views of learning do not dismiss individual cognition, but rather situate it in the learning community or learning culture. Cognitive feedback supports learning understood in this way if it is used by the community of practice (e.g., in work sessions of a small group of peers, in whole-class discussions, in classroom moderation of work quality goals by exhibiting and discussing models of good and poor work).

Information from Measurement

Readers of this chapter will already understand that the meaning conveyed by quantitative measurement differs according to the type of scale. For example, assigning a score of 3 to a student might mean she is in group 3, or that her grade-point average ranks third in her class, or that her writing performance places her at level 3 on a rubric with four levels, or that she got three problems correct on a five-point quiz, and so on. The information communicated is different in each case.

Stevens (1946) showed that the rules by which numbers are applied to observations determine the kind of information the numbers communicate, and applied the terms nominal, ordinal, interval, and ratio to different kinds of scales. Some discussions of types of numerical data add a fifth type of scale, binary or binomial data. Binary data has just two values, 0 and 1, to codify right/wrong, yes/no, true/false, and other dichotomous classifications. Binary data are useful for this discussion because the designation of right/wrong has been an important part of the feedback literature.

If observations are classified into groups that share common characteristics and the groups are numbered, they are on a nominal scale. Some quantitative methodologists call nominal data "qualitative," even though the data are numerical. Stevens (1946) considered nominal data quantitative, based on empirical observation of equality and, mathematically, subject to one-to-one substitution of any member in the group. This chapter will adopt that designation, reserving the designation of "qualitative" for non-numerical information. If observations are placed into rank order and the ranks are reported, they are on an ordinal scale. If equal differences are determined and numbers are assigned, they are on an interval scale. If equal ratios are determined and numbers are assigned, they are on a ratio scale. The nature of the scale supports the use of certain statistics and, with the exception of ratio scales, precludes the meaningful use of others.

For the discussion in this chapter, the concern is less with allowable statistical treatment of the numbers than with the meaning they communicate, namely: group membership (nominal), rank order (ordinal), location on an equal-interval scale with an arbitrary (or with no) meaningful zero point (interval), and location on an equal-interval scale with a meaningful zero point (ratio). The focus is on what the numbers mean because that meaning determines what message the score is able to send. This is important for the purpose of the chapter, to explore the relationship between feedback and measurement in the context of classroom learning, focusing on the information communicated about student progress toward classroom learning goals.

Synthesis: Relationships between Types of Feedback and Types of Measurement

Table 4.1 charts the relationship among the types of feedback information, types of measurement information and relevant learning theories. It synthesizes the discussion to this point. Table 4.1 is organized according to the types of feedback described above: outcome, cognitive, and personal. Each type of feedback sends a different message, which is described in the second column, and is particularly relevant for or compatible with certain views of learning, noted in the third column.

Messages containing information about student work can come in several forms. Sometimes students get information about their learning from test scores or other forms of measurement. Sometimes students get information from substantive comments about their work in the form of oral or written verbal feedback.

Sometimes students get messages about the quality of their work and potential next steps in both numerical *and* verbal form. Classroom rubrics give students both quantitative and qualitative information at the same time. Rubrics are assessment tools that include both criteria for appraising work and performance-level descriptions that describe work along a continuum of quality (Brookhart & Chen, 2015). When teachers and students use rubrics for formative or summative classroom assessment, meaning about the quality of student work is communicated via both ordinal quantitative data and written descriptions of the work. Whether rubrics use actual numbers for the performance levels (e.g., 1 through 4) or names (e.g., emerging, developing, proficient, exemplary), the levels on rubrics are ordered categories. The performance-level description for a particular level of a particular category describes the quality of student work relative to that category. Sometimes teachers add additional verbal comments as well.

Table 4.1 Relations between types of feedback and types of information

Types of Feedback	Meaning of Information Communicated	Learning Theory Implied or Assumed
Outcome feedback: Feedback for the verification of correctness, including:	Correct or not (Binary scale, e.g., R/W or 1/0) Which response option was correct? (Nominal scale, e.g., abcd)	Supports a behaviorist or transmissionist view of learning
	What level of achievement have I reached? (Ordinal scale, e.g., ABCDF; performance levels on rubrics)	Supports cognitive/constructivist views of learning for low-level skills (e.g., memorizing math facts)
• Knowledge of response	How well did I do? (Interval scale, e.g., total test score or percentage; ordinal scale, e.g., rubric performance level)	Supports cognitive/constructivist views of learning if coupled with additional student tools, such as instruction on reflection or how to look for patterns in their R/W answers
• Answer until correct		
• Knowledge of correct response		
Cognitive feedback: Feedback for elaboration on learning, describing current learning and suggesting avenues for improvement, including:	What does my work show about my learning? (Descriptive comments; performance-level descriptions in rubrics) What do I need to understand that my work doesn't yet show? (Expository comments)	Supports cognitive/constructivist views of learning Supports self-regulation of learning Supports situative views of learning
• Topic-contingent	What next steps might I take in my learning? (Expository comments explaining next steps, and sometimes argumentative comments taking a position about the work and supporting it)	
• Response-contingent		
• Bug-related		
• Attribute isolation		
• Specifying attainment		
• Specifying improvement		
• Constructing achievement		
• Constructing the way forward		
• Task-level feedback		
• Process-level feedback		
• Self-regulation-level feedback		
Self-level feedback: Feedback about the person, including:	Am I good at this? (Incomplete argumentative comments, taking an evaluative position without providing an explanation; misinterpreting student work as an indicator of the student personally instead of as an indicator of learning)	Not supportive of learning
• Rewarding		
• Punishing		
• Approving		
• Disapproving		

If feedback—whether qualitative, quantitative, or both—is closely tied to criteria that are shared between teachers and students, the contents of feedback can provide insights into decisions made on the basis of measures of learning, including applying large-scale measurement for classroom purposes (e.g., deciding on next instructional moves for a group of students based on benchmark assessment results) and using classroom measurement for instructional decisions (e.g., deciding on next instructional moves on the basis of graded [measured] performance on a unit test or performance assessment).

Table 4.1 interprets "text" broadly to include the words in oral as well as written feedback. Some feedback is in the form of a physical demonstration or a visual model. For example, a kindergarten teacher may rearrange a student's fingers as she grasps a pencil to show her how to hold it properly. A primary teacher may reference an ideal capital A on an alphabet chart to show students how to make a capital A. Since the purpose of most feedback that comes in the form of physical demonstration or visual models is to explain how to do something, such feedback would be considered expository.

Table 4.1 shows that outcome feedback is, or could be transformed to be, quantitative information recognizable as the kind of information conveyed by a scale of measurement. Cognitive feedback is largely—although not exclusively—verbal information, and therefore does not fit the definition of measurement used in this chapter.

Nevertheless, cognitive feedback is related to measurement in that the same learning goals or outcomes form the constructs or properties of reference behind both. The learning goal is the mechanism by which verbal, cognitive feedback and measurement are related. Most assessments that are not scored could be, given a clear domain definition and clear criteria. In a well-functioning classroom assessment system, formative assessments are done for learning and practice and receive verbal feedback throughout a unit. Then a similar assessment of the same learning outcome will be done as a summative assessment, which will be scored and issued a grade. In this way, the relationship between feedback and measurement is made concrete.

The discussion to this point has established that conveying information or sending a message about student standing, progress, or next steps relative to a learning goal is the underlying purpose for both feedback and measurement. Another question follows: How valid or sound is that information? The next section is not an exhaustive treatment of validity, but rather a preliminary discussion of some areas in validation that are related to both feedback and measurement.

Feedback and Validation

The validity of quantitative measures is concerned with score meaning and with the appropriateness of decisions based on score meaning. Consequential evidence for validity seeks to answer the question of whether decisions made on the basis of inferences about score meaning led to intended consequences and avoided unintended consequences, at least unintended consequences that are related to construct-relevant variance (Kane, 2006; Messick, 1989). As described earlier, intended learning goals or outcomes, of varying grain sizes, are the constructs of interest in measurement of achievement, in both classroom and large-scale assessment. The intended consequence is student learning—achievement of those outcomes. Intended learning outcomes are also the constructs of interest in feedback, whether numerical or verbal. If the construct is an intended learning outcome, then surely the major intended implication is that the student should learn the intended knowledge and skills (i.e., should reach the outcome) (Wilson, 2018).

Feedback information can be used as consequential evidence for the validation of quantitative measures used in classrooms. Feedback could comprise important evidence for validity, evaluating whether the use of a measure did in fact lead to student learning. Using feedback to improve is arguably the most important intended consequence of decisions based on formative classroom assessment information, and, as the NCME (2018) statement explained, of summative classroom assessment information as well. Consequential evidence for validity of educational measures would seek to answer questions such as the following: Did the measure provide meaningful feedback to the teacher and/or student? Did the teacher provide additional, elaborative feedback to the student? If either of these answers is yes, did the student use the feedback, and was the result an improvement in intended knowledge and skills? What did students learn? How did performance improve? Did knowing the results of measurement help students set goals and adjust their studying to reach them (i.e., did the results of measurement help support student self-regulation of learning)? Consequences might be direct, as when a student uses a test score to focus future studying, or indirect, as when a teacher uses a test score to help inform future instruction, which in turn helps students learn.

If feedback is a message or information to a student about current work quality and suggestions for next steps, based on what students are intending to learn, then feedback too may be subject to validation. Consequential evidence may be the most important evidence for the validation of feedback, because feedback is effective if it leads to improvement of learning. A treatise on establishing the validity (or soundness, authenticity, credibility, and importance) of qualitative information is beyond the scope of this chapter. However, it is important here to note that any information, including feedback, should convey intended meaning and support intended interpretations and uses, including students' own interpretations and uses. Questions that could be used to investigate the validity of inferences about learning from the use of feedback include: Was the feedback based on criteria directly related to progress toward the intended learning outcome? Did the students understand the feedback? Did they have an opportunity to use it in the manner the teacher intended? Did the quality of subsequent work demonstrate that further learning occurred?

Conclusion

There are many roles for measurement in the learning process, but measurement alone is inadequate to provide effective feedback for student learning. This accords with other research that has shown that teachers who are the most effective users of formative assessment collect and respond to evidence of student thinking, not the correctness of their responses (Hattie, 2009; Hattie & Timperley, 2007; Kroog, Ruiz-Primo, & Sands, 2014; Minstrell, Anderson, & Li, 2009). However, measurement has a large role to play in classroom learning, even if not as large a role as feedback.

What is the relationship between feedback and measurement in classroom learning? The argument and analysis set forth in this chapter support three conclusions. First, some feedback is in the form of quantitative measurement, and this type of feedback alone is not adequate to improve all types of learning. Outcome or verification feedback, in most if not all of its forms, provides feedback that is useful for monitoring some kinds of learning (e.g., the type of rote learning used in memorizing the multiplication facts). When teachers coach students to use cognitive and self-regulatory strategies to reflect on or track their learning, quantitative feedback can serve an even more useful role in classroom learning.

Second, feedback that is not quantitative should be based on the same learning goals, or aspects of the same learning goals, that are measured for summative assessment, and ideally those criteria are shared with students and become part of their learning. This is probably the most important conclusion of the three, defining the relationship between measurement and feedback in classroom learning and grounding both in the major purpose of schooling, namely student achievement of intended learning goals or outcomes.

Third, meaning derived from feedback could be an important part of the validity argument for classroom assessment because the use of feedback to improve is the most important intended consequence of decisions based on classroom assessment information. Feedback itself could be subject to validation. In fact, practitioners who study the effectiveness of their own feedback are doing a sort of action-research version of feedback validation (Brookhart, 2017).

This chapter has considered the relationship between measurement and feedback in the context of classroom learning. What should be the next steps? First, the argument in this chapter, and particularly the analysis summarized in Table 4.1, should be discussed among scholars in both the measurement and classroom assessment fields. The discussion chapter for this section will start that conversation. Second, if the argument and analysis in this chapter are anywhere near the mark, measurement scholars and classroom assessment scholars have a basis on which to look more broadly at the information about learning generated in the classroom context. This author believes that there is a lot more information about student learning available from student work in the classroom than currently gets measured, garners feedback, contributes to student learning, or contributes to the scientific understanding of learning. It should be possible to harness this information to make more powerful contributions to both student learning and the science of assessment. Third, and this is a hope, perhaps the argument and analysis in this chapter can help with the broader understanding of the relationship between measurement and assessment, which NCME is just now trying to mine for what it can tell us about student learning.

Note

1   In this chapter, the term "learning goal" is used to mean an intended learning outcome at any level of generality, whether a lesson-sized learning target, a unit or curricular goal, a state standard, or broad discipline-based achievement (e.g., "mathematics").

References

Balzer, W. K., Doherty, M. E., & O'Connor, R. (1989). Effects of cognitive feedback on performance. *Psychological Bulletin, 106*, 410–433.

Brookhart, S. M. (2001). Successful students' formative and summative use of assessment information. *Assessment in Education, 8*, 153–169.

Brookhart, S. M. (2017). *How to give effective feedback to your students* (2nd ed.). Alexandria, VA: ASCD.

Brookhart, S. M. (2018). Summative and formative feedback. In A. A. Lipnevich & J. K. Smith (Eds.), *The Cambridge handbook of instructional feedback* (pp. 52–78). Cambridge: Cambridge University Press.

Brookhart, S. M., & Chen, F. (2015). The quality and effectiveness of descriptive rubrics. *Educational Review, 67*(3), 343–368. http://dx.doi.org/10.1080/00131911.2014.929565

Butler, D. L., & Winne, P. H. (1995). Feedback and self-regulated learning: A theoretical synthesis. *Review of Educational Research, 65*, 245–281.

Gamlem, S. M., & Smith, K. (2013). Student perceptions of classroom feedback. *Assessment in Education: Principles, Policy & Practice, 20*, 150–169.

Glaser, R., & Baxter, G. P. (2002). Cognition and construct validity: Evidence for the nature of cognitive performance in assessment situations. In H. I. Braun, D. N. Jackson, & D. E. Wiley (Eds.), *The role of constructs in psychological and educational measurement* (pp. 179–192). Mahwah, NJ: Lawrence Erlbaum Associates.

Haertel, E. (1985). Construct validity and criterion-referenced testing. *Review of Educational Research, 55*, 23–46.

Hattie, J. A. C. (2009). *Visible learning*. London: Routledge.

Hattie, J., & Timperley, H. (2007). The power of feedback. *Review of Educational Research, 77*, 81–112.

Kane, M. T. (2006). Validation. In R. L. Brennan (Ed.), *Educational measurement* (4th ed., pp. 17–64). Westport, CT: Praeger.

Kroog, H. I., Ruiz-Primo, M. A., & Sands, D. (2014). *Understanding the interplay between the cultural context of classrooms and formative assessment*. Paper presented at the annual meeting of the American Educational Research Association, Philadelphia, PA.

Kluger, A. N., & DeNisi, A. (1996). The effects of feedback interventions on performance: A historical review, a meta-analysis, and a preliminary feedback intervention theory. *Psychological Bulletin, 119*, 254–284.

Kulhavy, R. W., & Stock, W. (1989). Feedback in written instruction: The place of response certitude. *Educational Psychology Review, 1*(4), 279–308.

Lorge, I. (1951). The fundamental nature of measurement. In E. F. Lindquist (Ed.), *Educational measurement* (pp. 533–559). Washington, DC: American Council on Education.

Mason, B. J., & Bruning, R. (2001). *Providing feedback in computer-based instruction: What the research tells us.* University of Nebraska-Lincoln. Retrieved from http://dwb.unl.edu/Edit/MB/MasonBruning.html

Messick, S. (1989). Validity. In R. L. Linn (Ed.), *Educational measurement* (3rd ed., pp. 13–103). New York: Macmillan.

Minstrell, J., Anderson, R., & Li, M. (2009). *Assessing teacher competency in formative assessment.* Washington, DC: National Science Foundation.

National Council on Measurement in Education (NCME). (2018). *Position statement on K-12 classroom assessment.* Retrieved from https://higherlogicdownload.s3.amazonaws.com/NCME/c53581e4-9882-4137-987b-4475f6cb502a/UploadedImages/Classroom_assessment_position_statement_-_Board_approved.pdf

Panadero, E., Andrade, H., & Brookhart, S. (2018). Fusing self-regulated learning and formative assessment: A roadmap of where we are, how we got here, and where we are going. *Australian Educational Researcher, 45*(1), 13–31. https://doi.org/10.1007/s13384-018-0258-y

Pellegrino, J. W., Chudowsky, N., & Glaser, R. (Eds.). (2001). *Knowing what students know: The science and design of educational assessment.* Washington, DC: National Academies Press.

Ruiz-Primo, M. A., & Brookhart, S. M. (2018). *Using feedback to improve learning.* New York: Routledge.

Sadler, D. R. (1989). Formative assessment and the design of instructional systems. *Instructional Science, 18,* 119–144.

Shepard, L. A. (2000). The role of assessment in a learning culture. *Educational Researcher, 29*(7), 4–14.

Shepard, L. A. (2008). Formative assessment: Caveat emptor. In C. A. Dwyer (Ed.), *The future of assessment: Shaping teaching and learning* (pp. 279–303). New York: Lawrence Earlbaum.

Shepard, L. A., Penuel, W. R., & Pellegrino, J. W. (2018). Using learning and motivation theories to coherently link formative assessment, grading practices, and large-scale assessment. *Educational Measurement: Issues and Practice, 37*(1), 21–34.

Shute, V. J. (2008). Focus on formative feedback. *Review of Educational Research, 78,* 153–189.

Skinner, B. F. (1958). Teaching machines. *Science, 128,* 969–977.

Stevens, S. S. (1946). On the theory of scales of measurement. *Science, 103,* 677–680.

Thorndike, E. L. (1913). *Educational psychology. Vol. I: The original nature of man.* New York: Columbia University Teachers College.

Tunstall, P., & Gipps, C. (1996). Teacher feedback to young children in formative assessment: A typology. *British Educational Research Journal, 22,* 389–404.

Van der Kleij, F. M., Feskens, R. C. W., & Eggen, T. J. H. M. (2015). Effects of feedback in a computer-based learning environment on students' learning outcomes: A meta-analysis. *Review of Educational Research, 85,* 475–511.

Wiliam, D., Lee, C., Harrison, C., & Black, P. (2004). Teachers developing assessment for learning: Impact on student achievement. *Assessment in Education: Principles Policy & Practice, 11*(1), 49–65.

Wilson, M. (2018). Making measurement important for education: The crucial role of classroom assessment. *Educational Measurement: Issues and Practice, 37*(1), 5–20.

Wright, B. D., & Stone, M. H. (2004). *Making measures.* Chicago, IL: Phaneron Press.

Zimmerman, B. J. (2000). Attaining self-regulation: A social cognitive perspective. In M. Boekaerts, P. R. Pintrich, & M. Zeidner (Eds.), *Handbook of self-regulation* (pp. 13–40). San Diego, CA: Academic Press.

5

Discussion of Part I
Assessment Information in Context

James H. McMillan

Introduction

Teachers gather a wealth of information from classroom assessment and use it for numerous purposes in unique, local contexts. These multiple purposes reflect the need, in classroom assessment, to do more than document and report student proficiency. Teachers use assessment information to improve student learning outcomes, including but not limited to knowledge and understanding; to enhance traits such as self-regulation, perseverance after making mistakes and being wrong, and responsibility; and to diagnose student weaknesses and provide feedback. Contextual characteristics, unique to each teacher and class, influence the meaning and usefulness of assessment information for these multiple purposes. Furthermore, as Wilson (2016) emphasized, the primary purpose of assessment information is "to help in the educational progress of *each student* as they learn" (p. 2, emphasis added). These realities—multiple purposes, contextual differences, and improvement of learning for individual students—have a significant impact on the nature of classroom assessment information.

My main aim in this chapter is to discuss elements of three factors in light of key points from the chapters in this part, in order to suggest implications for improving classroom assessment. The first factor is that the foundation of assessment intended to improve learning must be based on contemporary theories of learning and motivation. The second is that classroom assessment is context-embedded, and the context influences assessment. The third factor explores implications of the intention that assessment should improve learning for individual students, which means that individual students' perceptions about assessment are important. The chapter ends with a discussion of how educators can conceptualize and overcome threats to making reasonable validity arguments for classroom assessment information.

Emphasis on Learning *and* Motivation

Contemporary theories of learning and motivation should help identify what assessment information is most needed and how it should be used. Many (notably Pellegrino, Chudowsky, & Glaser, 2001; Penuel & Shepard, 2016; Shepard, 2000; Shepard, Penuel, & Pellegrino, 2018) have argued convincingly for the importance of cognitive, constructivist, and sociocultural principles of learning for classroom assessment. The claim is that if assessment is not grounded in theories of cognition and sociocultural factors in learning and motivation, the information derived from the assessment will not be as valid, from a measurement perspective, nor as useful to identify and implement instruction that promotes further learning.

Learning Theory

When assessment is based on how students come to know, to understand, and to perform skills, the information derived can be interpreted and used in ways that are closely aligned to those learning processes. Two extensively researched theories of learning, constructivist and socio-cultural, have been endorsed as essential to classroom assessment. I summarize them briefly to show how the processes of learning and motivation, when used as a basis for classroom assessment, enhance the extent to which information that is generated from the assessments can be used to improve learning.

Constructivist

Constructivist learning theory stresses the significance of meaningfulness of information in the development of new knowledge structures and mental representations. When assessments are designed to reflect the manner in which individual students "develop knowledge structures, construct mental representations, and in turn access these resources to answer questions, solve problems, and develop new understandings" (Shepard et al., 2018, p. 23), the information derived is closely tied to how learning occurs, and will be more helpful in enhancing learning.

Brookhart (this volume) illustrates this principle. She indicates that effective feedback is "information students can use to move [the] learning process forward" (p. 65). The purpose of feedback is to enhance learning by conveying information about student performance that can be internalized and acted on *by the student*. To achieve this purpose, students need to perceive the information as meaningful, connected to what they know and how they have learned. The information from assessment needs to be in a form that makes it possible for teachers to provide qualitative information that will have meaning to the student.

Examples of this principle in practice include creating test items that pinpoint specific misunderstandings and differentiate between levels of understanding (e.g., to distinguish between simple recall knowledge, comprehension, and application). In both cases, meaningfulness of the results is improved by matching feedback to each student's capability and performance. Rubrics, as Brookhart (this volume) points out, can be structured so that feedback helps students see what they understand and/or can do and what further learning is needed. Finally, carefully constructed criteria for evaluating performance that students can understand and apply themselves can be used to enhance the effectiveness of feedback.

Leighton (this volume) contends that learning in classrooms is *fluid* and *fine-grained*. To improve what students know, understand, and can do, the focus of instruction is on relatively small learning targets and learning gains that develop over time, often in unpredictable ways. In contrast to what is needed for measuring longer-term learning (e.g., semester exams or common or accountability tests), classroom teachers need good evidence of what has transpired during the process of learning fine-grained, incremental learning targets. Classroom assessment data, then, need to be "proximal," generated and used in ways that inform the learning process. This suggests that teachers need expertise in measuring and interpreting the outcomes of short learning segments. How is this best achieved to result in valid interpretations and uses of classroom assessment information (e.g., describing a student's partial understanding and designing the most effective further instruction)? If based on observation of performance, how is observation planned and implemented? How can assessment accommodate the fluid nature of learning?

Sociocultural

The emphasis of sociocultural learning theory is on how social roles, experiences, and interactions influence emotion and cognition (Shepard et al., 2018). The nature of personal identity, quality of interpersonal relationships, normative expectations regarding learning and assessment, and emotional well-being of students is intertwined with cognition and influences how students perform. Furthermore, recent Elementary and Secondary Education Act (ESSA) guidelines require attention to social and emotional learning outcomes.

Leighton (this volume) contends that the basic goal of classroom assessment is to provide teachers with information that they can use to enhance learning. She points out that, in contrast to cognitive understanding and skills, emotional and social relatedness aspects of learning have not been as extensively researched and operationalized. While one could quibble with whether self-regulation and metacognition are solely or mainly cognitive, not socio-emotional, her contention is critical to our understanding of how classroom assessment, with a focus on learning, needs accurate measurement of social and emotional factors that are integral to cognitive performance. The point is that learning is a socio-constructivist process, and as a result classroom assessment information is only fully understood by consideration of social interaction and emotions. In her conclusion to Chapter 2, Leighton makes a compelling case:

> Classroom assessments and socio-emotional measures should be used jointly by teachers. Socio-emotional data serve to contextualize student assessment results so as to yield valid claims about what students need to help them learn. Classroom assessments together with socio-emotional data provide sufficiency of information for making diagnoses of a fluid and fine-grained learning process, and planning interventions that are more likely to succeed in the presence of socio-emotional data to help delivery and support of the student implementing the intervention.
>
> (p. 42)

The argument is that effective classroom assessment generates information that relates meaningfully to the socio-emotional view of learning. It follows, then, that there is a need to study how to assess emotional and social factors, for both formative and summative classroom assessment. Bailey and Durán (this volume) argue that teacher observation of social interaction during the process of learning is essential, particularly in formative assessment, to ensure "that the construct they intend to gather evidence about is fully represented, includes all the important dimensions of the construct, and is sufficient for drawing fair and unbiased inferences about a student's performance" (p. 49). They point out that a sociocultural approach to assessment, with a focus on interactional and other social aspects of learning, is needed to show "how students convey their knowledge and learning as social beings when interacting with others" (p. 52).

As argued by Leighton (this volume), incorporating social-emotional and social interaction traits into the development and interpretation of classroom assessment information is difficult for several reasons. Leighton's learning and assessment model suggests an approach to incorporating these elements, though it is focused mostly on misconceptions and errors in learning. As related to learning theory, the model could be expanded to include important social-emotional factors in classroom assessment more broadly. For example, it would be useful for teachers to know how to measure those social-emotional traits that are essential to building an effective learning environment. Bailey and Durán (this volume) contend that discourse analysis techniques and close observation of social interactions are needed for language assessment. Their example showcases how formative assessment that attends to social interactions is effective for making valid inferences about language proficiency.

Together, cognitive and sociocultural theories suggest principles for how assessment in the classroom is best designed and implemented. The argument is that if these theories are not used to influence the nature of classroom assessment there may be a disconnect between how learning occurs, how it is measured, and how information from assessment can enhance learning. That is, classroom assessment must be based on theories of learning to provide the kind of information students and teachers can use to promote further learning.

In summary, learning needs to be meaningful to students socially, emotionally, and cognitively, and classroom assessment needs to be aligned with all of these realms to generate information that will improve learning. This is the reason moment-to-moment formative assessment can be a powerful influence on learning. With a focus on learning as it occurs, with attention to meaningfulness and social interactions, the information is closely tied to learning and likely to be used by students.

Motivation

Most would agree that proper student motivation is critical to learning, though it has received much less attention in the classroom assessment literature than learning theory. It is common, for example, to think about classroom assessment as assessment *for* learning (AfL). It is uncommon to say assessment *for* learning *and* motivation (AfLM). Recently, authors have argued that motivation is a key construct linked to classroom assessment (Brookhart, 2017; Panadero, Andrade, & Brookhart, 2018; Ruiz-Primo & Brookhart, 2018). Shepard et al. (2018) posit that sociocultural theories provide a basis for understanding "how motivational aspects of learning, such as self-regulation, self-efficacy, sense of belonging, and identity are completely entwined with cognitive development" (p. 23). Perhaps there has been less attention to motivation because it is a difficult construct to measure; thought of as less important than learning in our accountability-oriented educational culture with an emphasis on cognitive knowledge, understanding, and skills; or not valued much as an educational outcome. Whatever the reasons, most teachers realize the importance of motivation in learning. They do what they can to engage students, cultivate appropriate levels of effort, and promote further interest in learning.

Self-regulation, a process that is clearly associated with learning, student engagement, and feedback (Andrade, 2010; Andrade & Brookhart, 2016; Andrade & Heritage, 2017), is one well-researched, motivation-related trait with important implications for classroom assessment. It is also a part of many researchers' conceptions of effective formative assessment (Panadero et al., 2018). Self-regulation is a process in which students monitor, control, and regulate their cognitions, emotions, and actions through self-reflection and self-evaluation to improve learning (Zimmerman & Schunk, 2011). Motivational factors such as goal-setting, attributions to causes, and self-efficacy influence the nature and quality of self-regulation (Schunk & Zimmerman, 2012). When students can set personal learning goals that are consistent with learning targets and at the right level of difficulty (e.g., challenging), they are more likely to have confidence in their ability to learn, connect performance to effort, and develop internal attributions that portend future learning and influence self-efficacy. Effective assessment that involves the student, in turn, provides opportunities for students to self-regulate.

Brookhart (this volume) connects cognitive-oriented feedback to self-regulation: "Feedback that helps students interpret the task and connect it with their understandings and performance gives students information they can use to set new goals and self-regulate" (p. 70). Brookhart also points out that Hattie and Timperley (2007) identified self-regulation feedback that involves "the student's self-direction and self-monitoring" (p. 71) as an important type of feedback for learning.

The importance of self-regulation presents many opportunities for classroom assessment research. For example, what types of assessments are best for developing self-regulation? There is some evidence that constructed-response items and performance-based assessment generate more self-regulation than selected-response assessments (Dinsmore & Wilson, 2016), but the differences are not well understood. Does age make a difference in what assessments will enhance self-regulation? What type of feedback is best (e.g., self, peers, teacher)? When students make mistakes, how do they interpret their performance? Are results used to self-reflect and set new learning goals? As Dinsmore and Wilson (2016) pointed out in their review of research, the relationship between self-regulation and assessment is multidimensional, depending on context, subject, age, teacher, and other variables.

There are compelling reasons to include motivation as well as learning in discussions of classroom assessment. Motivation is needed to promote effort so that performance is accurate; it is needed for the development of vital student dispositions such as self-regulation; it is a key part of formative assessment in which student reflection, goal-setting, and self-evaluation are used; it is consistent with more general purposes of schooling; and it is a contributor to learning. Gathering evidence of motivation for these purposes is primarily a classroom assessment task, guided by what information teachers need for individual students.

Contextual Complexity

As Leighton (this volume) reminds us, Messick (1984) recognized that appropriate interpretations based on classroom assessment information are made with consideration of the complexity of teaching and learning in specific contexts, as well as student individual differences. Alonzo (this volume) contends that "classroom assessment is inextricable from an associated classroom environment" (p. 123). Fulmer, Lee, and Tan (2015) operationalize this admonition in their review of research describing how contextual factors influence teachers' assessment practices. Their study concluded that research has documented the relationship between "micro-level" differences that exist between classrooms, including teachers' assessment literacy, teaching styles, beliefs and values, student characteristics that encompass age, ability, race and ethnicity, special needs, and social skills, and classroom supports such as technology and the physical setting. Add to that subject matter differences and whether accountability tests are used, and contextual complexity becomes a compelling reality. Each classroom has its own unique set of characteristics that influence teaching, learning, and assessment. In addition, there may be school, school district, and statewide policies and initiatives that impact assessment practices, as well as local community-level factors. There is some evidence, for example, that a school-wide culture that promotes teacher collaboration and autonomy facilitates the implementation of a focus on assessment for learning (Heitink, Van der Kleij, Veldkamp, Schildkamp, & Kippers, 2016).

Classroom assessment information is collected and evaluated (Alonzo, this volume; Kane and Wools, this volume) within complex contexts. The implication of this process is that like effective teaching, effective assessment may vary from one classroom to another. Unlike the purpose of large-scale measurement that provides mostly context-free interpretations, classroom assessment practices are tailored to contextual factors. That is, the impact of classroom assessment on learning is dependent on gathering information that reflects the interplay of these factors. The challenge is in understanding how to accommodate assessment based on multiple contextual influences and interpret results with these factors in mind.

Each of the chapters in this part address contextual complexity, either directly or indirectly. Bailey and Durán (this volume) address the importance of social and cultural dimensions of learning for English language learners, and make a strong case for how classroom assessment, in contrast to large-scale assessment, is able to accommodate these students. The primary purpose of classroom assessment is to support learning, and learning in turn depends significantly on teacher–student relationships; therefore, teachers' assessment of learning depends on being able to account for language and cultural differences. Bailey and Durán believe that formative, socially embedded assessments are needed to obtain valid information for linguistically and culturally different students. For this purpose, sociocultural theories of learning that emphasize the importance of student dialog and engagement can guide the design of assessment. As Bailey and Durán comment, "classroom assessment can offer the advantages of being 'proximal' to learners in terms of their learning needs . . . matching the language of assessment tasks to students' own language complexity levels" (p. 52).

Leighton (this volume) highlights the need to incorporate students' socio-emotional states for effective classroom assessment. She argues that these states, because they an inherent part of learning, must be considered for classroom assessment that targets the improvement of learning. Leighton contends that socio emotional information contextualizes student assessment to result in more credible and useful next steps for students' subsequent learning. This suggests the need to interpret assessment in light of these states. Leighton emphasizes the value of academic errors, mistakes, and misconceptions in the LEAFF model to incorporate socio-emotional states in classroom assessment. Often student receptivity to feedback from being wrong is dependent on emotional states, attitudes, and a willingness to receive and act on the information (McMillan, 2018).

Both Brookhart (this volume) and Kane and Wools (this volume) address context indirectly. Brookhart contends that both feedback and measurement need to provide information that is *meaningful* to students to help them learn. Brookhart states, "it is important here to note that any information, including feedback, should convey intended meaning and support intended interpretations and uses, including students' own interpretations and uses" (p. 76). While meaningfulness may be primarily a cognitive activity, the proclivity to use the information depends on contextual factors such as the normative expectations in the classroom for why feedback is provided and how it can be used (see Alonzo, this volume). For example, the extent to which students are expected to explain how their performance relates to criteria and learning goals, an important component of formative assessment, depends on whether the teacher has established this use as an expectation. Similarly, teachers can create an environment that promotes the positive use of mistakes and errors, or one that denigrates being wrong and celebrates being right.

Kane and Wools chapter (this volume) recognize context early in their chapter with this key statement:

> The bottom line in validating classroom assessments (as in all assessments) is to identify the qualities that the assessment results need to have, given their particular interpretations and uses in the context at hand, and then to examine whether the assessment results meet these requirements.
>
> (p. 12)

Kane and Wools emphasize that the warrants used to draw inferences to support a functional validity argument focus on intended outcomes *in each classroom*. The evidence needs to be generated and evaluated with respect to the classroom context. Throughout their chapter, Kane and Wools emphasize teacher and student as unique, localized units. The implication is that assessment information that promotes appropriate instruction and learning in classrooms could be, and perhaps should be, diverse across different contexts. Their major point about the functional validity perspective is that it is primarily a qualitative judgment about whether intended instructional and learning outcomes have been attained within each classroom.

I agree with Leighton (this volume) that it would be helpful for testing specialists to advance assessment guidelines that reflect contextualization. This could include, for example, the development and availability of test item formats and item banks that provide sufficient choice to enable teachers to use items that are appropriate for their specific context.

Student-Centric Focus

All the chapters in this part stress that the central role of classroom assessment is to enhance student learning. The focus is on the student and how assessment impacts learning. The degree to which classroom assessment information is useful for learning depends in turn on how each student perceives, prepares for, and reacts to assessment, and how assessment affects each student's learning and motivation. In this chapter, I refer to this emphasis as being "student-centric."

The role of student perceptions is particularly important because what students think and feel about an assessment mediates the impact it will have on their behavior, as well as their receptivity to feedback (Brookhart, this volume; Crooks, 1988; McMillan, 2016). Perceptions refer to beliefs, cognitions, and understandings, and are accompanied by emotion, such as enjoyment, engagement, hope, and anxiety (Vogel & Pekrun, 2016). Perceptions and emotions influence the way students process an assessment event, which can often result in an array of different thoughts and reactions to the same assessment event within a classroom (Chu, Guo, & Leighton, 2014).

The power of student perceptions is reflected in the processes of formative assessment, student self-assessment, and learning from making mistakes and misconceptions. In each of these, the critical element of effectiveness is how each student perceives and reacts to the assessment event and results.

Student Perceptions in Formative Assessment

An integral part of both informal and formal formative assessment is that students reflect on their performance and feedback in relation to learning goals and criteria. This involves cognitive interpretations of the meaning of results and feedback. As Brookhart (this volume) notes, "Feedback and measurement are information *about* learning that are intended to be used to *interpret* learning" (p. 68, emphasis in original). Interpretation is a cognitive process that helps determine the meaning of results and feedback to the student. It is influenced by both the nature of the results and feedback as well as by student expectations. For example, the role of effort in determining meaning is well established. Students interpret "success" and "failure" in part by how much effort they have exerted in preparation and completing the assessment (Wise & Smith, 2016). When little effort is exerted, results are less valid; with moderate levels of effort, results are more valid, leading to appropriate, accurate perceptions. Minimal effort is detrimental if it leads to students' inaccurate conceptions of ability in the face of success and disregard for feedback when wrong.

Here is where the student's perceived purpose of the assessment is critical. There is good evidence that students know the difference between assessment targeted to improve their learning and assessment for external purposes, such as semester exams for grades, college entrance exams, and accountability tests (Brown, 2011; Brown, Irving, Peterson, & Hirschfeld, 2009). When students perceive assessment as connected to learning and aligned with learning goals and criteria, they are more engaged, exert more effort, and take results and feedback more seriously (Dorman, Fisher, & Waldrip, 2006; Irving, Peterson, & Brown, 2008). This is consistent with the purpose of formative assessment, which is one reason why it can be a powerful tool to increase learning and motivation. Assessments that are viewed as relevant, authentic, challenging, and engaging increase student attention to errors and misconceptions (McMillan, 2018). Their perceptions are more accurate and meaningful, enhancing the connections students are able to make between their learning and performance. Appropriate research is needed to better understand and operationalize how these dimensions of assessment affect student learning and motivation. For example, performance-based assessment is typically viewed as relevant, and constructed-response items in general are seen by students are more challenging than selected-response items. Do these finding suggest greater use of the performance-based assessments and constructed-response items? There is also evidence that novel assessments that are perceived positively enhance student engagement (Struyen & Devesa, 2016).

Bailey and Duŕan (this volume) address the importance of being student-centric in their discussion of how language mediates the classroom assessment experiences of linguistically and culturally diverse students. They argue that culturally diverse students are better able to demonstrate proficiency "through authentic language practices that they have exercised during content learning" (p. 51). In contrast to large-scale assessment, authentic and innovative classroom assessment practices can find meaningful evidence of learning using the lens of students' individual linguistic expressions. Furthermore, by focusing on proficiency in the context of linguistic skills, teachers can more accurately understand learning strengths and weaknesses and provide appropriate feedback. This is especially important in informal, ongoing formative assessment, during which teachers continually interpret behavior in relation to learning goals and criteria and provide feedback that incorporates student perceptions of their performance.

The challenge for classroom teachers is to efficiently understand and account for individual student differences in designing and implementing their assessments. In a classroom with a diverse set of linguistic skills and English language proficiencies, how is it possible to appropriately differentiate assessment? Working together, the measurement and classroom assessment communities can translate principles of fair and valid large-scale summative assessment to classroom assessment (see Chapter 13, this volume) to account for student differences. Effective classroom assessment happens at the intersection of learning theory, pedagogy, and individual student perception differences. We may ask: What principles of accommodation for students' individual characteristics are important to the design and implementation of student-centric classroom assessments that will result in meaningful student engagement and subsequent action on the part of both teachers and students?

Another illustration of the importance of student perceptions—in formative or summative assessment—is the need to understand students' perceptions of the level of difficulty and challenge of questions and required demonstrations of proficiency. Assessments that are viewed as very easy, for example, may result in lower effort, less meaningfulness of results, disregard for feedback, and external attributions (McMillan, 2018).

Student Self-Assessment

While there are multiple views of student self-assessment (Panadero, 2017) and how it should be labeled (e.g., self-evaluation, self-monitoring, self-reflection), it is generally agreed that self-assessment posits the central role of the student in describing, evaluating, and taking actions based on their performance (Andrade & Brown, 2016; Brookhart, 2016; Brown & Harris, 2013; Harris & Brown, 2018). Self-assessment is a student-centered activity in which the student evaluates his or her performance. Wylie and Lyon (this volume) describe three steps in self-assessment: understanding the desired performance, monitoring progress, and taking action to improve their proficiency. As such, it is clearly related to self-regulation: evaluating and setting goals, being aware of learning, and comparing performance to intended learning (Brown & Harris, 2013).

While there are many benefits of self-assessment (e.g., on self-regulation and metacognition, as summarized by Schneider and Lyons, this volume), it is influenced by myriad factors, including age, ability, intrapersonal and interpersonal characteristics, teacher support, and feedback (Andrade & Brown, 2016), and it is difficult to implement successfully. Both Leighton (this volume) and Bailey and Durán (this volume) suggest that socio-emotional factors, especially social interactions in the classroom, should be assessed and monitored. Relatively little is known, however, about how this is best accomplished and what skills teachers need to be able to assess and utilize these factors for self-assessment.

Kane and Wools's (this volume) conceptualization of validity suggests that it may be helpful to separate the accuracy of information students use to assess their level of proficiency (measurement perspective) from how they use the information (functional perspective). It would also be helpful for teachers to know how to evaluate the evidence from students' use of self-assessment.

Learning from Mistakes and Misconceptions

Leighton (this volume) presents the Learning Errors and Formative Feedback (LEAFF) model to show how three components—the classroom social environment, students' mental models (such as attributions), and academic performance—relate to the ability of misconceptions, mistakes, and errors to facilitate learning. A significant aspect of the model is how students' emotional and belief systems impact perceptions about being wrong and making mistakes. Are wrong answers viewed as an opportunity to learn? Do mistakes mean a lack of proficiency? Do misconceptions suggest low knowledge or ability? When wrong, how important is it to relearn? Is being wrong viewed as a negative, as something to be avoided? These student perceptions about making mistakes and getting wrong answers (assessment information) have important consequences. They affect self-efficacy, self-confidence and motivation, and subsequent effort, as well as performance (McMillan, 2018). Wrong answers also provide opportunities for self-regulation. In a larger sense, being wrong can promote persistence in the face of barriers or roadblocks, and develop a healthy growth mindset (Dweck, 2006).

Leighton (this volume) suggests that the assessment climate in the classroom is important to how students perceive being wrong. Established classroom norms and expectations create an environment that influences students' perceptions. In a classroom climate that embraces errors, mistakes and being wrong are viewed positively as a part of learning; they are accepted, valued, and helpful. Teachers who establish a positive error climate are tolerant of mistakes and errors, provide support, and discourage other students' disapproval of those who have been wrong. These social and emotional dimensions of the classroom are very important and directly related to the use of assessment information and feedback. Students are more willing to disclose their knowledge and engage in self-assessment in classrooms characterized by interpersonal trust and respect (Tierney, 2013).

Because each student experiences being wrong differently, and each is uniquely affected, it is important to know how to respond to students individually, especially with feedback. Except in the field of test anxiety, however, research provides little information about student perceptions of errors and mistakes. There is a need to investigate how classroom assessment can be designed and implemented to facilitate further learning when students are wrong. How can teachers understand student reactions when they make incorrect answers? How can a series of assessments scaffold different levels of ability with increasingly more difficult tasks to reveal errors and misconceptions for all students? How is cultural background related to being wrong? How should teachers design assessments to capture student misconceptions and interpret students' partial understanding? How should the classroom culture's treatment of mistakes be conceptualized and measured?

The previous sections have discussed important factors that influence the nature of classroom assessment information and the extent to which it may result in improved learning and motivation. I now turn to considering how measurement and functional validity arguments can be conceptualized to provide a basis for individual teachers to evaluate the meaning and value of that assessment information.

Threats to Classroom Assessment Validity

In this section, I discuss the validity of classroom assessment in light of the aforementioned factors that differentiate classroom assessment from large-scale assessment—the primacy of learning and motivation theory, the importance of context, and the focus on individual students—to suggest an approach for evaluating the validity of information that teachers gather and act on to improve learning.

Classroom Assessment Validity

Classroom assessment is complex and serves multiple purposes. That in itself provides a foundation for how classroom assessment validity can be conceptualized. It is in the transition of the meaning of validity from traditional psychometric views to those that apply to classroom assessment, as exemplified by Kane and Wools (this volume) and Alonzo (this volume), that a useful, practical way of conceptualizing classroom assessment validity can be implemented to include both accurate measurement and appropriate uses, consequences, and outcomes.

As explicated by Newton and Shaw (2014) and reprised in a series of articles in *Assessment in Education: Principles, Policy & Practice* (2016, Vol. 23), there continues to be debate and controversy about validity, despite its longstanding status as a pillar of measurement. Significantly, for our purpose here, much has been written about whether the dual dimensions of validity as an argument about both intended *inferences* and *uses* about assessment evidence makes sense (Newton & Shaw, 2016). Much of the debate stems from considering how broadly the psychometric perspective focused on achievement and aptitude can be applied. The traditional psychometric emphasis on inferences and interpretations related to test scores has led to a technical, measurement-oriented meaning of validity. Here, the validity argument focuses on evidence that test scores can be used to infer conclusions about student proficiency on what is measured, taking into account possible error and bias. I would argue that this meaning of validity is indispensable for classroom assessment validity. Appropriate functional uses of the information gathered (e.g., for improving learning and motivation, determining grades, making decisions about instruction, feedback, placement, accountability) depends on accurate inferences about the nature and level of student performance. In classroom assessment, however, the landscape changes in many ways. The psychometrically based conceptualization of validity becomes a necessary but not sufficient principle for teachers and other educators to determine the adequacy and appropriateness of how they gather, interpret, and use the evidence for multiple purposes (Alonzo, this volume; Bonner, 2013; Leighton, this volume; McMillan, 2018).

As many in this volume argue (e.g., Alonzo; Brookhart; Kane & Wools), *use* of information is an essential component of validity for classroom assessment because the main purpose of classroom assessment is consequential, namely to improve student learning. Use and consequences imply an action-oriented conceptualization, one that has clear relevance to the nature of classroom assessment information. As Bonner (2017) points out, classroom assessment by its very nature includes a "classroom" component, one that is grounded in learning theory, context, and pedagogy. Assessment use refers to how teachers plan to apply assessment information to student learning and instruction; assessment consequences, both intended and unintended, result from what is implemented in the classroom. As Koretz (2016) noted, the psychometric quality of the inference is quite separate from the impact of the assessment and requires different types of evidence. For classroom assessment, then, it seems clear that validity of information concerns not only the soundness of inferences about proficiency, but also the appropriateness of uses and consequences.

Kane and Wools (this volume) have suggested a provocative way of conceptualizing validity for classroom assessment that includes both performance inferences and uses/consequences.

They conclude that it is most important to focus on the functional perspective of assessment (e.g., use/consequences for learning and teaching), rather than the measurement perspective (accuracy). As Brookhart (this volume) contends: "Consequential evidence may be the most important evidence for the validation of feedback, because feedback is effective if it leads to improvement of learning" (p. 76). Alonzo (this volume) emphasizes that trustworthiness, as an alternative criterion to validity for large-scale testing, depends on the extent to which the purposes for which the assessment is intended are achieved. It follows, then, that if classroom assessment results do not provide information that can be translated to actual use, there is a lack of validity (or trustworthiness).

Furthermore, as Leighton (this volume) points out in her discussion of validity, accurate diagnosis of students' psychosocial learning processes and planning for subsequent interventions and feedback requires appropriate evidence. She contends that this evidence for validity requires attention to *how* students learn, not only *what* they learn, and that this requires assessment information about states of emotion, relatedness to others, and other states that influence the learning process. Leighton has essentially extended the importance of cognitive learning theory for assessment to psychosocial factors to contextualize teachers' interpretations of performance and subsequent interventions to enhance learning.

Threats to Classroom Assessment Validity

I would argue, then, that validity of classroom assessment should be based on both measurement and functional perspectives, incorporating the importance of theories of student learning *and* motivation, contextual complexity, and a student-centric emphasis that includes psychosocial factors. In other words, validity needs to include both a psychometric measurement perspective and a consequences/use evaluation grounded in sociocultural learning theory and specific contexts. The emphasis on functionality in specific contexts suggests that validity arguments, to some extent, will be unique for each classroom. That is, the evidence that needs to be gathered and evaluated to make a reasonable validity argument becomes teacher-/class-centric. This presents a conundrum of sorts: How, as a profession, do we establish generalized principles of validity for classroom assessment that are implemented individually in specific contexts, generating unique information on an ongoing basis?

One answer to this question is to emphasize to teachers the importance of Kane and Wools's (this volume) conceptualization of validity for classroom assessment and then develop teachers' expertise in making validity arguments for their context and students by systematically examining possible alternative explanations for inferences and uses (Alonzo, this volume). Consistent with Bonner (2013), Kane (2006), Kane and Wools (this volume), and Mislevy (2003), this is essentially a process to attempt to falsify claims by consideration of evidence that would refute the inference or use. That is, alternative explanations should be considered and evaluated as possible or plausible. This is what Kane and Wools (this volume) contend when stating that assessment validation depends on "identifying potential challenges . . . and evaluating their impact" (p. 14). The approach is also what is stressed in the "Validity" chapter of the current *Standards for Educational and Psychological Testing* (American Educational Research Association [AERA], American Psychological Association [APA], & National Council on Measurement in Education [NCME], 2014): "Identifying the propositions implied by a proposed test interpretation can be facilitated by considering rival hypotheses that may challenge the proposed interpretation" (p. 12).

Alternate explanations or rival hypotheses about what scores mean and whether intended purposes and uses are appropriate constitute so-called "threats" to validity. As for threats for experimental validity (Campbell & Stanley, 1963), the goal is to identify ways of thinking about how certain sources of invalidity could influence the accuracy of interpretations, uses, and consequences that teachers could address as a way of ongoing evaluation of evidence specific to their context and consistent with multiple purposes and theories of learning and motivation. This essentially extends Kane and Wools's (this volume) important point that "If the IUA is found wanting, because it lacks coherence and completeness or because the evidence does not support some of its inferences and assumptions, the interpretation and use would not be accepted as valid" (p. 13).

In what follows, I suggest five possible threats to classroom assessment validity. The intent is to describe the threats in a way that allows teachers to focus on major issues that could strengthen validity arguments by eliminating "legitimate challenges to proposed interpretations and uses" (Kane & Wools, this volume, p. 14). The threats are not presented as a comprehensive list; rather, they illustrate the kinds of categories that could be used to approach validity arguments that consider multiple purposes, contextual influences, and the essential role of the student and his or her perceptions of assessment events.

Inadequate Construct Explication

Much has been written about the importance of specifying the precise nature of whatever construct is being measured. Careful construct definitions are needed in the development of assessments to assure that all important elements are included (avoiding construct under-representation) and that contamination is avoided (construct irrelevance). This is achieved somewhat via a test blueprint for content-related evidence, which can also be used to identify the depth of learning and/or thinking skills required. The essential questions for teachers would be: (1) Are all important elements of the learning goal included in the assessment? (2) Are there elements being measured that are not a part of the construct? Answering these questions can prompt teachers to consider how the measure could lead to inaccurate inferences about student proficiency. Traditional measurement has focused considerably on construct clarity, though mostly for summative assessments that cover large chunks of learning; this expertise can be applied to classroom assessments where the information gathered is more fine-grained and formative. A good example of this approach is the use of learning progressions or trajectories that break down constructs to be able to assess aspects of the construct that need to be measured as students learn (see Briggs & Furtak, this volume).

Error Underestimation

The measurement perspective (Kane & Wools, this volume) concerns the accuracy of obtained scores. As Kane and Wools point out, since quantitative estimates of reliability are not commonly used in classroom assessment, this is mostly a qualitative judgment. Once teachers are aware of the sources of error (such as bias, poorly written items, language deficiencies, student illness, guessing, and cultural norms), the question is simply: Are there any sources of error that have contributed to the "observed" score? It would be helpful for teachers to understand common errors for different types of classroom assessment, as well as protocols for ruling out such errors. For example, much is known about observer error, but there is little research on how teacher observation during formative assessment could be biased or contain other types of error, such as observer fatigue.

Nonalignment with Learning Targets and/or Instruction

According to Kane and Wools (this volume), validity of classroom assessment information depends on the veracity of predictions about what further learning is needed for students. These predictions will be accurate only to the extent that there is alignment between learning targets and instruction received, and the nature of the assessment information that is subsequently used for identifying strengths and weaknesses and providing feedback. For instance, if assessments are not aligned with what has been taught, judgments about what feedback to provide and what further instruction is needed will not be accurate. Furthermore, student perceptions about an assessment, reactions to their performance, and acceptance of feedback depend on alignment. If students believe that an assessment is inconsistent with learning targets and/or instruction, they are likely to ignore their feedback. If their effort in studying is not aligned with the assessment, they are unlikely to use their performance, whatever it is, in the processes of self-assessment and self-regulation, with no important consequences for further learning.

Single Exemplar Error

One of Kane and Wools's (this volume) proposed functions for classroom assessment validity concerns the evaluation of a student's general level of performance of a fine-grained task; another is to make inferences about a student's level of achievement in a defined domain. In both cases, the evaluation is based on whether the action based on assessment information is helpful for instruction that will improve student learning and motivation. The single exemplar error occurs when teachers base feedback and instructional decisions on the results of one assessment.

It is difficult to imagine a situation where a single exemplar of student proficiency should be used to draw a conclusion about student proficiency, let alone for determining important uses. Whether a brief formative classroom assessment or summative test, there are simply many sources of error that can accompany a single assessment (Alonzo, this volume). Effective teachers know this intuitively and use multiple measures of a single learning target to verify what the performances mean for future instruction. That is because there are a multitude of factors that could influence the accuracy of a single performance. For example, the nature of a single assessment may not match well with the target; it may not be administered or scored properly, students may be distracted, exert low effort, or be ill; scoring could be biased; cultural background may unduly influence interpretations; cheating can occur; and the nature of the assessment may impact student performance. In other words, there are many confounding factors that could accompany a single assessment, and when only one assessment is administered there is a danger that these influences could unduly impact performance, leading to flawed decisions about subsequent instruction. When several assessments of the same target are used, the deleterious impacts of such factors on interpretations and uses are minimized.

Inappropriate Assessment Task Difficulty

Kane and Wools (this volume) stress the importance of task difficulty for the purpose of identifying strengths and weaknesses: "[For identifying strengths and weaknesses] ... the tasks presented to the student would probably need to be at a level that the student finds somewhat difficult" (p. 21). Moderate levels of difficulty, as perceived by students and operationalized in assessment tasks, promote accurate inferences about what students need for further learning. From the standpoint of learning theory, motivation, self-regulation, student engagement, and receptivity to feedback, assessment tasks that result in both successful and unsuccessful performance are needed. Perceived and actual levels of difficulty are context-bound and student-centered. For teachers, the question would be: Are the assessment tasks for these students at the right level of difficulty? Tasks that are too difficult or too easy will reduce validity by leading to inaccurate determinations of what further instruction is needed to enhance learning. Such tasks also mitigate the accuracy of conclusions about student proficiency. Assessment tasks within a single class are generally the same for all students. Perhaps differentiated assessment tasks, based on different levels of difficulty, would be most effective for learning and motivation.

Summary and Implications

The chapters in this part suggest that assessment information needs to be based on what will result in improved instruction, feedback, learning, and motivation, with some specific examples of how that can be accomplished. This chapter situated these ideas and arguments in realities of classroom assessment (i.e., multiple purposes, theories of learning and motivation, contextual differences, student perceptions) and addressed classroom assessment validity arguments.

Constructivist and sociocultural theories of learning *and* motivation show that assessment and feedback must be aligned with *how* learning occurs, not simply with what is targeted. This suggests that assessment should examine short learning segments with questions that meaningfully connect what is asked with existing knowledge, taking into account sociocultural contextual factors that influence learning. Motivation, student perceptions of the difficulty, relevance, and value of assessment, and social and emotional factors must be incorporated into the design, implementation, and uses of assessment.

Contextual factors that create unique classroom environments influence how learning occurs and need to be incorporated into decisions about what information concerning student proficiency is gathered. The implication is that, to a certain extent, classroom assessment that is effective may vary from one class to another and from one student to another. What is most meaningful and most motivating for some students may not be appropriate for others. Cultural and language barriers need to be accommodated.

Since the locus of learning outcomes and motivation is individual students, it is important for assessment to be student-centric. Assessment that is accommodated to what is best for students, rather than having students accommodate to assessment, will result in improved functional validity. In particular, attention to information related to student self-assessment, self-regulation, and authentic assessment may enhance student engagement and learning. Formative and summative assessment, and subsequent evaluations of validity, must be based primarily on how assessment affects student learning and motivation, what some have called learning-oriented assessment (LOA). LOA is an approach in which the emphasis of assessment changes from primarily summative to formative, and assessment as, of, and for learning are considered together as a process to enhance learning (Zeng, Huang, Yu, & Chen, 2018). This is consistent with a greater emphasis on functional aspects of classroom assessment validity (Kane & Wools, this volume).

If effective classroom assessment is based on theories of learning and motivation, contextualized, and student-centered, and is designed to achieve multiple purposes, the best evidence for making validity arguments may rest on how well individual teachers eliminate threats to validity for their situation, students, and goals. Five possible threats to validity were presented as a starting point for how this might be structured. Further consideration of how threats differ for various types of assessment is needed (e.g., informal and formal formative assessment, summative tests, measures of social and emotional factors, informal observation). This would establish the origin of validity arguments within individual contexts and for different purposes. Teachers would view validity as an argument about the reasonableness of inferences, uses, and impacts for their students and situation.

The chapters in this part address some key considerations about what kind of assessment information both supports and measures student learning and motivation. The challenge for classroom assessment to progress as a field is to merge theories of learning and motivation with relevant principles of measurement.

References

American Educational Research Association (AERA), American Psychological Association (APA), & National Council on Measurement in Education (NCME). (2014). *Standards for educational and psychological testing.* Washington, DC: American Educational Research Association, American Psychological Association, & National Council on Measurement in Education.

Andrade, H. L. (2010). Students as the definitive source of formative assessment: Academic self-assessment and the self-regulation of learning. In H. L. Andrade & G. J. Cizek (Eds.), *Handbook of formative assessment* (pp. 90–105). New York: Routledge.

Andrade, H. L., & Brookhart, S. M. (2016). The role of classroom assessment in supporting self-regulated learning. In D. Laveault & L. Allal (Eds.), *Assessment for learning: Meeting the challenge of implementation* (pp. 293–309). Cham: Springer International.

Andrade, H. L., & Brown, G. T. L. (2016). Student self-assessment in the classroom. In G. T. L. Brown & L. R. Harris (Eds.), *Handbook of human and social conditions in assessment* (pp. 319–334). New York: Routledge.

Andrade, H. L., & Heritage, M. (2017). *Using formative assessment to enhance learning, achievement, and academic self-regulation.* New York: Routledge.

Bonner, S. M. (2013). Validity in classroom assessment: Purposes, properties, and principles. In J. H. McMillan (Ed.), *SAGE handbook of research on classroom assessment* (pp. 87–106). Thousand Oaks, CA: SAGE.

Bonner, S. M. (2017, April). *Using learning theory and validity theory to improve classroom assessment research, design, and implementation.* Paper presented at the Annual Meeting of the National Council on Measurement in Education, New York.

Brookhart, S. M. (2016). Building assessments that work in the classroom. In G. T. L. Brown & L. R. Harris (Eds.), *Handbook of human and social conditions in assessment* (pp. 351–365). New York: Routledge.

Brookhart, S. M. (2017). *How to give effective feedback to your students* (2nd ed.). Alexandria, VA: ASCD.

Brown, G. T. L. (2011). Self-regulation of assessment beliefs and attitudes: A review of the students' conceptions of assessment inventory. *Educational Psychology, 31*(6), 731–748. doi:10.1080/0143410.2011.599836

Brown, G. T. L., & Harris, L. R. (2013). Student self-assessment. In J. H. McMillan (Ed.), *SAGE handbook of research on classroom assessment* (pp. 367–393). Thousand Oaks, CA: SAGE.

Brown, G. T. L., Irving, S. E., Peterson, E. R., & Hirschfeld, G. H. F. (2009). Use of interactive-informal assessment practices: New Zealand secondary students' conceptions of assessment. *Learning and Instruction, 19*(2), 97–111.

Campbell, D. T., & Stanley, J. (1963). Experimental and quasi-experimental designs for research on teaching. In N. L. Gage (Ed.), *Handbook of research on teaching* (pp. 171–246). Chicago, IL: Rand McNally.

Chu, M. W., Guo, Q., & Leighton, J. P. (2014). Students' interpersonal trust and attitudes towards standardized tests: Exploring affective variables related to student assessment. *Assessment in Education: Principles, Policy & Practice, 21*(2), 167–192. doi:10.19080/0969594X.2013.844094

Crooks, T. J. (1988). The impact of classroom evaluation on students. *Review of Educational Research, 58*(4), 438–481.

Dinsmore, D. L., & Wilson, H. E. (2016). Student participation in assessment: Does it influence self-regulation? In G. T. L. Brown & L. R. Harris (Eds.), *Handbook of human and social conditions in assessment* (pp. 145–168). New York: Routledge.

Dorman, J. P., Fisher, D. L., & Waldrip, B. G. (2006). Classroom environment, students' perceptions of assessment, academic efficacy and attitude to science: A LISREL analysis. In D. Fisher & M. S. Khine (Eds.), *Contemporary approaches to research on learning environments* (pp. 1–28). Singapore: World Scientific.

Dweck, C. (2006). *Mindset: The new psychology of success.* New York: Ballantine Books.

Fulmer, G. W., Lee, I. C. H., & Tan, K. H. K. (2015). Multi-level model of contextual factors and teachers' assessment practices: An integrative review of research. *Assessment in Education: Principles, Policy & Practice, 22*(4), 475–494. doi:10.1080/0969594X.2015.1017445

Harris, L. M., & Brown, G. T. L. (2018). *Using self-assessment to improve learning.* New York: Routledge.

Hattie, J., & Timperley, H. (2007). The power of feedback. *Review of Educational Research, 77*, 81–112.

Heitink, M. C., Van der Kleij, F. M., Veldkamp, B. P., Schildkamp, K., & Kippers, W. B. (2016). A systematic review of prerequisites for implementing assessment for learning in classroom practice. *Educational Research Review, 17*, 50–62.

Irving, S. E., Peterson, E. R., & Brown, G. T. L. (2008). *Feedback and academic achievement: The relationship between students' conceptions of feedback and achievement.* Paper presented at the 6th Biennial Conference of the International Test Commission, Liverpool, UK.

Kane, M. T. (2006). Validation. In R. L. Brennan (Ed.), *Educational measurement* (4th ed., pp. 17–64). Westport, CT: Praeger.

Koretz, D. (2016). Making the term "validity" useful. *Assessment in Education: Principles, Policy & Practice, 23*(2), 290–292. doi:10.1080/0969594X.2015.1111193

McMillan, J. H. (2016). Section discussion: Student perceptions of assessment. In G. T. L. Brown & L. R. Harris (Eds.), *Handbook of human and social conditions in assessment* (pp. 221–243). New York: Routledge.

McMillan, J. H. (2018). *Classroom assessment: Principles and practice that enhance student learning and motivation* (7th ed.). Boston, MA: Pearson.

Messick, S. (1984). The psychology of educational measurement. *Journal of Educational Measurement, 21*(3), 215–237.

Mislevy, R. J. (2003). Substance and structure in assessment arguments. *Law, Probability, and Risk, 2*(4), 237–258.

Newton, P. E., & Shaw, S. D. (2014). *Validity in educational and psychological assessment.* London: SAGE.

Newton, P. E., & Shaw, S. D. (2016). Agreements and disagreements over validity. *Assessment in Education: Principles, Policy & Practice, 23*(2), 316–318. doi:10.1080/0969594X.2016.1158151

Panadero, E. (2017). A review of self-regulated learning: Six models and four directions for research. *Frontiers in Psychology, 8*, 1–28. doi:10.3389/fpyg.2017.00422.

Panadero, E., Andrade, H., & Brookhart, S. (2018). Fusing self-regulated learning and formative assessment: A roadmap of where we are, how we got here, and where we are going. *Australian Educational Researcher, 45*(1), 13–31. https://doi.10.1007/s13384-018-0258-y

Pellegrino, J. W., Chudowsky, N. M., & Glaser, R. (2001). *Knowing what students know: The science and design of educational assessment.* Washington, DC: National Research Council.

Penuel, W. R., & Shepard, L. A. (2016). Assessment and teaching. In D. H. Gitomer & C. A. Bell (Eds.), *Handbook of research on teaching* (5th ed., pp. 787–850). Washington, DC: American Educational Research Association.

Ruiz-Primo, M. A., & Brookhart, S. M. (2018). *Using feedback to improve learning.* New York: Routledge.

Shepard, L. A. (2000). The role of assessment in a learning culture. *Educational Researcher, 29*(7), 4–14.

Shepard, L. A, Penuel, W. R., & Pellegrino, J. W. (2018). Using learning and motivation theories to coherently link formative assessment, grading practices, and large-scale assessment. *Educational Measurement: Issues and Practice, 37*(1), 21–34.

Schunk, D. H., & Zimmerman, B. J. (Eds.). (2012). *Motivation and self-regulated learning: Theory, research and applications.* New York: Lawrence Erlbaum Associates.

Struyen, K., & Devesa, J. (2016). Students' perceptions of novel forms of assessment. In G. T. L. Brown & L. R. Harris (Eds.), *Handbook of human and social conditions in assessment* (pp. 129–144). New York: Routledge.

Tierney, R. D. (2013). Fairness in classroom assessment. In J. H. McMillan (Ed.), *SAGE handbook of research on classroom assessment* (pp. 125–144). Thousand Oaks, CA: SAGE.

Vogel, E., & Pekrun, R. (2016). Emotions that matter to achievement: Student feelings about assessment. In J. H. McMillan (Ed.), *SAGE handbook of research on classroom assessment* (pp. 111–128). Thousand Oaks, CA: SAGE.

Wilson, M. (2016, June). The importance of classroom assessment. *NCME Newsletter, 24*(2), 2–3.

Wise, S. L., & Smith, L. F. (2016). The validity of assessment when students don't give good effort. In J. H. McMillan (Ed.), *SAGE handbook of research on classroom assessment* (pp. 204–220). Thousand Oaks, CA: SAGE.

Zeng, W., Huang, F., Yu, L., & Chen, S. (2018). Towards a learning-oriented assessment to improve student learning: A critical review of literature. *Educational Assessment, Evaluation and Accountability, 30*(3), 211–250. doi:10.1007/s11092-018-9281-9

Zimmerman, B. J., & Schunk, D. H. (2011). Self-regulated learning and performance: An introduction and an overview. In B. J. Zimmerman & D. H. Schunk (Eds.), *Handbook of self-regulation of learning and performance* (pp. 1–11). New York: Routledge.

Part II

The Use of Classroom Assessment Information to Enhance Learning

6

Guidance in the *Standards* for Classroom Assessment

Useful or Irrelevant?

Steve Ferrara, Kristen Maxey-Moore, and Susan M. Brookhart

Introduction

Researchers and thought leaders in classroom assessment have called for reconceptualizing psychometric formulations of fundamental measurement concepts in the *Standards for Educational and Psychological Testing* (American Educational Research Association [AERA], American Psychological Association [APA], & National Council on Measurement in Education [NCME], 2014)[1] for the realities of classroom assessment (e.g., Brookhart, 2003; Moss, 2003; Shepard, 2006; Smith, 2003). The introduction to the *Standards* contains the claim that they "may . . . be usefully applied in varying degrees to a broad range of less formal assessment techniques" (AERA et al., 2014, p. 2), and a commentary on the *Standards* development process claimed that "classroom teachers would benefit from reading the *Standards*" (Plake & Wise, 2014, p. 6). In response, Ferrara (2014) observed that "the standards are written in our technical language . . . [not teacher language, and] . . . a translation of relevant *Standards* into standards for classroom assessment practice could be valuable" (p. 25).

In this chapter, we explore the hypothesis that there may be value in translating time-tested psychometric requirements as articulated in the *Standards* into formulations that make sense to teachers and are useful for teachers' classroom assessment to support student learning. This analysis represents a proof of concept test of the potential relevance of the *Standards* for classroom assessment.

We are aware of the *Classroom Assessment Standards* (Joint Committee on Standards for Educational Evaluation, 2015) and recommendations in the various widely used textbooks on classroom assessment for teachers. We do not consider these sources in the proof of concept, but discuss them later in comparison to the psychometric standards. In addition, a widely used textbook on classroom assessment (Brookhart & Nitko, 2019) provides criteria for improving validity for classroom assessment used for student grading (p. 41, Figure 3.1) and reliability concerns for classroom assessment (p. 69, Figure 4.1). Likewise, we do not consider those guidelines here.

We present 12 standards, translated for classroom assessment, for the proof of concept. We selected the standards primarily from the three "Foundations" chapters in the *Standards*.

We selected additional standards that address teacher and student behavior that occurs in classroom assessment practices that are related to fairness and interpretation validity.

In the following sections, we define classroom assessment, translate the 12 standards, and apply the translated standards to four types of classroom assessment. We end the chapter with a broader discussion of the role that the measurement community and the *Standards* could play in supporting pre-service and in-service teachers in integrating effective classroom assessment practices into the teaching-learning process.

Definition of Terms, and Some Debate

Published Definitions of Classroom Assessment to Support Instructional Decisions and Student Learning

Thought leaders and researchers in classroom assessment from the measurement community offer definitions of classroom assessment to support instruction and learning. We consider two examples, first McMillan (2013) and then Wiliam (2011):

> CA [classroom assessment] is a broad and evolving conceptualization of a process that teachers and students use in collecting, evaluating, and using evidence of student learning for a variety of purposes, including diagnosing student strengths and weaknesses, monitoring student progress toward meeting desired levels of proficiency, assigning grades, and providing feedback to parents. That is, CA is a tool teachers use ... It is distinguished from large-scale or standardized, whether standards based, personality, aptitude, or benchmark- or interim-type tests. It is locally controlled ...
>
> (McMillan, 2013, p. 4)

Classroom assessment, as the name implies, involves gathering, interpreting, and using assessment information within a classroom. Teachers are the primary designers of classroom assessment, and along with their students use the information to support learning. Thus, one of the distinguishing features of classroom assessment is that it is situated in a particular learning community (e.g., a classroom), and classroom assessment information derives its meaning in large part from that context.

Context is important for the evidentiary process. Both informal formative assessment strategies and summative unit assessments provide meaning closely tied with the way concepts and skills are considered, in particular contextualized lessons, the instructional methods used to develop students' understandings and capabilities, and the ways in which students developed their understandings of lesson content. Only the teacher and students in a classroom have a complete understanding of what they have discussed or done during classroom lessons. Consider an assessment question that is intended to require higher-order thinking and understanding of primary sources, in which students are asked to analyze a passage or phrase in the Gettysburg Address. No matter the question's design, if that passage had already been analyzed in classroom discussion, the question assesses mostly recall of the conclusions reached in class. Information from that question would mean something different in classrooms, depending on whether students have or have not analyzed part of the Gettysburg Address, and how deeply parts of the passage or phrase were examined. These experiences, in turn, would shape the effect that the assessment has on their understanding and grasp of the content. This is part of the co-regulation of learning (Allal, 2016), where "co" means regulation of learning from influences external to the learner. All of this is part of the situated nature of learning and assessment, in addition to the more sociocultural aspects of learning and assessment (e.g., whether the classroom climate fosters risk-taking or defensiveness in academic discourse).

The situated nature of classroom assessment, then, affects interpretation of assessment results, which in turn informs the validity of the interpretations. This is one of the major differences between classroom and large-scale, cross-context assessment. Validity in the contextualized nature of classroom assessment can be defined as the trustworthiness of the information (see Alonzo, this volume) and its usefulness to support learning (see Kane & Wools, this volume). In contrast, large-scale, standardized assessments are designed to be administered across classrooms, with the accompanying need to demonstrate standardization, reliability, and validity to facilitate interpretation, aggregation, and comparisons for varied contexts.

Wiliam's (2011) definition of classroom formative assessment acknowledges that classroom assessment is situated in the classroom, specifically in instructional situations focusing on teachers and learners using assessment information to guide instructional decisions:

> An assessment functions formatively to the extent that evidence about student achievement is elicited, interpreted, and used by teachers, learners, or their peers to make decisions about the next steps in instruction that are likely to be better, or better founded, than the decisions they would have made in the absence of that evidence.
>
> (p. 43)

Most definitions of classroom assessment have at least three common elements, tools, or processes for: (a) gathering information about student learning; (b) interpreting that information within the context of a classroom learning community; and (c) using that information to identify and address student needs to support and promote learning.

The Authors' Debate: Two Positions on What Is and Is Not Classroom Assessment

Both of the aforementioned definitions focus more on the evidentiary process in classroom assessment than on the tools used to collect the evidence. The co-authors of this chapter disagree on the answer to an important related question: Are externally delivered assessment tools that are intended to provide information to guide instructional decisions considered classroom assessments? One position is that assessments that are used across classrooms, regardless of the intended uses of the assessment information, cannot be regarded as classroom assessment because they are not "locally controlled" (McMillan, 2013, p. 4). In this view, local control is seen as a defining characteristic of classroom assessment, in part because of the situated nature of the meaning of the assessment questions and tasks, and assessment results. McMillan (2013, p. 4) specifically categorizes interim and benchmark assessments as large-scale, standardized assessments, not classroom assessments.

An opposing position is that what matters in determining whether an assessment type is a classroom assessment is the *use* of the assessment information, regardless of the origin of the assessment. As long as the information is used formatively to make instructional decisions and promote further learning, it is a classroom assessment practice. For example, commercially provided "formative" and "interim" assessments (e.g., the widely used MAP, Aspire, eMPower, and i-Ready assessments) that are used to guide curriculum and instruction decisions could be considered classroom assessments. State accountability tests that are used almost exclusively for public accountability purposes would not be considered classroom assessments.

If the idea that the core of what defines classroom assessment is whether the assessment information is used by teachers and students to enable further learning, then commercial classroom assessment products are classroom assessments *because of their use.*[2] The intended use of information from commercial classroom assessment products is specifically to guide and enable further learning. Obviously, the further learning based on this information cannot take place at the moment of a lesson or unit. In this view, commercial classroom assessment information is a way in which teachers, teacher teams, and school leaders can make decisions about curriculum, instructional focus, grouping, and so forth for the next quarter, for example. Student learning objective (SLO; see below) processes are not, because they focus on teacher effects on student learning.

In summary, the authors of this chapter disagree on what should be included in a scholarly definition of classroom assessment. One view is that only localized classroom formative and summative assessment (described below) should be considered classroom assessment. The other view is that three of the purposes described below (classroom formative and summative assessment and commercial classroom assessment products) can be considered classroom assessment. The SLO process would not qualify as classroom assessment, and yet it is something teachers engage in regularly in their classrooms and cannot be ignored.

In the end, we set aside these distinctions for the purposes of this chapter. We include all four assessment types (classroom formative, classroom summative, commercial, and SLO) because they are prevalent assessment functions in which teachers engage, whether or not they want to. For example, participation in the SLO process has been mandated in several states, partly to counter educators' uneasiness with top-down mandates about using external standardized test information for teacher evaluation. The SLO process gives teachers some level of control over the student achievement data that are used in evaluations of their teaching. This "accountability creep" moves the locus of information for teacher evaluation from large-scale accountability tests to classroom-based measures, and the locus of decision-making control from the state to local teachers and administrators. However, the purpose (i.e., teacher evaluation) remains the same.

Four Types of Classroom Assessment

Teacher Inferences about Student Understanding of Skills, Concepts, and Procedures during Instruction

When teachers pose questions during instruction, they typically intend to make inferences about the degree to which students have learned targeted learning outcomes and what additional instruction (e.g., clarification, re-explanation) and learning (e.g., more accurate understanding of concepts and skills) they may need. This type of assessment is called informal classroom formative assessment, short-cycle formative assessment (Wiliam, 2010), or assessment for learning (AfL).

Wiliam (2011) cites study results that indicate that 57% of elementary teachers' classroom questions are about classroom management, 33% require only recall of information provided previously, and 8% require analyzing, inferencing, and generalizing. As Wiliam (2011) highlighted, "less than 10 percent of questions . . . actually caused any new learning" (p. 79). Within that 10% estimate, teachers may pose questions to students during instruction both to assess student learning and learning needs and to promote and extend learning. Frameworks for questions to assess students' knowledge of facts, understanding of concepts, and ability to apply concepts, skills, and procedures abound—and they focus as much on questions intended to help students learn as to help teachers assess student learning. For example, McTighe and Wiggins (2013, p. 14, Figure 1.2) offer four types of classroom questions: questions that hook, lead, and guide students during instruction and essential questions that encourage students to develop and refine their understanding of key ideas and processes continuously. Chappuis, Stiggins, Chappuis, and Arter (2012) propose "instructional questions" (p. 27) to assess student knowledge and understanding and assess reasoning. Zwiers and Crawford (2011) propose five core skills to make classroom conversations "more academic" (p. 31), around which classroom assessment questions can be built: (a) elaborate and clarify; (b) support ideas with examples; (c) build on and/or challenge a partner's idea; (d) paraphrase; and (e) synthesize conversation points.

Teachers use a range of other formative assessment methods, in addition to questioning, to make inferences about student understanding during instruction, to help students make sense of their learning. These methods include clarifying learning targets and criteria for success, student self- and peer assessment, feedback based on teacher observations of student work processes and products, and more formal methods such as periodic quizzes. Students and teachers are the primary users of classroom formative assessment information.

Teacher-Made or -Selected Unit Summative Assessments

Teachers typically construct or select tests and assessments to ascertain levels of student acquisition of knowledge and skills at the completion of units of instruction, and for grading. A unit test may include multiple-choice and short constructed response items, essay prompts, multiple-step problems, write-ups of a laboratory investigation or library and Internet research, or other assessment activities. Teachers may use performance assessments such as oral presentations, research papers, and long-term projects as well. Teacher-selected unit tests typically accompany curriculum materials (e.g., textbooks). The types of items included in teacher-made and -selected unit tests (e.g., binary choice, matching, multiple-choice, short constructed response) can differ considerably across elementary, middle, and high school instructional units, elementary curriculum areas (e.g., language arts, mathematics, social studies), and secondary subjects (e.g., English, mathematics, algebra, U.S. history) (Brookhart, 2004).

When teachers administer unit tests, they typically intend to make summative inferences about what students know, understand, and can do at the conclusion of the instructional unit. They use this information for grading and reporting. Students, teachers, parents, and other educators are the primary users of classroom summative (i.e., graded) assessment information.

Student Learning Objectives Aligned with Competencies Used for High-Stakes Decisions for Teachers

In some states and school systems, student learning objectives (SLOs) are course-long learning objectives set by teachers to identify and monitor student progress toward critical learning outcomes. In the SLO process, student growth is determined by comparing student readiness for content at the beginning of the course (i.e., the preparedness level) with their mastery of content at the end of a course (i.e., the expectation level). For example, according to the Colorado Academic Standards, which incorporate the Common Core State Standards (see www.cde.state. co.us/contentareas/ccss_in_the_colorado_standards), the goal of SLOs is to focus teachers on setting ambitious, realistic, and measurable objectives toward student mastery of standards.

Throughout the school year, teachers use a variety of assessments to monitor student progress toward mastery of the SLOs. At the end of a course or school year, teachers may use a body of evidence to determine students' expectation levels for the specific standards within the SLO (there is also use of simple pre-/post-testing to monitor progress on SLOs). Expectation levels are closely aligned to the specific content and grade-level standards and the learning progression for the SLO. Not all assessments used in SLO processes involve classroom-based assessment. Some schools use cross-class, large-scale measures to assess student progress on SLOs.

Commercial Classroom Assessment Products

Commercial curriculum and testing companies offer classroom assessment products, some of which are labeled interim and benchmark assessments. Interim assessment products, offered to schools and school districts by commercial vendors, typically include parallel test forms that cover the content standards for an entire school year and can be administered at multiple times throughout the school year (e.g., fall, winter, spring). Their intended use is to track student learning and achievement growth toward a desired level of performance by the end of the school year (e.g., the proficient standard on a state summative test). Benchmark formative assessments typically are non-parallel test forms that cover a selected portion of the content standards for an entire school year (e.g., quarter 1), and are intended to be administered at a specified point in the school year, consistent with the scope and sequence of a curriculum. Commercial interim and benchmark assessments are intended to provide achievement information to guide teachers, schools, and districts in making instructional grouping decisions, curriculum planning, and staff and other resource allocation decisions. Typically, they are purchased by a school or district; teachers are required to administer them and use the information from each administration to guide planning. Commercial or locally developed interim and benchmark assessments can be considered large-scale measures and are guided by psychometric requirements in the *Standards*. For example, they typically are supported by technical manuals that report psychometric information, as required by the *Standards*, on reliability, validity, and scaling.

In addition, other commercial assessment products include item banks for constructing classroom assessments. Sometimes teachers use such item banks to construct classroom embedded tests, for one of several purposes. For example, some teachers may use item banks for more formal formative assessment methods, such as weekly quizzes (Ruiz-Primo & Furtak, 2004). Wiliam (2010) calls this medium-cycle formative assessment. Other purposes for classroom teachers' use of item banks include course summative assessment or SLO assessment.

Selected Standards, Translated for Classroom Assessment

For this chapter, we translated 12 standards that are relevant to effective classroom assessment. Each chapter author nominated standards deemed relevant to gathering, interpreting, and using high-quality information about student learning in the classroom, including issues of validity, fairness, and students' rights and responsibilities. The authors then reached consensus on the 12 standards listed in Table 6.1.

Table 6.1 Psychometric standards and categories translated for classroom assessment

Score Interpretation Validity
Content-oriented evidence (standards 1.11 and 12.4)
Evidence regarding cognitive processes (standard 1.12)
Construct alignment and relevance (standard 3.2)
Inappropriate test preparation (standard 12.7)
Fairness and Validity
Testing process (standard 3.1)
Test administration accommodations (standard 3.9)
Reliability of Inferences about Student Proficiency and Learning Needs
Testing procedure replications as evidence (standard 2.1)
Decision consistency (standard 2.16)
Test-Takers' Rights and Responsibilities
Intended test purposes and impacts (standards 8.1 and 8.2)
Test security, data integrity, and cheating (standard 8.9)

We began by translating each of the 12 standards from the wording in the *Standards* to language that would be appropriate for classroom assessment. Following translation, we evaluated each standard in terms of relevance for the aforementioned four types of classroom assessment:

- Teacher inferences about student understanding of skills, concepts, and procedures during instruction (i.e., classroom formative assessment).
- Teacher-made or teacher-selected instructional unit tests and assessments (i.e., classroom summative assessment or grading).
- Student learning outcomes (SLOs) aligned with competencies used for high-stakes decisions for teachers.
- Commercial formative assessment products, when the information is used by a teacher for within-classroom decisions.

Table 6.2 contains the verbatim standard, our translation of the standard, and our application of that translation to the four classroom assessment types. We ask readers to work simultaneously with Table 6.2 and the text in this section so that we do not have to duplicate content from the table in the text. In the text below, we summarize the translations to help the reader. Also, we explain the translation, provide a rationale for translating each standard, and evaluate the efficacy of translating each psychometric standard for classroom assessment. We have organized the 12 standards into four categories that are relevant to classroom assessment practice and inferences that may make sense to teachers and that are useful for teachers' classroom assessment to support student learning: score interpretation validity, fairness and validity, reliability of inferences about student proficiency and learning needs, and test-takers' rights and responsibilities. In some cases, we created a combined translation of two related standards.

Table 6.2 also illustrates how a teacher could apply each of the selected standards to the four types of classroom assessment, in the form of evaluative questions they could pose to themselves. We expect that teachers' responses to these questions would be mostly positive for the 8% of teacher classroom questions that result in new learning in the Wiliam (2011) study citation. We also expect that teachers' responses to these questions would be mostly negative for the other 92% of teacher classroom questions. To the extent that these standards are applied routinely in classroom assessment practice, the percentage of classroom questions that result in new learning would increase.

Score Interpretation Validity

The field of educational measurement is in general agreement that validity is not a quality of a test. Rather, interpretations made and actions taken on behalf of examinees, based on test scores, are more or less valid and supportable by evidence. The *Standards* refers to this view as "interpretations of test scores for proposed uses of tests" (AERA et al., 2014, p. 11). The same goes for classroom assessment, though the standards for validation and evidence are different, as we have tried to point out in this chapter. The four standards in this group address prerequisite conditions to enable valid interpretations and uses of test scores. These prerequisites apply to large scale and classroom assessments.

Content-Oriented Evidence (Standards 1.11 and 12.4)

The first sentence in standard 1.11 can be parsed as follows: (a) appropriateness of test content; (b) procedures to specify and generate test content; (c) the intended testing population; and (d) the construct to be measured or domain that is represented. The references to "importance, frequency, or criticality" in the second sentence are relevant to, for example, justifying the score

Table 6.2 Teacher-oriented translations of selected standards applied to four classroom assessment practices

Translations of the *Standards* for:

Teacher Inferences about Student Understanding of Skills, Concepts, and Procedures during Instruction	Teacher-Made or -Selected Unit Assessments	SLOs Aligned with Competencies Used for High-Stakes Decisions for Teachers	Commercial Classroom Assessment Products

Score Interpretation Validity

Content-Oriented Evidence (standards 1.11 and 12.4)

1.11 *When the rationale for test score interpretation for a given score use rests in part on the appropriateness of test content, the procedures followed in specifying and generating test content should be described and justified with reference to the intended population to be tested and the construct the test is intended to measure or the domain it is intended to represent. If the definition of the content sampled incorporates criteria such as importance, frequency, or criticality, these criteria should also be clearly explained and justified.*

12.4 *When a test is used as an indicator of achievement in an instructional domain or with respect to specified content standards, evidence of the extent to which the test samples the range of knowledge and elicits the processes reflected in the target domain should be provided. Both the tested and target domains should be described in sufficient detail for their relationship to be evaluated. The analyses should make explicit those aspects of the target domain that the test represents, as well as those aspects that the test fails to represent.*

Translation of Both Standards

The content and format of classroom assessment activities and the knowledge and skills targeted in instruction should be aligned. All classroom assessment activities, taken together, cover all knowledge and thinking skill outcomes I targeted in instruction or reading and homework assignments, and do not cover outcomes I did not require of my students.

Is the assessment evidence I've gathered relevant to determining the degree to which students have mastered each of the learning outcomes in this lesson or unit?	Do the items on this test reflect all the important learning outcomes in this unit? Do the items reflect what I taught?	Is the evidence gathered to illustrate mastery of each SLO aligned with each SLO?	Do the items on this assessment cover all learning outcomes adequately? Are the item response demands consistent with the content standards targeted during the period of instruction prior to test administration?
Do I pose questions or assign work to students that require knowledge and thinking skills I've not covered in instruction?	What portion of the learning outcomes in this unit of instruction do the test items cover? Do they items require knowledge or thinking skills I didn't cover?	What portion of the learning outcomes in this unit of instruction do the SLOs cover? Do any SLOs require knowledge or thinking skills I didn't cover?	What portion of the learning outcomes in this unit of instruction do the test items cover? Do the items require knowledge or thinking skills I didn't cover?
When I do pose questions or make assignments like that, do I make it clear that this is a learning activity as well as an assessment activity?			

Evidence Regarding Cognitive Processes (standard 1.12)

If the rationale for score interpretation for a given use depends on premises about the psychological processes or cognitive operations of test takers, then theoretical or empirical evidence in support of those premises should be provided. When statements about the processes employed by observers or scorers are part of the argument for validity, similar information should be provided.

Translation

The thinking skills required to respond to assessment activities should be consistent with the thinking skills specified in the learning outcome and targeted in instruction.

Do the questions I ask and the work students do during instruction require the level of thinking described in the content standards? Can the tasks be completed without using those thinking skills? Do I give students enough time to think before they respond? Does student classroom discussion and classroom work produce evidence of how students are thinking about the concepts, and not just correctness?

Do the items on the test reflect the thinking skills identified or implied in the content standard?

Do I have evidence that students have mastered the thinking skills indicated in the SLOs?

Are the thinking skills targeted in the test items aligned with the thinking skills in the targeted content standards and the corresponding Achievement Level Descriptor?

Construct Alignment and Relevance (standard 3.2)

Test developers are responsible for developing tests that measure the intended construct and for minimizing the potential for tests' being affected by construct-irrelevant characteristics, such as linguistic, communicative, cognitive, cultural, physical, or other characteristics.

Translation

Classroom assessment information about student learning focuses on mastery of targeted learning outcomes that is not unduly affected by extraneous factors in the assessment activities, such as a student's current oral language development, limited writing capability, visual impairment, etc.

When I require students to explain their understanding of mathematics, science, and social studies concepts, do I remove the influence of expression limitations, grammatical errors, and other irrelevant factors from my conclusion about their conceptual understanding?
In my observation of a student performance or evaluation of a student product, am I certain that students with different backgrounds would interpret the task as I intend?

Are the items on this test written to minimize barriers and maximize flexibility for all (or most) learners?
Conversely, do the items on this unit test contain impediments to some students that may obscure what they know and can do in relation to the targeted learning outcomes?

Is any SLO or evidence associated with an SLO influenced by impediments that obscure what students know and can do?

Do the items on this assessment product contain impediments to some students that may obscure what they know and can do in relation to the targeted learning outcomes?

Inappropriate Test Preparation (standard 12.7)

In educational settings, test users should take steps to prevent test preparation activities and distribution of materials to students that may adversely affect the validity of test score inferences.

(Continued)

Table 6.2 *(Continued)*

Translations of the *Standards* for:

Teacher Inferences about Student Understanding of Skills, Concepts, and Procedures during Instruction	Teacher-Made or -Selected Unit Assessments	SLOs Aligned with Competencies Used for High-Stakes Decisions for Teachers	Commercial Classroom Assessment Products
Translation			
During instruction, students should be clear on the knowledge and skills they are learning. In classroom formative assessment situations, they should be aware of the learning outcomes that the teacher is assessing because it is part of the teaching-learning process. In classroom summative assessment situations, students should know what knowledge and skills are eligible on a test but not know the actual test content ahead of time.			
(Any opportunity that helps students learn the knowledge and thinking skills targeted during and in addition to my teaching is likely to be appropriate.)	Did my students have inappropriate access to the questions on this unit test?	Did my students complete on their own, without undue assistance, the work that is used as evidence for each SLO?	Did my students have inappropriate access to the questions on this assessment?

FAIRNESS AND VALIDITY

Testing Process (standard 3.1)

Those responsible for test development, revision, and administration should design all steps of the testing process to promote valid score interpretations for intended score uses for the widest possible range of individuals and relevant subgroups in the intended population.

Translation			
Teachers should conduct classroom formative and summative assessments that are accessible to all students in the classroom.			
Have I posed questions during instruction that are appropriate for all of my students? Did I have to adjust some questions for some students?	Are all items on the test appropriate for all of my students? Can I interpret test questions for those students who need it without invalidating the item and test?	Did I collect evidence for each SLO that shows what students know and can do without undue assistance?	Are all items on the test appropriate for all of my students? Can I interpret test questions or provide other accommodations for those students who need it without invalidating the item and test?

Test Administration Accommodations (standard 3.9)

Test developers and/or test users are responsible for developing and providing test accommodations, when appropriate and feasible, to remove construct-irrelevant barriers that otherwise would interfere with examinees' ability to demonstrate their standing on the target constructs.

Translation

Teachers should provide accommodations when they assess students in the classroom for those students who need them, without unduly influencing student performance, to ensure that students can show what they have learned, know, and can do and have a trustworthy idea of their learning needs.

Are there any requirements in this classroom assessment activity that might obscure what this student knows and can do around these learning outcomes? If so, have I made accommodations to the task to ensure student access?	Are there any requirements in this unit test that might obscure what this student knows and can do around these learning outcomes? If so, have I made accommodations to the task to ensure student access?	Is any of the evidence about mastery of SLOs about what this student knows and can do around these learning outcomes obscured by impediments (e.g. writing requirements beyond a student's current capability)? If so, have I made accommodations to the task to ensure student access? Is any of the evidence unduly influenced by support from another student or an adult?	Are there any requirements in this assessment that might obscure what this student knows and can do around these learning outcomes? If so, have I made accommodations to the task to ensure student access?

RELIABILITY OF INFERENCES ABOUT STUDENT PROFICIENCY AND LEARNING NEEDS

Testing Procedure Replications as Evidence (standard 2.1)

The range of replications over which reliability/precision is being evaluated should be clearly stated, along with a rationale for the choice of this definition, given the testing situation.

Translation

Teachers should use systematic procedures to assess work and assign scores or course grades. Teachers should be clear about factors over which appraisals should not vary (e.g., whether I graded a paper on Monday or Tuesday) and factors over which appraisals could vary (e.g., how much instruction a student has had before producing the work). Teachers should gather sufficient evidence for each assessment purpose.

Do I have enough items or tasks to get a consistent picture of what my students know and can do? Would another teacher give the same score or appraisal to the student work that I would?	Do I have enough items or tasks to get a consistent picture of what my students know and can do? Would another teacher give the same score or appraisal to the student work that I would?	Would students do about as well on this test if I gave it later today? Next week?
Would students do about as well on this unit test if I gave it later today? Next week?	Could my students produce similar evidence for the targeted SLOs at another time, with support from different people?	
Will students be able to demonstrate at another time that they've learned the knowledge and thinking skills I targeted during instruction?		

(Continued)

Table 6.2 *(Continued)*

Translations of the *Standards* for:

Teacher Inferences about Student Understanding of Skills, Concepts, and Procedures during Instruction	Teacher-Made or -Selected Unit Assessments	SLOs Aligned with Competencies Used for High-Stakes Decisions for Teachers	Commercial Classroom Assessment Products

Decision Consistency (standard 2.16)

When a test or combination of measures is used to make classification decisions, estimates should be provided of the percentage of test takers who would be classified in the same way on two replications of the procedure.

Translation

Information about student learning should be sufficiently trustworthy and in the best interest of students to support my decisions about providing or not providing additional instruction on the outcomes.

Teacher Inferences	Teacher-Made	SLOs	Commercial
Do I have enough evidence to conclude confidently that these students have mastered the targeted learning outcomes or decide what additional instruction they need? Have I accurately identified those students who do and do not need additional instruction?	Does this unit test score accurately distinguish students who have and have not mastered the instructional content? How confident am I that these decisions are correct? Does other student work evidence point to the same decision(s)?	Are the assessment data relevant to each SLO adequately rigorous, when aggregated, to support accurate identification of students who have and have not met graduation-readiness decisions?	Does information from this assessment accurately distinguish students who are and are not progressing toward end of school year proficiency standards?

TEST-TAKERS' RIGHTS AND RESPONSIBILITIES

Intended Test Purposes and Impacts (standards 8.1 and 8.2)

8.1 *Information about test content and purposes that is available to any test taker prior to testing should be available to all test takers. Shared information should be available free of charge and in accessible formats.*

8.2 *Test takers should be provided in advance with as much information about the test, the testing process, the intended test use, test scoring criteria, testing policy, availability of accommodations, and confidentiality protection as is consistent with obtaining valid responses and making appropriate interpretations of test scores.*

Translation of Both Standards

Students need information about assessment in order to participate in the assessment process in a way that yields valid, interpretable information (for both the student and the teacher) and informs their learning.

My students know what they are trying to learn in each lesson (their learning target) and the success criteria by which both they and their teacher will be able to judge the quality of their learning and what they need to learn next. My students are aware that mistakes are opportunities for learning and interpret their formative assessment evidence in that light. I do not penalize or grade students for mistakes made during learning.	I give my students enough notice before each test or graded assignment that they can prepare properly. Notice about a test includes what the test will be about, when it will be given, and what the grade will be used for. Notice about projects or performances include directions, scoring criteria, due date, and what the grade will be used for. As appropriate, I prepare study guides and other scaffolds for students' preparation.	I give my students enough notice before each SLO test or performance assessment that they can prepare properly. Notice about a test includes what the test will be about, when it will be given, and what the grade will be used for. Notice about projects or performances include directions, scoring criteria, due date, and what the grade will be used for. As appropriate, I prepare study guides and other scaffolds for students' preparation.	I inform my students about when a formal formative assessment will be given, what will be covered on the test, and how the results will be used.

Test Security, Data Integrity, and Cheating (standard 8.9)

Test takers should be made aware that having someone else take the test for them, disclosing confidential test material, or engaging in any other forms of cheating is unacceptable and that such behavior may result in sanctions.

Translation

Students should be reminded that they should not cheat on tests and other classroom assessment activities because they are part of the teaching-learning process. They should be helped to understand that cheating on classroom assessment denies themselves the opportunity to identify their learning needs.

My understanding of what students have learned is accurate and not influenced by student cheating (e.g., copying from another student) or undue influence of another student or adult. I know the difference between cheating and legitimate collaboration on work designed for collaboration.	My understanding of what students have learned is accurate and not influenced by student cheating (e.g., copying from another student). I know the difference between cheating and legitimate collaboration on work designed for collaboration. For grades or other individually identified scores or marks, I have evidence of individual students' learning.	My understanding of what students have learned is accurate and not influenced by student cheating (e.g., copying from another student) or undue influence of another student or adult.	My understanding of what students have learned is accurate and not influenced by student cheating (e.g., copying from another student) or undue influence of another student or adult.

point weights assigned to various instructional objectives based on their importance and/or their emphasis in instruction. Standard 12.4 refers to the degree to which a test samples from a content subdomain of knowledge and thinking skills and being explicit about what is and is not covered.

References in standard 1.11 to test development procedures, intended testing population, target construct, sampling, importance, frequency, and criticality ratings are psychometric terms and concepts. References to the appropriateness and importance of test content are relevant to aligning test content to what has been covered and emphasized during instruction. The reference to specifying content can be construed as an oblique consideration of aligning assessment formats (e.g., multiple-choice items, work product creation tasks) with the learning outcomes targeted during instruction.

A caution is in order here. The authors have observed that because the word "alignment" in the United States has come to be associated with alignment studies for state accountability tests, some teachers and administrators have a narrow view of alignment as categorizing (i.e., simply of identifying a state standard that a particular assessment item or task matches). "Alignment," as we use the term in Table 6.2, means a true, more nuanced match with standards that include, in addition to a content match, considerations of learning progressions or trajectories and grain size (see Briggs & Furtak, this volume). In other words, for an assessment item or task to align with a standard, it is not enough for it simply to reference appropriate content. It must also ask the students about that content at an appropriate time in their sequence of learning, and the specific content must be at the appropriate grain size for the intended inferences and decision (smaller for lesson-embedded formative assessment, slightly larger for unit assessments).

TRANSLATION OF BOTH STANDARDS

The content and format of classroom assessment activities and the knowledge and skills targeted in instruction should be aligned. All classroom assessment items and tasks, taken together, constitute a representative sample of all the knowledge and thinking skill outcomes targeted in instruction or reading and homework assignments, and do not cover outcomes not targeted. For example, in a unit on graphing linear equations, a unit test might ask students to graph linear equations and solve problems in which graphing linear equations constitute effective solution strategies.

EXPLANATION AND RATIONALE

Alignment between content (e.g., conceptual understanding) and process learning outcomes (e.g., writing and mathematical procedures) and test content and item formats is fundamental. This type of alignment is crucial to support intended interpretations of performance on classroom assessments and how the interpretations are used for grading and other decisions. Making learning outcomes clear to students is required for effective teaching and learning. It is equally important to designing tests, including classroom assessments. Teachers can form useful inferences about student learning and learning needs when they have made learning outcomes clear and assess those outcomes in appropriate ways.

EVALUATION

These translations can be effective only if the references to technical terms (e.g., target construct) and procedures (e.g., specifying content) are recast for teachers and classroom assessment, as in learning outcomes targeted in instruction and creating classroom assessments. The concepts of alignment and representativeness are crucial to the conclusions that teachers can draw about student learning and learning needs.

Evidence Regarding Cognitive Processes (Standard 1.12)

This standard requires that evidence must be provided to support claims about cognitive processes to support score interpretations. This standard is particularly important when teachers (and psychometricians) assess process standards in the Common Core and Next Generation Science Standards.

TRANSLATION

The thinking skills required to respond to assessment items and tasks should be consistent with the thinking skills specified in the learning outcome and what is targeted in instruction. For example, if students are expected to be able to draw conclusions about Hamlet's character from what he says and does in the play, then an assessment needs to ask them to do that—as opposed to, for example, repeating conclusions about Hamlet's character that were provided in lecture notes or literary analyses students were asked to read.

EXPLANATION AND RATIONALE

Ongoing, in-the-moment assessment of student learning and other, more structured classroom assessments require teachers to observe student behavior, verbalizations, performances, and work products and draw conclusions about thinking skill proficiency. That is, along with standard 1.11, classroom assessment activities must demonstrably elicit student thinking skills (e.g., problem-solving, analysis) as well as content knowledge to support teacher conclusions about conceptual understanding and higher-order thinking skills.

This standard is particularly important for teacher-made tests and performance assessment tasks so that the assessment response demands align with the cognitive process specified in learning outcomes and targeted during instruction. Our experience is that most teachers understand this but find it difficult to construct test items or performance tasks that in fact tap intended cognitive processes. For example, a significant classroom performance assessment "trap" is retelling tasks, in which students simply copy and paste information into a presentation, paper, or poster without having to understand or process it. Many classroom assignments and assessments (e.g., do a presentation on a planet, a U.S. state, or a simple machine) do not meet standard 1.12.

EVALUATION

This translation supplements the translation of standard 1.11 to emphasize the importance of aligning classroom assessment with both content knowledge and cognitive processes that are specified in content standards and targeted during instruction. It should be recognizable to teachers who are familiar with and may use Bloom's taxonomy, the depth of knowledge framework, and other thinking skills frameworks (e.g., the essential questions in Wiggins & McTighe, 2013).

Construct Alignment and Relevance (Standard 3.2)

In state and other testing programs, psychometricians and content specialists strive to reduce and avoid sources of construct irrelevance, using review processes such as bias and sensitivity reviews, language simplification edits, differential item functioning analyses, and by providing test administration accommodations. Item difficulty modeling research (e.g., Ferrara, Steedle, &

Frantz, 2018) provides an extensive list of content, cognitive, linguistic, and other item response demands that are related to item difficulty, though some are construct-irrelevant and should be accounted for in test development.

TRANSLATION

Classroom assessment information about student learning focuses on mastery of targeted learning outcomes that is not unduly affected by extraneous factors (i.e., factors not related to the intended construct/learning outcome) in the assessment, such as a student's current oral language proficiency, limited writing capability, visual impairment, etc. For example, word problems intended to assess problem-solving in mathematics should be written at or below students' current reading levels so that reading comprehension is not confounded with student problem-solving achievement.

EXPLANATION AND RATIONALE

Teachers choose classroom assessment activities that target content area learning outcomes, though those activities may not align well with cognitive process outcomes (Brookhart, 2004). Teachers who know their students well make adjustments for individual student capabilities and learning needs during the teaching-learning process, when they assess student learning, and when they assign grades to students. Teachers may not be aware of construct-irrelevant factors, even when they make adjustments for students. They may not be aware of unobservable cognitive processes that, for example, discussion questions and assessment activities require of learners, but they can adjust in the moment as part of the teaching, learning, and assessment process.

EVALUATION

Translation of this standard is particularly important because it highlights considerations for alignment with higher-order thinking skills and other cognitive processes and the need to minimize construct-irrelevant factors, both obvious and subtle, in assessment activities.

Inappropriate Test Preparation (Standard 12.7)

Inappropriate test preparation (e.g., knowing test items ahead of testing) is important for the inferences that teachers make from classroom assessment activities about student learning and learning needs. Likewise, it is important to making valid inferences about student achievement from large-scale, summative assessments.

TRANSLATION

During instruction, students should be clear about the knowledge and skills they are learning. In classroom formative assessment situations, they should be aware of the learning outcomes that the teacher is assessing because it is part of the teaching-learning process. In classroom summative assessment situations, students should know what knowledge and skills are targeted in a test but not know the specific questions and tasks ahead of time. For example, students should be told that their unit test on the Revolutionary War period will cover the historical events, important historical figures, and political contexts from 1764 to 1789, which were studied in their social studies unit. However, they should not be told what specific questions might be asked about George Washington, the Boston Tea Party, etc. In measurement terms, students should know what the assessment domain is, so they can study appropriately and effectively, but not what items or tasks are going to be sampled from the domain. In this way, their performance on the unit test can be generalized to represent their knowledge of the domain of learning for the whole unit.

EXPLANATION AND RATIONALE

In the teaching-learning process, which includes formative assessment, clarity of goals is of utmost importance. In summative assessment, clarity of inferences about what students know, can do, and need help with is of utmost importance.

EVALUATION

Teachers' abilities to focus students on lesson-sized learning targets and on broader, unit-sized learning goals varies widely (Brookhart, 2004). To the extent that learning goals are clear to both teachers and students, learning and assessment is enhanced. This translation is potentially valuable because it highlights the differences in effective classroom assessment practices for formative purposes, where domain sampling is less of an issue, versus summative purposes, where domain sampling is crucial to inferences and generalizations about student achievement.

Fairness and Validity

We address fairness in this chapter because it is fundamental to the education process, class-room assessment, and to students' sense of being treated equitably. For a more in-depth treatment of the fairness standards, see Herman and Cook (this volume).

Testing Process (Standard 3.1)

In large-scale assessment programs, fairness is needed to support valid score interpretations for all students and subgroups. In classroom assessment, validity of inferences about student learning and learning needs is important. To students, fairness in summative classroom assessments also means fair treatment (i.e., knowledge of eligible test content on which student grades are based).

TRANSLATION

Teachers should conduct classroom formative and summative assessments that are accessible to all students in the classroom.

EXPLANATION AND RATIONALE

Classroom teachers face the challenge of posing questions during instruction and on summative tests that enhance learning and that all students, including struggling learners, students with special needs, and English learners, can understand and respond to. Teachers can reformulate questions for students and can provide standard accommodations for students who need it.

EVALUATION

In translating this standard, it is important that we in the measurement community acknowledge the student perspective on the fairness of classroom assessment as well as our interest in sup-porting score interpretation validity. This is part of the difference between situated, classroom assessment and standardized, large-scale assessment. Students are central in a classroom learn-ing community. In fact, there is no classroom learning community without them. Teachers' actions create the classroom assessment environment to a large extent (Stiggins & Conklin,

1992), but it is the student interaction with that environment, including their use of assessment information, that leads to learning. Students' perceptions of assessment can have a significant impact on learning, motivation, and performance on assessments (McMillan, 2016).

Test Administration Accommodations (Standard 3.9)

Providing test administration accommodations that enhance accessibility without undermining validity is standard practice for psychometricians. In the classroom, teachers routinely accommodate their students during instruction and assessment.

TRANSLATION

Teachers should provide test administration accommodations in the classroom for those students who need them, without unduly influencing student performance. This ensures that students are able to show what they have learned, know, and can do, and to have a trustworthy idea of their learning needs. For example, some qualifying students may be given extra time to complete a classroom test.

EXPLANATION AND RATIONALE

Teachers have great latitude in providing accommodations to their students. Accommodations are provided in large-scale assessment presentation (e.g., reading directions aloud), materials (e.g., using a glossary or dictionary), response methods (e.g., having a scribe), scheduling (e.g., extra time), and setting (e.g., using a separate room). Teachers must be aware of the need to provide accommodations in classroom assessment situations and those accommodations that undermine the purposes of a classroom assessment activity.

EVALUATION

Translating this standard is important both to acknowledge that teachers accommodate their students and emphasize the importance of preserving the intended interpretations and uses of classroom assessment information.

Reliability of Inferences about Student Proficiency and Learning Needs

Testing Procedure Replications as Evidence of Score Reliability (Standard 2.1)

In psychometric terms, standard 2.1 defines score reliability by referring to testing conditions that are fixed and those that are allowed to vary, and by alluding to the classical test theory concepts test-retest reliability and alternate forms reliability. More specifically, it is a reference to the precision of an observed test score as an estimate of an examinee's true score over time and measurement conditions. In the classroom assessment context, measurement precision is less about testing conditions and more about sufficiency of information and the quality of scorer (teacher) judgment.

TRANSLATION

Teachers should use systematic procedures to assess work and assign scores or course grades. Teachers should be clear about factors over which appraisals should not vary (e.g., whether I graded a paper on Monday or Tuesday) and factors over which appraisals could vary (e.g., how much instruction a student has had before producing the work). Teachers should gather sufficient evidence for each assessment purpose.

EXPLANATION AND RATIONALE

The concepts of a true score and score precision obviously are valuable in psychometrics. In classroom assessment, "trustworthiness" may be a more useful concept (see Alonzo, this volume), as in: How much do I trust what this classroom assessment has told me about student mastery of the learning outcomes in this instruction and their learning needs? Trustworthiness as we intend its meaning encompasses and interprets psychometric conceptions of score reliability and validity. And its everyday meaning and usage is readily accessible for teachers, is true enough to the corresponding psychometrics concepts, and does not require training in psychometrics.

EVALUATION

Replication in the psychometric context may not be as useful in classroom assessment as a conception of score reliability as other conceptions (e.g., see standard 2.16, decision consistency, below). Other psychometric conceptualizations (e.g., internal consistency, generalizability, standard errors, and reliability coefficients and standard error estimates) likewise may not be useful. Those concepts remain to be tested, using our translation approach. Scorer consistency and accuracy (see standards 2.7 and 2.8), on the other hand, are relevant in classroom assessment.

Decision Consistency (Standard 2.16)

Standard 2.16 requires psychometricians to provide estimates of the percentages of examinees who would be classified in the same way in two replications of the same testing procedure. The translation is relevant to classroom assessment information that teachers use to "correct" homework, "grade" papers and projects, and assign subject or course grades to students. Furthermore, it has to do with evaluating students fairly and providing accurate feedback about the quality of their work, performances, and learning.

TRANSLATION

Information about student learning should be sufficiently trustworthy and in the best interest of students to support decisions about providing or not providing additional instruction on targeted learning outcomes. For example, having more than one source of evidence (say, a unit test and a performance assessment) for decisions about mastery at the end of a unit enhances the reliability of those decisions. At the same time, using these two different sources of evidence increases the depth and breadth of the sample from the domain, and thus contributes to validity.

EXPLANATION AND RATIONALE

The stakes are high for some classroom assessments for students (in sharp contrast to statewide accountability tests, where the stakes apply to teachers and school, district, and state educators). Teachers use what they know about student learning and learning needs from their ongoing classroom assessment to guide decisions such as providing additional help in the classroom to be sure students have learned important course content, referring students for special services (e.g., special education, English language programs) or gifted and talented programs, and recommendations for grade promotion. That information must be adequately trustworthy to support those decisions. Teachers may need to undervalue that information if they are concerned about its trustworthiness—and they would need to reconsider their assessment practices.

In addition, this standard and its translation focus explicitly on decision consistency. Smith (2003) proposed "sufficiency of information . . . [that is], Do I have enough information here to make a reasonable decision about this student?" (p. 30). Combining Smith's formulation of reliability for classroom assessment for making decisions about students, standard 2.16 can be translated as: *Sufficiency of information about learning outcomes for students so that classroom decisions are accurate and in the best interest of the students.*

EVALUATION

This standard's focus on classification consistency and accuracy is clearly relevant to interpreting and using classroom assessment information for the important decisions that teachers make.

Test-Takers' Rights and Responsibilities

Intended Test Purposes and Impacts (Standards 8.1 and 8.2)

TRANSLATION OF BOTH STANDARDS

Students need information about assessment to participate in the assessment process in a way that yields valid, interpretable information (for both the student and the teacher) and informs their learning.

EXPLANATION AND RATIONALE

If students' responses to questions and tasks are to provide interpretable and scorable information for formative and summative assessments about their achievement of intended learning outcomes, they must have the opportunity to be prepared properly for assessment, whether during learning (i.e., formative purposes) or following learning (i.e., summative purposes). This is the measurement rationale for translating these two standards. There is also a fairness rationale: informing all students about the assessments they will encounter.

Educational assessments are, in general, intended to be opportunities for students to perform at their maximum level. For students to do that on summative assessments, they must prepare (e.g., study). To prepare effectively, students need information about when a test will be given, testing conditions, the content and skills that will be assessed, what the assessment will emphasize, the level of performance expected, how the assessment will be scored, and how the results will affect them (Brookhart & Nitko, 2019). The principle of opportunity to learn, now a part of case law in the United States for large-scale assessments (*Debra P. v. Turlington*, 1979, 1981, 1984), applies to students' summative classroom assessments as well. Consequences to students from summative classroom assessments (e.g., course grades) can have deep and long-lived effects. In the formative assessment process, the assessment purpose is interpretation of student responses and provision of feedback; the intended consequence is students' continued progress toward learning outcomes. If students are not clear on what they are supposed to learn, they will not be able to give evidence of their current thinking, and the formative assessment purpose will be thwarted.

EVALUATION

These standards are directly related to interpretation validity and treating students fairly in the classroom.

Test Security, Test Data Integrity, and Cheating (Standard 8.9)

Cheating is a widespread problem in classroom assessment as well as in large-scale testing (e.g., Ferrara, 2017). Cheating is often treated primarily as an ethical issue, which can obscure its impact on the conclusions teachers can draw about student learning and learning needs. In state accountability testing programs, cheating undermines the integrity of the accountability data. In classroom assessment, cheating undermines what teachers can conclude about student learning and learning needs (not to mention the trust relationship).

TRANSLATION

Students should be reminded that they should not cheat on tests and other classroom assessments because they are part of the teaching-learning process. Students should understand that cheating on classroom assessments denies them the opportunity to identify their learning needs.

EXPLANATION AND RATIONALE

Students know they should not cheat on classroom assessments. They know that copying another student's homework is a form of cheating. They may not view it as an ethical issue, but simply a necessary evil to pass a course, compete for the highest grades in a class, or maintain their self-image (e.g., Hamilton, 2015). Teachers and students may not attend to the role of cheating in drawing trustworthy conclusions about student learning and learning needs.

EVALUATION

Cheating is such a prevalent problem in education and testing that providing a separate standard for classroom assessment that addresses the issue is crucial. This translation acknowledges the ethical component of cheating and highlights its impact on identifying students' learning needs.

Discussion and Conclusions

How successfully were we able to translate these selected psychometric standards for the realities of classroom assessment? For this chapter, we chose standards that seemed obviously relevant to real classroom assessment. The translations of these standards seem reasonably relevant to classroom assessment types, as indicated by our explanations, rationales, and evaluations of each translated standard. How successful was our translation of these selected psychometric standards for the realities of classroom assessment? We leave it to the reader to decide whether our translations are adequately reformulated so that they make sense to teachers and are useful for classroom assessment in support of student learning. Generally, some standards are clearly relevant to classroom assessment (e.g., the 12 we translated here), and some less so or clearly not at all (e.g., see Chapter 5 of the *Standards*: "Score, Scales, Norms, Score Linking, and Cut Scores").

Identifying which standards may be relevant to classroom assessment and then translating them is challenging, and the translations that we or anyone would propose are debatable. The challenge comes from the complexity of the standards themselves, the profound concepts they represent, and the difficulty of shifting from psychometric thinking and applications to classroom assessment and teacher thinking.

Would a translation of all relevant standards provide comprehensive coverage of the concepts teachers need to know about measurement (e.g., reliability and validity of inferences and fairness) and practice in their daily classroom assessment? The *Standards* are not as comprehensive as the *Classroom Assessment Standards* (Joint Committee on Standards for Educational Evaluation, 2015). The *Classroom Assessment Standards* cover foundations (e.g., assessment purpose, student engagement in assessment), uses (e.g., analysis of student performance, effective feedback), and quality (e.g., cultural and linguistic diversity, reliability and validity), some of which are not addressed in the psychometric standards. For example, one of the foundations standards in the *Classroom Assessment Standards* specifies that students should be meaningfully engaged in the assessment process (Joint Committee on Standards for Educational Evaluation, 2015).

These differences raise a question: Should we measurement professionals continue to translate the *Standards*? Or should we abandon them for the *Classroom Assessment Standards*? Answering these questions would require an evaluation of the comprehensiveness of the classroom standards in relation to relevant psychometric standards. Logically, the most productive approach would involve combining the most useful and translatable standards from both sources. That way, the larger set of standards would represent the best thinking of both the joint committee that wrote the classroom standards and represent the classroom assessment point of view, and the measurement concepts necessary for classroom assessment. In any case, it is likely that teachers will be expected to become more and more competent in assessment, and therefore attuned to guidance from both sets of standards, in the future (Campbell, 2013).

What else have we learned from this exercise? Perhaps a little humility. The psychometric standards are rigorous and sound, and they are written for the use of measurement professionals who conduct research and operate testing programs with high degrees of psychometric rigor. They are written in technical language and address practices and concepts that are relevant to many testing programs. The *Standards* are not automatically relevant or comprehensible to teachers and their practice of classroom assessment to support student learning. Our measurement expertise, represented by the *Standards*, must be translated to the language and concepts of teachers and their classroom practices and informed by teachers' situated knowledge to help support effective inferences about student learning.

And what can we learn from teachers? As measurement professionals turn their attention to research, training, and classroom assessment practice, it would be best to start by observing and listening, not by insisting on application of the *Standards* and imposing our views on teachers. If we are going to be able to collaborate with teachers on classroom assessment, we first must understand their information needs, assessment practices, tools, goals, and challenges. Only then will we be able to bring our expertise to bear in ways that help them improve classroom assessment and support student learning.

Finally, how do we convey the translated standards to teachers so that they can learn them and maybe use them? Translating and publishing is only a start. The likely most effective tactic is to convince teacher educators to incorporate classroom assessment standards into their curriculum and instruction and methods courses, and into the few stand-alone classroom assessment courses in teacher education programs.

Notes

1 Hereafter referred to as the *Standards* or the "psychometric standards."
2 *Disclosure*: During development of this chapter, Steve Ferrara had design and psychometric responsibilities for eMPower, a commercial classroom formative assessment product.

References

Allal, L. (2016). The co-regulation of student learning in an assessment for learning culture. In L. Allal & D. Laveault (Eds.), *Assessment for learning: Meeting the challenge of implementation* (pp. 259–273). New York: Springer.

American Educational Research Association (AERA), American Psychological Association (APA), & National Council on Measurement in Education (NCME). (2014). *Standards for educational and psychological testing.* Washington, DC: American Educational Research Association, American Psychological Association, & National Council on Measurement in Education.

Brookhart, S. M. (2003). Developing measurement theory for classroom assessment purposes and uses. *Educational Measurement: Issues and Practice, 22*(4), 5–12.

Brookhart, S. M. (2004). Classroom assessment: Tensions and intersections in theory and practice. *Teachers College Record, 106*, 429–458.

Brookhart, S. M., & Nitko, A. J. (2019). *Educational assessment of students* (8th ed.). Boston, MA: Pearson.

Campbell, C. (2013). Research on teacher competency in classroom assessment. In J. H. McMillan (Ed.), *SAGE handbook of research on classroom assessment* (pp. 71–84). Thousand Oaks, CA: SAGE.

Chappuis, J., Stiggins, R., Chappuis, S., & Arter, J. (2012). *Classroom assessment for student learning: Doing it right—using it well* (2nd ed.). Boston, MA: Pearson.

Debra P. v. Turlington, 474 F. Supp. 244 (M.D. Fla. 1979).

Debra P. v. Turlington, 644 F.2d 397, 408 (5th Cir. 1981) (Unit B).

Debra P. v. Turlington, 730 F.2d 1405 (11th Cir. 1984).

Ferrara, S. (2014). Formative assessment and test security: The revised *Standards* are mostly fine; our practices are not (invited commentary). *Educational Measurement: Issues and Practice, 33*(4), 25–28.

Ferrara, S. (2017). A comprehensive framework for policies and practices to improve test security programs: Prevention, detection, investigation, and resolution (PDIR). *Educational Measurement: Issues and Practice, 36*(3), 5–23.

Ferrara, S., Steedle, J., & Frantz, R. (2018). *Item design with test score interpretation in mind.* Coordinated session at the annual meeting of the National Council on Measurement in Education, New York.

Hamilton, J. O'C. (2015, September/October). Why we cheat. *Stanford Magazine*, 59–64.

Joint Committee on Standards for Educational Evaluation. (2015). *Classroom assessment standards for preK-12 teachers.* Kalamazoo, MI: Joint Committee on Standards for Educational Evaluation.

McMillan, J. H. (2013). Why we need research on classroom assessment. In J. H. McMillan (Ed.), *SAGE handbook of research on classroom assessment* (pp. 3–16). Los Angeles, CA: SAGE.

McMillan, J. H. (2016). Student perceptions of assessment. In G. T. L. Brown & L. R. Harris (Eds.), *Handbook of human and social conditions in assessment* (pp. 221–243). New York: Routledge.

McTighe, J., & Wiggins, G. (2013). *Essential questions: Opening doors to student understanding.* Alexandria, VA: Association for Supervision and Curriculum Development.

Moss, P. A. (2003). Reconceptualizing validity for classroom assessment. *Educational Measurement: Issues and Practice, 22*(4), 13–25.

Plake, B. S., & Wise, L. L. (2014). What is the role and importance of the revised AERA, APA, NCME *Standards for Educational and Psychological Testing*? *Educational Measurement: Issues and Practice, 33*(4), 4–12.

Ruiz-Primo, M. A., & Furtak, E. M. (2004, August). *Informal formative assessment of students' understanding of scientific inquiry.* CSE Report 639. CRESST: University of California Los Angeles.

Shepard, L. A. (2006). Classroom assessment. In R. L. Brennan (Ed.), *Educational measurement* (4th ed., pp. 623–646). Westport, CT: Praeger.

Smith, J. K. (2003). Reconsidering reliability in classroom assessment and grading. *Educational Measurement: Issues and Practice, 22*(4), 26–33.

Stiggins, R. J., & Conklin, N. F. (1992). *In teachers' hands: Investigating the practices of classroom assessment.* Albany, NY: State University of New York Press.

Wiggins, G., & McTighe, J. (2013). *Understanding by design* (2nd ed.). Alexandria, VA: Association for Supervision and Curriculum Development.

Wiliam, D. (2010). An integrative summary of the research literature and implications for a new theory of formative assessment. In H. L. Andrade & G. J. Cizek (Eds.), *Handbook of formative assessment* (pp. 18–40). New York: Routledge.

Wiliam, D. (2011). *Embedded formative assessment.* Bloomington, IN: Solution Tree Press.

Zwiers, J., & Crawford, M. (2011). *Academic conversations: Classroom talk that fosters critical thinking and content understandings.* Portland, ME: Stenhouse.

7

Defining Trustworthiness for Teachers' Multiple Uses of Classroom Assessment Results[1]

Alicia C. Alonzo

Developed in the context of large-scale assessment, psychometric considerations of quality focus on the validity and reliability of scores derived from standardized tests. As such, these criteria have been defined in ways that are well-suited to describe measurements designed to be decontextualized (i.e., comparable across contexts) but may be poorly suited to other forms of assessment, including classroom assessment (e.g., Brookhart, 2003). With increased interest in and recognition of classroom assessment, psychometric definitions of validity and reliability have been translated and adapted for this application. However, such efforts have, for the most part, retained the psychometric criteria of validity and reliability (e.g., Brookhart, 2003; Taylor & Nolen, 1996), and thus classroom assessment has continued to be framed from a psychometric perspective. In this chapter, I explore *trustworthiness* as a broader, alternative criterion for considering classroom assessment, one that incorporates some aspects of the psychometric criteria but not others.

My conception of trustworthiness emerges from consideration of two features of classroom assessment (as compared to large-scale assessment). First, classroom assessment has multiple, sometimes conflicting, purposes. Although large-scale assessment has a number of different uses (e.g., college admissions, school accountability, international comparisons), these are mainly concerned with summative *measurement*. In contrast, *assessment* in classroom assessment (for both formative and summative purposes) may include, but is broader than, measurement. Second, classroom assessment is contextualized. While large-scale assessment is designed to be as standardized (i.e., context-independent) as possible (e.g., Moss, 2003), classroom assessment is embedded in a particular classroom teaching and learning environment (e.g., Bell & Cowie, 2001; Brookhart, 2003; Gipps, 1994). Both of these features lead to a broader conceptualization of quality for classroom assessment, as compared to that for large-scale assessment.

I expand on these two features of classroom assessment in the next section. In the following section, I provide a brief overview of approaches to applying psychometric criteria in the classroom context, illustrating how psychometric criteria—particularly reliability—do not align well with this context. In the bulk of the chapter, I lay out an argument for my conception of trustworthiness as applicable to a wide range of classroom assessment activities and illustrate this conception by unpacking how one might conduct an inquiry into one element of trustworthiness: the formative effects of classroom assessment.[2] I conclude by highlighting key aspects of trustworthiness through a brief case study of a high school physics teacher's consideration of learning progression-based assessment items for both formative and accountability purposes.

Features of Classroom Assessment

Classroom Assessment Purposes

Adopting Buhagiar's (2007) framing, this chapter "concerns assessment that—irrespective of the level of formality, the assessors and the types of tasks involved—originates inside the classroom as opposed to outside it" (p. 44). I focus on classroom-level assessment that is constructed, administered, and scored by classroom actors (i.e., teachers and perhaps their students). Thus, I include assessment tasks that teachers construct using items from externally developed test banks or other resources, as well as common assessment tasks constructed by teachers across a school or district. I also include teacher-made pre-/post-tests that are increasingly used to satisfy student growth requirements for teacher evaluation because—although required by outside policies—they are constructed, administered, and scored by teachers themselves. I exclude student growth measures that are externally generated, as well as "interim assessments," which are typically required and managed at the district level and often developed outside of the classroom (e.g., Perie, Marion, & Gong, 2009).[3] Therefore, I consider three purposes for classroom assessment: formative, summative, and, where applicable (i.e., in contexts in which such pre-/post-tests are teacher-made), accountability for student growth. In the subsections below, I provide a brief description of each purpose.

Formative Assessment

Ideally, the most frequent purpose of classroom assessment is formative. According to the Chief Council of State School Officers (CCSSO), "formative assessment is a process used by teachers and students during instruction that provides feedback to adjust ongoing teaching and learning to improve students' achievement of intended instructional outcomes" (McManus, 2008, p. 3). As a process, formative assessment has been described as consisting of a set of practices (e.g., eliciting, interpreting, and responding to evidence of student ideas; Ruiz-Primo & Furtak, 2007). These practices are undertaken by both teachers and students, and may occur on a continuum of formality (Shavelson et al., 2008), from taking advantage of on-the-fly, informal opportunities to engaging in formal, planned-for assessment events.

Eliciting gets student ideas "on the table." This is most commonly thought of in terms of teachers eliciting students' responses to tasks or questions, posed either formally (e.g., through a mid-unit quiz) or informally (e.g., in the midst of a classroom discussion). However, evidence may also be collected through observations (e.g., of students' work during a lab activity). These interactions may be planned (e.g., a specific question designed to check student understanding, an observation checklist), or they may be more spontaneous (e.g., a follow-up question to clarify a student comment, noticing unexpected behaviors; Bell & Cowie, 2001). Students may also engage in this practice by asking a question (Cowie, 2005) or making some other unsolicited contribution.

Interpreting entails making sense of the student ideas that have been elicited. Student work has many features, and classrooms are complex places, such that it would not be possible to attend to all evidence that is available (e.g., Erickson, 2007). Rather, the teacher and students must identify which evidence is most relevant and fruitful for improving student learning (e.g., particular features of a student's essay, particular student ideas in a class discussion). Then students and teachers must figure out what that evidence means. What does it say about what students know and can do? About where students are still struggling? What does it suggest that students might need to learn in order to make progress? This sense-making may be undertaken by the teacher, the student, and/or peers, but the student has a crucial role in the process. Even if others provide support (e.g., feedback), students' own sense-making is *required* for any meaningful learning to result (e.g., Nicol & Macfarlane-Dick, 2006).

Finally, *responding* involves the teacher and students acting on their interpretations. Teachers may change their instruction (e.g., Shepard, 2000) or provide feedback to students (i.e., an interpretation of the evidence that is communicated to students; Black & Wiliam, 1998), whether formally (e.g., written feedback on student work) or informally (e.g., reacting to students during a class discussion). However, students are the only ones who "can take the actions necessary to improve. The teacher cannot learn 'for' the student" (Brookhart, 2003, p. 7). Whether students respond directly to interpretations from an assessment event (e.g., adjust their thinking about a given topic) or engage in instruction that the teacher has implemented based on such interpretations, students are ultimately responsible for any learning that results. Thus, while the teacher's response in formative assessment is optional, the student's is not (e.g., Black & Wiliam, 1998).

Summative Assessment

In contrast to formative assessment, which focuses on how to promote learning *beyond* students' current knowledge and skills, summative assessment focuses on evaluating the knowledge and skills that have been attained by some point in time (e.g., the end of an instructional unit). Students encounter a range of different summative assessment instruments in their classrooms, including state-level standardized tests; however, in this chapter, I consider only summative assessment that is relatively close to classroom instruction (i.e., tasks constructed, administered, and scored by the classroom teacher, whether individually or in collaboration with colleagues). Hence, with the narrower scope of this chapter, summative assessment occurs as part of classroom instruction, and thus it must be viewed in light of the larger goal of improving student learning. If nothing else, the time that is spent on summative assessment could be spent on learning activities, so there should be some justification in terms of its educational value. Indeed, Bennett (2011) argues that summative assessment, if carefully designed, can not only "fulfil its primary purpose of documenting what students know and can do," but also "meet a secondary purpose" of supporting learning (p. 7). Brookhart (2003) goes further, arguing that most classroom assessment, even that which is primarily summative, has at least some formative component.

Accountability for Student Growth in Contexts with Teacher-Made Pre-/Post-Tests

Through criteria articulated for the awarding of competitive grants, Race to the Top (RTTT) incentivized state adoption of particular teacher evaluation policies. States were expected to "differentiate effectiveness using multiple rating categories that take student achievement growth into account as a significant factor and are designed with teacher involvement" and "use evaluations to inform decisions about staff development, compensation, promotion, tenure, certification, and removal of ineffective teachers" (Hallgren, James-Burdumy, & Perez-Johnson, 2014, p. 2). In many states/districts, this has resulted in the requirement that teachers administer and report data from pre-/post-tests to be used as part of their annual evaluations (Popham, 2013). Policies differ across contexts, but in some schools and districts, policies allow (or even require) teachers to "devise and administer their own classroom assessments" for this purpose (Popham, 2013, p. 35).[4] While required for accountability purposes, these tests may serve formative and summative purposes as well.[5] Evidence from the pre-test may be used by a teacher (e.g., Carless, 2007) and his or her students to plan teaching and learning strategies for an upcoming unit. Evidence from the post-test may also be used to summarize student learning across the unit and thus may be incorporated into students' grades.

Comparison to Large-Scale Assessment: Beyond Measurement

Similar to large-scale assessment, classroom assessment for summative and accountability purposes entails measurement of—i.e., "assigning numbers to" (Wu, Tam, & Jen, 2016, p. 3)—student achievement and growth, respectively. However, formative purposes require "more than mere documentation (i.e., measurement)" (McMillan, 2003, p. 39; see also Moss, 2003; Nichols, Meyer, & Burling, 2009). This is true not only of formative assessment, but also of assessment that is summative and/or designed for accountability purposes, but that may be used secondarily for formative purposes. Support for future learning requires not only information about students' knowledge and skills, but also diagnostic information (i.e., not just that students need to learn what they do not yet know, but identification of specific learning needs and causes for learning difficulties). Indeed, Shepard, Penuel, and Pellegrino (2018) argue that measurement information may actually be *detrimental* for formative purposes if there is "emphasis . . . on quantification rather than the qualities of student thinking" (p. 21).[6] Thus, even consideration of classroom assessment for summative and accountability purposes must take into account the overarching goal of student learning; hence, there is a need for qualitative, diagnostic information, not solely quantitative measurements.

Classroom Assessment Context

Despite the somewhat disparate purposes of classroom assessment, its forms are unified by (and differentiated from large-scale assessment in terms of) their contextualized nature. While large-scale assessment must provide consistent results across many contexts, classroom assessment prioritizes "desirable consequences . . . for (relatively) small groups of students" (Black & Wiliam, 1998, p. 54), requiring classroom assessment to be tailored to a particular teaching and learning environment. Classroom assessment "is embedded in the social and cultural life of the classroom" (Gipps, 1994, p. 158). Not only does classroom assessment reflect the teaching and learning environment in which it is embedded, but "classroom assessment information and uses become part of the daily realities of the classroom" (Brookhart, 2003, p. 8). These complementary influences mean that classroom assessment is inextricable from an associated classroom environment. Therefore, any consideration of classroom assessment must account for this larger context (e.g., Moss, 2003; Nichols et al., 2009).

A significant dimension of the classroom context concerns "interactions among teachers and students around content" (National Research Council, 2001, p. 313)—i.e., instruction—as depicted in the "instructional triangle" (p. 314). Because classroom assessment "is integral to the teaching [and learning] process" (Gipps, 1994, p. 158), it can be viewed as one of many instructional interactions occurring among the teacher and his or her students (Tierney & Charland, 2007). While students and teachers typically have no contact with those responsible

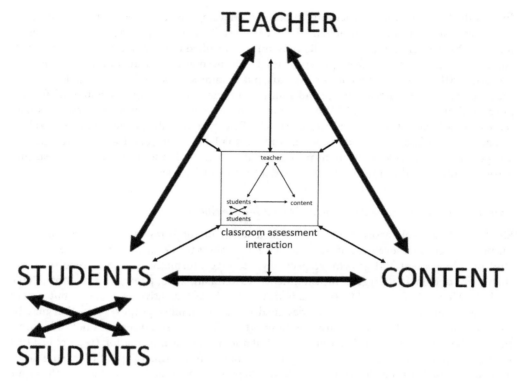

Figure 7.1 Classroom assessment triangle, within the larger instructional triangle, showing relationships among teacher, students, and content.

for large-scale assessment, classroom assessment occurs *as an interaction* among classroom actors (between teacher and students, among students). Teachers pose assessment tasks to their students, students respond to their teacher, etc. Indeed, as Moss (2003), points out, "anytime I interact with my students is an opportunity for me (and them) to learn about what they are learning and about the quality and effects of my own teaching" (p. 16). Thus, as shown in Figure 7.1, classroom assessment—as an instructional interaction—can be depicted in an "assessment triangle" that connects teacher, students, and content *and* that relates to a larger instructional context characterized by longer-term relationships among teacher, students, and content. Any consideration of the quality of classroom assessment must attend to these relationships, which are largely irrelevant for decontextualized large-scale assessment.

Summary

As compared to large-scale assessment, investigations of classroom assessment require a much broader (and somewhat different) set of considerations. Although some forms of classroom assessment require measurement of what students know and can do, information that can (and does) inform teaching and learning processes is central to the overarching classroom goal of promoting student learning and thus to classroom assessment. Therefore, quality considerations must extend beyond precise and accurate measurement to include the utility and use of information for improving teaching and learning. Because teaching and learning are embedded in a classroom context, such considerations necessarily include a much broader set of elements as compared to those for decontextualized large-scale assessment. Below, I develop the notion of trustworthiness in terms of ways student learning may be affected by classroom assessment. I introduce these ideas by first (in the next section) providing a brief overview of some prior efforts to articulate quality criteria for classroom assessment in terms of the psychometric criteria of validity and reliability. My consideration of trustworthiness (in the following section) builds on some of the misalignment between these traditional criteria and the features of classroom assessment.

Framing Classroom Assessment in Terms of Validity and Reliability

Prior efforts to translate psychometric principles to the classroom have started with the constructs of validity and reliability (Brookhart, 2003). Amidst laments about teachers' lack of assessment preparation (e.g., Stiggins, 1988), there are numerous textbooks (e.g., Linn & Gronlund, 2012; Oosterhof, 2009) and other resources that attempt to "translate" these psychometric constructs into language and situations more familiar to teachers. Such efforts typically target teachers' summative assessment practices (i.e., their ability to design tests and quizzes that will gauge what students know and can do *after* some unit of instruction). For example, the assigned reader for a course I taught a number of years ago included the following example to introduce consideration of reliability:

> *Monday*: After a unit on the bone structures of both birds and dinosaurs, Ms. Fowler asks her students to write an essay explaining why many scientists believe that birds are descended from dinosaurs. After school, she tosses the pile of essays in the back seat of her cluttered '57 Chevy.
>
> *Tuesday*: Ms. Fowler looks high and low for the essays both at home and in her classroom, but she can't find them anywhere.
>
> *Wednesday*: Because Ms. Fowler wants to use the essay to determine what her students have learned, she asks the class to write the same essay a second time.
>
> *Thursday*: Ms. Fowler discovers Monday's essays in the back seat of her Chevy.
>
> *Friday*: Ms. Fowler grades both sets of essays. She is surprised to discover that there is very little consistency between them: Students who wrote the best essays on Monday did not necessarily do well on Wednesday, and some of Monday's poorest performers did quite well on Wednesday.
>
> (Ormrod, 2000, p. 642)

This example was then used to motivate consideration of a wide variety of "temporary conditions unrelated to the characteristic being measured" (p. 643), such as variation in students' mood, in the conditions under which the task was administered, in students' interpretation of the task (e.g., due to ambiguous instructions), and in scoring (e.g., due to vague criteria). While such considerations are certainly relevant in considering the reliability of scores resulting from a teacher's test or quiz, my teaching interns struggled to understand how this was relevant to their classroom work, other than as a cautionary tale to keep track of their students' papers.

More recently, psychometricians have begun to call for a reformulation of these traditional constructs, in ways appropriate for the classroom—"'classroometric' measurement theory" (Brookhart, 2003, p. 8) or "edumetrics" (Gielen, Dochy, & Dierick, 2003, p. 38). This work, while still using the language of validity and reliability, highlights important differences in the definitions of these terms for classroom versus large-scale applications (e.g., McMillan, 2003;

Stobart, 2012). For example, while still focusing only on classroom summative assessment, reliability for classroom assessment has been recast as "sufficiency of information" (Taylor & Nolen, 1996, p. 11)—i.e., "Do I have enough information here to make a reasonable decision about this student with regard to this domain of information?" (Smith, 2003, p. 30).

However, the most fundamental shift entailed in adapting concepts of validity and reliability for classroom use stems from the recognition of formative assessment as a critical aspect of classroom assessment. Consideration of validity and reliability of large-scale assessment focuses primarily on the accuracy and precision of scores resulting from a particular instrument, in relation to a particular use (e.g., Frisbie, 2005). In contrast, consideration of classroom assessment (particularly formative classroom assessment) must include its consequences (i.e., the extent to which student learning is supported).[7] In addition, formative assessment cannot be considered solely in terms of an assessment "instrument."[8] Indeed, formative classroom assessment may not even involve a traditional assessment instrument, as it includes "everyday learning tasks and activities, as well as routine observation and dialogue" (e.g., Third International Conference on Assessment for Learning Participants, 2009, p. 2). In contrast to large-scale assessment, as a one-time event, formative classroom assessment is happening all the time (Taylor & Nolen, 1996), with continuous opportunities for new evidence (Moss, 2003) and refinement of diagnoses of students' learning needs (Bennett, 2011); therefore, for (formative)[9] classroom assessment, the quality of any one interpretation becomes much less important.

Returning to the construct of reliability, a focus on more formative, informal forms of classroom assessment has several implications that reduce the usefulness of many traditional forms of reliability evidence. First, because formative assessment is embedded in the ongoing work of teaching and learning, we hope that students will be continually learning and thus that reliability from one assessment event to the next (i.e., test-retest reliability) is not a particularly meaningful concern. As Moss (2003) explains:

> For much of what I do, I have no need to draw and warrant fixed interpretations of students' capabilities; rather, it is my job to make those interpretations obsolete. What I need to do is make decisions—moment-to-moment, day-to-day, course-to-course—that help students learn.
>
> (p. 16)

Second, reliability refers to the *consequences* of an assessment process, rather than to the reliability of the scores that are generated:

> Formative assessment is reliable to the extent that the assessment processes being used generate evidence that consistently lead to better, or better founded decisions . . . The same assessment process, administered by different teachers, might result in different evidence of achievement, which jeopardizes the summative function, but as long as the instructional decisions based on this evidence are equally appropriate, they can be different from one teacher to another.
>
> (Black & Wiliam, 2012, pp. 260–261)

In other words, the target of reliability considerations for formative assessment is the learning that results, rather than students' scores on the assessment instrument that is used. For example, if a group of teachers develops a formative assessment prompt, the process of using the prompt to elicit, interpret, and respond to students' ideas may be reliable if it allows most of the teachers to help their students to understand a difficult concept, even if they disagree on how to interpret the ideas that were elicited (i.e., low inter-rater reliability).

Finally, as students are learning, the information that is gathered is not likely to "be tidy, complete and self-consistent, but fragmentary and often contradictory" (Harlen & James 1997, as quoted in Rea-Dickins, 2007, p. 508). Indeed, there is ample evidence to suggest that student thinking—particularly as they are learning—is *not* reliable, i.e., consistent from one context to another (e.g., diSessa, 1996; National Research Council, 2000). Thus, while reliability of student performance (i.e., internal consistency) and generalizability from one task to another (i.e., task reliability) are desirable in large-scale assessment contexts, at the fine-grained level of information required for formative assessment (e.g., Shepard, et al., 2018) this may not accurately reflect the student thinking one is seeking to capture. In order to obtain an accurate diagnosis of student learning needs, formative assessment should reflect the "unreliability" of student thinking:

> The fact that a pupil can do something in one context but apparently not in another is a positive advantage, since it gives clues to the conditions which seem to favor better performance and thus can be the basis for taking action.
>
> (Harlen & James, 1997, as quoted in Rea-Dickins, 2007, p. 508)

What large-scale assessment might view as "noise" (and thus a threat to reliability), classroom assessment may consider "signal" (and thus part of what assessment seeks to uncover). Because formative assessment seeks to provide information to inform *learning*—rather than precisely report measurements of achievement—and because that information can easily be revised, inconsistencies in student thinking are not to be avoided, but sought out, as potential targets of instruction. To the extent that students exhibit consistent thinking within a given context, reliability of finer-grained diagnoses is desirable; however, the nature of students' thinking often precludes neat patterns, and classroom assessment results are still valuable for the hints they provide to guide teachers' further interactions with students.

Framing Classroom Assessment in Terms of Trustworthiness

Although great progress has been made in applying psychometric criteria to consideration of classroom assessment, there still exists some degree of mismatch in this endeavor. Thus, to develop the concept of trustworthiness, rather than starting from psychometric considerations and adapting them to classroom assessment, I start with essential features of classroom assessment and consider how they might be used to explore quality criteria more tailored to this type of assessment. I use "trustworthiness" as an alternative criterion to validity and reliability for large-scale assessment, in the sense that if scores from a large-scale assessment are valid and reliable, we expect that they will consistently reflect accurate measures of a given construct, and thus we can trust them. This use also reflects the colloquial definition of trustworthiness, which the *Oxford English Dictionary* lists as a derivative of the adjective "trustworthy": "worthy of trust or confidence; reliable, dependable" (Trustworthy, n.d.). In turn, "trust" is defined as "firm belief in the reliability, truth, or ability of someone or something; confidence or faith in a person or thing, or in an attribute of a person or thing" (Trust, n.d.).

Applying similar considerations to classroom assessment, trustworthiness centers around the extent to which classroom assessment can be relied upon for the various purposes for which it is intended. While this certainly includes some consideration of the measurement properties of classroom assessment (i.e., providing valid, reliable measures of a given construct), ultimately all classroom assessment must be considered in terms of the broader goals of the classroom instruction in which it is embedded. Therefore, trustworthiness centers around the extent to which classroom assessment can be relied upon to play a "constructive role in the educational process" (Murphy & Torrance, 1988, as quoted in Buhagiar, 2007, p. 41).

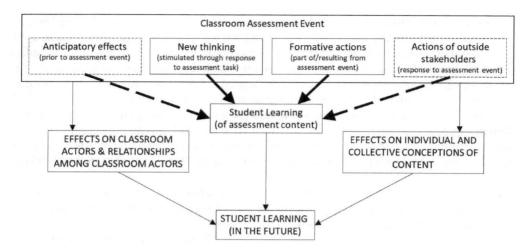

Figure 7.2 Model of the impact of classroom assessment on student learning. Direct effects are indicated with bold arrows; indirect effects are indicated with regular arrows. Dashed lines indicate effects that apply only to summative and/or accountability assessment (i.e., not to formative assessment). Lower-case labels indicate effects that take place in the context of a given classroom assessment event. Upper-case labels indicate effects beyond a single classroom assessment event.

As part of instruction, when students and teachers engage in classroom assessment by "dipping into the stream of learning from time to time to evaluate student progress and performance" (Wilson & Carstensen, 2007, p. 319), they actively shape the flow. All classroom assessment—not only that which is explicitly formative—affects the teaching and learning in a given classroom (Brookhart, 2003). Therefore, as depicted in Figure 7.2, student learning is affected directly (as all forms of classroom assessment impact student learning of assessment content, which contributes to students' overall learning) *and* indirectly (as all forms of classroom assessment affect components of the instructional triangle, which impact students' future learning). The trustworthiness of classroom assessment concerns the extent to which these impacts have a positive effect on student learning. In the subsections below, I discuss the impacts (both direct and indirect) that classroom assessment can be expected to have on student learning.

Direct Impact on Student Learning of Assessment Content

I consider four ways classroom assessment is thought to have a direct impact on student learning. These are depicted in the top box of Figure 7.2. As indicated by the solid lines around "new thinking" and "formative actions," these impacts are expected for all forms of classroom assessment, while—as indicated by dashed lines—"anticipatory effects" and "actions of outside stakeholders" are expected only for summative and/or accountability assessment.

Anticipatory Effects on Student Learning

Because classroom assessment signals to students what their teachers view as important for them to learn, summative assessment (including post-tests to measure student growth) may have anticipatory effects on students' learning (e.g., Gielen et al., 2003; McMillan, 2003).

Students are likely to "adapt their approach to learning . . . in order to gain the highest possible scores" (Taylor & Nolen, 1996, p. 4) on summative assessment tasks; therefore, students' expectations about the way they will be assessed likely have an impact on what is learned during a given unit of instruction: "When students are motivated to prepare, studying encourages consolidation and organisation of knowledge, rehearsal of domain-relevant processes and strategies, stronger links to conditions of use, and greater automaticity in execution; in other words, the development of expertise" (Bennett, 2011, p. 7).

Elicitation as an Occasion for Student Learning

"Good classroom assessments are not only measures of learning, but genuine episodes of learning themselves" (Brookhart, 2003, p. 7). While informal formative assessment occurs in conjunction with classroom instruction, even summative assessment may serve as an opportunity for student learning. In particular, responding to assessment tasks may support students in making connections between concepts (Struyf, Vandenberghe, & Lens, 2001) or transferring their knowledge to new situations (Gielen et al., 2003; McMillan, 2003), or may strengthen students' mental representations of content (Bennett, 2011).

Formative Actions to Enhance Student Learning

Following Brookhart (2003), I assume that most (if not all) classroom assessment—even that with primarily summative purposes—has at least some formative component. Students and their teacher continue to interact in the same classroom environment after a summative assessment event. If nothing else, summative assessment signals to students "what they were 'supposed to learn'" (Brookhart, 2003, p. 8). Although the class may not revisit the content of a particular summative assessment, "lessons learned" may carry forward to the learning that occurs in the next unit. Teachers may use summative assessment results to reflect on their teaching of a particular unit (i.e., how to teach the same content differently to future students) or to reflect on student learning needs that can be addressed with subsequent instruction (i.e., how to teach new content to the same students). Students may use summative assessment results to reflect on their learning of a particular unit (thus learning some of the content that may not have been mastered at the time of the summative assessment) or more general learning in a particular classroom context (i.e., how to approach learning of future content). As Bennett (2011) points out, formative use of summative assessment is more likely to occur when this has been designed for (e.g., through connections to learning progressions).

Effects Due to Actions of Other (Non-Classroom) Actors

For summative and accountability assessment, classroom actors are not the only stakeholders. Others—such as parents or administrators—may impact student learning through actions taken in response to classroom assessment. For example, in response to students' grades (reports of classroom summative assessment), parents may directly intervene (e.g., hiring a tutor, helping students with homework).

Indirect Impact through Internalization of Disciplinary Criteria

Adopting a sociocultural perspective on classroom assessment (e.g., Shepard et al., 2018), one can see all assessment practices as "develop[ing] patterns of participation that subsequently contribute to pupils' identities as learners and knowers" (Cowie, 2005, p. 140). The teacher and students jointly define content and disciplinary practices in ways specific to their classroom community. Part of students' learning is adopting the shared understandings of the class-room community and coming to participate in the community following shared norms for participation. In turn, those understandings and norms come to represent for students what the discipline entails: "Internalizing what criteria mean in a particular discipline is not just about learning the rules for grading—it literally means learning the discipline itself" (Shepard, Hammerness, Darling-Hammond, & Rust, 2005, p. 298).

Of course, the teacher plays a large role in shaping the class construction of the discipline being studied. At the most basic level, relative importance of different aspects of content may be communicated by the relative emphasis that a teacher places on each (Cowie, 2005). In addition, the way that content is treated in a teacher's assessments "instantiate[s] what it means to know and learn" (Shepard, 2000, p. 7) in that discipline for students in a given classroom community. For example, if classroom assessments in a history class focus pri-marily on students' recall of key dates, history becomes about facts rather than historical thinking (Weinburg, 2010). Or if students in a science classroom are pressed to explain *why* phenomena occur (e.g., Braaten & Windschitl, 2011), this may come to define what it means to provide a scientific explanation. In order to have a positive impact on student learning, classroom assessments (of all types) must portray the content in ways that are consistent with disciplinary norms.

Indirect Impact through Classroom and Non-Classroom Actors and Their Relationships

Students make visible what they know and can do through interaction with the teacher—whether responding in writing to a question or task posed by the teacher, answering a question orally, engaging in a dialog, asking a question, or saying/doing something that catches the teacher's attention. Students may also be interacting with their peers (e.g., as fellow participants in a class discussion, as participants in peer assessment). Because of these interactions, class-room assessment may have an impact on both individuals (i.e., teacher, students) as well as the relationships among them.

Social-Motivational Effects on Classroom Actors

As for other forms of assessment, social interactions that occur during classroom assessment have "non-cognitive" effects on students—"impacting their effort, engagement, motivation, and self-efficacy" (McMillan, 2003, p. 37) in relation to subsequent learning. For example, Cowie (2005) describes negative impacts on students' confidence and self-efficacy as a result of participation in class discussions (i.e., formative assessment). Students felt embarrassed and belittled by their teachers' responses to questions and other contributions during class and, through listening to other pupils' contributions, concluded, "everyone else probably under-stands it and I don't" (p. 148). She also described how feedback made students feel "useless" and so "undermine[d] pupils' views of themselves as learners" (p. 142). As a result of such interactions, classroom assessment "impacted on how [pupils] felt about themselves as learners and knowers" (p. 150).

Classroom assessment can clearly impact teachers in similar ways. As Taylor and Nolen (1996) explain, "Classroom teachers have a vested interest in the outcomes of instruction—many believing that student failure is a reflection on their teaching" (p. 4). Thus, students' responses to assessment may have a positive or negative influence on teachers' self-efficacy regarding their own teaching. In turn, teachers' sense of themselves as teachers impacts their classroom work and thus student learning (e.g., Tschannen-Moran, Hoy, & Hoy, 1998).

Effects on Relationships between Classroom Actors

Not only does classroom assessment affect individual students, it also impacts "whether or not individual pupils are judged capable and competent" and thus shapes the social construction of their capabilities in the classroom community (Cowie, 2005, p. 140). Not surprisingly, students' impressions of teacher feedback impact their relationships with teachers. Students in Cowie's (2005) study indicated that "rude" feedback "undermined their inclination to interact with the teacher" (p. 142). In contrast, supportive feedback was perceived as sustaining "relationships of respect and trust" (p. 148). Students' perceptions of the "fairness" of a given summative assessment event may influence how they feel about the teacher (e.g., whether or not a teacher is "on their side").[10] As depicted in the instructional triangle (Figure 7.1), students learn through interactions with their teacher and peers. Therefore, any impact on these relationships due to classroom assessment will likewise impact student learning.

Effects on Relationships with Non-Classroom Actors

Outside stakeholders may also affect student learning through their relationships with classroom actors. For example, in response to a student's grades (i.e., reports of classroom summative assessment), parents may express approval or disapproval, both of which may impact student motivation. Less directly, although doubts have been cast on the efficacy of this approach (e.g., Gardner, 2012), policymakers have enacted teacher evaluation policies to encourage student growth. If teachers are indeed motivated by such policies, administrators' responses to pre-/post-test scores (in the form of teacher evaluations), or teachers' anticipations of these responses, may also have an impact on student learning.

Summary

With trustworthiness of classroom assessment primarily an indicator of the extent to which there is a positive impact on student learning, the effects above can be used to identify a set of broad questions to guide consideration of the trustworthiness of a given episode of classroom assessment:

1) *Anticipatory effects on student learning*: [Summative only] Do students learn by preparing for the classroom assessment? (Do the content and format of the assessment represent worthy goals for student learning?)
2) *Elicitation as an occasion for student learning*: Do students learn by engaging in the classroom assessment task itself? (Do the content and format of the assessment stimulate student learning?)
3) *Formative actions to enhance student learning*: Do formative actions taken as part of the classroom assessment improve student learning?
4) *Effects due to actions of other (non-classroom) actors*: [Summative and accountability only] Do outside stakeholders respond to classroom assessment results in ways that directly improve student learning?
5) *Internalization of disciplinary criteria*: Does the classroom assessment portray content in ways consistent with disciplinary norms? Does the classroom assessment help students to internalize disciplinary norms?
6) *Social-motivational effects on classroom actors*: Do social interactions entailed in the classroom assessment have a positive (or at least not negative) impact on students' and teacher's motivation?

7) *Effects on relationships between classroom actors*: Does the classroom assessment have a positive (or at least not negative) impact on relationships between teacher and students and among students?

8) *Effects on relationships with non-classroom actors*: [Summative and accountability only] Do classroom assessment results cause changes in relationships between classroom and outside stakeholders that improve student learning? Do outside stakeholders respond to classroom assessment results in ways that indirectly improve student learning?

To the extent that these questions can be answered affirmatively in a given classroom context, an episode of classroom assessment (or a classroom assessment process) may be considered to be trustworthy. To the extent that changing the context does not change the answers to these questions, the classroom assessment may be considered trustworthy in other contexts as well; however, it is important to note that because of the contextualized nature of classroom assessment, this generalizability may be quite limited. For example, a teacher may consider a given formative assessment prompt to be trustworthy for use in his conceptual physics course, but not his honors physics course, given differences in students' motivations and/or the relationships that exist within the two groups of students. Or a teacher may judge a summative assessment used by another teacher to be untrustworthy because it would not be consistent with the disciplinary norms she has been developing with her students.

In this section, I have laid out a number of ways that classroom assessment may affect student learning. In the next section, I drill down a bit further, to explore factors that underlie these influences on student learning. In particular, because the formative purpose of classroom assessment ideally has a central role in classroom assessment, I focus on the formative effects of classroom assessment on student learning, unpacking question 3 above to consider more specifically what questions must be asked in order to investigate this aspect of trustworthiness.

Application of Trustworthiness to an Inquiry into Formative Effects of Classroom Assessment

Drawing a parallel to discussion of validity and Kane's (2013) argument-based approach to validation of test score interpretation and use, I consider the elements above to be important in establishing a trustworthiness argument for classroom assessment. However, drawing on Kane's earlier work, Stobart (2012) distinguishes between validation and a "validity inquiry" (p. 235). Validation entails "evaluat[ing] the plausibility of the claims . . . inherent in the proposed interpretations and uses of . . . test scores" (Kane, 2013, p. 1). In contrast, a validity inquiry relates to what actually happened (i.e., whether and why an intended interpretation or use was accomplished):

> The task of any validity inquiry is to find out what helped and what hindered the intention being realized . . . For example, we may give feedback with the intention of "closing the gap" between desired and actual performance, yet in many cases it may have the opposite effect (Kluger & DiNisi, 1996). While a validation argument may have made the case for feedback, a validity inquiry may have to investigate why it did not work in these circumstances.
>
> (Stobart, 2012, pp. 234–235)

Because the validity inquiry is more contextualized (i.e., relating to the impact of a particular classroom assessment under particular circumstances, rather than a general argument for its likely efficacy), it is particularly relevant for a teacher's consideration of trustworthiness with respect to assessment in his or her classroom.

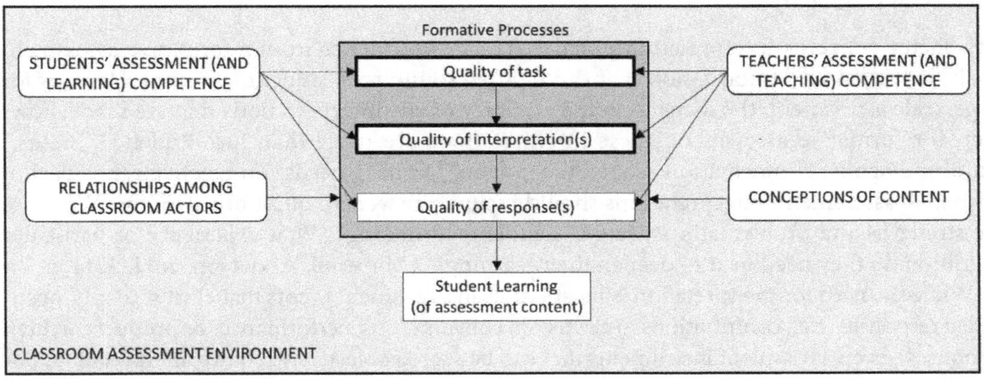

Figure 7.3 Model of the underlying factors influencing the relationship between formative processes (undertaken as part of all types of classroom assessment) and student learning of assessment content. Lower-case labels indicate influences within a given classroom assessment event. Upper-case labels indicate influences that exist in the broader classroom context. Traditional considerations of validity and reliability are indicated by bold boxes (quality of task and quality of interpretation).

In this section, I illustrate what a validity inquiry for classroom assessment might entail by exploring the factors influencing just one part of the model above: the formative effects of classroom assessment on student learning.[11] As shown in Figure 7.3, I "unpack" both the formative assessment process—to consider the quality of the "task," of interpretations derived from the task, and of response(s) to those interpretations—and factors that influence that process (i.e., the classroom assessment environment, student and teacher competences, relationships among classroom actors, and the conception(s) of content available in the classroom community). In considering student and teacher competences, I draw on Blömeke, Gustafsson, and Shavelson's (2015) model of competence, which considers one's competence to act in any given situation to comprise a set of "cognitive, conative, affective, or motivational" resources (p. 5) and "situation-specific skills" (p. 6) that lead to performance (i.e., observable behavior). Thus, in addressing student and teacher competencies, I consider both cognitive and non-cognitive competencies ("different constituents of competence," p. 5), including knowledge, beliefs, and skills.

Unpacking the Formative Assessment Process

Task Quality

This factor concerns elicitation practice. Task, here, is broadly construed to include not only formal assessment events (e.g., quizzes), but also students' contributions to class discussions (including student-initiated questions) and student behavior during class activities. Quality, of course, relates to purpose. For assessment, that purpose is "the generation and display of relevant evidence" (Black & Wiliam, 1998, p. 31). For both large-scale and formative assessment purposes, "relevant evidence" concerns what students know and can do. However, relevant evidence for formative assessment also includes evidence that could be used to support student learning. In other words, evidence must indicate not just where students are, but how to get them further (e.g., what difficulties students might be experiencing and clues as to how those might be addressed).

Interpretation Quality

This factor concerns interpretation practice (i.e., how evidence from a formative assessment "task" is turned into information that can be used to improve student learning). Here, as for large-scale assessment, the focus is on the accuracy of any interpretations that are made; however, for formative assessment, these interpretations are more than just students' "status," but also diagnostic information related to students' learning needs. To be effective as part of formative assessment, interpretations should include answers to questions such as: "What are the strengths and problematic aspects of [students'] thinking? What experience or particular cognition do they need next to deepen their learning?" (Minstrell, Anderson, & Li, 2011, p. 2).

While the need for interpretation is most visible in assessment events that elicit students' open-ended responses (e.g., contributions to classroom conversations, performances or products, written responses), even assessment instruments that can be scored objectively require interpretation. For example, a class set of student responses to a series of multiple-choice questions contains complexity as teachers consider variation in responses across students and across items. While psychometric theory may help to identify "misfit" (e.g, a group of students answering an "easy" question incorrectly but demonstrating understanding of more difficult concepts), it cannot explain why. Is the context of the question unfamiliar to some students? Is the wording difficult for English language learners? Were those students absent the day a particular concept was discussed in class?

Response Quality

Finally, this factor concerns response practice, considering how students and/or their teacher act on their interpretations. An inquiry into this practice concerns both what these classroom actors did and how (given everything that influences student learning) their actions did or did not have an impact on student learning.

There has been extensive research on characteristics of teachers' feedback (e.g., Hattie & Timperley, 2007; Kluger & DeNisi, 1996). Heritage (2010) summarizes two key characteristics of feedback to improve student learning: that "it is focused on the task and provides the student with suggestions, hints, or cues, rather than offered in the form of praise or comments about performances" (p. 5). However, Carless (2006) notes that (for summative assessment) it may be more useful to provide students with general rather than task feedback, as the former can more easily be transferred to future learning. Indeed:

> Whether feedback has positive learning effects depends on many interacting factors: motivation, the complexity of the task, the expertise of the learner, and the level and quality of the feedback. This makes it highly situational; the same feedback given to two learners could have opposite effects.
>
> (Stobart, 2012, p. 239)

Because the effectiveness of feedback depends on its interpretability to the learner who is receiving it (e.g., Carless, 2006; Cowie, 2005), and thus specific learner characteristics, effective feedback is tailored to specific students. In addition, "the feedback the student receives becomes meaningful only when the student gets the opportunity to improve his or her performance" (Struyf et al., 2011, p. 220). Thus, response quality also entails the environment for and opportunities to respond to feedback.

Unpacking Factors Influencing the Formative Assessment Process

The formative assessment process (and all other processes related to classroom assessment) takes place within the context of a given classroom environment. Thus, the quality of the components of this process—i.e., task, interpretation(s), response(s)—are heavily influenced by the characteristics of that environment. This includes characteristics of classroom actors and relationships among classroom actors, as well as how the classroom community constitutes both the content under consideration and "assessment cultural practices" (Shepard et al., 2018, p. 28). These practices refer to "the social norms and meanings associated with assessment processes" (p. 28) in a given classroom and evolve within the classroom community as a "network of (largely implicit) expectations and agreements" (Black & Wiliam, 1998, p. 56). Such expectations include which classroom actors have responsibilities for which parts of classroom assessment processes (Black & Wiliam, 1998)—e.g., whether students are responsible for alerting teachers when they are confused or whether teachers are responsible for monitoring student understanding (Cowie, 2005)—as well as assumptions about the purpose of classroom assessment—i.e., whether it is "a source of insight and help" or "an occasion for meting out rewards and punishments" (Shepard, 2000, p. 10). This larger *classroom assessment environment* is depicted as the large shaded box around all of the components in Figure 7.3. In the subsections below, I explore each of the other factors (depicted as rounded rectangles in Figure 7.3).

Teacher Assessment (and Teaching) Competence

Teachers' role throughout the formative assessment process means that the quality of the formative process (and thus the trustworthiness of a given formative assessment event) depends heavily on the teacher's competencies, including knowledge, beliefs, and skills. Of special importance is teachers' pedagogical content knowledge (PCK)—the "particular form of content knowledge that embodies the aspects of content most germane to its teachability" (Shulman, 1986, p. 9). This includes both knowledge of student learning difficulties and knowledge of instructional approaches that can be used to address those difficulties (e.g., van Driel, Verloop, & de Vos, 1998). Many models of PCK explicitly include a component related to assessment (e.g., Magnusson, Krajcik, & Borko, 1999), emphasizing the importance of content-specific knowledge about assessment. Teachers' beliefs, are also influential; these may include beliefs about their role in the classroom, about the nature of learning and of assessment, and about their students (Black & Wiliam, 1998; McMillan, 2003; Shepard, 2000). Clearly, teachers' perceptions of what it is that they *should* be doing will influence what it is that they do when engaging in classroom assessment.

During elicitation, the teacher has a significant influence on the quality of the task (i.e., the extent to which it makes visible diagnostic evidence of what students know and can do). Even when the event is initiated by the student (e.g., by asking a question), he or she does so in the context of an instructional lesson that the teacher likely had a significant role in shaping. Teachers' ability to construct/orchestrate quality tasks depends on their beliefs (e.g., about the purpose of assessment), as well as their PCK (e.g., knowing what difficulties students are likely to experience with particular content, knowing how to elicit evidence of student knowledge and skills related to that content) and situation-specific skills (e.g., being able to orchestrate a class discussion that surfaces students' ideas about particular content).

What a teacher is able to identify and interpret with respect to a given assessment task depends on his or her PCK (e.g., knowledge of common student learning difficulties to attend to) and beliefs about assessment (e.g., whether the purpose of assessment is to reveal *whether* students know something or *how* they are reasoning about it; Minstrell et al., 2011), as well as situation-specific skills such as *noticing* (van Es & Sherin, 2002). Black and Wiliam (1998) suggest "a sound model of students' progression in the learning of the subject matter" as a requirement for interpreting assessment results "in a formative way" (p. 37). Teachers may have internalized such a model (as part of their PCK), or assessment materials may provide support for such interpretations. For example, multiple-choice items may be linked to levels of a learning progression (e.g., Briggs, Alonzo, Schwab, & Wilson, 2006), or curriculum materials may provide information to help teachers interpret student responses in light of such models (e.g., Shepard et al., 2018). Teachers' competence may also be "boosted" by various other types of support for interpretation—even those built in by the teacher when designing the assessment. For example, analysis of student responses to multiple-choice items may be more easily analyzed for formative interpretations using grading software, or rubrics may be used to aid analysis of more open-ended tasks.

Finally, responding to interpretations requires both planning (i.e., deciding what to do) and execution (i.e., actually enacting instruction or giving feedback). Both are relevant, in that a teacher might come up with a brilliant plan for supporting student learning needs but be unable to actually enact that plan in the classroom (e.g., due to poor classroom management). Teachers' beliefs are implicated here (e.g., beliefs about whether students or the teacher is responsible for responding to information from assessment, general beliefs about teaching and learning). Clearly, responses also depend on teachers' PCK, particularly the instructional component, and on teachers' situation-specific judgments to select/adapt a strategy for use in a particular classroom assessment event. Teachers' instructional responses and feedback are based on existing models of learning; thus, the effectiveness of teachers' responses depends on the validity of these models (e.g., Black, 1998). In this regard, having an interpretative framework (such as a learning progression) may be helpful in identifying "instructional moves that help to connect with students' current understandings" (Shepard et al., 2018, p. 24). Without such a framework, it can be difficult to identify productive next steps, and therefore easy for teachers to resort to providing feedback or instruction that simply tells students the right answer (e.g., Stahnke, Schueler, & Roesken-Winter, 2016).

Student Assessment (and Learning) Competence

Given students' central role in the formative assessment process, their competencies also play an important role in determining the quality of tasks, interpretations, and responses that comprise an assessment event. A distinguishing feature of classroom assessment (as compared to large-scale assessment) is that the "student is not the 'subject' whose achievement is measured but an active participant in the process, such that the meaning of the assessment information itself cannot be fully understood apart from the student who is using it" (Brookhart, 2003, p. 8). Of particular importance are beliefs and affective-motivational characteristics related to their own learning (Black & Wiliam, 1998, p. 59).

Elicitation depends critically on students' willingness and ability to articulate what they are thinking. When responding to teachers' questions, "whether the student believes ability to be incremental or fixed will have a strong influence on how the student sees a question—as an opportunity to learn or as a threat to self-esteem" (Black & Wiliam, 1998, p. 57). What students identify and interpret with respect to a given assessment task depends on their content knowledge—in particular, their developing sense for what constitutes quality work in a given domain (e.g., their understanding of goals, skills to evaluate their own work; Heritage, 2010). Students' metacognitive skills (e.g., ability to be self-reflective) are also important for using assessment information to derive useful interpretations for improving their own learning (National Research Council, 2000). Feedback (from teachers and peers), as well as tools such as rubrics, can aid students in identifying and interpreting relevant aspects of their own performances/responses. Finally, students' responses (i.e., how they make adjustments to their learning) are highly dependent on factors such as self-efficacy, goal orientation, and beliefs about the nature of learning and about effort (Black & Wiliam, 1998).

Relationships among Classroom Actors

In contrast to large-scale assessment, in which those developing/administering and scoring students' work are outsiders, teachers and students are intimately involved in all aspects of a classroom assessment event. Their familiarity with each other allows contextual knowledge to become part of the assessment event. Teachers' knowledge of students impacts the kinds of tasks that are posed—and to whom—and how both teacher and students interpret responses. For example, a contribution from a student who is generally regarded as "smart" or knowledgeable may be treated differently (by both teacher and students) than a similar contribution from a student who is regarded as struggling. In responding, there is "no simple recipe for effective feedback; there is just no substitute for the teacher knowing their students" (Wiliam, 2013, p. 18). With knowledge of his or her students, a teacher can provide feedback that will be most informative and motivating to a particular student, given his or her personal characteristics.

In addition, relationships in the classroom (especially as related to trust) affect students' engagement in the formative assessment process (e.g., Carless, 2009; Stobart, 2012). Students' willingness to share ideas or ask a question during elicitation may be heavily influenced by their fear that doing so will expose them to ridicule or other sanctions versus confidence that their contributions will be met with "teacher and peer reactions" that are "considerate and well intentioned" (e.g., Cowie, 2005, p. 148). Similarly, students may be more likely to act on feedback received from teachers with whom they have a mutually trusting and respectful relationship (Cowie, 2005; Wiliam, 2013) and whose judgments they regard as fair (Carless, 2006). Students' perceptions of their teacher:

> influence the ways in which students interact with the teacher, and those interactions in turn influence how the students come to be seen through the eyes of the teacher . . . [S]tudent judgments of and reactions to the teacher . . . are a constitutive feature of the fundamental social ecology of classroom teaching.
>
> (Erickson, 2007, p. 193)

In order to put forth effort to make revisions as indicated through a formative assessment event or to engage in learning experiences offered by the teacher as a result, students need to trust that their efforts will have some benefit. Students are more likely "to take risks to learn from a trusted adult and classmates" (Shepard et al., 2018).

Conception(s) of Content in the Classroom Community

As discussed above, classroom assessment contributes to conceptions of content in a particular classroom community, but such conceptions also influence classroom assessment. The meaning of a given classroom assessment event can only be interpreted through the content lens of that classroom. Has a particular example been discussed in class or are students being asked to apply their knowledge to a new context? What does it mean to provide an explanation in a particular classroom? The construction of content in a particular classroom influences the tasks that teachers pose, the way that students interpret and respond to those tasks, and the ways that their responses are subsequently interpreted. If a classroom assessment deviates significantly from the way that content has been constructed in a particular context, students may view it as "unfair, illegitimate or even meaningless" (Black & Wiliam, 1998, p. 56).

Summary

Above, I have laid out a set of factors underlying one influence on the trustworthiness of classroom assessment: its formative effects (whether the assessment is intended primarily for formative, summative, or accountability purposes). Unpacking the formative assessment process, we can first identify three factors—task quality, interpretation quality, and response quality—and associated questions to guide consideration of the trustworthiness of a given episode of classroom assessment in terms of its formative effects on student learning:

1) *Task quality*: Does the task elicit diagnostic evidence related to students' knowledge and skills?
2) *Interpretation quality*: Are interpretations of student responses to the task accurate—in terms of both what students know and can do and what support they need to progress further?
3) *Response quality*: Are responses to the interpretations (by teacher and/or students) likely to (and do they) support student learning?

However, this is just one part of a consideration of this influence on the trustworthiness of classroom assessment. As discussed above, another set of factors influences task, interpretation, and response quality, and thus another set of questions can be asked to guide consideration in terms of formative effects on student learning:

4) *Classroom assessment environment*: Does the classroom assessment environment support formative effects on student learning (task quality, interpretation quality, and response quality)?
5) *Teacher assessment (and teaching) competence*: Do the teacher's competencies (PCK, beliefs, and situation-specific skills) support formative effects on student learning (task quality, interpretation quality, and response quality)?
6) *Student assessment (and learning) competence*: Do students' competencies (evolving understanding of disciplinary norms, beliefs and affective-motivational characteristics, and metacognitive skills) support formative effects on student learning (task quality, interpretation quality, and response quality)?
7) *Relationships among classroom actors*: Do relationships among students and the teacher's relationships with students support formative effects on student learning (task quality, interpretation quality, and response quality)?
8) *Conception(s) of content in the classroom community*: Do conceptions of content in the classroom community support formative effects on student learning (task quality, interpretation quality, and response quality)?

This section has unpacked and identified questions associated with the factors underlying just one effect of classroom assessment on student learning. A similar exercise could be carried out with each of the other factors, in order to expand questions 1–2 and 4–8 identified to guide broad consideration of trustworthiness (pp. 131–132).

Conclusion: Trustworthiness from a Teacher's Perspective

The discussion above highlights the complexity of trustworthiness, and thus the multitude of considerations entailed in classroom assessment. To further highlight this complexity, and to illustrate some key points in the discussion above, I conclude this chapter with a brief case study of a physics teacher's consideration of learning progression-based assessment items.

As described in more detail elsewhere (e.g., Alonzo & Elby, 2019), Tim[12] is a high school physics teacher who worked with me for several years on design research involving learning progressions. After presenting some of his work at a science education research conference, Tim reflected on his use of learning progression-based assessment items for a variety of potentially conflicting purposes. In particular, he discussed his perception of how researchers reacted to his use of learning progression-based items; these reflections often referred to concerns about (psychometric) validity. Data from this interview (Alonzo & Elby, 2019) provide a window into one teacher's detailed consideration of the trustworthiness of learning progression-based assessment items in his classroom and a contrast between the construct of trustworthiness developed in this chapter and the traditional psychometric criteria of validity and reliability.

Tim's Assessment Practice in Terms of Trustworthiness

Tim constructed a multiple-choice assessment instrument covering topics in mechanics, with learning progression-based items (e.g., Alonzo & Steedle, 2009) and items pulled from concept inventories (e.g., Force Concept Inventory; Hestenes, Wells, & Swackhamer, 1992). He used this instrument, with modifications from year to year, for formative and summative purposes, as well as to document student growth to meet accountability requirements. By drawing on these existing items, Tim's *assessment competence* was bolstered by a learning progression that provided a framework for "the different ways students understand something," as well as items for eliciting those understandings.

Formative Use

Tim used the assessment instrument primarily for formative purposes, emphasizing the importance of the qualitative information he gained about his students' understanding (i.e., *interpretation quality*), rather than the quantitative information about their learning progression levels: "I don't care about what level they're at. I will never look at that piece of information. What I care about is how they are understanding the idea." In contrast to more commonly available materials, Tim was able to obtain diagnostic information from students' responses to the learning progression-based multiple-choice items:

> I guess for me, the [non-learning progression] materials that I have currently for formative assessment I find . . . not as useful because it's the binary they know this or they don't know this . . . That doesn't tell me why they're not getting it . . . If it doesn't help me figure out what they're not getting or how they're thinking about it, so that way I can redirect them and help them get back on track, then it's not as useful.
>
> What I normally look at, in terms of what I'm going to teach the next day . . . [is what] their responses are saying about their understanding . . . Each answer [choice] tells me something about what the student knows—that's useful . . . It tells me something about how they're thinking about it . . . One question there tells me about as much as four questions on a standard right or wrong test because it says, "Okay, yeah, they don't have a complete understanding, but this is what their understanding is right now." . . . I look for what are they thinking [based on the answer that they chose] and then I try and discern why are they thinking that?

Tim described the benefits of his formative use of the learning progression-based items in terms of three effects on student learning: *formative actions* (as mentioned above), *elicitation as an occasion for student learning*, and *affective-motivational effects* for students. Tim explained the learning progression-based items to his students as having answer choices that "all have some bits of truth to them" and as representing "different levels of correctness." He felt that this made his students think more as they engaged with the items:

A student taking an evaluation know[s] that these all have some semblance of truth to them, that these are different levels of correctness, rather than . . . like guessing all the rest of them are wrong. I think that will get them thinking a lot more as opposed to . . . saying, "I don't know this," they say, "Okay, which one of these makes the most sense? Because it's got to be at least a little bit true." And I just feel . . . that will help them actually think more through questions rather than just getting [the item] and saying, "I don't know this one." He also felt that the items had affective-motivational benefits for his students:

It seems as if they feel a lot more comfortable saying, "Well, you know, this is what people, this is common to think this. I'm not stupid. This is actually a pretty good thought right here because this is what a lot of other people think . . ."

I think there's value to be able to say, "Okay, you're almost there . . . These are really good ideas you have and you're almost there. You're really close but this is where we want to get you."

Accountability Use

While providing formative evidence to shape his instruction, results from Tim's assessment instrument also served as evidence for his district's accountability requirements. He presented his approach to these requirements as a contrast to what he perceived other teachers to be doing:

[The] legislature is saying we have to show the growth of a single student in every classroom. And the main way that [teachers are] doing that is pre-test and post-test and that's just not good information. It's not useful information. Of course, [students] didn't know anything about it when they came in and of course they know more when they leave . . . You're going to find that in almost any class, especially [since it's] the teachers that are the ones writing the pre-test, post-test . . . I know there are teachers out there that do—just, "Okay, here's your pre-test. I'm going to turn on some music and open the door and bang this pot while you're taking it," you know what I mean? "I'm not going to be so worried about my kids doing great on the pre-test." That is an issue—teachers are worried about their kids doing too well on the pre-test.

This approach to accountability requirements (i.e., seeking to minimize students' pre-test performance) is consistent with Shepard's (2000) observation that teachers often do not use pre-test results (elicited to demonstrate student growth) to inform their instruction. In contrast, Tim found that learning progression-based pre-/post-tests allowed him to obtain real information about his students' understanding, as well as providing a much better way of demonstrating students' growth:

I can actually track, are my students improving in terms of their understanding? I can get a student from a [level] 1 to a [level] 3 understanding—it's true they might not be . . . to the four and five levels where I want them, but I've still shown growth. So that's useful for me in terms of showing to my administrators . . . I don't have to show a binary—either they know it or they don't . . . I can show growth because every student might not get it [i.e., reach the standard], but almost every student . . . in my class is going to [move up] at least, hopefully at least a level on the majority of the topics.

This approach allowed Tim to continue teaching in ways that he knew were beneficial to his students because he was able to demonstrate to his administrator that he was having an impact on their learning without wasting time on contrived assessment events. In other words, Tim's pre-/post-tests allowed him to manage his *relationship with a non-classroom actor* (i.e., his building principal) in ways supportive of student learning.

Tim's Assessment Practice in Terms of Validity and Reliability

In addition to illustrating aspects of *trustworthiness*, Tim's discussion highlighted both the difficulty with and the unsuitability of traditional notions of validity and reliability for considering his classroom assessment. Traditional notions of reliability (and thus validity) are difficult because:

> A student's level really doesn't tell me a lot about what they're thinking. I can go to that level and say, "Okay, this is what a level 2 thinks," but in reality, if I look across the board, that student might, you know, if these are eight items, they might be 5 on these two and, like, 1 on this one . . . So the student's level isn't as valuable to me. I don't feel like it gives me enough because the thinking is so- . . . they might understand this chunk really well but not this chunk of, um, and so that's less valuable to me.

However, in line with the discussion above, it is exactly this unreliability that was most valuable to him: "That's where it's useful to me because then I can say, 'What is it about this particular question that maybe links it to a different concept,' you know?" Indeed, in another interview, Tim was asked to think aloud while examining a score report for responses to a set of learning progression-based items (Alonzo, de los Santos, & Kobrin, 2014). During the interview, he used apparent inconsistencies in students' responses to posit hypotheses about the nature of their ideas. For example:

> So it's interesting to me that when it's on a table they . . . don't recognize that gravity is acting on it. But when it's in the air they recognize that gravity's acting on it. So maybe just associating gravity with falling and only with falling and not as a force that's always there . . . [But] down here, we have big objects—gravity and weight tend to come in a little more . . . Gravity is holding it down on the ground. So it's interesting that when it's off the ground they aren't worried about gravity, but when it's on the ground and it's heavy, now gravity is really important . . . I'd have to think about that idea a little bit more, but it certainly gives me a little bit more insight . . . We've talked about gravity and normal force, but this idea of gravity coming from the ground and having to be in contact with the ground to feel gravity—because that's when they feel gravity the most, is, you know, as weight, the ground. That's interesting.

In addition to providing valuable information, students' "unreliability" is not a threat to Tim's work in the way it is to large-scale assessment because he has the opportunity to interact with students to check any interpretations he may have about their thinking: "And so knowing what they're thinking, or at least an approximation of what they're thinking about a topic, that's what's useful. Because then I can say, 'This is, I observed you thinking in this way. Is that true?'" Even if he wants to use the learning progression level indicated by students' responses to inform instruction, Tim has the opportunity to check whether this is appropriate before proceeding.

Tim *did* acknowledge that some reliability (i.e., consistency of information about student performance) was necessary for reporting to his administrator and differentiated between: (a) the inconsistency that appears when student ideas are examined at a small grain size (as above); and (b) the overall consistency that he expected at the larger grain size for reporting to his administrator. Similarly, Tim recognized that it was important for him to be able to justify the validity of his approach to his administrator ("research says this is valid"). However, he was frustrated by what seemed like researchers' over-concern with validity, as it seemed to deny his own experiences with the assessment items:

> A lot of times people come up with a great idea and then . . . there's a tendency of "No, no, no . . . I haven't proven validity . . . No, no, no, it's bad, it's bad, it's bad." But what I'm saying is, "But I have used it and it is helpful regardless of if it has, for me it's been very helpful anecdotally in my class and I've seen improvement," you know what I mean? Like, I've, as much as a teacher can claim, like, this was awesome for me . . . And just because it hasn't yet been validated in that way . . . This is a great tool, and even though it's not perfect, no tool is ever going to be perfect. You know, in my eyes, from what I've seen, it's a pretty decent model at this point . . . it still shows me these are the ideas that the student has . . . And these ideas tend to be better informed than those ideas. That's really close enough for what we're doing . . . education isn't an exact science, so if you can at least make it valid enough . . . [it] only has to fit so well before it's going to be useful.

Thus, consistent with the definition of trustworthiness developed in this chapter, Tim was primarily concerned with his students' learning. He trusted his assessment instrument, even if it may not have satisfied psychometric criteria, because it had a number of important benefits for student learning, particularly when used formatively. In contrast, considerations of validity and reliability for large-scale assessment may focus only on test score interpretation (e.g., Cizek, 2016)—i.e., task quality and interpretation quality. As illustrated by the discussion of formative effects of classroom assessment described above, consideration of these criteria is only part of an inquiry into the trustworthiness of classroom assessment. Thus, as Tim acknowledges, it is not so much that traditional psychometric criteria are not applicable to classroom assessment, but that the pieces that are applicable are only a small part of a much larger network of concerns that must be considered. From a teacher's perspective, both emphasis on student learning *and* consideration of the influences on student learning are important. Classroom assessment has significant potential to impact student learning, but it is not a "magic bullet." Consideration only of scores on classroom assessment "instruments" not only leaves out the vast majority of teachers' formative assessment work, but also ignores the factors that may be much more important in determining whether student learning results, such as teachers' professional competencies (and perhaps need for resources and/or professional development), students' self-efficacy and ability to affect their own learning, and attention to classroom relationships and shared understandings of disciplines.

Notes

1 This work was supported in part by grants from NCS Pearson, Inc. and the National Science Foundation (Grant No. DRL-1253036). Any opinions, findings, and conclusions or recommendations expressed in this chapter are those of the author and do not necessarily reflect the views of the funding agencies.

2 As discussed below, these effects may occur for all types of classroom assessment, not only assessment activities that are explicitly labeled "formative assessment."

3 As compared to other forms of classroom assessment, interim assessment also has a more limited role for students (Brookhart, 2009) and thus does not involve the whole classroom in the same way.

4 For example, see the Illinois guidebook on the use of student growth in teacher evaluation (Illinois State Board of Education, 2014) and two examples of resulting district-level policies (Performance Evaluation Reform Act Joint Committee, 2015, 2016).

5 Pre-/post-tests developed outside of the classroom may also serve formative and summative purposes. However, these forms of assessment are outside the scope of this chapter.

6 This is a broader argument than the more common one regarding the negative impact of grades or feedback on student learning (e.g., Black & Wiliam, 1998).

7   Considerations of consequences as part of psychometric validity (e.g., Kane, 2002; Messick, 1995) do attend to the broader context and use of assessment; however, there is not consensus about use of this criterion in large-scale contexts (e.g., Moss, 2003; Nichols et al., 2009; Stobart, 2012). In addition, consequences may be considered primarily "if they can be traced to a source of construct under-representation or construct irrelevant variance" (Moss, 2003, p. 14), and in general are not as central a consideration as they must be in the classroom assessment context (e.g., Moss, 2003; Nichols et al., 2009).

8   Although consistent with the definition of formative assessment cited above, reference to formative assessment (and thus classroom assessment) as a process, rather than an instrument, is not universally accepted (e.g., Bennett, 2011).

9   Even for more summative purposes, classroom assessment often involves multiple measures. Grades for a given instructional unit are rarely based solely on performance on a single unit test, and grades for a semester/trimester or year are made up of those for multiple instructional units. If, as Taylor and Nolen (1996) recommend, multiple sources of information are used to create (and revise) judgments about student learning and performance, decisions that are reliable (i.e., based on sufficient information) can be made, even if individual measurements are not as reliable as those for large-scale assessments.

10 Traditional notions of validity and reliability may play a role in students' perceptions of fairness, in that a test that does not measure what students have learned (whether because it measures something else or because it cannot be generalized to provide an adequate representation of learning) is likely to be perceived as unfair (e.g., Sambell, McDowell, & Brown, 1997).

11 Although these effects occur primarily through (formal and informal) formative assessment, they may also occur when summative and/or accountability assessment is used for formative purposes.

12 This is a pseudonym.

References

Alonzo, A. C., de los Santos, X. E., & Kobrin, J. L. (2014, April). *Teachers' interpretations of score reports based upon ordered-multiple choice items linked to a learning progression.* Paper presented at the annual meeting of the American Educational Research Association, Philadelphia, PA.

Alonzo, A. C., & Elby, A. (2019). Beyond empirical adequacy: Learning progressions as models and their value for teachers. *Cognition and Instruction, 37*, 1–37.

Alonzo, A. C., & Steedle, J. T. (2009). Developing and assessing a force and motion learning progression. *Science Education, 93*, 389–421.

Bell, B., & Cowie, B. (2001). The characteristics of formative assessment in science education. *Science Education, 85*, 536–553.

Bennett, R. E. (2011). Formative assessment: A critical review. *Assessment in Education: Principles, Policy & Practice, 18*(1), 5–25.

Black, P. (1998). *Testing: Friend or foe? Theory and practice of assessment and testing.* London: Falmer Press.

Black, P., & Wiliam, D. (1998). Assessment and classroom learning. *Assessment in Education: Principles, Policy & Practice, 5*(1), 7–74.

Black, P., & Wiliam, D. (2012). The reliability of assessments. In J. Gardner (Ed.), *Assessment and learning* (2nd ed., pp. 243–263). London: SAGE.

Blömeke, S., Gustafsson, J.-E., & Shavelson, R. J. (2015). Beyond dichotomies: Competence viewed as a continuum. *Zeitschrift für Psychologie, 223*(1), 3–13.

Braaten, M., & Windschitl, M. (2011). Working toward a stronger conceptualization of scientific explanation for science education. *Science Education, 95*(4), 639–669.

Briggs, D. C., Alonzo, A. C., Schwab, C., & Wilson, M. (2006). Diagnostic assessment with ordered multiple-choice items. *Educational Assessment, 11*, 33–63.

Brookhart, S. M. (2003). Developing measurement theory for classroom assessment purposes and uses. *Educational Measurement: Issues and Practice, 22*(4), 5–12.

Brookhart, S. M. (2009). Editorial. *Educational Measurement: Issues and Practice, 28*(3), 1–4.

Buhagiar, M. A. (2007). Classroom assessment within the alternative assessment paradigm: Revisiting the territory. *The Curriculum Journal, 18*(1), 39–56.

Carless, D. (2006). Differing perceptions in the feedback process. *Studies in Higher Education, 31*(2), 219–233.

Carless, D. (2007). Conceptualizing pre-emptive formative assessment. *Assessment in Education: Principles, Policy & Practice, 14*(2), 171–184.

Carless, D. (2009). Trust, distrust, and their impact on assessment reform. *Assessment & Evaluation in Higher Education, 34*(1), 79–89.

Cizek, G. J. (2016). Validating test score meaning and defending test score use: Different aims, different methods. *Assessment in Education: Principles, Policy & Practice, 23*(2), 212–225.

Cowie, B. (2005). Pupil commentary on assessment for learning. *The Curriculum Journal, 16*(2), 137–151.

diSessa, A. A. (1996). What do "just plain folk" know about physics? In D. R. Olson & N. Torrance (Eds.), *The handbook of education and human development: New models of learning, teaching, and schooling* (pp. 709–730). Cambridge, MA: Blackwell.

Erickson, F. (2007). Some thoughts on "proximal" formative assessment of student learning. *Yearbook of the National Society for the Study of Education, 106*(1), 186–216.

Frisbie, D. A. (2005). Measurement 101: Some fundamentals revisited. *Educational Measurement: Issues and Practice, 24*(3), 21–28.

Gardner, J. (2012). Quality assessment practice. In J. Gardner (Ed.), *Assessment and learning* (2nd ed., pp. 103–121). London: SAGE.

Gielen, S., Dochy, F., & Dierick, S. (2003). Evaluating the consequential validity of new modes of assessment: The influence of assessment on learning, including pre-, post-, and true assessment effects. In M. Segers, F. Dochy, & E. Cascallar (Eds.), *Optimising new modes of assessment: In search of qualities and standards* (pp. 37–54). New York: Kluwer Academic Publishers.

Gipps, C. (1994). *Beyond testing: Towards a theory of educational assessment.* London: Falmer Press.

Hallgren, K., James-Burdumy, S., & Perez-Johnson, I. (2014, April). *State requirements for teacher evaluation policies promoted by Race to the Top.* NCEE Evaluation Brief 2014-4016. Washington, DC: Institute of Education Sciences. Retrieved from https://files.eric.ed.gov/fulltext/ED544794.pdf

Hattie, J., & Timperley, H. (2007). The power of feedback. *Review of Educational Research, 77*(1), 81–112.

Heritage, M. (2010, September). *Formative assessment and next-generation assessment systems: Are we losing an opportunity?* Washington, DC: Council of Chief State School Officers. Retrieved from https://files.eric.ed.gov/fulltext/ED543063.pdf

Hestenes, D., Wells, M., & Swackhamer, G. (1992). Force concept inventory. *The Physics Teacher, 30*(3), 141–166.

Illinois State Board of Education. (2014, February). *Joint committee guidebook: Implementing the student growth component in teacher and principal evaluation systems.* Retrieved from www.isbe.net/documents/14-4-student-growth-component.pdf

Kane, M. (2002). Validating high-stakes testing programs. *Educational Measurement: Issues and Practice, 21*(1), 31–41.

Kane, M. T. (2013). Validating the interpretations and uses of test scores. *Journal of Educational Measurement, 50*(1), 1–73.

Kluger, A. N., & DeNisi, A. (1996). The effect of feedback interventions on performance: A historical review, a meta-analysis, and a preliminary feedback intervention theory. *Psychological Bulletin, 119*, 254–284.

Linn, R. L., & Gronlund, N. E. (2012). *Measurement and assessment in teaching* (11th ed.). Upper Saddle River, NJ: Pearson.

Magnusson, S., Krajcik, J., & Borko, H. (1999). Secondary teachers' knowledge and beliefs about subject matter and their impact on instruction. In J. Gess-Newsome and N. G. Lederman (Eds.), *Examining pedagogical content knowledge* (pp. 95–132). Dordrecht: Kluwer Academic.

McManus, S. (2008). *Attributes of effective formative assessment.* Washington, DC: Council of Chief State School Officers. Retrieved from http://ccsso.org/Documents/2008/Attributes_of_Effective_2008.pdf

McMillan, J. H. (2003). Understanding and improving teachers' classroom assessment decision making: Implications for theory and practice. *Educational Measurement: Issues and Practice, 22*(4), 34–43.

Messick, S. (1995). Validity of psychological assessment: Validation of inferences from persons' responses and performances as scientific inquiry into score meaning. *American Psychologist, 50*(9), 741–749.

Minstrell, J., Anderson, R., & Li, M. (2011, May). *Building on learner thinking: A framework for assessment in instruction.* Commissioned paper for the Committee on Highly Successful STEM Schools or Programs for K-12 STEM Education, National Academy of Sciences.

Moss, P. A. (2003). Reconceptualizing validity for classroom assessment. *Educational Measurement: Issues and Practice, 22*(4), 13–25.

National Research Council. (2000). *How people learn: Brain, mind, experience, and school.* Washington, DC: National Academy Press.

National Research Council. (2001). *Adding it up: Helping children learn mathematics.* Washington, DC: National Academy Press.

Nichols, P. D., Meyers, J. L., & Burling, K. S. (2009). A framework for evaluating and planning assessments intended to improve student achievement. *Educational Measurement: Issues and Practice, 28*(3), 14–23.

Nicol, D. J., & Macfarlane-Dick, D. (2006). Formative assessment and self-regulated learning: A model and seven principles of good feedback practice. *Studies in Higher Education, 31*, 199–218.

Oosterhof, A. (2009). *Developing and using classroom assessments* (4th ed.). Upper Saddle River, NJ: Pearson.

Ormrod, J. E. (2000). *Educational psychology: Developing learners* (3rd ed.). Upper Saddle River, NJ: Prentice Hall.

Performance Evaluation Reform Act Joint Committee. (2015, April). *Student growth-model.* Bremen HS District 228, Illinois. Retrieved from www.bhsd228.com/UserFiles/Servers/Server_736353/File/District%20Departments/Performance%20Evaluation%20Plan/Student%20Growth%20Model.pdf

Performance Evaluation Reform Act Joint Committee. (2016, April). *Ewing grade school student growth and SLO guide-book 2018–2019*. Ewing-Northern Community Consolidated School District #115, IL. Retrieved from www.ewinggradeschool.org/UserFiles/Servers/Server_20448887/Image/Student%20Growth%20Handbook%202018-2019-%20Ewing%20Grade%20School.pdf

Perie, M., Marion, S., & Gong, B. (2009). Moving toward a comprehensive assessment system: A framework for considering interim assessments. *Educational Measurement: Issues and Practice, 28*(3), 5–13.

Popham, W. J. (2013). Can classroom assessments of student growth be credibly used to evaluate teachers? *English Journal, 103*(1), 34–39.

Rea-Dickins, R. (2007). Classroom-based assessment: Possibilities and pitfalls. In J. Cummins & C. Davison (Eds.), *International handbook of English language teaching* (pp. 505–520). Boston, MA: Springer.

Ruiz-Primo, M. A., & Furtak, E. M. (2007). Exploring teachers' informal formative assessment practices and students' understanding in the context of scientific inquiry. *Journal of Research in Science Teaching, 44*(1), 57–84.

Sambell, K., McDowell, L., & Brown, S. (1997). "But is it fair?" An exploratory study of student perceptions of the consequential validity of assessment. *Studies in Educational Evaluation, 23*, 349–371.

Shavelson, R. J., Young, D. B., Ayala, C. C., Brandon, P. R., Furtak, E. M., Ruiz-Primo, M. A., Tomita, M. K., & Yin, Y. (2008). On the impact of curriculum-embedded formative assessment on learning: A collaboration between curriculum and assessment developers. *Applied Measurement in Education, 21*(4), 295–314.

Shepard, L. A. (2000). The role of assessment in a learning culture. *Educational Researcher, 29*(7), 4–14.

Shepard, L., Hammerness, K., Darling-Hammond, L., & Rust, F. (2005). Assessment. In L. Darling-Hammond & J. Bransford (Eds.), *Preparing teachers for a changing world: What teachers should lean and be able to do* (pp. 275–326). San Francisco, CA: Jossey-Bass.

Shepard, L. A., Penuel, W. R., & Pellegrino, J. W. (2018). Using learning and motivation theories to coherently link formative assessment, grading practices, and large-scale assessment. *Educational Measurement: Issues and Practice, 37*(1), 21–34.

Shulman, L. S. (1986). Those who understand: Knowledge growth in teaching. *Educational Researcher, 15*(2), 4–14.

Smith, J. K. (2003). Reconsidering reliability in classroom assessment and grading. *Educational Measurement: Issues and Practice, 22*(4), 26–33.

Stahnke, R., Schueler, S., & Roesken-Winter, B. (2016). Teachers' perception, interpretation, and decision-making: A systematic review of empirical mathematics education research. *ZDM, 48*(1), 1–27.

Stiggins, R. J. (1988). Revitalizing classroom assessment: The highest instructional priority. *Phi Delta Kappan, 69*(5), 363–368.

Stobart, G. (2012). Validity in formative assessment. In J. Gardner (Ed.), *Assessment and learning* (2nd ed., pp. 233–242). Thousand Oaks, CA: SAGE.

Struyf, E., Vandenberghe, R., & Lens, W. (2001). The evaluation practice of teachers as a learning opportunity for students. *Studies in Educational Evaluation, 27*, 215–238.

Taylor, C., & Nolen, S. B. (1996). What does the psychometrician's classroom look like? Reframing assessment concepts in the context of learning. *Education Policy Analysis Archives, 4*(17). Retrieved from https://epaa.asu.edu/ojs/article/viewFile/640/762

Third International Conference on Assessment for Learning Participants. (2009, March). *Position paper on assessment for learning from the Third International Conference on Assessment for Learning*. Dunedin, New Zealand: Authors. Retrieved from www.fairtest.org/sites/default/files/Assess-for-Learning-position-paper.pdf

Tierney, R. D., & Charland, J. (2007, April). *Stocks and prospects: Research on formative assessment in secondary classrooms*. Paper presented at the annual meeting of the American Educational Research Association, Chicago, IL.

Trust. Def. 1a. (n.d.). In *Oxford English dictionary online*. Retrieved from www.oed.com

Trustworthy. (n.d.). In *Oxford English dictionary online*. Retrieved from www.oed.com

Tschannen-Moran, M., Hoy, A. W., & Hoy, W. K. (1998). Teacher efficacy: Its meaning and measure. *Review of Educational Research, 68*(2), 202–248.

van Driel, J. H., Verloop, N., & de Vos, W. (1998). Developing science teachers' pedagogical content knowledge. *Journal of Research in Science Teaching, 35*, 673–695.

van Es, E. A., & Sherin, M. G. (2002). Learning to notice: Scaffolding new teachers' interpretations of classroom interactions. *Journal of Technology and Teacher Education, 10*, 571–596.

Weinburg, S. (2010). Thinking like a historian. *Teaching with Primary Sources Quarterly, 3*(1), 2–4. Retrieved from www.loc.gov/teachers/tps/quarterly/historical_thinking/pdf/historical_thinking.pdf

Wiliam, D. (2013). Assessment: The bridge between teaching and learning. *Voices from the Middle, 21*(2), 15–20.

Wilson, M., & Carstensen, C. (2007). Assessment to improve learning in mathematics: The BEAR assessment system. In A. Schoenfeld (Ed.), *Assessing mathematical proficiency* (pp. 311–332). London: Cambridge University Press.

Wu, M., Tam, H. P., & Jen, T.-H. (2016). What is measurement? In *Educational measurement for applied researchers: Theory into practice* (pp. 1–18). Singapore: Springer Nature.

8

Learning Progressions and Embedded Assessment

Derek C. Briggs and Erin Marie Furtak

Learning Progressions and Embedded Assessment

It has been nearly two decades since the publication of the seminal National Research Council report *Knowing What Students Know* (NRC, 2001), and during this time interest in the topic of learning progressions has rapidly increased (Alonzo, 2011; Shepard, Penuel, & Pellegrino, 2018a; Wilson, 2018). Learning progressions are empirically grounded and testable hypotheses about how students' understanding of core concepts within a subject domain grows and becomes more sophisticated over time with appropriate instruction (Corcoran, Mosher, & Rogat, 2009). As such, research on learning progressions represents one tangible response to a key recommendation from *Knowing What Students Know*, namely that all assessment activities should be motivated by, or at least motivate reflection about, theories for how students learn in a given subject domain. The presence of a learning theory is important because once established, it is more general and comprehensive than any single assessment event. A good theory helps teachers to pose the questions best suited to their students, so ideally it is learning theory that eventually drives student assessment, and not the other way around (Shepard, Penuel, & Pellegrino, 2018b). Moreover, theories about how students learn can help teachers discern instructionally relevant insights from the answers that students give on assessment items. Because learning progressions are premised on testable hypotheses, the learning theories that they embody can and should be modified and refined over time. This is especially important when learning is viewed as a sociocognitive or sociocultural phenomenon (Penuel & Shepard, 2016), because the theory that may best explain changes in student understanding in one situated context may not have the same explanatory power in another.

There are numerous challenges to the use of learning progressions as an organizing framework for classroom instruction and assessment (cf. Alonzo & Gotwals, 2012). In this chapter, we focus on one challenge in particular: the challenge of developing a curriculum-embedded assessment system. Designing good student assessments is always challenging, but it is especially so in a learning progression context for at least two related reasons. The first reason is that, almost by definition, the greatest utility of a learning progression is an orientation to teaching that focuses on growth over status. A good learning progression marks out one (or more) likely path(s) that students are expected to traverse as they become more sophisticated in their understanding of a core concept. It follows that for teachers to gain insights about the actual path that students take over the course of an instructional period, it is necessary to organize *multiple* assessment events along the way, and it can be challenging to find a way to ensure that each assessment is appropriately targeted and aligned to the different levels of the progression. The second reason assessment design in this context is challenging (closely related to the first reason) is that the middle to top ends of most learning progressions are typically characterized by expectations of cognitive complexity that go beyond the recall of isolated facts or the application of these facts as part of standard procedures. Consequently, distinguishing between a student or a group of students at different locations on a continuum from novice to expert can require more complex tasks (e.g., constructed-response items, performance-based tasks) that are time-consuming to design, administer, and evaluate. Taken together, to the extent that an ideal use of learning progressions could involve lengthy assessment events on multiple occasions, it is little wonder that prior research on learning progressions tends to involve cross-sectional data collected at one point in time, rather than longitudinal data collected at multiple time points. This is unfortunate because it limits the benefits teachers are likely to get from using the learning progression as a tool for formative assessment,[1] and because it provides for a fairly weak test of the theory underlying the learning progression.

We argue that one way for a learning progression framework to realize its full potential is through the development of curriculum-embedded assessments (hereafter, we refer to these simply as embedded assessments). Embedded assessments serve dual purposes as part of a comprehensive assessment system. On the one hand, they are proximal to a teacher's curriculum and can be used to provide immediate feedback that facilitates student learning. On the other hand, they include scorable tasks that can be used to reliably monitor growth in student understanding over time, and to evaluate what students have learned at some given point in time. Ideally, there will be coherence between assessments used for both formative and summative purposes. In this chapter, we describe work from an ongoing project in which we were faced with the challenge of building a system of embedded assessment in support of a learning progression in science. The learning progression at the heart of this project pertains to the modeling of energy flows, a "big idea" in science that crosses disciplinary boundaries, and which we are presently implementing and evaluating as part of structured professional development activities with classroom teachers of physics, chemistry, and biology in a high school setting. Following the development of a learning progression for the modeling of energy flows, four of the key ingredients of our approach include: (1) mapping and aligning the scientific content of the learning progression to both the content standards and the curricula of the participating teachers; (2) building a system of assessments targeted to the learning progression that can provide teachers with relevant insights about their students; (3) bringing teachers together to discuss student ideas that emerge from embedded assessments; and (4) linking the assessments within and across the courses taught by participating teachers in physics, chemistry, and biology with a subset of common tasks.

Motivating Context

The context for our illustration comes from the first two years of a research project funded by the National Science Foundation (NSF). This project is itself situated within an ongoing research–practice partnership between a medium-sized Colorado school district (total enrollment of about 40,000 students) and researchers at the University of Colorado Boulder. The partnership was formed around the need, from the school district's perspective, to support secondary science teachers in developing, using, and interpreting student assessments for a variety of purposes, ranging from those that were low-stakes (involving primarily formative classroom use by teachers) to those that could be higher-stakes (involving summative uses to grade and compare students, or even as a basis for teacher evaluations). From our perspective as researchers, we saw the partnership as an opportunity to both study and challenge what, in the United States at least, has become a conventional teacher view about student assessment. Two aspects of this conventional view are especially salient to our work. The first is that assessment is something that is "done" to students and that it comes from an external source outside a teacher's control. The second is that the point of assessing students is to find out if they get it or they don't (Otero, 2006). We view learning progressions, and the approach to student assessment that they require, as a promising way to challenge this conventional view to the benefit of both teachers and their students.

The intervention at the heart of our NSF-funded project was to directly engage high school science teachers in a process of using learning progressions as a framework for iteratively designing, enacting, and reflecting upon student assessment. This engagement took place during regularly scheduled meetings in teachers' *professional learning communities* (PLCs) (Gröschner, Seidel, & Katharina, 2014; Loughran, Mulhall, & Berry, 2004; McLaughlin & Talbert, 2001). Over the course of two years, our team took over facilitation of a subgroup of six "focus" PLCs, two in each of the disciplinary content areas of physics, chemistry, and biology. Historically, although the activities within each PLC varied, a major emphasis had been placed on what the district referred to as "data cycling," which involved teachers administering assessments, collecting data, and analyzing results in rapid cycles lasting two to four weeks. To create these assessments, teachers were expected to draw upon a variety of resources, including their curriculum materials, test item banks from textbook publishers, and released state test items. One challenge, then, was to demonstrate to the district that it was still possible to make "data-based decisions" using assessments designed using a learning progression framework. A second challenge was to make the case to teachers that this framework could help them to teach and assess the content of the NGSS more effectively and efficiently. We suspect that our district's context would be familiar to most researchers who engage with teachers around issues of classroom assessment.

Two other aspects of national and local context informed our work. First, in 2012, the National Research Council released the report *A Framework for K-12 Science Education*, and a year later a collaboration between the National Science Teachers Association and the American Association for the Advancement of Science, facilitated by the organization Achieve, Inc., led to the release of the Next Generation Science Standards (NGSS). A defining feature of the NGSS relative to previous approaches such as the National Science Education Standards or the Benchmarks for Scientific Literacy is the view that the teaching and learning of science should be conceptualized as an interwoven three-dimensional enterprise in which students generate, or are presented with, a real-world phenomenon and then use some combination of disciplinary core ideas (DCIs), scientific and engineering practices (SEPs), and crosscutting concepts (CCCs) to make sense of it. At the start of our project, Colorado had just adopted the NGSS, and the district was just beginning to grapple with the implications of this for its curriculum, instruction, and assessment structures and activities.

A second salient aspect of our context was that our partner district uses a "physics-first" curricular sequence, in which physics is taught to ninth grade students, chemistry to tenth grade students, and biology to eleventh grade students. The physics-first structure to the science curriculum, which is contrasted with the traditional sequence of biology-physics-chemistry, is intended to help students establish a foundation in core physical concepts such as energy and force, and then use these concepts to facilitate subsequent learning about chemical reactions and molecules, all of which are the foundations of modern biology (Popkin, 2009). An implicit premise here is the notion that one should revisit student understandings of certain core concepts even as they cross disciplinary boundaries, and this echoes a premise of the NGSS. In this sense, adopting the NGSS helped the district make their implicit premise an explicit hypothesis. The desire to find a scientific concept that would be central to all three discipline-specific courses was a key reason that we chose to develop a learning progression around energy. In the next section, we explain how we went about this development.

Development of a Learning Progression for the Modeling of Energy Flows

This section describes our development of a learning progression for the modeling of energy flows. We show how prior research on energy as a learning progression and how energy is treated in the NGSS lead to a learning progression for modeling energy flows in high school.

Prior Research on Energy as a Learning Progression

The law of energy conservation is deceptively simple, requiring that initial energy is equal to final energy in any isolated system. The implications of this law are tremendously useful to scientific investigations of both natural and human-generated phenomena, since it introduces a fixed constraint. Whenever the energy of a system increases, we know that the additional energy had to have come from some other source outside the system. Whenever the energy in a system decreases, we know that the lost energy must have gone to some other system. At the same time, as a scientific concept the term "energy" is vague and abstract, as much a label that gets attached to a process as it is a specific thing that is tangible and observable at some fixed moment in time. The physicist Richard Feynman famously remarked, "It is important to realize that in physics today, we have no knowledge what energy is" (Feynman, Leighton & Sands, 1989, section 4-1).

To really understand what energy is and how it comes to be requires, among other things, an understanding of the particulate nature of matter, an understanding of force and the relationship between force and potential energy, an understanding of electric and magnetic fields, chemical reactions among molecules, and an understanding of the concept of a system (Chen et al., 2014; Nordine, 2016). Because of this, when children begin to receive formal instruction about energy, they come to understand it almost exclusively by where it comes from and what it does, leaving the lingering question of what it *is* to sit in a black box, to be revisited at some later date. At the same time, children enter school settings having already developed intuitive understandings about where energy comes from (e.g., the sun, a battery, food) and what it does (e.g., makes things move and grow). As Nordine (2016) points out, students are likely to perceive some cognitive dissonance when they first encounter the law of energy conservation, because it is likely to conflict with a previously established mental model that conceives of energy as a thing that gets acquired, used up, and reacquired. Because this mental model may well predict many observable phenomena with reasonable accuracy, teachers are faced with the challenge of helping students integrate this flawed (but useful) model with a more complex and seemingly counterintuitive account.

One approach to meeting this challenge is to conceptualize the understanding of energy as a learning progression, defined with respect to some combination of four interrelated big ideas (Herrmann-Abell & DeBoer, 2018; Neumann, Viering, Boone, & Fischer, 2013; Nordine, 2016):

1. Energy comes in different forms and manifestations.
2. Energy can be transformed from one form to another or transferred from one object to another.
3. Energy is conserved. It is never destroyed—only transformed or transferred.
4. Energy is degraded or dissipated in all macroscopic processes.

In one of the earliest studies to adopt this perspective and examine it empirically, Liu and McKeough (2005) conducted a secondary analysis of TIMMS multiple-choice items written to assess students' understanding of energy. Liu and McKeough coded these energy items to correspond to one of the four big ideas listed above, and subsequently found that comparisons among the items with respect to their difficulty for students to answer them correctly supported the hypothesis that the ideas had some hierarchical structure: items related to the identification of energy forms tended to be easier to solve than items related to energy transformation and transfer, which in turn tended to be easier to solve than items related to energy conservation and dissipation. The core findings from this study were subsequently replicated in follow-up studies involving performance assessments (Liu & Collard, 2005) and constructed-response items (Lee & Liu, 2010).

Neumann et al. (2013) built upon these results to develop a more elaborated learning progression that they sought to validate as part of a prospective study. A partial order was hypothesized to exist across the four big ideas about energy, along with a hierarchical order *within* each of the four big ideas. The "within big idea" order was to be related to the degree of scaffolding (in the form of hints) that a student would need to correctly solve a selected-response item. The results from this study showed mixed support for the hypothesized partial order between the big ideas. While items associated with the identification of energy forms tended to be easiest for students to solve, and items associated with energy conservation tended to be hardest, there was no significant difference between items associated with energy transfer and transformation and those associated with energy dissipation. Beyond this, Neumann et al. (2013) found no evidence of hierarchies within the big idea items associated with scaffolding (though this may have been due to acknowledged confounds in their item design and administration).

The results from these early studies, and others that followed by Herrmann-Abell and DeBoer (2018) and Park and Liu (2016) were, perhaps not surprisingly, inconclusive, but they can be characterized as groundbreaking in the sense that they represented early, exploratory attempts to connect the design of student assessments to Piagetian or neo-Piagetian theories of how students become more sophisticated in their understanding of energy. To a great extent, these studies raised more questions than they answered about both the nature of a learning progression that could (or should) be posited for energy, the nature of the assessments that should be used to test the learning progression, and the nature of the evidence one would expect to find in order to validate—or invalidate—the learning progression. An important limitation of these early efforts is that they do not situate the assessment of a student's location on the learning progression within any particular context for curriculum and instruction. Neither was there any theory of action for how teachers could use the information from these assessments for formative or summative purposes. Instead, the assessment efforts were exclusively focused on high-level theory validation.

Energy in the Next Generation Science Standards

Energy is the only concept in the NGSS that is named as both a disciplinary core idea (DCI) and a crosscutting concept (CCC). That is, on the one hand, energy is one of four major DCIs situated within the physical sciences, and the NGSS sketches out a rough learning progression for American students from kindergarten through high school in terms of four smaller grain ideas about energy, depicted in the rows of Table 8.1 labeled PS3.A, PS3.B, PS3.C, and PS3.D. On the other hand, the NGSS casts energy (together with matter) as one of seven CCCs that can play a role in understanding phenomena related to DCIs across not only physical science, but also across earth and space science and life science. The NGSS's suggested progression of energy and matter across grade bands is depicted in the last row of Table 8.1.

Table 8.1 NGSS progressions of energy concepts across grade bands

	K–2	3–5	6–8	9–12
Energy as a DCI				
PS3.A Definitions of energy PS3.B Conservation of energy and energy transfer	N/A Sunlight warms earth's surface.	Moving objects contain energy. The faster the object moves, the more energy it has. Energy can be moved from place to place by moving objects, or through sound, light, or electrical currents. Energy can be converted from one form to another form.	Kinetic energy can be distinguished from the various forms of potential energy. Energy changes to and from each type can be tracked through physical or chemical interactions. The relationship between the temperature and the total energy of a system depends on the types, states, and amounts of matter.	The total energy within a system is conserved. Energy transfer within and between systems can be described and predicted in terms of energy associated with the motion or configuration of particles (objects). Systems move toward stable states.
PS3.C Relationship between energy and forces	Bigger pushes and pulls cause bigger changes in an object's motion or shape. Sunlight warms earth's surface.	When objects collide, contact forces transfer energy so as to change the objects' motions.	When two objects interact, each one exerts a force on the other, and these forces can transfer energy between them.	Fields contain energy that depends on the arrangement of the objects in the field.
PS3.D Energy in chemical processes and everyday life		Energy can be "produced," "used," or "released" by converting stored energy. Plants capture energy from sunlight, which can later be used as fuel or food.	Sunlight is captured by plants and used in a reaction to produce sugar molecules, which can be reversed by burning those molecules to release energy.	Photosynthesis is the primary biological means of capturing radiation from the sun; energy cannot be destroyed, it can be converted to less useful forms.
Energy as a CC Energy and matter	Observe objects may break into smaller pieces, be put together into larger pieces, or change shapes.	Matter is made of particles and energy can be transferred in various ways and between objects. Students observe the conservation of matter by tracking matter flows and cycles before and after processes and recognizing the total weight of substances does not change.	Matter is conserved because atoms are conserved in physical and chemical processes. They also learn within a natural or designed system, the transfer of energy drives the motion and/or cycling of matter. Energy may take different forms (e.g. energy in fields, thermal energy, energy of motion). The transfer of energy can be tracked as energy flows through a designed or natural system.	The total amount of energy and matter in closed systems is conserved. They can describe changes of energy and matter in a system in terms of energy and matter flows into, out of, and within that system. They also learn that energy cannot be created or destroyed. It only moves between one place and another place, between objects and/or fields, or between systems. Energy drives the cycling of matter within and between systems. In nuclear processes, atoms are not conserved, but the total number of protons plus neutrons is conserved.

The NGSS were written to support a laudable vision for K-12 science instruction, one that calls for students to actively engage in the practices of scientists to answer puzzling questions about the world around them. Rather than promoting the view that science is constituted by a set of facts and procedures that need to be memorized, the NGSS were designed to promote the goal of students graduating from high school with both a curiosity about the world around them and the ability to use a small set of core ideas and practices about science that they have begun to master to investigate and understand novel phenomena. Few would argue that these are not worthwhile ambitions.

At the same time, the "three-dimensional" structure of the NGSS presents a significant challenge to student assessment, and a little bit of arithmetic can illustrate the issue at hand. If making sense of a phenomenon always involves some combination of one or more interrelated DCIs, SEPs, and CCCs, then prospectively, if we simply count up all the unique DCIs at the smallest available grain size (44) and cross them by unique SEPs (8) and CCCs (7), there are a total 2,464 combinations that might, in theory, be brought to the table to characterize the means by which a student makes sense of any given phenomenon. The proper construct for assessment, and the grain size of the construct, thus becomes an open question. Is it the ability of a student to understand and explain a specific phenomenon? Is it some underlying DCI abstracted from a motivating phenomenon but specific to a subset of SEPs or CCCs? Is it some underlying DCI generalized across all SEPs or CCCs? In an attempt to mitigate this issue, the NGSS specifies *performance expectations*, organized by grade band and discipline, that represent a purposeful crossing of some subset of DCIs, SEPs, and CCCs. Still, the number of unique performance expectations remain daunting from an assessment perspective. In grades K–2, there are 33 unique performance expectations; in grades 3–5, there are 45; in middle school, there are 59; and in high school, there are 72. And since each performance expectation comes with a detailed set of evidence standards that stipulate what a student should know and be able to do to demonstrate mastery, the design and administration of an assessment for just one performance expectation is likely to be a time-intensive activity.

To the extent that teachers wish to assess their students for the purpose of gaining insights about their learning within the course of a semester or academic school year, the NGSS, if viewed in isolation, are unlikely to be sufficient. As argued at the outset of this chapter, when there is a desire to use student assessments to gain insights about learning, it helps to have a learning theory in mind. Although the NGSS does provide some learning progression markers for each DCI, SEP, and CCC dimension across grade bands, the dimensions have not been integrated and there is no hypothesis available for what a progression might look like *within* a grade or course. In some sense, then, each NGSS performance expectation could be cast as the "upper anchor" of a within- or across-grade learning progression, with the trajectory that leads to this upper anchor left unspecified. For example, in high school, there are 14 unique performance expectations that include energy and matter as a CCC, nine unique performance expectations that include energy as a DCI, and just one that includes energy as *both* a CCC and a DCI. Each of these 24 performance expectations could, in principle, be the basis for a learning progression related to the understanding of energy within and across the high school grades.

A Learning Progression for Modeling Energy Flows in High School

The learning progression (LP) we developed builds upon consensus positions (e.g., NGSS) and the extant research literature in science education (Herrmann-Abell & DeBoer, 2018; Neumann et al., 2013), but also breaks new ground. Our proposed LP maintains a link to the big ideas about energy that have been the basis for previous large-scale investigations. That is, we posit that student conceptions of energy are some function of these big ideas, and that some of the big ideas are easier to grasp and interrelate than others. For example, students are likely to be able to identify different forms of energy that they encounter when presented with canonical cycles in the natural world (i.e., the rock cycle, the water cycle, the carbon cycle), or with the motion of an object or objects in a closed system (i.e., the swinging of a pendulum). Following Herrmann-Abell and DeBoer (2018), we distinguish between five main types of energy forms: kinetic energy, gravitational potential energy, thermal energy, elastic potential energy, and chemical energy. Prior to high school, we can expect that students have previously come into contact with these different labels and hence can recognize that energy comes in multiple forms. Forms of energy go hand in hand with the transformation and transfer of energy. For example, when a student sees a pendulum swinging, the reason a student identifies different forms of energy is the recognition that energy is changing as the pendulum swings. Being able to *connect* ideas about energy forms, transformation and transfer, and the law of energy conservation represents an important conceptual demarcation, one that hinges upon the ability to recognize and distinguish between a *system* and its *surroundings*. Another important demarcation is an understanding of the *mechanism* through which energy is transferred and how this can lead to dissipation or degradation. These would include transfer by conduction, convection, radiation, forces, electricity, or sound.

Distinctions among levels of our LP depend upon the ability of a student to *develop and use a model* that interrelates the big ideas about energy for the purpose of explaining and predicting a *phenomenon*, where we define a phenomenon as an observable event or state that can be explained or predicted through scientific investigation. In including the scientific and engineering practice of developing and using models in our LP for energy, we draw upon a recent revision by Pierson, Clark, and Sherard (2017) to a well-known LP for modeling in science first developed by Schwarz et al. (2009). This modeling LP was defined with respect to five different categories, with each category further delineated with respect to a hierarchy of discrete levels. We pull from the "mechanistic-generative" category which distinguishes between models that:

- describe only (lowest level);
- illustrate patterns;
- represent a mechanism to explain a predicted phenomenon; and
- predict and generate questions about possible new phenomena (highest level).

The center column in Table 8.2 depicts the five levels of our modeling energy flows LP,[2] with the lowest entry level at the bottom and the highest level at the top. Each level represents differences in the sophistication of a model a student could develop and/or use to make sense of a phenomenon of interest in terms of the flows of energy into, within, and out of the system. Implicit is the scenario in which a student is presented with a phenomenon in the physical world that can be linked to a specific DCI, but the generic progression as specified here is, at this point, agnostic about the specific nature of the phenomenon and its associated DCI that would be required to illustrate the mechanism of energy transfer or transformation. What *is* assumed is that the student is receiving instruction and practice in using what Lacy, Tobin, Wiser, and Crissman (2014) refer to as an "energy lens" when thinking about the phenomenon at hand. Taking an energy lens means that before developing and/or using a model to make sense of a phenomenon, students get used to asking themselves the following questions:

- What is the system of interest?
- What observable or measurable changes or other interesting behaviors are taking place?
- Where in the system are energy changes occurring?
- Where does the energy come from?
- Where does the energy go to?
- What is the evidence for our answers?

Table 8.2 A learning progression for modeling energy flows in systems

Level	Description	Key Indicators
5: Modeling energy flows for generalizing and predicting	• Students are able to *generalize their model* to unknown or multiple phenomena, and can *explain limitations of applying the model* to a new *phenomenon*.	• Multiple phenomena or predictable changes within given phenomenon. • Limitations to generalization in scope or intensity.
4: Modeling energy flows, including the mechanisms by which energy is stored or changed, to account for changes in a phenomenon	• Students *develop a model* that illustrates a *mechanism* that can explain or predict the *phenomenon*, and *use* the model to make predictions about how changing one part of the model would influence energy flows elsewhere in the *system*. • Students can explain how the total energy of the *system* constrains the magnitude of change possible. • Students can *describe limitations of the model* in explaining or predicting the phenomenon.	• Multiple scales within model (zoom out or zoom in). • Kinetic energy represented as molecular motion. • Potential energy represented as stored in fields within a system. • Radiation represented as particles or waves. • Describes how the total energy constrains the system in some way, either by requiring energy into the system, loss due to degradation/dissipation, or limits to the amount of change possible.
3: Modeling energy flows to account for changes in a phenomenon	• Students *use* or *develop* a model that relates changes in the phenomenon directly to changes in energy through transfers/transformations by identifying specific *indicators*. • Students begin to show evidence that their model is accounting for conservation and dissipation. • Model includes energy flows into, within, and out of the *system*.	• Explicitly relate changes in energy to changes in phenomenon. • Transfers into and/or out of the system.
2: Modeling energy flows to illustrate the pattern of energy flow	• Students *use* or *develop* a model to illustrate a relationship or pattern between the increase in one form of energy and the decrease in another form, or the transfer of energy from one location or object to another. • Students identify the most relevant components and relationships in the model *and* distinguish between the *system and surroundings*. • Model focuses on energy flows within the *system* only.	• Transfers start in an object and end in another object. • Transformations start in one form and end in another form. • System and surroundings clearly identified and justifiable.
1: Using models as literal representations	• Students *use* or *develop* a model that shows, through drawings or labels, the components involved in a *phenomenon*, and some (but not necessarily all) relevant energy forms, transfers, or transformations.	• Literal components. • Energy forms labeled. • Energy transfers may not start or end in an object. • No clear source for transformations (energy created or destroyed).

Phenomenon: An observable event or state that can be explained or predicted through scientific investigation.

System and surroundings: The system includes the part of the universe under investigation and the surroundings include everything outside of the investigation. A system is an organized group of related objects or components that form a whole. Systems can consist, for example, of organisms, machines, fundamental particles, galaxies, ideas, and numbers.

Indicator: How changes in energy are manifested. These are the observable differences in a phenomenon (e.g., when an object speeds up or slows down) that let students know there is a transfer or transformation of energy.

Mechanism: The entities and activities that produce the changes in energy flow (e.g., changes in kinetic energy can best be explained through particle motion).

And to these questions we might add, for high school students, what are the limitations of the evidence we have available? Though Lacy et al. (2014) frame the questions that accompany an energy lens as an activity for students in elementary school grades, the same habits of mind surely apply to developing a good model of an energy flow in high school and beyond.

Returning to the learning progression in Table 8.2, we focus on the critical distinctions between each level. At level 1, a student can develop a model to answer some of the above questions but will generally only be able to do so by showing or identifying physical components of a phenomenon, specific energy forms, or transformations motivated by a change they have observed. The key change at level 2 of the progression is the ability to identify and distinguish the appropriate system and surrounding, and to show that there is a relationship between the increase in one form of energy and the decrease in another form. At this level, students can use their model to show patterns that are suggestive of energy sources and destinations, even if they remain hazy about the evidence that connects one to the other. At level 3, a student can develop a model that shows the total energy of the system is conserved either by accounting for all transfers or transformations within the system or by dissipation out of the system. At level 4, a student can develop a model to illustrate a mechanism that can explain and predict the phenomena in question in terms of a transfer of energy. It is at this level that the student is able to use the law of energy conservation as a constraint on the system, explain the role of energy in a given phenomenon through an interaction between all the big ideas of energy, and describe limitations of the model. Finally, at level 5, a student is able to generalize the model to other phenomena beyond that which spurred the need for a model, and to recognize limitations in the model with this novel purpose in mind.

With respect to the structure of the NGSS, the LP above weaves together many of the different dimensions that are used to characterize the core ideas and concepts of science. It clearly combines the idea of energy and matter as a CCC with designing and using models as an SEP. But it also incorporates aspects of others CCCs and SEPs. To be at levels 3–5 of the LP will typically require some students to rely on practices related to modeling, practices that include analyzing and interpreting data, using mathematical and computational thinking, constructing explanations, and engaging in argument from evidence. Similarly, progress up the levels will typically invoke other crosscutting concepts, most notably patterns, cause and effect, scale, systems, and stability and change. The LP is not meant to be applied to *all* DCIs, only those that have been flagged by the NGSS as belonging within a performance expectation that includes some combination of energy and matter as a CCC, modeling as an SEP, and any of the four energy-specific DCIs. In the next section, we show how this is used to constrain the content domain to which the LP can be applied while also mapping to units of our participating school district's curriculum.

We conclude this section by pointing out that the modeling of energy flows LP is intended to be used to support the development of assessments for a mixture of formative and summative purposes both within a particular grade and course in high school, and across courses in high school. A general hypothesis of this LP is that when it comes to modeling energy flows, the order of the five levels of sophistication remain the same, irrespective of the scientific discipline of a high school course. This does not, however, imply an assumption that the progress across levels will be linear, or that it does not depend upon the course sequence. A linear progression would imply that once a student has demonstrated an ability to model the energy flow for some sample of phenomena by the end of a ninth grade course at level 4, they will be able to do so at level 4 or 5 in their tenth grade course. This would be possible but seems unlikely. More plausibly, practice with modeling energy flows in one disciplinary context should make it easier to do so in the next disciplinary context. When students follow a physics-first curriculum, one can track the implied longitudinal progression associated with modeling energy flows of phenomena from a physical science perspective (courses in physics and chemistry), followed by life science perspective (course in biology). This is probably the ideal curricular sequence for the modeling of energy learning progression, because physics and chemistry give students the tools to model the mechanisms behind energy transfers at the particulate level, and this can then be gainfully applied to biological phenomena.

Mapping the Learning Progression to Standards and Curricular Units of Instruction

To be relevant and useful as basis for either formative or summative assessment, an LP must not only align with, but also help to bolster, the instructional activities that are part of planned curricular units, and teachers must be able to see that. Although teachers in most school districts are often given considerable flexibility with respect to the structure of these units and their timing, they are expected to demonstrate that the units have been linked to the district's content standards for science. In this context, those standards are the performance expectations of the NGSS. Our goals were to show teachers the connections between the modeling energy flows LP and the NGSS performance expectations, and to use this link to show teachers how the LP (and its associated assessment tasks) can be used to make connections across units that might not have been visible otherwise.

We established a manageable domain for this learning progression by filtering the performance expectations for grades 9–12 to include, with one exception, only those that include the SEP of modeling and either the CCC of energy and matter or one of the four DCIs associated with energy.[3] This resulted in a total of 11 unique performance expectations that could, in principle, be matched to the disciplinary focus of high school courses of physics (4), chemistry (3), and biology (4). We chose two performance expectations per discipline as a basis for focal curricular units and associated student assessments, and these are listed in Table 8.3. Each of these performance expectations can be readily associated with the modeling of energy flows for a given phenomenon, but they can differ with respect to the DCIs a student would encounter in coming to a sophisticated understanding of the mechanism behind energy transfer.

Each of the performance expectations in Table 8.3 is related to the modeling energy flows LP in the following way: mastery of any of the performance expectations can always be associated with level 4 of the LP. More specifically, every performance expectation can be fleshed

Table 8.3 Map of performance expectations and unique DCIs relevant to assessments of modeling energy flows LP in high school

Course	Performance Expectation	Associated DCIs and Unique CCs
Physics (ninth grade)	HS-PS3-2 Energy Develop and use models to illustrate that energy at the macroscopic scale can be accounted for as a combination of energy associated with the motions of particles (objects) and energy associated with the relative positions of particles (objects).	PS3.A Definitions of Energy
Physics (ninth grade)	HS-ESS2-3 Earth's Systems Develop a model based on evidence of earth's interior to describe the cycling of matter by thermal convection.	ESS2.A Earth Materials and Systems ESS2.B Plate Tectonics and Large-Scale Interactions PS4.A Wave Properties
Chemistry (tenth grade)	HS-PS1-4 Matter and Its Interactions Develop a model to illustrate that the release or absorption of energy from a chemical reaction system depends upon the changes in total bond energy.	PS1.A Structure and Properties of Matter PS1.B Chemical Reactions

Chemistry (tenth grade)	HS-PS3-4 Energy Plan and conduct an investigation to provide evidence that the transfer of thermal energy when two components of different temperature are combined within a closed system results in a more uniform energy distribution among the components in the system (second law of thermodynamics).	PS3.B Conservation of Energy and Energy Transfer PS3.D Energy and Chemical Processes CC Systems and System Models
Biology (eleventh grade)	HS-LS1-7 From Molecules to Organisms: Structures and Processes Use a model to illustrate that cellular respiration is a chemical process whereby the bonds of food molecules and oxygen molecules are broken and the bonds in new compounds are formed resulting in a net transfer of energy.	LS1.C Organization for Matter and Energy Flow in Organisms
Biology (eleventh grade)	HS-LS2-5 Ecosystems: Interactions, Energy, and Dynamics Develop a model to illustrate the role of photosynthesis and cellular respiration in the cycling of carbon among the biosphere, atmosphere, hydrosphere, and geosphere.	LS2.B Cycles of Matter and Energy Transfer in Ecosystems PS3.D Energy in Chemical Processes CC Systems and System Models

out into a DCI-specific LP with levels that characterize a student's most likely pathway to an understanding of energy flows that demonstrates an integration of the four big ideas about energy. Our conjecture is that, with respect to the ability of students to model energy flows, these levels would track with the ones specified in our general LP (see Table 8.2). A great advantage of this perspective, if it can be validated, is that it lends greater coherence across NGSS performance expectations and associated curricular units by emphasizing the way that energy is a concept that cuts across them, and how models can be used as a tool for sense-making and explanation.

Designing a System of Assessments

Because the modeling energy flows LP has a three-dimensional structure, in keeping with the ethos of the NGSS, building a system of assessments aligned to it is challenging. In 2014, the National Research Council released the report *Developing Assessments for the Next Generation of Science Standards*, and one of its principal conclusions underscores this challenge:

> Measuring the learning described in the NGSS will require assessments that are significantly different from those in current use. Specifically, the tasks designed to assess performance expectations in the NGSS will need to have the following characteristics:
>
> 1. Include multiple components that reflect the connected use of different scientific practices in the context of interconnected disciplinary ideas and cross-cutting concepts;
> 2. Address the progressive nature of learning by providing information about where students fall on a continuum between expected beginning and ending points in a given unit or grade; and
> 3. Include an interpretive system for evaluating a range of student products that are specific enough to be useful for helping teachers understand the range of student responses and provide tools for helping teachers decide on next steps in instruction.
>
> (NRC, 2014, p. 3)

The necessary features of assessment tasks described in *Developing Assessments for the Next Generation* make clear the desirability of building a system of embedded assessment opportunities, wherein assessments are included at multiple junctures within a given curricular unit as part of planned classroom activities that promote learning. The assessment tasks themselves would be expected to vary with respect to their format, their duration, and their use. To this end, we envisioned and developed three types of assessment tasks: performance-based tasks and labs, phenomenon-based item clusters, and conceptually oriented multiple-choice items.

Performance-Based Tasks and Labs

Performance-based tasks are most closely aligned with the vision for science assessment sketched out by the National Research Council. These tasks are always premised on a motivating question or scenario that presents students with a real-world phenomenon and then poses questions about the phenomenon that ideally should lead students to invoke the three dimensions of disciplinary core ideas, crosscutting concepts, and scientific practices in their answers. Figure 8.1 provides an example of a performance-based task we developed to elicit evidence about students' ability to model energy flows across multiple disciplinary contexts. The task is premised on a scenario in which students are asked, "How can corn provide energy to power a bus?" They are informed that corn is grown for many purposes, not just for food; it can also be made into fuel. Next, they are asked to develop a diagrammatic model that traces energy as it flows from the sun to the corn, is processed into ethanol, and then flows from ethanol to the movement of the bus. Finally, they are asked to use the model to explain how energy flows through these systems, including all energy inputs, outputs, transfer, and transformations (for more details on the development of this task, see Furtak, Binder, & Henson, 2018).

The task has some notable characteristics. It includes three different stages that could correspond to distinct system models, and in each one a flow of energy could be depicted with respect to different transfers and transformations. At the same time, the mechanisms by which these energy transformations and transfers take place would potentially require a student to invoke DCIs specific to physics, chemistry, and biology. One could argue that the ability to fully complete a task such as this would represent an ideal end goal for a student after three years of instruction in physics, chemistry, and biology, provided that the instruction was able to consistently emphasize the role of energy as a crosscutting concept and the role of modeling as a practice that can be used to depict and understand energy flows. In this kind of idealized scenario, we would still expect to see considerable variability in the sophistication of student responses, and these responses would be scorable with respect to the levels of the modeling energy flows LP previously depicted in Table 8.2.

A problem that we soon discovered when piloting this task with high school students in physics and biology courses as a stand-alone assessment was that very few students were able to engage with it in the way that we had intended. One reason for this was because it provides minimal scaffolding or points of entry for students who are just developing their understandings about energy flows and how to describe them with a model. As a classroom assessment, a task such as this works best in the context of an activity that could incorporated into a project or lab-based investigation that could span multiple days of class time.

An example of this that can serve as a template is provided by Eisenkraft (2016) with the "cheese puff lab." The motivation for the activity is showing students the food label with the nutrition facts about a bag of cheese puffs and then asking them to speculate about how the number of calories associated with a single cheese puff is determined. How do calories

Corn is grown for many purposes, not just for food; it can also be made into fuel.

How can corn provide energy to power a bus?

Draw and label arrows to trace energy as it is transferred and transformed from the **sun to corn** and, after the corn is processed into ethanol, from the **ethanol to the moving bus.**

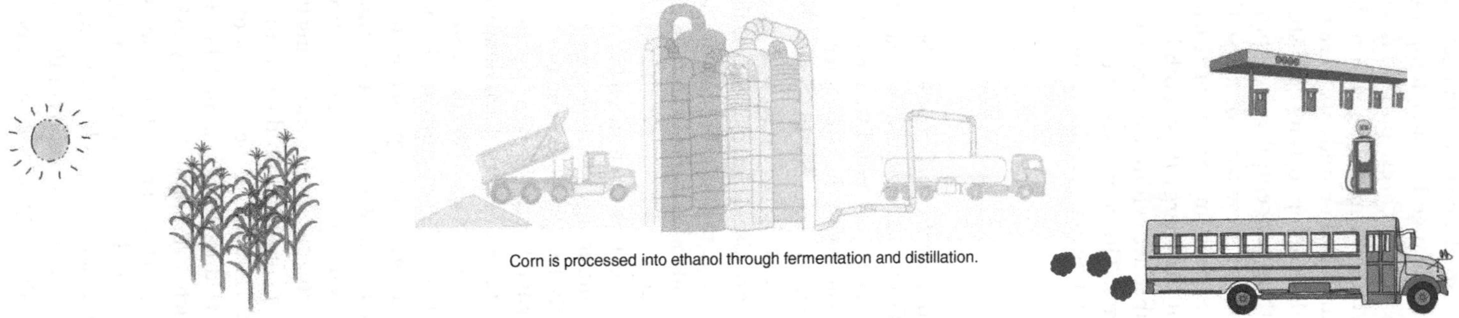

Corn is processed into ethanol through fermentation and distillation.

Explain how energy flows through these systems including all energy inputs, outputs, transfers and transformations.

Figure 8.1 Biofuels Performance-based Task

provide a representation of energy content? From there, students participate in a lab in which they are asked to attach a cheese puff to a small apparatus that sits below a container of water, light it on fire, and then measure the change in water temperature before and after the cheese puff has finished burning. Eisenkraft's cheese puff lab is a great example of a phenomenon that could be readily connected to the modeling energy flows LP, because it invokes multiple DCIs that would be relevant whether students were taking a course in physics, chemistry, or biology, because it provides an opportunity for students to practice model development, and because the crosscutting concept of energy provides the critical framing for answering the motivating question. In these sorts of lab settings, assessment is still at the center of the activity in that it remains important for teachers to elicit and attend to the differences in student ideas about the energy flows both before and after the central lab activities. But the assessment is embedded within the larger lab activity, which could (and probably should) span multiple days. The responses students give to targeted questions about the data they have collected can become the basis for *student-work focus sessions* (described later).

Phenomenon-Based Item Clusters

Phenomenon-based item clusters (PBICs) are similar to the performance-based tasks described above in that they are also associated with a specific motivating question related to some observable phenomenon, but they are broken into a sequence of items intended to provide students with scaffolding so they are better equipped to engage with the phenomenon even if they only have a limited understanding of the underlying energy concepts. In a sense, they are intended to mimic an interaction with a teacher who is able to help the students see and make connections between the phenomenon and disciplinary core ideas related to energy flows. These ideas can be brought to the fore by helping students engage the task through the development and use of a model of energy flow, so item clusters are intended to provide students with the information and prompts necessary to set this in motion.

All PBICs are based on a common design template[4] that can be used to create an assessment for any of the six PE-specific versions of the modeling energy LP shown previously in Table 8.3. Figures 8.2 and 8.3 provide two examples of a motivating phenomenon, one that invokes a DCI specific to biology (LS1.C Organization for Matter and Energy Flow in Organisms) and one that invokes a DCI specific to physics (PS3.A Definitions of Energy).[5] Each figure also includes the next two items that follow the opening scenario as students are asked to identify and distinguish between the system and surroundings. Not depicted in these figures are the next four items in the PBIC in which students are asked to identify the forms of energy in the phenomenon and to characterize the patterns that suggest energy is being transferred or transformed. The opening six items of each PBIC, which ask for selected responses from the student, probe the extent to which the student understands the mechanism of energy transfer underlying this scenario and can use the law of the conservation of energy as a constraint on the system. These are items that help make distinctions primarily between levels 1 and 2 of the LP. In addition, these items provide students with the vocabulary they will need to develop a model of the energy flow. The culmination of each PBIC are three constructed-response items that ask the student to: (1) draw a model that shows the phenomenon (e.g., "Draw a model that shows how an energy bar provides a runner with energy to move"); (2) describe in words how energy is being transferred or transformed (e.g., "Use your model to describe in words how the energy bar provides a runner with energy to move"); and (3) characterize the limitations of the model as a way of explaining the phenomenon. These are the items that help to distinguish between levels 2–4 of the LP.

How does an energy bar help a runner move?

Olivia runs on her high school's track and field team. Her coach suggests that she eat a glucose energy bar before her last race to help her when she is tired. Olivia asks her coach how glucose will help her run. To help explain the science to her, Olivia's coach has asked you for help.

In biology, a **system** is the part of the world that is under investigation and the **surroundings** are anything outside of the investigation. Circle the best answer.

1. Which of the following is part of the *system* where the cellular respiration reaction occurs?

   (a) air outside Olivia's body only   (b) glucose only
   (c) Olivia's cells and O_2 in the cells only   (d) glucose, Olivia's cells, and O_2 in the cells

2. Which of the following is part of the *surroundings*?

   (a) air outside Olivia's body only   (b) glucose only
   (c) Olivia's cells and O_2 in the cells only   (d) glucose, Olivia's cells, and O_2 in the cells

Figure 8.2 Scenario and first two items from a phenomenon-based item cluster in biology

Where does a skydiver's energy to break the sound barrier come from?

Stuntman Felix Baumgartner holds the world record for the fastest speed achieved by a human without an engine. He broke the sound barrier and reached a top speed of 377 m/s. He used a balloon to fly approximately 39,000 m above earth, and, wearing a special suit, jumped down.

In physics, a **system** is the part of the world that is under investigation and the **surroundings** are anything outside of the investigation. Circle the best answer.

1. Which of the following is included in the *system* where Felix gets energy to fall?

   (a) the air around Felix's body only   (b) Felix's body only
   (c) the earth only   (d) Felix's body and the earth

2. Which of the following is part of the *surroundings*?

   (a) the air around Felix's body only   (b) Felix's body only
   (c) the earth only   (d) Felix's body and the earth

Figure 8.3 Scenario and first two items from a phenomenon-based item cluster in physics

Conceptually Oriented Multiple-Choice Items

The last type of items that comprise our assessment system are multiple-choice (MC) items that focus on students' conceptual knowledge. Here, we generally pull from preexisting items with a focus on DCIs in the physical sciences. Many of these are described in the published studies by Herrmann-Abell and DeBoer (2018), Neumann et al. (2013), and Park and Liu (2016). Some of these items are publicly available from a website maintained by the American Association for the Advancement of Science (AAAS).[6] We also use or adapt multiple-choice items for chemistry from Jim Minstrell's diagnoser assessment system (Thissen-Roe, Hunt, & Minstrell, 2004). On the one hand, these items are more limited in the depth of information they can elicit about the ability of

---

Jody left a half-filled glass of sweet (sugar added) tea with ice on her dresser for two days. The ice has melted and the tea is now at room temperature. If you could look inside the glass and see the molecules of sugar, tea, and water, what would you see?

A. The sugar, tea, and water molecules are motionless. There is no movement or change at this point.
B. The sugar, tea, and water molecules are in constant, random motion, even though the ice has entirely melted.
C. The water, tea, and sugar molecules are reacting with each other, and will eventually form a new substance.

Figure 8.4 Example of a conceptually oriented multiple-choice item

students to develop and use models to describe and explain energy flows in the three-dimensional manner envisioned by the NGSS. However, they can provide very relevant information about students' understandings of DCIs and sometimes certain SEPs and CCCs. In addition, in some cases, the distractors (incorrect answer options) have been written to reflect common student misconceptions, so there may be more diagnostic information that can be gleaned beyond whether the student got the item correct or not (cf. Briggs, Alonzo, Schwab, & Wilson, 2006). Finally, they are easy to score, and with respect to the AAAS items there is normative information available to compare the frequency distribution of students in a given classroom to a national sample of students in at least the same age range. An example of a conceptually oriented MC item, taken from the diagnoser assessment system, is depicted in Figure 8.4.

Creating Assessment Events for Different Uses

The three assessment formats described above—performance-based tasks and labs, PBICs, and conceptually oriented MC items—are the raw ingredients that comprise a system of embedded assessments. In this system, different assessment events could be used in support of different purposes. The NRC panel responsible for the report *Developing Assessments for the Next Generation Science Standards* makes the distinction between a *classroom assessment* and an *assessment for monitoring*. A classroom assessment is one that is selected by teachers and typically given to students at the culmination of a curriculum activity or unit. Two defining features are its timing (within or immediately following related instructional topics) and who controls it (teachers). In contrast to a classroom assessment, an assessment for monitoring is one that has typically not been developed by a teacher who is being asked to administer it and is less likely to be as closely related to the curriculum and instruction that immediately preceded its administration. Two defining features of an assessment for monitoring are its standardization and reliability. Although both classroom assessments and assessments for monitoring *can* be used for formative and summative purposes, on balance classroom assessments are better suited for formative use, and assessments for monitoring are better suited for summative use. In our ideal vision of an embedded assessment system, a learning progression provides a framework that promotes coherence between the two different types of assessment events. That is, whether an assessment is given for formative purposes with the timing and content at the local discretion of a classroom teacher or given for summative purposes with the timing and content at the discretion of a school district or state, the assessment should be written to provide insights about student conceptions relative to the theory of learning embodied by the learning progression. To the extent that performance-based tasks and labs, PBICs, and conceptually oriented MC items have all been designed to elicit this information, any one of these assessment formats, or a mixture of them, could be used for either classroom assessment or assessment for monitoring. However, as we discuss later, the evidence needed to validate an assessment created for these different uses is likely to differ.

Professional Development and Teacher Ownership

In this section, we describe the professional development we provided to help teachers use the embedded assessment. We describe how teachers used the formative assessment design cycle and how they conducted student-work focus sessions.

Formative Assessment Design Cycle

The LP, its connection to curricular units, and a system of assessment tasks are the key ingredients that support working collaboratively with teachers in their PLCs to enact the *formative assessment design cycle* (Furtak & Heredia, 2014; Furtak, Morrison, & Kroog, 2014). The cycle, illustrated in Figure 8.5, is intended as a sense-making space for teachers to iteratively work with the LP as they learn to design, enact, and use information from the LP to inform their instruction. The cycle begins with teachers *setting goals* and *exploring student thinking*. In this initial phase, teachers use the LP as a model for how student learning can unfold in a domain of interest. Next, teachers *design* and *revise formative assessment tasks* using the LP to create prompts that target specific levels of understanding. Next, teachers *collect data* in their own classrooms, enacting the tasks as common formative assessments (Ainsworth & Viegut, 2006), and collect evidence of what students know and are able to do relative to the LP to later discuss in their PLC. The cycle concludes when the teachers *reflect* on their classroom enactment and *make inferences* about what students know and are able to do. In this crucial final step, teachers' interpretations are guided by the LP as they categorize student responses before identifying the types of instructional feedback that will be most useful to help each cluster of students move forward.

In our research project, we tailored this design cycle to an LP framework in the following ways. First, teachers were not expected to create a learning progression "from scratch." Instead, our starting point for the cycle was the general modeling energy flows learning progression developed by our research team, where (as described above) this development was informed by the research literature on energy in science education and the framework for science education established by the NGSS. In this case, the LP development went through several revisions informed by the results from piloting performance-based tasks, PBICs,

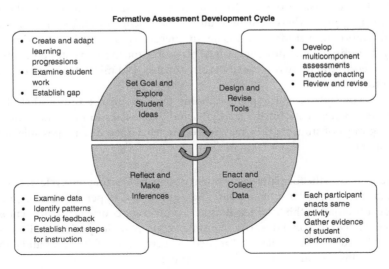

Figure 8.5 Illustration of the Formative Assessment Design Cycle

and conceptually oriented multiple-choice items to teachers' students. To provide teachers an opportunity for ownership, we collaborated with them to develop a list of performance expectation-specific indicators that help them easily identify the specific ideas that they will be expecting to see at each level of the learning progression for a given performance expectation. Second, teachers are also provided with templates and examples of performance-based tasks and PBICs that they could use directly with their students as part of energy-related curricular units, or that they could use as basis for writing new tasks and items. The idea here was that while we wanted to empower teachers to write their own assessment tasks, they needed to be given a starting point and some guidelines for the principles that should inform these tasks. We also provided checklists derived from prior research on effective formative assessment to help teachers learn about scaffolds that can help students make their reasoning explicit to their teachers (e.g., Kang, Thompson, & Windschitl, 2014). One overarching principle is that assessment tasks should be chosen deliberately such that they can be used to elicit differences about the ways students model energy flows in their disciplinary context, and that this information should be useful in giving teachers ideas about what to do next. With this in mind, we have teachers engage in *student-work focus sessions* as part of the "collect data" and "reflect and make inferences" stages of the formative assessment design cycle.

Student-Work Focus Sessions

During student-work focus sessions,[7] teachers meet together to discuss student responses to common assessment tasks with the goals of: (a) making visible the qualitatively different ways that students make sense of energy as a crosscutting scientific concept; (b) seeing the connections between the assessment tasks and the levels of the learning progressions; and (c) suggesting revisions that improve the assessment tasks and learning progression. The inputs for these sessions are a small number of student responses to assessment tasks that have been written to align to the LP. The responses are specifically selected by the organizer of the session to characterize the variability in the ways that students answer the questions that have been posed to them. There are two phases to a student-work focus session:

- In the first phase, all participating teachers make explicit connections between the scoring of the tasks, the student conceptions each task is expected to elicit, and how this relates to the levels of the LP. Next, teachers are asked to each score the same set of student responses where scoring requires the teacher to make a judgment about the sophistication of a student's ideas about energy flows and how they can be modeled. They then discuss any differences in their scores for the same student, come to a consensus score, and discuss ideas to modify the task and minimize score discrepancies in the future.
- In the second phase, participants examine the consensus scores and student work to generate a better sense for the strengths and weaknesses in individual students as well as the groups of students they may represent. They then discuss possible next steps for instruction.

A key to the success of the formative assessment design cycle is that the cycle needs to fit within the timeframe of a curricular unit emphasizing a known NGSS performance expectation. The challenge of coordinating this with teachers across different courses and different schools was considerable. To see if this could work as a proof of concept in our project, we limited ourselves in each discipline to one curricular unit related to energy in the fall/winter and another in the winter/spring demarcations of the academic calendar.

The Question of Validity

In line with recommendations from the National Research Council (NRC, 2014), a comprehensive and coherent assessment system should be able to support both formative and summative assessment purposes. But these represent two different use cases, and although some of the evidence needed to validate an assessment assembled for each use may overlap, much of it will be distinct, requiring the conduct of uniquely constituted studies. As a brief example of validity evidence that should overlap, the connection to a common learning progression implies that the information about students being elicited for a formative purpose should not conflict or be inconsistent with that which is elicited for a summative purpose. This requires evidence that the content and cognitive complexity of items in an assessment for monitoring learning (e.g., a district or state-administered interim assessment) is aligned with what is found in the items used for classroom assessments.

As an example of validity evidence specific to formative classroom use, consider the use case of a teacher including one of the performance-based tasks our team had developed as part of multi-day lab activity in her instructional unit. Students work in groups on the lab activity, and in the process they discuss and write up responses to questions that focus on identifying forms of energy, explaining energy transformations, and creating diagrammatic models that describe the phenomenon motivating the lab (e.g., the burning of a cheese puff). A teacher may walk around different stations in the classroom to listen to student discussions and/or read written responses in real time. By noticing differences in how students are making sense of the energy-related phenomenon, and by connecting what is being heard or read to distinctions suggested by the learning progression, the teacher decides on the next instructional move to take (e.g., ask probing questions to a specific student or student group, convene the full class to have the different groups share their answers, etc.). In this hypothetical use case, assessment is happening in the moment, yet nothing is being formally scored, and if a teacher makes the wrong initial inference about what a student or group of students understands about the phenomenon in question and its relationship to the more general concept of energy flows, there will be other opportunities to adjust this inference by collecting additional information. For the assessment to be valid for this formative use, critical sources of evidence to gather are whether students find the task engaging, whether the task and questions posed are accessible to all students (e.g., English language learners, students with disabilities), and whether the assessment is successful at surfacing distinct student conceptions the teacher is able to use to provide feedback and adjust instruction.

As an example of validity evidence specific to the more summative use of monitoring student learning, consider the use case of two different forms of an assessment targeting the modeling energy flows LP, with each form comprised of a combination of a unique PBIC along with a collection of conceptually oriented MC items. Every student in the school district taking a ninth grade course in the physical sciences will take the assessment once a few months into the school year, and then again near the end of the school year. On each occasion, the scores from the assessment will be used to assign students' grades, and the growth in scores across occasions is intended to be used by district staff to make comparisons across classrooms and schools. For the assessments to be valid for these uses, considerable scrutiny needs to be placed on the psychometric properties of the assessments as measures of a student's location on the modeling energy flows construct. Critical sources of evidence would include:

- the alignment of the PBIC and MC items with the different levels of the modeling energy LP;
- the distribution of item difficulty and whether variability in item difficulty can be explained by intentional design features of the assessment;

- the intercorrelation of assessment items and whether this can be accounted for by a single dimension of student ability or whether multiple dimensions are needed;
- the reliability of assessment scores and the distinctions among individual students that they support;
- the comparability of scores from two different assessment forms; and
- whether a common scale could be created to depict growth across the two assessment forms.

Importantly, any single assessment item (or even groups of items) that might contribute to the validity of one particular use may not necessarily contribute to the validity of another. For example, when administered in tandem with a PBIC, a single MC item may contribute supporting information about specific student conceptions that help to increase the generalizability of the score inferences from the assessment. But if the same MC item is used in isolation as a concept question to spur discussion at the start of class, it may not support valid inferences relative to an LP for modeling energy if it has not been connected to either a motivating phenomenon or an intent to focus on diagrammatic or explanatory modeling.

A full discussion of the concept of building and testing interpretive arguments for assessment use is outside the scope of this chapter, but see Kane (2006), NRC (2014, Chapter 3), Pellegrino, DiBello, and Goldman (2016), and Shepard (1993). In the specific context of an LP for energy, past empirical research has focused on using student response data and psychometric models not so much to validate a specific use of scores to make inferences about individual students, but to validate the developmental theory underlying the delineation of levels (Hermann-Abell & DeBoer, 2018; Neumann et al., 2013; Park & Liu, 2016). Such work is also relevant in the particular context we have described here, and we think it has the potential to be even more informative and defensible to the extent data collection is embedded within a known curricular sequence, something that was a focal point of our project. For more on issues related to the use of psychometric modeling to validate a learning progression hypothesis, see Briggs (2012).

Conclusion

In this chapter, we have used the context of our work building an assessment system for a research project with a school district to illustrate the way that a learning progression and a system of curricular embedded assessments can be used to both provide feedback about student understanding and to monitor evidence of student learning in the context of NGSS performance expectations. The particular learning progression that we introduce here on modeling energy flows has some important defining characteristics. The first characteristic is that it is an embodiment of a sociocognitive learning theory. It draws from the research literature to speculate about a path students are likely to traverse as they are exposed to instruction about energy within and across a disciplinary sequence. The second characteristic is that the learning progression can be mapped to both the content standards that represent the coin of the realm in most school districts, as well as to the curricular units to which it best applies. In this particular example, it was important to appreciate that the learning progression could be seen as an elaboration of a given NGSS performance expectation that includes energy as a crosscutting concept and modeling as a focal practice. The elaboration comes in the specification of levels that fall below and above the statement of what it entails for students to meet the performance expectation. The third characteristic is that the learning progression contains information that teachers can use to "move" students from one level to the next. These are three characteristics (embodiment of a learning theory, aligned with content standards and curriculum, and providing instructionally relevant feedback) that should generalize to any learning progression if it is under consideration for use in classroom settings.

Taken together, a learning progression with embedded assessments has the potential to comprise a powerful framework for professional development, and we presented the formative assessment design cycle that takes places within teacher PLC meetings as the location where this framework is realized. In these design cycles, teachers have the opportunity to revise or tailor the learning progression to the specifics of their curricular units and use or develop assessment tasks to support these units, so long as the tasks are designed with an eye toward making the distinctions in student thinking hypothesized by the learning progression. Student-work focus sessions provide teachers with opportunities to make these distinctions visible and to take a critical look at the quality of their available assessment tasks. All of this is intended to give teachers greater ownership over the assessment of their students.

The assessment system that we introduce as part of the infrastructure of the learning progression contains three types of assessment tasks: performance-based tasks and labs, phenomenon-based item clusters, and conceptually oriented multiple-choice items. Performance-based tasks can be written with a generality that cuts across disciplinary boundaries and may be the most authentic to the ideal the NGSS might have for students as scientists in training. However, they can be very time-consuming to administer, and without the right supports may be unlikely to elicit useful distinctions in student thinking. A rich use for performance-based tasks is as a basis for multi-day scaffolded projects or labs. The PBICs attempt to mimic these scaffolded lab activities, but over a more constrained domain and in a much more limited amount of time. Finally, conceptually oriented MC items remain an important tool because they are efficient to administer while still having the potential to provide insights about student misconceptions. We argue that assessments for both formative and summative purposes can be supported within a single assessment system when the assessments are motivated by a common learning progression hypothesis. It is the learning progression that, in principle, can help maintain the coherence of the assessments for these different purposes. However, the validity of any learning progression and the assessments that are motivated by the progression are always a subject for ongoing investigation and improvement.

Notes

1   We define formative assessment following Bennett (2011) as both the processes and instruments that elicit what students know and are able to do for the purpose of informing subsequent classroom instruction.

2   The modeling energy flows learning progression was the product of the collaborative iterations of our research team, and, in addition to the lead authors, involved contributions from Jason Buell, Kate Henson, Rajendra Chattergoon, Kelsey Tayne, Amy Burkhardt, Caitlin Fine, and Borbala Mahr. A more detailed report on its development can be found at www.colorado.edu/cadre/report.

3   The one exception was the performance expectation for Energy (PS3-4), which is linked to the SEP "Planning and Carrying Out Investigations." It is nonetheless clearly aligned with our modeling energy flow LP given its CC of systems and systems models and its energy-specific DCIs.

4   The development of the PBIC template was spearheaded by Rajendra Chattergoon and Jason Buel. For details, see www.colorado.edu/cadre/report.

5   We thank Knut Neumann and Jeffrey Nordine for their permission to use this "Stuntman Felix" scenario, which they developed as part of a different research project.

6   See http://assessment.aaas.org/topics/1/EG#/0.

7   We have developed a guidebook for student focus sessions, which is available on the website for the Center for Assessment, Design, Research and Evaluation (www.colorado.edu/cadre/learning-progressions-project).

References

Ainsworth, L., & Viegut, D. (2006). *Common formative assessments: How to connect standards-based instruction assessment.* Thousand Oaks, CA: Corwin Press.

Alonzo, A. C. (2011). Learning progressions that support formative assessment practices. *Measurement: Interdisciplinary Research & Perspective, 9*(2–3), 124–129.

Alonzo, A. C., & Gotwals, A. W. (2012). *Learning progressions in science: Current challenges and future directions.* Rotterdam: Sense Publishers.

Bennett, R. E. (2011). Formative assessment: A critical review. *Assessment in Education: Principles, Policy & Practice, 18*(1), 5–25. doi:10.1080/0969594X.2010.513678

Briggs, D. C. (2012). Making progress in the modeling of learning progressions. In A. Alonzo & A. Gotwals (Eds.), *Learning progressions in science* (pp. 293–316). Rotterdam: Sense Publishers.

Briggs, D., Alonzo, A., Schwab, C., & Wilson, M. (2006). Diagnostic assessment with ordered multiple-choice items. *Educational Assessment, 11*(1), 33–64.

Chen, R. F., Eisenkraft, A., Fortus, D., Krajcik, J., Neumann, K., Nordine, J., & Scheff, A. (2014). *Teaching and learning of energy in K-12 education.* Cham: Springer. doi:10.1007/978-3-319-05017-1

Corcoran, T., Mosher, F. A., & Rogat, A. (2009). *Learning progressions in science: An evidence-based approach to reform.* Philadelphia, PA: Consortium for Policy Research in Education.

Eisenkraft, A. (2016). Teaching about energy as a crosscutting concept. In J. Nordine (Ed.), *Teaching about energy across the sciences* (pp. 39–60). Arlington, VA: National Science Teachers Association Press.

Feynman, R. P., Leighton, R. B., & Sands, M. L. (1989). *The Feynman lectures on physics. Vol. 1.* Redwood City, CA: Addison-Wesley. Retrieved from www.feynmanlectures.caltech.edu/I_04.html

Furtak, E. M., Binder, T., & Henson, K. (2018). Designing from outer space: Tensions in the development of a task to assess a crosscutting concept. In J. Kay & R. Luckin (Eds.), *Rethinking learning in the digital age: Making the learning sciences count. 13th International Conference of the Learning Sciences (ICLS) 2018, Vol. 3* (pp. 528–535). London: International Society of the Learning Sciences.

Furtak, E. M., & Heredia, S. (2014). Exploring the influence of learning progressions in two teacher communities. *Journal of Research in Science Teaching, 51*(8), 982–1020.

Furtak, E. M., Morrison, D. L., & Kroog, H. (2014). Investigating the link between learning progressions and classroom assessment. *Science Education, 98*(4), 640–673.

Gröschner, A., Seidel, T., & Katharina, A. P. (2014). Facilitating collaborative teacher learning: The role of "mindfulness" in video-based teacher professional development programs. *Gruppendynamik und Organisationsberatung, 45*(3), 273–290.

Herrmann-Abell, C. F., & DeBoer, G. E. (2018). Investigating a learning progression for energy ideas from upper elementary through high school. *Journal of Research in Science Teaching, 55*(1), 68–93.

Kane, M. T. (2006). Validation. In R. Brennan (Ed.), *Educational measurement* (4th ed., pp. 17–64). Westport, CT: Praeger.

Kang, H., Thompson, J., & Windschitl, M. (2014). Creating opportunities for students to show what they know: The role of scaffolding in assessment tasks. *Science Education, 98*(4), 674–704. https://doi.org/10.1002/sce.21123

Lacy, S., Tobin, R. G., Wiser, M., & Crissman, S. (2014). Looking through the energy lens: A proposed learning progression for energy in grades 3–5. In R. F. Chen, A. Eisenkraft, D. Fortus, J. Krajcik, K. Neumann, J. C. Nordine, & A. Scheff (Eds.), *Teaching and learning of energy in K-12 education* (pp. 241–265). New York: Springer International.

Lee, H. S., & Liu, O. L. (2010). Assessing learning progression of energy concepts across middle school grades: The knowledge integration perspective. *Science Education, 94*(4), 665–688.

Liu, X., & Collard, S. (2005). Using the Rasch model to validate stages of understanding the energy concept. *Journal of Applied Measurement, 6*(2), 224–241.

Liu, X., & McKeough, A. (2005). Developmental growth in students' concept of energy: Analysis of selected items from the TIMSS database. *Journal of Research in Science Teaching, 42*(5), 493–517.

Loughran, J., Mulhall, P., & Berry, A. (2004). In search of pedagogical content knowledge in science: Developing ways of articulating and documenting professional practice. *Journal of Research in Science Teaching, 41*(4), 370–391.

McLaughlin, M. W., & Talbert, J. E. (2001). *Professional communities and the work of high school teaching.* Chicago, IL: University of Chicago Press.

National Research Council (NRC). (2001). *Knowing what students know: The science and design of educational assessment.* Washington, DC: National Academies Press. https://doi.org/10.17226/10019

National Research Council. (2012). *A framework for K-12 science education: Practices, crosscutting concepts, and core ideas.* Washington, DC: National Academies Press. https://doi.org/10.17226/13165

National Research Council (NRC). (2014). *Developing assessments for the Next Generation Science Standards.* Committee on Developing Assessments of Science Proficiency in K-12. Board on Testing and Assessment and Board on Science Education, J. W. Pellegrino, M. R. Wilson, & A. S. Beatty (Eds.). Division of Behavioral and Social Sciences and Education. Washington, DC: National Academies Press.

Neumann, K., Viering, T., Boone, W. J., & Fischer, H. E. (2013). Towards a learning progression of energy. *Journal of Research in Science Teaching, 50*(2), 162–188.

Nordine, J. (2016). *Teaching energy across the sciences.* Arlington, VA: NSTA Press.

Otero, V. K. (2006). Moving beyond the "get it or don't" conception of formative assessment. *Journal of Teacher Education, 57*(3), 247–255. https://doi.org/10.1177/0022487105285963

Park, M., & Liu, X. (2016). Assessing understanding of the energy concept in different science disciplines. *Science Education, 100*(3), 483–516.

Pellegrino, J. W., DiBello, L. V., & Goldman, S. R. (2016). A framework for conceptualizing and evaluating the validity of instructionally relevant assessments. *Educational Psychologist, 51*(1), 59–81, doi:10.1080/00461520.2016.1145550

Penuel, W. R., & Shepard, L. A. (2016). Assessment and teaching. In D. H. Gitomer & C. Bell (Eds.), *Handbook of research on teaching* (5th ed., pp. 787–850). Washington, DC: American Educational Research Association.

Pierson, A. E., Clark, D. B., & Sherard, M. K. (2017). Learning progressions in context: Tensions and insights from a semester-long middle school modeling curriculum. *Science Education, 101*, 1061–1088.

Popkin, G. (2009). *Physics first battles for acceptance.* APS News. Retrieved from www.aps.org/publications/aps news/200907/physicsfirst.cfm

Schwarz, C. V., Reiser, B. J., Davis, E. A., Kenyon, L., Achér, A., Fortus, D., & Krajcik, J. (2009). Developing a learning progression for scientific modeling: Making scientific modeling accessible and meaningful for learners. *Journal of Research in Science Teaching, 46*(6), 632–654.

Shepard, L. (1993). Evaluating test validity. *Review of Educational Research, 19*, 405–450.

Shepard, L., Penuel, B., & Pellegrino, J. (2018a). Using learning and motivation theories to coherently link formative assessment, grading practices, and large-scale assessment. *Educational Measurement: Issues and Practice, 37*(1), 21–34.

Shepard, L., Penuel, B., & Pellegrino, J. (2018b). Classroom assessment principles to support learning and avoid the harms of testing. *Educational Measurement: Issues and Practice, 37*(1), 52–57.

Thissen-Roe, A., Hunt, E., & Minstrell, J. (2004). The DIAGNOSER project: Combining assessment and learning. *Behavior Research Methods, Instruments, & Computers, 36*(2), 234–240. https://doi.org/10.3758/BF03195568

Wilson, M. (2018). Making measurement important for education: The crucial role of classroom assessment. *Educational Measurement: Issues and Practice, 37*(1), 5–20.

9

The Role of Technology-Enhanced Self- and Peer Assessment in Formative Assessment

E. Caroline Wylie and Christine J. Lyon

Introduction

In the opening paper to a special issue on student agency in assessment, Adie, Willis, and Van der Kleij (2018) pose some questions for future exploration, one of which asks, "Can innovative structural environments such as digital tools, new generation learning spaces or authentic assessment designs enable greater student agency in classroom assessment?" (p. 9). In this chapter, we seek to explore the role of digital tools to support self- and peer assessment as a means of supporting student agency. More specifically, the goal of this chapter is to explore the structures and supports that are necessary for students to engage with self-assessment and peer feedback activities that are consistent with the underlying framework of formative assessment, to examine how technology has been used to support the use of these practices, and to present an argument that merging technology processes with rich content tasks has the potential to maximize the impact of these practices on both student engagement and learning.

We begin the chapter by situating self-assessment and peer feedback within a formative assessment framework. We examine the research that supports the use of these two practices, defines necessary supports, and identifies implementation challenges. Next, we identify how technology has been used to support student contributions in the classroom and engagement in self-assessment and peer feedback. Finally, we will illustrate, through the examination of one prototype, "Gathering Evidence to Support Noticing, Interpretation, and Use" (GENIUs), how advances in technology and the integration of rich content tasks have the potential to better reflect best practices and address the limitations in previous technological approaches. We conclude the chapter with implications for future technology development, classroom-based practices, teacher professional learning needs, and research.

Research and Theory on Formative Assessment, Self-Assessment, and Peer Assessment and Feedback

Formative Assessment

Formative assessment is an important classroom-based practice in which the teacher and students analyze and interpret evidence of learning so that adjustments can be made to teaching and learning in support of the emerging learning needs of students. Effective use of formative assessment is a driver of learning (Black & Wiliam, 1998a, 1998b; Brookhart, 2005; Hattie, 2009; Hattie & Timperley, 2007) and involves several categories of practices: (a) sharing learning goals and expectations; (b) eliciting evidence of learning; (c) structuring opportunities for self-assessment; (d) structuring opportunities for peer feedback; and (e) providing actionable formative feedback (Leahy, Lyon, Thompson, & Wiliam, 2005; Wylie & Lyon, 2012).

In addition to the classroom processes that support formative assessment as a tool for learning, effective formative assessment also requires the integration of these processes with deep cognitive-domain understanding or disciplinary content (Bennett, 2011, 2013; Coffey, Hammer, Levin, & Grant, 2011; Council of Chief State School Officers [CCSSO], 2018; Penuel & Shepard, 2016). By situating formative assessment within a cognitive domain model that includes learning progressions and domain-specific tasks and activities, teachers have access to a richer set of resources that support the elicitation of key knowledge and misconceptions, guide what teachers should look for in student performance, support teachers as they make inferences about student knowledge, and guide the identification of instructional adjustments (Bennett, 2011). The provision of these types of rich content resources is consistent with a sociocognitive approach to leaning, whereby student understanding and skill is assessed as students participate in practices that are common to disciplinary experts, and the sequence of instructional activities can be designed to support a specific group of students as they develop proficiency with the identified knowledge and skill (Penuel & Shepard, 2016). Therefore, when combining rich content with tools and processes, formative assessment can help both teachers and students attend to whether or not students provide evidence, but also, more importantly, the quality of that evidence (Coffey et al., 2011). Finally, the integration of formative assessment processes with rich disciplinary tasks supports the development of what Shepard, Penuel, and Davidson (2017) term "horizontal coherence." The authors define horizontal coherence as the "conceptual integration of assessments with a shared model of learning" (p. 48). They argue that horizontal coherence should be considered across standards, accountability assessments, curriculum, professional learning opportunities, and instruction. When horizontal coherence is achieved, formative assessment can provide teachers with insights that can be used immediately by providing students with specific feedback and instructional support to develop understanding in specific academic domains (Shepard et al., 2017).

In addition to the integration of formative assessment practices with deep cognitive-domain understanding or disciplinary content, it is also helpful to consider how teachers implement the breadth of formative assessment practices (the operationalization of the full set of practices). While each of the defined practices is vital to formative assessment, it is also important to recognize the interdependencies between the strategies and how those interdependencies and the breadth of implementation can impact the quality of formative assessment practice (Wylie & Lyon, 2015). And while the specific approach to implementation will vary by teachers' context and the disciplinary content, each of the larger categories of practice should be relevant in all situations (Thompson & Wiliam, 2007). Wylie and Lyon (2015) provide the following example to illustrate the importance of this integration:

> If a teacher implements classroom practices related to the activation of students as resources in the learning process, but fails to communicate the learning expectations, the quality of implementation may be weakened . . . A teacher who focuses solely on the provision of formative feedback is missing opportunities to utilise the formative assessment process in other aspects of her practice.
>
> (p. 144)

There is evidence that these larger categories of formative assessment practices are not evenly implemented by teachers as they learn to incorporate more formative assessment into their instruction (Jonsson, Lundahl, & Holmgren, 2015; O'Leary, Lysaght, & Ludlow, 2013; Wylie & Lyon, 2015). For example, while teachers often report the use of learning goals and success criteria, the implementation of these strategies is often superficial (Lyon, Nabors Oláh, & Wylie, in press; Lyon, Wylie, Brockway, & Mavronikolas, 2018; Wylie & Lyon, 2015). Research has also shown that while teachers are more likely to increase their use of formative feedback and effective questioning, changes to practice related to self-assessment and peer feedback appear to be more infrequent and more difficult (Lyon et al., 2018; O'Leary et al., 2013; Wylie & Lyon, 2015). While there is evidence, then, that formative assessment practices are an effective means to improve student learning, there is a need to more closely examine self-assessment and peer feedback, the impacts of these practices on student learning, the relevant implementation challenges, and the supports that are necessary for both teachers and students.

Self-Assessment

Students engage in self-assessment when they "judge their own work to improve performance as they identify discrepancies between current and desired performance" (McMillan & Hearn, 2008, p. 40). This judgment involves a range of processes, including the self-assessment of one's own work, metacognitive awareness, and self-regulation. The overall process of self-assessment has been characterized as having three steps: monitor, evaluate, and decide on next steps (Bailey & Heritage, 2018). Both descriptions of self-assessment (Bailey & Heritage, 2018; McMillan & Hearn, 2008) imply three distinct steps in the process: (1) students understand what the desired performance is; (2) they are able to monitor their own work against that desired performance to identity differences; and (3) they are able to take action to improve their work product.

Some concerns have been raised about the use of self-assessment for consequential or high-stakes decisions, such as grouping students, curriculum planning, or even retention or promotion decisions (Brown & Harris, 2014). When self-assessment evidence is used in these ways, there is a challenge to the validity of the interpretations that can be made and the actions that are made as a result of those interpretations. These concerns center on the mixed results regarding the consistency of evidence provided by student self-assessment and other measures, such as test scores, teacher judgments, or peer ratings (Brown & Harris, 2013). To avoid these concerns, self-assessment should be used as a self-regulation tool to help students develop and deepen their ability to establish learning goals and to monitor and evaluate progress toward those goals (Andrade, Du, & Wang, 2008; Zimmerman, 2008), and not used for grading (Panadero, Jonsson, & Strijbos, 2016).

While Brown and Harris (2013) raise some concerns about the potential negative impacts of self-assessment, there are also a number of studies that support positive impacts on the self-regulation of learning. Empirical studies have shown that when students are provided with opportunities to develop self-assessment skills, with clear descriptions of the learning target or desired performance, and are encouraged to be introspective, independent, and empowered, they improve their self-regulation and self-efficacy (Andrade, Du, & Mycek, 2010; McDonald & Boud, 2003), are more motivated and engaged (Munns & Woodward, 2006), and develop a sense of autonomy (Brookhart, Andolina, Zuza, & Furman, 2004). Furthermore, there are positive impacts on learning outcomes associated with self-assessment (Andrade et al., 2010; Andrade & Valtcheva, 2009; McDonald & Boud, 2003) and students learn material more deeply when they are metacognitively aware (Everson & Tobias, 1998; Lin & Lehman, 1999; Zhao, 1998).

Despite the literature describing the potential benefits of self-assessment and metacognitive awareness, research has shown that students rarely employ metacognitive processes that foster learning, and that teachers will limit self-assessment in favor of other types of classroom assessment (Everson & Tobias, 1998; Jonsson et al., 2015; Lin & Lehman, 1999; Zhao, 1998). In addition, even when teachers use self-assessment thoughtfully with students, there is evidence that negative student behavior can occur. One early study by Ross, Rolheiser, and Hogaboam-Gray (1998) indicated that students were concerned about cheating and a lack of accuracy in evaluations. Furthermore, students had misconceptions about the purpose of the self-evaluation and self-assessment. One conclusion from the researchers was that teachers underestimated the amount of time and training that students required to engage in self-assessment. More recently, in a study by Harris and Brown (2013), some students admitted to not being honest with the teacher in their self-assessment to either avoid disappointing the teacher or to avoid losing face in front of the teacher or other students. These results were similar to findings from Cowie (2005), who noted that students were sometimes embarrassed by a teacher's reaction to a question when they indicated a lack of understanding. This embarrassment was further exacerbated when the teacher brought the whole class together for an explanation based on a question from an individual student. Additionally, there was evidence in the Harris and Brown (2013) study that the students' self evaluations were often superficial, even when the teacher provided a learning intention and models for students to use. While there was evidence in the study that students understood how self-assessment could be valuable both to themselves and to the teacher, there were also some misunderstandings about its role.

The challenges to effective implementation of self-assessment suggest that teachers need greater awareness of the social dynamics around the use of self-assessment, the importance of clarity with students about the purpose, and the need for sufficient scaffolding of the process so that students develop an appropriate understanding of their role. Given these challenges, we turn next to a more detailed description of the structures that are needed to support self-assessment by unpacking three steps that are important to scaffold the process for students.

First, self-assessment requires that students understand the nature of the desired performance. This requirement is central to the broader concept of formative assessment, which posits that students who can identify and understand the learning expectations for a lesson or set of lessons are better prepared to support one another, to take responsibility for their own learning, and make more progress toward the learning goals (Tell, Bodone, & Addie, 2000; White & Frederiksen, 1998). Identifying or developing with students and understanding the learning expectations for a lesson or set of lessons involves two related practices: (1) identifying or developing and sharing the learning goals for the lesson (i.e., what students should know or understand by the end of the lesson); and (2) specifying or developing the success criteria (i.e., how students would know if they have met the learning goals by the end of the lesson). It is critical for both of these components that the expectations are focused on what the students know, understand, and are able to do (i.e., what they are learning). This is consistent with the first recommendation made by Panadero et al. (2016) for actions and supports that teachers need to provide for the successful implementation of self-assessment: "define the criteria by which students assess their work" (p. 318).

However, studies have also shown that, in general, teachers fail to engage in the practice (Lyon et al., in press). When they do share information about the intended learning it is often in an inaccessible form, such as a state standard or only conveys information about what students will do instead of what they will learn (e.g., a class agenda) (Lyon, Nabors Oláh, & Brenneman, submitted; Wylie & Lyon, 2015). It is also critical that these learning goals are meaningful, coherently building on previous and future learning goals, as well as appropriately challenging (Moss & Brookhart, 2012). For students to meaningfully internalize goals, the goals must be appropriate for the content being covered and the age of the students, written in language that is accessible to the students, and use structures and routines to support students' interpretations and understanding of the goals. Structures and routines that can support students in the internalization of learning goals can include a discussion of what meeting the goals entails, unpacking of the goals to define new vocabulary or processes, and the provision of or co-development of the goals and associated criteria with students (Moss & Brookhart, 2012).

Second, self-assessment requires that students are able to use the learning goals and associated criteria to monitor their own work against the expressed desired performance and identify differences. Panadero et al. (2016) argue that defining the criteria is insufficient to meet this step. In order for students to monitor their own work against the criteria, teachers need to teach students how to apply the criteria so that they can understand gaps between their own performance and the criteria to help them identify next steps. Teaching students how to apply the criteria generally involves providing opportunities to practice using the criteria with exemplars or previous assignments, and providing time to use the criteria on current work. In addition, they argue that teachers should provide students with feedback on their self-assessments.

The third step in the self-assessment process requires students to take action to improve their work product based on the self-assessment. Panadero et al. (2016) note that it is not enough to simply require students to take action, but that teachers need to provide students with help in using self-assessment data to improve performance and must provide sufficient time for revision after self-assessment. Much of the research evidence supporting self-assessment focuses on the impact of students revising their work (e.g., Andrade & Boulay, 2003; Andrade & Valtcheva, 2009) rather than on the specifics of different approaches to support the revision process. However, drawing a parallel with research on teachers, this step of moving from analysis of assessment information to action to determine the next instructional steps based on the assessment evidence has been shown to be difficult for teachers (Heritage, Kim, Vendlinski, & Herman, 2009; Herman, Osmundson, & Silver, 2010; Osmundson, Dai, & Herman, 2011; Wylie & Lyon, 2012). The challenges outlined previously would suggest that students also need significant scaffolding and modeling to understand why and how to engage in a revision process.

Each of these steps draws attention to the partnership that is required between teachers and students. Initially, teachers help students engage with the process and then deepen that engagement through feedback, which highlights self-assessment as a skill that is learned and improved over time. Furthermore, students' use of self-assessment and peer feedback will be influenced by the classroom climate and norms around collaboration, with trust between student and teacher and among students being an important factor in learning (James, Kobe, & Zhao, 2017; Van Maele, Van Houtte, & Forsyth, 2014). As a result, for self-assessment to be successful, students need to value the process and work in a classroom environment where they feel safe to reveal lack of understanding to either the teacher or other students (Cowie, 2005).

Teachers need professional learning opportunities to help them engage students in self-assessment, together with models of practice such as rich video exemplars (Bliss & Reynolds, 2003) that support professional discussions around classroom implementation. In addition, teachers need opportunities to explore the ways in which students may be sensitive to self-assessment (Brown & Harris, 2013; Cowie, 2005) so that they can ameliorate rather than exacerbate those issues by how they position the role of self-assessment, the supports they provide to students, and how they respond to students. Finally, having access to tools and prompts that support meaningful self-assessment within the context of rich learning and assessment tasks will provide models for teachers and students that they can use and adapt (Shepard et al., 2017).

Peer Assessment

The three steps identified for self-assessment (i.e., monitor, evaluate, and decide on next steps) have close parallels for peer assessment and feedback, except that the focus is on the evaluation of a peer's work by another student, rather than the student examining his or her own work (Black & Wiliam, 1998b; Topping, 2010). In our research and professional learning programs, we use the terms peer assessment and peer feedback interchangeably to emphasize the process of students reviewing the work of a peer to provide feedback to the originator of the work, with the focus on helping that student improve the work. The use of peer feedback allows for more timely and frequent feedback to students than teacher feedback alone, even if the quality is not as high (Topping, 1998). Similar to what was noted for self-assessment, we distinguish this process from peer evaluation where one student gives a score or a grade on another student's work, a process that we do not consider part of formative assessment (Liu & Carless, 2007), and which can lead to negative impacts on student relationships (Panadero et al., 2016).

A benefit of peer assessment, when students are able to take on both the roles of provider and receiver of feedback, is that it can help "students develop internal standards for quality work and support their capacity to make better judgments of their own work" (Bourgeois, 2016, p. 350) and develop greater levels of accountability (Tell et al., 2000). A study by Lu and Law (2012) on the impact of peer feedback on both the assessor and assessee provides evidence that the greatest benefit is to the assessor, and suggests that the process of identifying problems in a peer's work or constructing a suggestion for how to improve it helped the assessor better understand the assessment criteria, which in turn resulted in higher-quality work. As noted by Topping (1998), the assessor is able to "consolidate, reinforce, and deepen understanding" (p. 254). These results are similar to those identified by van Popta, Kral, and Camp (2016).

Another benefit of peer assessment, noted by Nicol and Macfarlane-Dick (2006), is that "by commenting on the work of peers, students develop detachment of judgment (about work in relation to standards) which is transferred to the assessment of their own work (e.g., 'I didn't do that either')" (p. 211). McLuckie and Topping (2004) also point out that students may be motivated to make the effort to revise work in recognition of the effort that peers made to provide feedback. Beyond these specific benefits, evidence suggests more generally that student learning outcomes are improved as a result of these experiences (e.g., Graham, McKeown, Kiuhara, & Harris, 2012).

The challenges that were described earlier for self-assessment are similar to those documented for peer assessment. While some have argued that students may view peer feedback as less threatening than teacher feedback (Ellman, 1975), students may be reluctant to disclose their performance to their peers, do not always trust the accuracy of peer evaluation, and may respond differently to peer and teacher feedback (Cowie, 2005, 2009). Even in a higher education context with older students, Williams (1992) showed that students found criticizing their friends difficult. Peer assessment requires teachers to give up some control to their students and trust students' abilities to be honest and to give meaningful feedback (Noonan & Duncan, 2005). Researchers have used rubrics, criteria, or exemplars to help students internalize performance standards and to provide a structure for meaningful feedback (Tell et al., 2000). Furthermore, another challenge for implementation is teacher content knowledge (Andrade & Brookhart, 2016). Teachers need to have a sufficient grasp of the discipline to develop or select tasks that are appropriate for the learning goals and that provide opportunity for peer feedback. In addition, they need to be able to support students in the process and provide feedback on student feedback.

There are also parallels to self-assessment in terms of the supports that are needed to support meaningful engagement with the provision and use of peer assessment, particularly around the importance of clear assessment criteria, scaffolds, and coaching for students. More specifically, Panadero et al. (2016) proposed a series of eight recommendations for teachers to support peer assessment:

(1) Clarify the purpose of PA [peer assessment], its rationale and expectations to the students; (2) Involve students in developing and clarifying assessment criteria; (3) Match participants (e.g., individuals, groups) in a way that fosters productive PA; (4) Determine the PA format (e.g., rating with or without comments) and mode of PA interaction (e.g., face-to-face or online); (5) Provide quality PA training, examples and practice (including feedback about PA); (6) Provide rubrics, scripts, checklists, or other tangible scaffolding for PA; (7) Specify PA activities and timescale; (8) Monitor the PA process and coach students.

(p. 322)

Both students and the teacher have critical roles to ensure that students get the maximum benefit from this process. Steps 1, 2, and 5 are similar to the first self-assessment step, helping students to understand what the desired performance is before they begin to provide feedback for a peer. Also similar to self-assessment, although not stated as explicitly in this sequence of steps, students must have the opportunity to apply the feedback they receive to make it meaningful and useful.

Integration of Self-Assessment and Peer Feedback with Rich Disciplinary Content

While the literature outlined above describes the impact and the structures and supports necessary for self-assessment and peer feedback, these practices are situated within the larger framework of formative assessment. As previously reviewed, formative assessment, and as a result self-assessment and peer feedback, are more likely to be effective if integrated with deep cognitive-domain understanding or disciplinary content (Bennett, 2011; CCSSO, 2018; Penuel & Shepard, 2016; Shepard et al., 2017). It is critical therefore that self-assessment and peer feedback activities are purposefully developed to provide opportunities for students to reflect on their learning and to provide feedback to peers on key standards at critical points in a learning progression. When accomplished successfully, this can provide one step toward achieving horizontal coherence between the standards, the assessments, and instruction (Shepard et al., 2017). It is important, however, to understand that this purposeful development takes time and support. The provision of tasks is one mechanism. Another support is the provision of teacher professional learning opportunities to support the purposeful and effective use of these tasks to help ensure that the tasks are implemented appropriately and that the evidence is used to advance student self-regulation and the development of knowledge and skill. In addition, as argued by Black and Wiliam (1998a), while resources can support teachers as they begin to understand and implement formative assessment, resources alone are not sufficient. Teachers also need to be able to move beyond the use of model resources to an understanding of how the resources are developed and how practices such as self-assessment and peer feedback can be implemented within their classroom context, the demands of their content area, and individual lessons.

What Technology Approaches Have Been Used to Support Student Engagement in the Formative Assessment Process?

It is clear that students have an active role to play in formative assessment (CCSSO, 2018; Cizek, Bennett, & Andrade, in press). Ensuring that students are able to play this role is largely the responsibility of teachers, who are the "designers and sustainers of the learning milieu; establishing the conditions in which students can operate with agency" (Boud & Molloy, 2013, p. 170). In this section, we explore some of the ways in which technology is being used to support teachers by creating conditions within which students can make their thinking more visible to the rest of the class. We identified two categories of online tools: those that support increasing student contributions in the classroom, and those that focus on peer feedback and peer grading processes.

The first set of technology-based tools focus on the concept of increasing contributions from students during a lesson by changing the ways in which a teacher might solicit evidence of understanding from students. One approach, popularized in higher education classes, gives students electronic clickers to provide anonymous responses to questions posed during a lecture (Schell, Lukoff, & Mazur, 2013). The approach engaged students in questions that helped uncover misunderstandings of the content, and provided opportunities for peers to engage with each other to explain their answer choices. Studies have shown improved learning gains for students using this approach (e.g., a meta-analysis of 225 studies by Freeman et al., 2014).

As online sharing technologies have increased, a proliferation of tools aimed more at K-12 classrooms have also emerged, although with significantly less research support. For example, Drost (2017) identified eight ways to use digital tools to provide ways for students to express ideas, ask questions, or respond quickly to polling or other kinds of questions. These tools allow students to contribute anonymously while providing the teacher and other students with greater insights into what students are thinking about, primarily as a support for classroom discussions.

The second category of technology-based tools includes tools that have been developed to support teacher and student use of peer assessment (see a classification by Luxton-Reilly, 2009). Topping (1998) noted in his review of peer assessment that the then-emerging use of computer tools to assist with peer assessment could serve as a useful tool in terms of organization and record-keeping. A few years later, as online peer learning opportunities expanded in higher education, McLuckie and Topping (2004) noted the importance of clarity about the roles students were expected to play in online peer learning opportunities and providing training to support student interactions. The identification of these structures and supports is consistent with the literature on supporting peer assessment when technology is not being utilized.

Luxton-Reilly (2009) conducted a review of 18 online tools that support both peer feedback and peer grading processes, primarily in the context of higher education computer science courses (although a number of the tools could be used in any context). Tools were classified according to flexibility of use, kind of work, and tailoring toward particular kinds of artifacts. The tools generally supported the use of a rubric or scoring criteria, and exemplars, and in some instances included a training phase before students were allowed to proceed to reviewing peers' work. Several tools supported multiple rounds of review and/or having multiple students review the same piece of work. A few of the tools also supported student self-assessment. Although the majority of the systems supported the provision of text-based comments on the work, the tools were primarily focused on supporting summative evaluations by peers, which often contributed to student grades. As a result, there was much less focus on formative feedback that could be used for revision purposes.

Across the two categories of technology-enhanced tools, there are some common challenges that teachers may encounter. First, content is generally left to the discretion of the teacher. While the technology may support classroom discussions, the teacher still needs to identify meaningful questions to use with the technology. Second, because the peer assessment tools tend to focus on peer evaluation and grading, the benefit of qualitative feedback and opportunities to revise response may be lost. In other words, the tool may model a practice that does not align with formative assessment practices.

Gathering Evidence to Support Noticing, Interpretation, and Use (GENIUs) Prototype

We have noted the importance of self-assessment and peer feedback within the formative assessment process and presented evidence that these two practices are less likely to be implemented by teachers than other aspects of formative assessment. While there are some technology supports (more so for peer assessment than self-assessment), we also identified several limitations: technology supports can send incorrect messages about how to use peer feedback to improve teaching and learning, and the need for teachers to develop appropriate content in which to enact that practices. Given these limitations, we wanted to understand how to increase the opportunities for both teachers and students to engage in the formative assessment process—and more specifically with self-assessment and peer feedback. As outlined above, we examined the underlying framework of formative assessment with respect to these practices, the specific considerations and steps put forth in the literature that are required for self-assessment and peer feedback to align with that framework and achieve the intended impacts, the affordances and constraints of the K-12 context, and available technological supports. From this review, we developed a new interface that combines advances in technology with rich content tasks. We use the results from a small pilot of this approach, the GENIUs prototype, to illustrate how this combination has the potential to better reflect best practices in the literature and address the limitations in previous technological tools.

The GENIUs prototype was developed following a design-based research approach (Bell, 2004; Brown, 1992; Cobb, Confrey, Lehrer, & Schauble, 2003; Collins, 1992), beginning with existing content-rich tasks developed through a previous initiative with the intention of developing new student and teacher interfaces. An overarching development goal was to support teachers in the full range of formative assessment practice, including student self-assessment and peer feedback, and specifically to address implementation challenges. The iterative design of the prototype included brainstorming in the light of the existing literature, the collection of feedback from teacher focus groups, and an external expert review. These processes resulted in the identification of nine key design decisions that address the gaps in previous technological approaches and support student self-assessment and peer feedback, including:

1. The integration of self-assessment and peer feedback activities with a well-designed and meaningful scenario-based assessment that is connected to appropriate grade-level standards and provides scaffolding to help students achieve the intended learning goals.
2. Provision and presentation of clear, accessible, and learning-focused goals for each task.
3. Provision, presentation, and use of success criteria to evaluate progress toward the learning goals (e.g., "I can" statements, exemplars, guidelines, rubrics).
4. Integration of opportunities for students to apply the criteria to exemplars or previous assignments.
5. Integration of self-assessment activities that occur at pivotal points in the learning process, provide opportunities for students to apply the criteria, and have no impact on overall grade or score.
6. Integration of peer feedback activities that occur at pivotal points in the learning process, allow multiple peers to provide feedback on the same work product, and that have no impact on overall grade or score.
7. The capability for the teacher to review all self-assessment data and peer feedback and provide feedback directly to the author.
8. The provision of revision opportunities based upon self-assessment evidence or peer feedback.
9. Reporting on student progress that is directly tied to the learning goal at the end of each task.

Eight classroom modules were developed and piloted as part of the GENIUs prototype, four mathematics modules and four English language arts (ELA) modules. Each module includes a single scenario-based assessment that is tied to key content standards and models of how student learning develops in key areas (Key Design Decision 1). Within each module, there are multiple activities (each of which includes multiple tasks) that follow a logical sequence based upon a progression of learning and the associated scenario. The modules can be completed over several lessons or integrated into the curriculum and instruction over a longer period of time. The teacher has a great deal of flexibility in terms of how to assign smaller parts of the module and to integrate the activities and tasks with instruction and other curricular resources. Activities can be assigned separately to students or assigned in a different order than originally presented to support the flexible grouping of students and attend to individual learning needs.

For each activity within a module, learning goals that clearly state what students will know or understand and success criteria that state what students will be able to do by the end of the activity were developed. These goals and criteria are presented directly to students before beginning the activity (Key Design Decisions 2 and 3). For example, in an ELA module focused on informational reading and writing, students learn about wind power from multiple sources and develop a synthesized written report. In activity 2, these students focus on the development of summaries and two learning intentions are presented, including:

1. Students will understand which parts of a text represent main ideas, supporting points, and details.
2. Students will know how to select main ideas and supporting points to develop an accurate summary.

The two success criteria presented for this activity include:

1. Students will correctly identify which parts of a text represent main ideas, supporting points, and details.
2. Students will correctly paraphrase this information to produce written summaries.

In addition, when appropriate, the success criteria were further explicated in the form of rubrics, guidelines, and checklists. For example, in the activity described above, students were also provided with a set of summary guidelines that provided more detailed criteria for producing written summaries. The five summary guidelines include:

1. State the central idea that the source discusses. (What is its main point?)
2. Report only the most important supporting ideas. (Leave out minor ideas and details.)
3. Report only what the author wrote. (Summaries do not include your own opinions on the subject.)
4. Be accurate. (Be careful not to distort information from the source.)
5. Use mostly your own words. (But if you do quote from the source, use quotation marks.)

These guidelines were available for students to use as a resource throughout the task, whether they were developing their own summaries or evaluating summaries. In addition, definitions for potentially unfamiliar key terms and vocabulary (e.g., source, distort) were defined using rollover technology.

Each module included opportunities designed to help students internalize the criteria through scaffolded learning opportunities or by applying the criteria to exemplars or previous assignments (Key Design Decision 4). Following through with the example above, before producing a summary of their own, students were asked to apply each individual criterion to exemplar responses. In one instance, students were presented with an exemplar summary of an article about wind power. Students were told that the summary doesn't follow the guidelines because it includes minor details. They were then asked to identify which sentence should be deleted from the summary. Only after scaffolding instruction and opportunities to apply each individual criterion to exemplars were students asked to write their own summary of a new article. To further support students as they consider success criteria and apply the content they are learning, the system included a highlight and annotate feature. This feature allows students to highlight text and add notes throughout the module in order to help students identify what is important and highlight aspects of the work that align with the success criteria.

The next set of design decisions focused on the integration of self-assessment and peer feedback activities (Key Design Decisions 5–8). To support these design decisions, several features were developed and implemented across all of the modules. Students viewed a completed piece of work from other peers in their group and provided feedback on that work (Key Design Decision 5) and reflected on their own learning to record and save those ideas (Key Design Decision 6). Students were provided with explicit success criteria and with opportunities to apply those criteria as outlined above. In addition, all feedback and responses to self-reflection prompts were available for the teacher to review and provide feedback on while students were completing their work and after completion of the activity (Key Design Decision 7). Table 9.1 shows two examples of peer feedback prompts, and Table 9.2 shows three examples of self-reflection prompts.

Table 9.1 Examples of prompts used to structure peer feedback

Module	Context/Prompt
ELA: Dolphin Intelligence Task	*Context*: Students are directed to write a three- to five-paragraph essay on the subject of dolphin intelligence following a series of research and inquiry tasks wherein students engaged with informative texts on the subject. After submitting their own essay, students are asked to review an essay written by a peer for the same prompt and access to the same resources.
	Prompt: Review your peer's essay. Using the rubric provided [focused on elements of a strong summary], identify two strengths and one area for improvement for your peer.
ELA: Learn about Wind Power	*Context*: Students are presented with a nonfiction text and are asked to write a summary. Following this, students were asked to give feedback to a peer on their summary.
	Prompt: Review the summary guidelines and read the summaries written by each member of your group. Did they follow the summary guidelines? If you see things that could be improved or things that your teammates did particularly well, let them know.

Table 9.2 Examples of prompts used to structure self-reflection

Module	Context/Prompt
ELA: Summarization	*Context*: Students are presented with a text and are asked to highlight the parts of the text that are most important to include in a summary. Then students are shown a model of what that highlighting might look like.
	Prompt: How similar was your highlighting to the highlighting provided? What did you highlight that was not highlighted in the example? What was highlighted in the example that you did not highlight? What does that tell you about what is, and is not, important—and why?
ELA: Wind Power	*Context*: Students are presented with two texts and asked to write summaries for each of them.
	Prompt: Reread both of your own summaries. Reflect on what you wrote. Did you fully follow the summary guidelines? If not, what do you need to change?
Mathematics: Write and Interpret Equations	*Context*: Students used the equation they wrote in an earlier part of the task to find the volume of the sink at a specific time. They are then asked to compare their solution to the graph.
	Prompt: Does my answer in (b) agree with the graph? Have I made a mistake?

While peer feedback and self-assessment features were explicitly built into each of the modules at pivotal points in the learning process, teachers could also choose to add additional peer feedback or self-reflection prompts at any point in the learning process, or pause the activity in order to give additional guidance on the quality of responses, peer feedback, or self-assessments. In addition, teachers could provide students with opportunities to collaborate on a single shared response, virtually chat with each other while completing work, or virtually chat with the teacher to ask questions, ask for help, or receive feedback on progress. Finally, following each instance of peer feedback or self-assessment, students were provided with an opportunity to revise their work (Key Design Decision 8). The final design decision relates to how student progress is reported. At the end of each task and activity, both teachers and students were provided with narrative feedback that highlights the learning goal and the success criteria. The student feedback provides suggestions to help students think about ways to improve their work.

In summary, we developed the GENIUs modules to use rich, engaging standards-based content to provide students with scaffolded learning opportunities, and to provide teachers with additional opportunities to develop inferences regarding student understanding. Additionally, the modules combined with the interface went beyond the provision of content or strategies, combining content, strategies, and scaffolding to encourage the implementation of the full breadth of the formative assessment framework (e.g., learning goals and success criteria were provided; students were provided opportunities to engage with success criteria to understand them and apply them to their own work or that of their peers; self-reflection and peer feedback opportunities were part of the student experience as they navigated through the task; revision opportunities were provided; and feedback was provided in a narrative form to help teachers and students identify meaningful next steps). The goal was that the interface, along with these formative assessment modules, would model strategies for teachers that they could apply to classroom learning experiences outside of the module use.

Formative Evaluation of the GENIUs Prototype

A small pilot was conducted to understand how students engaged in self-assessment and peer feedback, and how teachers used the GENIUs prototype to inform future development of the prototype and associated training for teachers and students. Fifteen teachers participated in the pilot. The pilot included two phases of implementation with the intention of allowing teachers to become familiar with the prototype, including both the content and features, during the first phase. During the second phase, we expected more sophisticated implementation given the experiences, training, and teacher familiarity gained in the first phase. Each teacher was asked to implement at least one module during each phase of the pilot and were provided with a number of training opportunities and supports throughout the pilot (i.e., a conference call focused on using the overall system, a content-specific case study that demonstrated possible implementations strategies, and one-on-one phone support). Individual implementation plans were left to the teachers' discretion to acknowledge their understanding of their students, curriculum, and context.

To explore the use of the prototype, specifically in terms of student self-assessment and peer feedback, we collected a variety of data, including a student engagement and usability survey, student ratings of the helpfulness of 10 different features of the prototype, and student responses to the peer feedback and self-assessments prompts. Multiple sources of data were collected from the teachers and analyzed to provide insight into how the teachers engaged with the prototype with their students. Participating teachers completed an online survey to collect information about implementation, student experiences, and perceptions regarding the overall usability of the prototype. To provide more detailed information, teachers also participated in one-on-one, semi-structured interviews.

Responses to the peer feedback and self-assessment prompts were reviewed and coded by the two authors to identify responses that indicated a hierarchy of sophistication. The first code identified responses in which the student (i.e., the student completing the self-assessment or the peer feedback) identifies something specific in the response, including whether it is correct or not, but does not connect to the success criteria or student understanding. This included responses that focused on procedural aspects (e.g., spelling) or provided a vague description of something done in the task. The second code identified responses in which the student highlights progress towards the task expectations/criteria for success or the content covered in the tasks that the student did well or incorrectly. The third code identified when a student identifies a suggestion for what to do next, encourages revision, or indicates why no revision is necessary. Finally, in some cases, a student redirected the student back to the teacher or to notes, rather than explicitly suggesting a revision. In these instances, the fourth code, redirect, was applied. In addition, three codes were used to indicate when a response was not scorable (i.e., random text or text not related to the prompt), a student indicated confusion, or the response provided nothing more than praise.

Across the collected data, three overall themes were identified: students' perception of the peer feedback and self-assessment features and opportunities, the role of scaffolding to support students' provision of quality self-assessment and peer feedback responses, and areas were students and teachers needed additional support.

Regarding the first theme of student perceptions of the system features, the majority of students who used each feature found them "very" or "somewhat" helpful (56% and 61% for peer feedback and self-assessment, respectively). From the open-ended survey questions, students provided insight into why they valued peer feedback:

I liked the peer review because you could see your response with some helpful criticism.

My favorite tool was the peer review because i got feedback from someone my age.

My favorite feature was how you can have a partner review. I found it to be very helpful and it made me realize my mistakes from a different perspective.

Fewer students commented on the self-assessment feature, but did provide some insights, with explanations such as:

My favorite feature was that the computer gave you a sample so you could compare your work to something. I liked this because you could figure out how well written you work was compared to a really good one.

Other aspects of the system that generated positive feedback from students included features that supported student engagement, such as being able to ask questions of a peer via a chat function and being able to resubmit questions after receiving feedback. In this way, the prototype provided students with alternative ways to make contributions to the teaching and learning opportunities and to self-regulate their own learning. The student comments indicated that students valued and took advantage of these opportunities.

The second theme related to the role of scaffolding to support students' provision of quality self-assessment and peer feedback responses. We considered quality self-assessment and peer feedback responses to be those responses that highlighted progress toward the task expectations/criteria for success, identified content covered in the tasks that the student did well or got incorrect, suggested what the student could do next, encouraged revision/indicated why no revision is necessary, or redirected the student back to the teacher or to notes.

Across all of the responses, only 20% met the criteria for a quality peer feedback response. Approximately 10% of the comments included a statement that described how the response related to the success criteria provided in the task. For example, one student commented:

This is a good summary. It gives the main idea of the whole paragraph and enough details to get more insight of what the writing was about.

Similarly, approximately 10% of the peer feedback responses described the next steps that a student could take to improve their response. For example, one student wrote:

Your summary is a little short compared to the sample paragraph. You should add some more details of the effect of barbed wire for American cowboys and Native Americans.

Interestingly, about 9% of peer feedback responses included a comparison of the peer's response to their own response or understanding. This type of response was not indicative of any specific level of quality, and in many cases the students simply commented that they got the "same answer." However, a few students commented on instances where they gained insight into how they should have responded themselves: (e.g., "I like how you explained what spoonerisms means and realize i should have included that in my summary"; "This makes a lot more snese then mine doesm and i understand it better now"). This is consistent with the research that suggests the process of internalizing the success criteria and applying it to someone else's work can help students to reflect on their own understanding (Bourgeois, 2016; Nicol & Macfarlane-Dick, 2006). Finally, while the statements that focused on a single aspect of a peer's work, either noting the correctness of the answer or providing feedback at a very high level (e.g., "it was a bit broad") did not meet the criteria for high quality, approximately one-third of the responses did rise to this level.

The quality of student feedback to a peer was not evenly distributed across the tasks or participating teachers. Three of the peer feedback prompts came from one ELA module and more than 50% of the student comments for these prompts included specific descriptions of strengths and weaknesses or suggested next steps. The teacher that used that module indicated in his interview that he used "turn and talk" type feedback previously with his students. He also decided to add the peer review feature to the module in addition to the self-reflection prompts that were already included, which suggests that students had prior experience. This teacher was very clear about the value that he expected students to get from the process:

[Using the module, students] actually got to read someone else's summary and then they got to say what they did well and what they, how they can improve. So not only do they have their own that they can look at, they have someone else's. And then, to give that critical feedback, and hopefully, carry it over to—well, I'm telling somebody else how to make it better, I could probably do the same thing on mine.

This teacher reported showing students how to provide feedback in the system but did not mention doing anything else specifically to support them. We cannot disentangle in this analysis whether the prompts that the teacher used or the students' prior experiences lent themselves to more insightful student feedback.

The analysis of the responses to the self-assessment prompts indicates some similar and more promising patterns. Just half of the responses included a high-level reference to the rubric or success criteria (e.g., "My summary has more detail than the computer's summary") and almost a quarter of the responses provided more detail in relation to the rubric (e.g., "My summary agrees with the sample, apart from the fact that mine is much longer and more fleshed out. Both summaries give a main idea and supporting details. Mine only disagrees where the length is"). Finally, about 10% of students' self-assessment comments indicated a specific next step to revise the work (e.g., "I need to restate my facts better and make sure that I do a brief summary and not add every detail. My summary was different because I talked to much about one thing"). Overall, this pattern indicates that the quality of the self-assessment responses was higher overall than the quality of the peer feedback statements.

Similar to peer feedback, the quality of students' self-assessment comments was not distributed evenly across prompts or participating teachers. However, the one module to which one teacher added the peer feedback prompts had several self-assessment prompts that were used by two other teachers. These prompts had the highest quality of student feedback. From the data we have, we cannot fully disentangle teacher effect from prompt effect, although the prompts were of a similar structure across most modules.

The third theme that we observed in the data indicates that while there were some successes in terms of the quality of students' self-assessment responses and peer feedback statements, additional support may be needed. Approximately half of the peer feedback statements were blank or superficial in nature. Superficial statements did not go beyond providing praise to the student, identifying whether something in the responses was correct or incorrect (without referencing the success criteria), identifying procedural aspects of the work that were incorrect (e.g., spelling), or providing a vague description of something done in the task.

While many of the peer feedback statements did not go beyond a superficial statement, one of the key design features included in the prototype explicitly addressed this challenge: the capability for teachers to review students' peer assessment statements so that they could provide greater support for students, if needed. One of the ELA teachers commented specifically on the superficiality of students' statements and described how she used that observation as a teaching moment with the students:

> I was noticing . . . they weren't giving feedback, they were giving compliments, they were giving criticism. And so one of the things that I did then was on the feedback. One of the slides, it says like, "Read the argument carefully and then ask this question." So I actually copied those questions. Those were the questions that students use to provide feedback directly from the [prototype] to their partners . . . We talked like a lot about the difference between feedback and compliments and criticism. And so I used the fact that I saw that . . . they were still giving those compliments and . . . I modeled that with them as well, like how to do it on from someone else's piece.

One of the mathematics teachers made a similar comment, reflecting on her students' prior experiences with peer assessment. Her realization, after the fact, was that the students needed some additional exposure to the idea of providing feedback for their peers:

> I found with seventh graders, they weren't . . . um, they didn't quite understand the student feedback portion or like how you look back at other people's work and how you give feedback on other work. So I definitely think I would do a separate maybe activity just on giving feedback . . . together, we would have maybe done an activity before we actually studied about giving feedback, introduce the activity, let them kind of go through it up to that first part where they get feedback and then I would have just been, I mean circulating the room, checking in, looking at their progress.

Although this teacher had not previously had students engage in peer assessment, she was willing to try it in the context of the module. She recognized that in the future, students needed some additional support to get the most benefit from the process. This same teacher commented later in her interview about the value that at least some of her students got from the process:

> I think when they have to explain it back to a peer it's more meaningful than it is coming from me sometimes. And I also feel like when they can explain it back then they have a solid and concrete understanding of what they are being asked to do . . . And I feel like good things come up when you have people that are willing to talk about it, because in their kid language they may understand that when someone else explains it to them.

As mentioned above, a large majority of the peer feedback statements that were considered quality statements came from one ELA module and students in one teacher's class. That teacher indicated that students had some previous experience providing feedback, and he added the peer review feature to the module (i.e., it was not part of the preprogrammed activity). This means that a larger proportion of lower-quality peer feedback statements came from other prompts and from students in other classes. This finding, combined with statements from teachers that they needed to provide more support and that some teachers used the functionality of the system to review student feedback statements and provide additional support, suggests that more may be needed either built into the modules or as professional learning opportunities for teachers to encourage the provision of quality peer feedback.

Given the higher number of quality self-assessment responses, it is not surprising that there were fewer blank or superficial responses (6% and 10%, respectively). Overall, students were much less likely to praise their own work than they were to praise a peer's work. However, students were more likely to express confusion with the self-assessment prompts, making comments such as "yes I don't really understand how to do this because I don't understand how to find the volume and its a little frustrating." While the prototype included a feature to allow teachers to review students' responses to self-assessment prompts, we do not know the extent to which the teachers monitored the responses or used the responses to provide additional help to those that needed it. Again, as mentioned above, the quality of the students' self-assessment comments was not distributed evenly across prompts or participating teachers. It is worth further investigation to understand why, in some instances, students were more likely to be confused and/or provide superficial responses and to identify which types of support were successful in prompting higher-quality responses.

Taken together, the pilot study findings illustrate the ways in which rich content-based tasks, integrated with formative assessment practices, and supported by a technology enhanced platform, have the potential to impact formative assessment practice. Teachers who might not necessarily have used peer feedback on their own, for example, were supported to use it because the prompt and rubric are provided, and the task is designed so that students are then encouraged to use the feedback. By also making it easy for the teacher to view the student comments, they are ideally able to directly see the value of it, or, if needed, they can intervene to support students engage in the practice.

We drew upon prior research on aspects of effective formative assessment practice to develop the GENIUs prototype. The prototype used tasks that grounded the learning and the assessment in disciplinary ways of knowing, acting, and reasoning, and modeled good teaching and learning practices. The system positions formative assessment as a process that is essential and integral to the practice of teaching and learning, and was developed to intentionally include and support all of the key processes and components for formative assessment. It can be integrated with rich curriculum and instruction, and invests in the development of teacher knowledge and skills that are needed to engage in the process of formative assessment (Bennett, 2011; Black & Wiliam, 2009; Leahy et al., 2005; Shepard et al., 2017).

Discussion

We reflect on what we have learned from the research literature on self- and peer assessment, examples of technology-based tools that have been developed to support these practices, and the more detailed view of the GENIUs prototype to consider implications for technology supports and for teacher professional learning needs. To structure this reflection, we modified a framework for data use (Coburn & Turner, 2011) to help us consider how the GENIUs prototype was used by students and teachers, and to extrapolate more broadly beyond the specific example to consider how teachers could engage students in more self- and peer assessment as a regular part of the learning process (see Figure 9.1). Given the uneven uptake of formative assessment practices (Wylie & Lyon, 2015), we paid attention to self-assessment and peer feedback to provide specific support for teachers who might otherwise avoid using these formative assessment practices.

At the center of Figure 9.1, we have the process of self-assessment and peer feedback, which we identify as three specific steps: notice, interpret, and use/action. These steps are parallel to frameworks for teacher noticing (van Es & Sherin, 2002) that distinguish among teachers' ability to: (1) identify what is important or noteworthy about a classroom situation and/or evidence of student understanding; (2) make connections between the specifics of classroom interactions, evidence of student learning, and the broader principles of teaching and learning they represent; and (3) use what one knows about the context to reason. For students engaging in either self- or peer assessment, they need to: (1) understand the important features to attend to in a piece of work (e.g., understand the learning goals and criteria for success); (2) make connections between the piece of work (their own or that of a peer) and the learning goals and criteria for success; and (3) identify appropriate next steps for their peer or for themselves (Black & Wiliam, 1998b; Panadero et al., 2016; Topping, 2010).

Figure 9.1 also illustrates both the school and classroom influences on self-assessment and peer feedback, along with the kinds of interventions that can also support those practices. Students' use of self-assessment and peer feedback will be influenced by the classroom climate and norms around collaboration, with trust between student and teacher and among students being an important factor in learning (James et al., 2017; Van Maele et al., 2014). Having clear

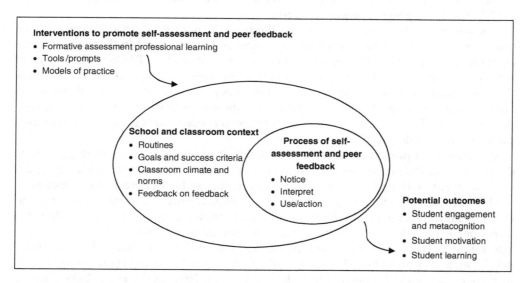

Figure 9.1 Framework for self-assessment and peer feedback (adapted from Coburn & Turner, 2011).

learning goals and/or success criteria is foundational to these practices, along with providing students with feedback on the quality of their feedback (Panadero et al., 2016). External to the classroom, teachers need support to help them engage students in these practices, and this support needs to include professional learning opportunities that emphasize the critical features of these practices along with models of practice such as rich video exemplars. These supports can foster professional discussions around how a teacher can implement these practices in the classroom (Bliss & Reynolds, 2003). Finally, having access to tools and prompts that support meaningful self-assessment and peer feedback within the context of rich learning and assessment tasks will provide models for teachers and students that they can use and adapt (Shepard et al., 2017).

The steps identified by Panadero et al. (2016) align with and perhaps expand the *school and classroom context* presented in Figure 9.1. The *process of self-assessment and peer feedback* can be supported by tasks such as those within the GENIUs prototype, which guide students through the steps of noticing, interpreting, and using evidence of their own or their peers' understanding. The tasks were designed to map clearly to the learning goals, illustrate the success criteria through rubrics or exemplars to scaffold the process, maintain the formative rather than evaluative nature of the task, and provide subsequent revision opportunities in the light of the feedback or reflection. Assessment tasks that incorporate self- and peer assessment themselves cannot ensure that the classroom climate and norms are supportive of self-assessment and peer feedback, so it will be important to provide professional learning opportunities for teachers to support these practices.

From the perspective of Figure 9.1, we recognize that any tools provided to teachers must be supported by *interventions to promote self-assessment and peer feedback*. It is critical to provide teacher-learning opportunities around how to teach students to apply success criteria to their own work or that of a peer, and to help them develop processes to monitor student feedback and to provide feedback on the student feedback. Learning opportunities that include models of practice, whether transcripts, case studies, or annotated video exemplars, can be useful to support teacher learning. Providing opportunities for teachers to learn to modify existing materials or develop their own prompts and routines around self-assessment and peer feedback, beyond what is provided in any tools, will help teachers and students extend these practices to the breadth of their teaching and learning. Finally, teachers also need opportunities to learn about the challenges of both self- and peer assessment, including student concerns about cheating, concerns of loss of face, embarrassment, and lack of trust of peer feedback. Teachers will need help to develop strategies to address these potential challenges so that they can be sensitive to how they respond to students. These strategies will vary according to the age and maturity of students, class dynamics, and previous experiences with self- and peer assessment.

There are also implications for technology-based approaches for supporting formative assessment. As we learned from the GENIUs prototype, students are willing to use technology to be both providers and receivers of feedback from peers and to engage in self-reflection. Teachers were able to work with the system and to identify areas where students needed additional supports to maximize their benefits from the self- and peer assessment processes. Having the formative assessment practices embedded within rich, engaging tasks enabled teachers to use them and identify ways to better support students. Even in a system that provided significant scaffolding for students (e.g., provision of learning goals, criteria for success, opportunities to practice using the rubrics), there is still a need for improvement to help students more routinely make connections between the rubric or success criteria and the work to strengthen the quality of their feedback. As we saw in our review of technology supports for peer assessment, a number of them focused on peer evaluation and did not incorporate opportunities for qualitative feedback and revision. Developers of future technology-based supports need to maintain both a clear focus on a theory of learning and on a framework for formative assessment. Supporting students engage in meaningful self- and peer assessment requires a time commitment to provide the appropriate structures and supports. Embedding the processes in rich content reduced the planning burden on teachers.

One final implication for teacher professional learning is related to teachers' opportunities to transfer ideas and skills from technology-based models to other aspects of classroom practice. If the tasks embedded in the technology are intended to serve models, teachers need explicit opportunities to make connections between the critical features of the model and how they can apply those features to their own practice. In other words, a model is only useful as a model if teachers recognize it as such and have supports to apply the lessons to other aspects of their practice.

Future research should investigate whether and how teachers expand their formative assessment practices when given technology tools that model these practices. In other words, to what extent are teachers able to learn from and apply features of the model to their own classroom practice? Additionally, future research could further explore extending the theory of teacher noticing to student noticing to better understand how to support students engaging in more insightful reflections of their own work or that of peers to support learning.

References

Adie, L. E., Willis, J., & Van der Kleij, F. M. (2018). Diverse perspectives on student agency in classroom assessment. *The Australian Educational Researcher*, 45(1), 1–12.

Andrade, H. L., & Boulay, B. A. (2003). Role of rubric-referenced self-assessment in learning to write. *The Journal of Educational Research*, 97(1), 21–30.

Andrade, H. L., & Brookhart, S. (2016). The role of classroom assessment in supporting self-regulated learning. In D. Laveault & L. Allal (Eds.), *Assessment for learning: Meeting the challenge of implementation* (pp. 293–310). Basel: Springer International.

Andrade, H. L., Du, Y., & Mycek, K. (2010). Rubric-referenced self-assessment and middle school students' writing. *Assessment in Education: Principles, Policy & Practice*, 17(2), 199–214.

Andrade, H. L., Du, Y., & Wang, X. (2008). Putting rubrics to the test: The effect of a model, criteria generation, and rubric-referenced self-assessment on elementary school students' writing. *Educational Measurement: Issues and Practice*, 27(2), 3–13. doi:10.1111/j.1745-3992.2008.00118.x

Andrade, H. L., & Valtcheva, A. (2009). Promoting learning and achievement through self-assessment. *Theory into Practice*, 48(1), 12–19. doi:10.1080/00405840802577544

Bailey, A., & Heritage, M. (2018). *Self-regulation in learning and the role of language and formative assessment*. Cambridge, MA: Harvard Education Press.

Bell, P. (2004). On the theoretical breadth of design-based research in education. *Educational Psychologist*, 39(4), 243–253.

Bennett, R. E. (2011). Formative assessment: A critical review. *Assessment in Education: Principles, Policy & Practice*, 18(1), 5–25.

Bennett, R. E. (2013). *Formative assessment: Process and tool*. Paper presented at the National Conference on Student Assessment, National Harbor, MD.

Black, P., & Wiliam, D. (1998a). Assessment and classroom learning. *Assessment in Education: Principles, Policy & Practice*, 5(1), 7–74.

Black, P., & Wiliam, D. (1998b). Inside the black box: Raising standards through classroom assessment. *Phi Delta Kappan*, 80(2), 139–144.

Black, P., & Wiliam, D. (2009). Developing the theory of formative assessment. *Educational Assessment, Evaluation and Accountability*, 21(1), 5–31.

Bliss, T., & Reynolds, A. (2003). Quality visions and focused imagination. In J. Brophy (Ed.), *Using video in teacher education* (pp. 29–51). Boston, MA: Elsevier.

Boud, D., & Molloy, E. (2013). Rethinking models of feedback for learning: The challenge of design. *Assessment & Evaluation in Higher Education*, 38(6), 698–712.

Bourgeois, L. (2016). Supporting students' learning: From teacher regulation to co-regulation. In D. L. L. Allal (Ed.), *Assessment for learning: Meeting the challenge of implementation* (pp. 345–363). Basel: Springer International.

Brookhart, S. M. (2005). *Research on formative classroom assessment*. Paper presented at the annual meeting of the American Educational Research Association, Montreal, Canada.

Brookhart, S. M., Andolina, M., Zuza, M., & Furman, R. (2004). Minute math: An action research study of student self-assessment. *Educational Studies in Mathematics, 57*(2), 213–227.

Brown, A. L. (1992). Design experiments: Theoretical and methodological challenges in creating complex interventions in classroom settings. *The Journal of the Learning Sciences, 2*(2), 141–178.

Brown, G., & Harris, L. R. (2013). Student self-assessment. In J. H. McMillan (Ed.), *SAGE handbook of research on classroom assessment* (pp. 367–393). Thousand Oaks, CA: SAGE.

Brown, G., & Harris, L. R. (2014). The future of self-assessment in classroom practice: Reframing self-assessment as a core competency. *Frontline Learning Research, 2*(1), 22–30. doi:10.14786/flr.v2i1.24

Cizek, G., Bennett, R., & Andrade, H. (in press). Formative assessment: History, definition, and progress. In G. Cizek, H. Andrade, & R. Bennett (Ed.), *The handbook of formative assessment in the disciplines*. New York: Routledge.

Cobb, P., Confrey, J., Lehrer, R., & Schauble, L. (2003). Design experiments in educational research. *Educational Researcher, 32*(1), 9–13.

Coburn, C. E., & Turner, E. O. (2011). Research on data use: A framework and analysis. *Measurement: Interdisciplinary Research & Perspective, 9*(4), 173–206.

Coffey, J. E., Hammer, D., Levin, D. M., & Grant, T. (2011). The missing disciplinary substance of formative assessment. *Journal of Research in Science Teaching, 48*(10), 1109–1136.

Collins, A. (1992). Toward a design science of education. In *New directions in educational technology* (pp. 15–22). Heidelberg: Springer.

Council of Chief State School Officers (CCSSO). (2018). *Revising the definition of formative assessment. Created by Caroline Wylie, ETS, for the Formative Assessment for Students and Teachers (FAST) collaborative.* Washington, DC: Council of Chief State School Officers.

Cowie, B. (2005). Pupil commentary on assessment for learning. *Curriculum Journal, 16*(2), 137–151.

Cowie, B. (2009). My teacher and my friends helped me learn: Student perceptions and experiences of classroom assessment. In D. M. McInerney, G. T. L. Brown, & G. A. D. Liem (Eds.), *Student perspectives on assessment: What students can tell us about assessment for learning* (pp. 85–105). Charlotte, NC: Information Age.

Drost, B. (2017). *Digital formative assessment tools to improve motivation.* Paper presented at the Presentation at the National Council on Measurement in Education (NCME) Special Conference on Classroom Assessment and Large-Scale Psychometrics, Lawrence, KS.

Ellman, N. (1975). Peer evaluation and peer grading. *The English Journal, 64*(3), 79–80.

Everson, H. T., & Tobias, S. (1998). The ability to estimate knowledge and performance in college: A metacognitive analysis. *Instructional Science, 26*(1–2), 65–79.

Freeman, S., Eddy, S. L., McDonough, M., Smith, M. K., Okoroafor, N., Jordt, H., & Wenderoth, M. P. (2014). Active learning increases student performance in science, engineering, and mathematics. *Proceedings of the National Academy of Sciences, 111*(23), 8410–8415.

Graham, S., McKeown, D., Kiuhara, S., & Harris, K. R. (2012). Meta-analysis of writing instruction for students in elementary grades. *Journal of Educational Psychology, 104*, 879–896.

Harris, L. R., & Brown, G. (2013). Opportunities and obstacles to consider when using peer- and self-assessment to improve student learning: Case studies into teachers' implementation. *Teaching and Teacher Education, 36*, 101–111.

Hattie, J. (2009). *Visible learning: A synthesis of over 800 meta-analyses relating to achievement.* New York: Routledge.

Hattie, J., & Timperley, H. (2007). The power of feedback. *Review of Educational Research, 77*(1), 81–112.

Heritage, M., Kim, J., Vendlinski, T., & Herman, J. L. (2009). From evidence to action: A seamless process in formative assessment? *Educational Measurement: Issues and Practice, 28*(3), 24–31.

Herman, J. L., Osmundson, E., & Silver, D. (2010). *Capturing quality in formative assessment practice: Measurement challenges.* CRESST Report 770. Los Angeles, CA: University of California, National Center for Research on Evaluation, Standards, and Student Testing.

James, J. H., Kobe, J. F., & Zhao, X. (2017). Examining the role of trust in shaping children's approaches to peer dialogue. *Teachers College Record, 119*(10), 1–34.

Jonsson, A., Lundahl, C., & Holmgren, A. (2015). Evaluating a large-scale implementation of Assessment for Learning in Sweden. *Assessment in Education: Principles, Policy & Practice, 22*(1), 104–121.

Leahy, S., Lyon, C. J., Thompson, M., & Wiliam, D. (2005). Classroom assessment: Minute by minute, day by day. *Educational Assessment, 63*(3), 19–24.

Lin, X., & Lehman, J. D. (1999). Supporting learning of variable control in a computer-based biology environment: Effects of prompting college students to reflect on their own thinking. *Journal of Research in Science Teaching, 36*(7), 837–858.

Liu, N., & Carless, D. (2007). Peer feedback: The learning element of peer assessment. *Teaching in Higher Education, 11*(3), 279–290.

Lu, J., & Law, N. (2012). Online peer assessment: Effects of cognitive and affective feedback. *Instructional Science, 40*(2), 257–275.

Luxton-Reilly, A. (2009). A systematic review of tools that support peer assessment. *Computer Science Education, 19*(4), 209–232.

Lyon, C. J., Nabors Oláh, L., & Brenneman, M. W. (submitted). A formative assessment focused observation protocol: Evaluating the scoring inference.

Lyon, C. J., Nabors Oláh, L., & Wylie, E. C. (in press). Working towards integrated practice: Understanding the interaction among formative assessment strategies. *Journal of Educational Research.*

Lyon, C. J., Wylie, E. C., Brockway, D., & Mavronikolas, E. (2018). Formative assessment and the role of teachers' content area. *School Science and Mathematics, 118*(5), 144–155. https://doi.org/10.1111/ssm.12277

McDonald, B., & Boud, D. (2003). The impact of self-assessment on achievement: The effects of self-assessment training on performance in external examinations. *Assessment in Education: Principles, Policy & Practice, 10*(2), 209–220.

McLuckie, J., & Topping, K. J. (2004). Transferable skills for online peer learning. *Assessment & Evaluation in Higher Education, 29*(5), 563–584.

McMillan, J., & Hearn, J. (2008). Student self-assessment: The key to strong student motivation and higher achievement. *Educational Horizons, 87*(1), 40–49.

Moss, C. M., & Brookhart, S. M. (2012). *Learning targets: Helping students aim for understanding in today's lesson.* Alexandria, VA: ASCD.

Munns, G., & Woodward, H. (2006). Student engagement and student self-assessment: The REAL framework. *Assessment in Education: Principles, Policy & Practice, 13*(2), 193–213. doi:10.1080/09695940600703969

Nicol, D. J., & Macfarlane-Dick, D. (2006). Formative assessment and self-regulated learning: A model and seven principles of good feedback practice. *Studies in Higher Education, 31*(2), 199–218.

Noonan, B., & Duncan, C. R. (2005). Peer and self-assessment in high schools. *Practical Assessment, Research and Evaluation, 10*(17), 1–8.

O'Leary, M., Lysaght, Z., & Ludlow, L. (2013). A measurement instrument to evaluate teachers' assessment for learning classroom practices. *International Journal of Educational and Psychological Assessment, 14,* 40–60.

Osmundson, E., Dai, Y., & Herman, J. L. (2011). *Year 3 ASK/FOSS efficacy study.* CRESST Report 782. Los Angeles, CA: University of California, National Center for Research on Evaluation, Standards, and Student Testing.

Panadero, E., Jonsson, A., & Strijbos, J. (2016). Scaffolding self-regulated learning through self-assessment and peer assessment: Guidelines for classroom implementation. In D. Laveault & L. Allal (Eds.), *Assessment for learning: Meeting the challenge of implementation* (pp. 311–326). Basel: Springer International.

Penuel, W. R., & Shepard, L. A. (2016). Assessment and teaching. In D. Gitomer & C. Bell (Eds.), *Handbook of research on teaching* (pp. 787–850). Washington, DC: AERA.

Ross, J. A., Rolheiser, C., & Hogaboam-Gray, A. (1998). Skills training versus action research in-service: Impact on student attitudes to self-evaluation. *Teaching and Teacher Education, 14*(5), 463–477.

Schell, J., Lukoff, B., & Mazur, E. (2013). Catalyzing learner engagement using cutting-edge classroom response systems in higher education. *Cutting-Edge Technologies in Higher Education, 6,* 233–261.

Shepard, L. A., Penuel, W. R., & Davidson, K. L. (2017). Design principles for new systems of assessment. *Phi Delta Kappan, 98*(6), 47–52.

Tell, C. A., Bodone, F. M., & Addie, K. L. (2000). *A framework of teacher knowledge and skills necessary in a standards-based system: Lessons from high school and university faculty.* Paper presented at the annual meeting of the American Educational Research Association, New Orleans, LA.

Thompson, M., & Wiliam, D. (2007). Tight but loose: A conceptual framework for scaling up school reforms. In E. C. Wylie (Ed.), *Tight but loose: Scaling up teacher professional development in diverse contexts* (pp. 1–44). Princeton, NJ: Educational Testing Service.

Topping, K. J. (1998). Peer assessment between students in colleges and universities. *Review of Educational Research, 68*(3), 249–276.

Topping, K. J. (2010). Peers as a source of formative assessment. In G. J. Cizek & H. L. Andrande (Eds.), *Handbook of formative assessment* (pp. 73–86). New York: Routledge.

van Es, E. A., & Sherin, M. G. (2002). Learning to notice: Scaffolding new teachers' interpretations of classroom interactions. *Journal of Technology and Teacher Education, 10*(4), 571–596.

Van Maele, D., Van Houtte, M., & Forsyth, P. B. (2014). Introduction: Trust as a matter of equity and excellence in education. In D. Van Maele, P. B. Forsyth, & M. Van Houtte (Eds.), *Trust and school life: The role of trust for learning, teaching, leading, and bridging* (pp. 1–33). Dordrecht: Springer Science+Business Media.

van Popta, E., Kral, M., & Camp, G. (2016). Exploring the value of peer feedback in online learning for the provider. *Educational Research Review, 20,* 24–34.

White, B. Y., & Frederiksen, J. R. (1998). Inquiry, modeling, and metacognition: Making science accessible to all students. *Cognition and Instruction, 16*(1), 3–118.

Williams, E. (1992). Student attitudes towards approaches to learning and assessment. *Assessment and Evaluation in Higher Education, 17*(1), 45–58.

Wylie, E. C., & Lyon, C. J. (2012). *Quality instruction and quality formative assessment: The same or different?* Paper presented at the annual meeting of the American Educational Research Association and the National Council on Measurement in Education, Vancouver, Canada.

Wylie, E. C., & Lyon, C. J. (2015). The fidelity of formative assessment implementation: Issues of breadth and quality. *Assessment in Education: Principles, Policy & Practice, 22*(1), 140–160.

Zhao, Y. (1998). The effects of anonymity on computer-mediated peer review. *International Journal of Educational Telecommunications, 4*(4), 311–345.

Zimmerman, B. J. (2008). Investigating self-regulation and motivation: Historical background, methodological developments, and future prospects. *American Educational Research Journal, 45*(1), 166–183. doi:10.3102/0002831207312909

10

Discussion of Part II

Should "Measurement" Have a Role in Teacher Learning about Classroom Assessment?

Lorrie A. Shepard

I agreed, with some trepidation, to write a commentary chapter for this volume on *Classroom Assessment and Educational Measurement*. My fears arose because I believe, based on evidence, that further intrusion of measurement into classroom assessment could very likely do more harm than good. Traditional "tests and measurement" conceptions of assessment are already hugely present in today's classrooms in the form of high-stakes test preparation, interim tests, and the multitude of worksheets and chapter tests that imitate standardized tests. Although there are innovations such as learning progressions that could redress some of these old conceptions, the question is whether measurement and data-focused interventions are the best way for teachers and districts to accomplish urgently needed instructional transformations. The editors and I agreed that fields of inquiry benefit when points of disagreement are clearly identified and actively engaged. They also agreed that I could be the more quarrelsome or negative commentator, given that the other two respondents in the volume would be more sanguine and enthusiastic in their attitudes toward measurement framings.

To begin, let me offer my own clarification regarding the province of classroom assessment. Virtually all educators as well as researchers who study *classroom assessment* agree that it includes both formative assessment, used by teachers and students to help with learning, and summative assessment, used primarily to assign grades. There is disagreement—as we see debated among the authors of the Ferrara, Maxey-Moore, and Brookhart chapter (this volume)—as to whether classroom assessment should also include interim tests and student learning objectives (SLOs) used to evaluate teachers. My own position, surprisingly, is that it is fine to allow these practices within the scope of a *scholarly analysis* of "classroom assessment," because teachers and students are forced to experience them. That doesn't mean that they are benign practices, however, nor that they can claim the support of research evidence. Formative assessment experts fought a significant definitional fight, over a decade ago, to distinguish interim tests (Perie, Marion, & Gong, 2009), which lacked a research base, from formative assessment (Kahl, 2005; McManus, 2008; Shepard, 2008), which had been shown to improve learning (Black & Wiliam, 1998). As I elaborate further in a later section of this chapter, this distinction in theory and empirical warrant is even more starkly drawn today.

In the sections that follow, I first present a conceptual framework intended to show the relationship between formative and summative assessment, and at the same time to highlight their quite different connections to theories of learning and motivation. All four of the chapters in this part offer summaries of research on formative assessment consistent with the framework I present. Indeed, chapters by Briggs and Furtak (this volume) and Wylie and Lyon (this volume) can be seen as field-based projects designed to enhance our understanding of specific elements of formative assessment that sit within this larger framework.

In the second, cautionary section of the chapter, I explain the sources of my worries about further intrusions of measurement into classrooms. I review what the research literature tells us about the kinds of feedback that have negative effects on learning and the counterproductive effects of interim tests and data-driven decision-making (DDDM). To a large extent, I am framing these concerns for the field rather than finding fault with the contributions of authors in this volume. In fact, I have only one major point of disagreement regarding contributions in this part. Despite the thoughtfulness of their translations, I want to argue against the use of measurement standards—even if offered in teacher language—as the primary way that teachers should learn about embedded formative assessment, student motivation, or grading practices. Because of this disagreement, in the third section of the chapter I review the history of "tests and measurement" courses as part of teacher preparation, and argue alternatively for a disciplinary and deep learning framing to help teachers develop a repertoire of assessment practices consistent with ambitious teaching.

In the fourth and final section of the chapter, I consider what measurement experts could best contribute to the improvement of teaching and learning. I argue for more synergistic projects such as that described by Briggs and Furtak (this volume) or earlier by Alonzo and Steedle (2009), whereby psychometric expertise is used to enhance summative assessments that are used to improve curriculum and instructional strategies at a different distance from daily student–teacher interactions.

Conceptual Framework: Learning Theory, Formative Assessment, and Grading Practices

A theoretical model is necessary to guide the development of learning and teaching innovations and to evaluate their efficacy. Quite a number of theoretical models have been offered specifically for formative assessment to help us understand how it works to improve learning. Two decades ago, I argued that present-day research on learning—based on cognitive, constructivist, and sociocultural theories—should be used to develop a learning culture in classrooms (Shepard, 2000). This was in contrast to prevailing test-focused practices (then and still) based on a behaviorist view of learning involving atomized bits of knowledge and extrinsic rewards and punishments. Focusing specifically on disciplinary learning, *Knowing What Students Know* (KWSK) (National Research Council [NRC], 2001) authors emphasized that assessments should be grounded in a cognitive model of learning reflecting the typical ways that students represent knowledge and develop competence in a subject domain.

More recently, Black and Wiliam (2009) offered a theory of formative assessment explaining how research on self-regulation and productive models of formative feedback fit within "more comprehensive theories of pedagogy" (p. 18). They considered, for example, how classroom discourse practices could serve to enact formative assessment strategies such as "activating students as the owners of their own learning" (p. 8). Building on both KWSK and Black and Wiliam (2009), Bennett (2011) argued that an explicit *theory of action* is needed before we can "meaningfully evaluate the underlying mechanisms that are supposed to cause the intended effects" (p. 14). Penuel and Shepard (2016) took up Bennett's theory of action idea, but we argued further that to be effective such a practical argument must be connected explicitly to a theory of learning. We explained the importance of discipline-specific sociocognitive models of learning and to this added the importance of sociocultural theory as a more integrative and equity-focused understanding of how learning and development occur.

Rather than seeing these as many competing and divergent theories, it is more useful to emphasize the extent to which these conceptualizations are compatible, which I attempt to do in the model I present next. Note that the contrast between a largely cognitive research base in KWSK versus a more contemporary emphasis on sociocultural theory reflects a general shift over time in the learning sciences—from recognizing mere social influences on individual cognition to a conception of learning that is socially situated, such that cultural values, ways of interacting, and identity development are completely entwined with intellectual development. Cognitive theory need not be at odds with sociocultural theory, and indeed it continues to provide important insights regarding transfer and knowledge use (NRC, 2012; Shepard, Penuel, & Pellegrino, 2018).

The picture in Figure 10.1 is intended to illustrate how—according to a sociocultural view of knowing and becoming—intrapersonal, cognitive, and interpersonal competencies are jointly developed (NRC, 2012). These interrelated competencies, shown on the left when a student first enters the classroom, are developed through an entwined learning progression and result in desired outcomes in these domains, which include affirmation and further development of a student's identity. Shepard et al. (2018) described the importance of sociocultural theory as the most appropriate overarching or "grand" theory of learning because it takes account of the assets from home and community that students bring with them to the classroom. Sociocultural theory is also the theoretical framing that best explains how expertise in disciplinary practices is developed, why collaborative and discourse-based instructional routines enhance deep learning, and how intrinsic motivation and self-regulation may be fostered by a sense of shared purpose and belonging. In short, sociocultural theory explains how a learning-focused classroom culture may be developed. This is the same idea that Alonzo (this volume) analyzes by referring to the norms and social meanings that shape the classroom assessment environment.

At the center of Figure 10.1, acting on the entwined learning progression, are both formative assessment and ambitious teaching practices. There is a growing literature on *ambitious teaching, high-leverage, and core teaching practices* that calls for ways of teaching that are interactive and discourse-based (Ball & Forzani, 2011; Lampert & Graziani, 2009). I provide a further summary of this literature in Shepard (2019), for which Figure 10.1 was first constructed. As an example of ambitious teaching, consider this excerpt where Windschitl, Thompson, Braaten, and Stroupe (2012) describe equitable and rigorous pedagogy:

> In the science classroom, this means that students learn to generate coherent explanations of natural phenomena using a variety of intellectual and social resources; they understand how claims are justified, how to represent their thinking to others, critique one another's ideas in ways that are civil and productive, and revise their ideas in response to evidence and argument. The hallmark of this pedagogy is its adaptiveness to students' needs and thinking . . .
>
> (p. 881)

Importantly, formative assessment is itself a high-leverage instructional practice. In many cases, specific strategies such as eliciting and building on students' thinking may be thought of as an example of both ambitious teaching and formative assessment practices.

The editors of this volume hoped to recruit chapter authors who were contributing new work to the development of classroom assessment. Indeed, Briggs and Furtak (this volume) describe the painstaking theoretical and empirical work that is required to create and test a discipline-specific learning progression that models the three dimensions of the Next Generation Science Standards (NGSS) (NRC, 2013). Learning progressions are one type of the more fine-grained

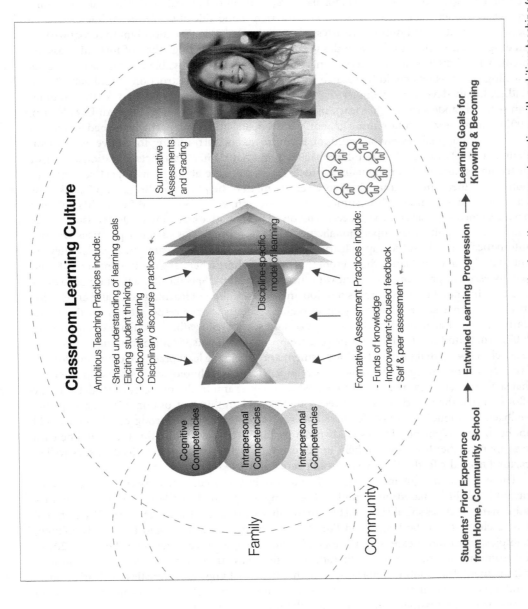

Classroom Learning Culture

Ambitious Teaching Practices include:

- Shared understanding of learning goals
- Eliciting student thinking
- Collaborative learning
- Disciplinary discourse practices

Summative Assessments and Grading

Discipline-specific model of learning

Formative Assessment Practices include:

- Funds of knowledge
- Improvement-focused feedback
- Self & peer assessment

Cognitive Competencies

Intrapersonal Competencies

Interpersonal Competencies

Family

Community

Students' Prior Experience from Home, Community, School → **Entwined Learning Progression** → **Learning Goals for Knowing & Becoming**

Figure 10.1 A progression-based model of a classroom learning culture connecting formative assessment practices with ambitious teaching (reproduced with permission from Shepard, 2019).

models of learning that can be used to coherently link curriculum, instruction, and assessment as recommended in KWSK (NRC, 2001). In Figure 10.1, I have attached the discipline-specific theory of learning label to the cognitive competencies strand, but in fact the intra- and interpersonal strands are also invoked by the NGSS vision, which entails participation in disciplinary practices and a student's developing identity as someone who can know and do science. Learning progressions also connect formative assessment to the goals and criteria used in summative assessments and grading, shown on the right-hand side of the figure. While coherence between formative and summative assessment is essential, it is also important to recognize that grading practices may undermine the positive, learning-affirming ethos of formative assessment, which I discuss in the next section. Note also that it is not possible to imagine that formal learning progressions could be created for every K-12 unit of instruction (Brookhart, 2018). Rather, highly developed examples such as that provided by Briggs and Furtak (this volume) can serve as models for teacher learning and, analogous to teacher noticing (van Es & Sherin, 2002), can prompt attention more generally to students' initial and partially formed ideas.

In his influential review of definitional controversies surrounding formative assessment, Bennett (2011) asserted that useful feedback requires both suitable artifacts (questions, tasks, or instruments) and well-conceptualized processes. In thinking about their respective contributions to the theoretical framing in Figure 10.1, it might be helpful to see Briggs and Furtak (this volume) as an example of "instrumentation" research, while Wylie and Lyon (this volume) have designed supports for the processes involved in formative assessment. Quite wisely, Wylie and Lyon recognize that "operationalizing" a list of formative assessment practices will not automatically result in the happy learning culture envisioned in theoretical models. They set out to design and evaluate a digital tool that would help teachers engage students in self- and peer assessment practices consistent with theoretical claims. Specifically, self- and peer assessment are intended to help learners develop an understanding of learning goals and criteria for success, enhance self-regulation by encouraging students to take responsibility for their own learning, and engage peers as social supports and sources of feedback (Wiliam & Thompson, 2007). Their findings from a pilot project are promising but also confirm findings from prior research showing that peer and self-assessment are among the least practiced of various formative assessment strategies. Moreover, merely providing a technological tool does not ensure that self- or peer assessment will be enacted well. For example, the majority of students in the pilot said that they liked giving and receiving feedback in this way, but only 20% gave quality feedback by attending to task features and success criteria. While strong conclusions could not be drawn, Wylie and Lyon's study provides hints about ways that this tool could be used to support teacher learning and help students improve the quality of their feedback, as well as learning from the feedback received from peers.

There is general agreement among the authors in this volume that assessment of and for learning should be based on a model of learning as specified in KWSK and that formative assessment practices should be used to gain insight to further the learning process. What should also be clear—from the Briggs and Furtak (this volume) and Wylie and Lyon (this volume) examples, from more extensive reviews of formative assessment (Penuel & Shepard, 2016), and from the ambitious teaching literature—is that these transformative changes are difficult to implement. It is doubly important, then, that their enabling characteristics be clearly understood. It is also essential, as I explain in the next section, that reform efforts and resources not be misspent on assessment products that lack these essential features.

Why a Measurement Framing Could Undermine Deep Learning Intentions

As illustrated by the central arrow in Figure 10.1, formative assessment and ambitious teaching practices must be coherently linked to summative assessments and learning goals. The danger of inviting the measurement community to create such linkages is that they might sometimes respond by building and selling traditional tests. The all-multiple-choice interim assessment products that proliferated in response to No Child Left Behind cannot adequately represent ambitious content goals and disciplinary practices called for by the Common Core State Standards (CCSS) or NGSS. For example, interim test items are insufficient as measures of mathematical or scientific practices such as modeling if they only ask students to select a right answer. Making assumptions about real-world contexts, creating diagrams and graphs, evaluating solutions, and revising a model are all aspects of the learning goal that cannot be captured adequately by multiple-choice test questions. Moreover, it reflects an outdated and inequitable theory of learning to say that learners must master low-level test content *before* they can go on to thinking about real-world contexts. A similar critique can be offered regarding the use of only multiple-choice items for virtually all of the disciplinary practices called for by contemporary standards.

In addition, there are socio-emotional consequences to predominantly quantitative systems that position many students as incapable learners by regularly reporting their below-proficiency status. Telling students how many more points they need to reach proficiency is not the kind of feedback that helps students know how to improve, and feedback in comparison to peers is antithetical to the features of formative assessment practices that most contribute to their efficacy in support of student learning. There is an extensive research literature on feedback (Shute, 2008) and on motivation (Ryan & Deci, 2000) showing that not all feedback is beneficial. In fact, feedback may sometimes have a negative rather than positive effect on learning. In the well-known meta-analysis by Kluger and DeNisi (1996), one-third of the 607 effect sizes were negative, meaning that in those studies students who received feedback learned less subsequently than controls who received no feedback. The pattern that was identified by Kluger and DeNisi and repeated in subsequent reviews (Hattie & Timperley, 2007) is that feedback (even praise) that focuses on the person tends to have negative effects on learning in contrast to feedback that focuses on specific features of the task and ways to improve.

Telling students where they stand compared to others is so unlikely to support new learning that in a review of feedback in computer-based learning environments, Van der Kleij, Feskens, and Eggen (2015) commented that "the number of studies examining feedback aimed at the level of self . . . is fortunately low" (p. 501). Yet the harm of these types of comparisons, especially when made in public, is not recognized in schools, and therefore has not stopped the proliferation of data walls in classrooms that publicly announce who is a red, yellow, or green learner. Data walls arose as a school practice in response to NCLB to communicate the importance of raising test scores (Koyama, 2013). They began in superintendents' offices by comparing schools and then moved to schools to compare teachers and finally children. *Data walls are a form of public shaming for low-performing students* (Strauss, 2014). Although many teachers believe that posting children's scores (in ways that clearly show their normative place compared to others) will motivate them to try harder (Marsh, Farrell, & Bertrand, 2016), such beliefs are clearly at odds with the motivation literature (Ames, 1992; Ryan & Deci, 2000).

Marsh et al. (2016) used an updated version of goal theory to analyze how teachers are currently using data with students and whether their approaches contribute to a performance or mastery orientation. Note that developing a mastery orientation is consistent with research on self-regulation whereby students are intrinsically motivated and believe that expending effort will help them become more adept. It is also worth emphasizing that mastery or performance orientations are not inborn personal traits, but rather can vary with learning contexts. Marsh et al. (2016) found that only one-quarter of the studied data use classrooms maintained a mastery orientation focused on meaningful and interesting learning activities, recognizing effort and student responsibility, and specific ways to improve one's work. In the one-third of cases that were performance-oriented, and somewhat in the mixed data use cases as well, teachers publicly displayed data to "incentivize" students, focused on status rather than growth, presented data in comparison to others, tied rewards to relative status, did not involve students in subsequent instructional decisions, and "gave low levels of support to help students bridge the gap between knowledge and action" (p. 262). It would be hard to think of a picture of classrooms more at odds with the literature on formative assessment. Marsh et al. (2016) acknowledged the disconnect between policy-level discourse derived from the organizational literature on continuous improvement and what is happening in classrooms. These efforts, they said, "failed to tap into extensive research on feedback and formative assessment about how to engage students in review of data in ways that promote motivation and productive work" (p. 271). A question worth asking is whether teachers simply need better training about thoughtful "data use" or whether it is the format of the test products themselves, plus an all-encompassing accountability culture and emphasis on quantification, that make undesirable practices so prevalent.

Data-driven decision making (DDDM)—which burgeoned under Race to the Top and philanthropic funding—is closely tied to interim tests and comes from a different theoretical source than the learning research that underpins formative assessment and disciplinary standards. DDDM derives from business and management research, specifically Deming's (1986) *total quality management* and Senge's (1990) conception of the "learning organization," and does not include a theory of learning (Penuel & Shepard, 2016). Despite a large number of published studies, including special issues of both the *American Journal of Education* (Coburn & Turner, 2012) and *Teachers College Record* (Mandinach & Gummer 2015; Turner & Coburn, 2012), very little attention has been paid to the nature of instructional changes or to the effects of DDDM on student learning. More often, DDDM studies focus on what Turner and Coburn (2012) referred to as data use interventions, looking at the policies, programs, and tools used to convene educators to examine and act on data.

In a rare large-scale, school-level randomized experiment, Konstantopoulos, Miller, van der Ploeg, and Li (2016) examined the effects of interim testing programs on mathematics and reading achievement. They found no significant differences between treatment and control schools in grades 3–8, but interim testing programs had a significant negative effect in grades K–2. In recent studies that attend to the nature of teachers' data use conversations, serious concerns have been raised about the opposing forces of an accountability culture in schools and equity goals (Datnow, Greene, & Gannon-Slaer, 2017). For example, teachers may use student characteristics to explain test results rather than looking for causes in their own instruction (Bertrand & Marsh, 2015), and they may abandon rich science learning experience when their district's data use initiative defines success narrowly in terms of improved test scores (Braaten, Bradford, Kirchgasler, & Barocas, 2017).

These negative findings about interim testing programs and DDDM are offered as a cautionary tale. The evidence does not prove that these initiatives are always harmful. In fact, many studies in the DDDM literature conclude with recommendations about the kinds of district-level supports and teacher professional development that might improve data use. The point I want to make here is that such data-focused efforts are misdirected because they are guided by flawed theory and rely on interim tests that do not help teachers gain insight into student thinking. Interim tests are not built to foster collaborative conversations, ambitious teaching practices, or a learning culture. It is with this set of worries in mind that I argue in the next section for teacher professional development regarding classroom assessment to be more closely connected to disciplinary curricular reforms and instructional professional development rather than as separate assessment literacy or data literacy initiatives.

Centering Teacher Learning in Disciplinary Curricular Reforms and Ambitious Teaching Practices Not Measurement

The discussion about how and whether to translate the *Standards for Educational and Psychological Testing* (American Educational Research Association [AERA], American Psychological Association [APA], & National Council on Measurement in Education [NCME], 2014) to make them accessible to classroom teachers is part of a much larger debate about what is meant by assessment literacy, how much it should be defined by traditional measurement principles, and, most importantly, who should be responsible for "delivering" assessment literacy as part of teacher preparation programs. Ferrara, Maxey-Moore, and Brookhart (this volume) did a reasonably good job of selecting 12 standards from the nearly 200 test standards relevant to educational testing, and their translations into teacher language reflect a thoughtful effort to imagine how the respective testing standards might play out in classrooms. Of course, we want practicing teachers and teacher candidates to be able to develop and select rich instructional activities and tasks that nurture progress toward intended learning goals and to be able to elicit and interpret evidence of student thinking. We also want there to be constancy in the criteria use to evaluate student work even as students' capabilities are changing; otherwise, there can't be a shared understanding about what success looks like and how to improve.

I disagree with Ferrara et al. (this volume), however, and with Alonzo's (this volume) renaming of validity about *whether translated measurement standards should be an organizing framework for teacher learning about classroom assessment*. Note that Alonzo's chapter provides an important review of previous efforts to translate standards plus an extensive analysis of the formative assessment literature—one that is entirely consistent with the overview and theoretical model I offered in the first section. Alonzo's validity framework would be entirely appropriate for "an *inquiry* into formative effects of classroom assessment" (p. 132, emphasis added) if, for example, researchers were to investigate whether a test product was validly serving formative purposes. The point of disagreement, then, is only about whether translated test standards should be at the center of teacher learning.

In addition to negative findings about data walls, interim tests, and DDDM outlined above, leaders in the National Council on Measurement in Education (NCME) and NCME's Classroom Assessment Task Force should consider the negative history of "tests and measurement" courses that historically were a routine part of teacher education requirements. In 2006, I reviewed the textbooks that had been used in these courses from the 1940s through the 1990s. Typical chapter headings shown here illustrate the technical measurement and instrumentation focus with the goal of making classroom tests in the image of standardized tests:

  I. The purpose of measurement and evaluation
  II. The statistical analysis of test results
  III. Validity
  IV. Reliability
  V. General principles of test construction (includes specifying instructional objectives)
  VI. Principles of objective test construction
  VII. Principles of essay test construction
  VIII. Item analysis for classroom tests
  IX. Grading and reporting
  X. IQ testing and scholastic aptitude
  XI. Standardized achievement tests
  XII. Measures of interest and personality
  XIII. Interpreting test norms

(Shepard, 2006, p. 625)

In that historical review, I also summarized the revolt against standardized testing by subject matter experts and the rise of assessment expertise within content disciplines (Shepard, 2006). The thoughtful treatment of assessment purposes and methods in the first *Curriculum and Evaluation Standards for School Mathematics* (National Council of Teachers of Mathematics, 1989) is but one example.

The question, then, is whether promulgation of the test standards as part of assessment literacy efforts will encourage again an instrumentation and test score focus. I said at the outset that interim tests and SLOs could be within the scope of a scholarly analysis of classroom assessment. But what should be apparent in Ferrara et al. (this volume) is the extent to which formative assessment processes have been pushed to the side to make room for these other practices along with summative testing. Though the authors strive valiantly not to make such a mistake, language in the formative assessment column occasionally lapses into conclusions about mastery status rather than insights about current thinking. More to the point, as the authors acknowledge in their concluding discussion, there are genuine questions about whether the standards categories are the right set of considerations. In my view, however, this should not be because they don't cover the relevant *psychometric* considerations, but because they don't address the more important things that teachers need to know about learning theory, motivation, and specific disciplinary models of knowledge development and knowledge use. The test standards do not consider learning processes, and it is arguably a distortion of disciplinary learning to consider content, cognitive process, and construct as if they should be separate standards.

As an exercise to consider what the content might be of a mandated assessment literacy course, I reviewed the table of contents for nine current classroom assessment textbooks identified through Google and Amazon searches. Classroom assessment textbooks represent a considerable range as to whether they reflect a traditional measurement perspective versus a shift toward more of a learning perspective. On the traditional end of the spectrum are chapter titles very similar to the historic list above, which include validity, reliability, and how to make tests, including multiple-choice and essay test questions. Improving on the past, the list of test types includes portfolios and performance assessments. In the middle of this continuum are textbooks that now include a chapter on formative assessment, although textbooks still vary in the extent to which a learning orientation shapes the overall approach of the book and whether research on motivation is specifically considered in the context of grading practices. As an example, Chappuis, Stiggins, Chappuis, and Arter (2012) have authored a text at the more learning-focused end of the continuum. A tenth textbook by Wiliam (2018) focuses exclusively on *embedded formative assessment*, which I would argue teacher candidates need most to overcome their own negative experiences with testing. If we treat this range of textbooks as proxies for what might be intended by assessment literacy, then I would ask the Classroom Assessment Task Force to join me in arguing for the learning-focused end of the continuum rather than the traditional end where validity and reliability standards are featured prominently. Chappuis et al. (2012) and Wiliam (2018), of course, care about validity, but they don't use that language, preferring to talk instead about the adequacy and accuracy of evidence gathered to represent intended learning goals.

As to who should be involved in teaching teacher candidates about classroom assessment, I believe it should be subject matter experts more often than measurement specialists. The number of university professors with expertise in psychometrics—who also have disciplinary expertise and know something about the formative assessment practices described earlier—is small. That limited set includes many of the authors in this volume, but there aren't such measurement specialists at many institutions. The question of how to represent learning goals (and progress toward them) is conceptually the same whether planning for instructional activities or assessment strategies. Therefore, the ability to jointly construct instruction and assessment is heavily dependent on subject matter expertise and more often found in content methods teacher education courses.

The demands on pre-service teachers for new learning are enormous. Three-dimensional science standards and Common Core State Standards in mathematics and English language arts are consistent with ambitious teaching practices but often are very different from teacher candidates' own experiences in school. In the case of veteran teachers, Bill Penuel, Jim Pellegrino, and I (Shepard et al., 2018) have argued for the importance of *coherence* in learning opportunities for teachers as well as for students. The need is even greater for pre-service teachers. Novices should not have to figure out by themselves how new standards and research on learning and motivation integrate with assessment practices.

In presenting Figure 10.1, I made the case that formative assessment practices such as eliciting student thinking and improvement-focused feedback should be coherently linked to ambitious teaching practices such as clarifying learning goals and facilitating disciplinary discourse practices. From the perspective of sociocultural learning theory, they are part of the same fabric. Although some high-leverage teaching practices such as leading a discussion might ultimately generalize across disciplines, providing opportunities for teacher candidates to rehearse and develop the sense-making behind such practices invariably requires discipline-specific enactments. Boerst, Sleep, Ball, and Bass (2011), for example, created a framework to identify different purposes for teacher questions from which teacher candidates could then generate classroom *talk moves* in kid-friendly language. Purposes for questioning included "checking whether right answers are supported by correct understanding, focusing students to listen and respond to others' ideas, extending students' current thinking and assessing how far they can be stretched" (p. 2860), etc. Similarly, in their efforts to create tools to support novice teachers in developing core discourse practices in science, Windschitl et al. (2012) illustrated the close connection between learning high-leverage instructional routines and formative assessment. In learning to enact discourse practices, for example, novices moved from traditional IRE question-and-answer routines to using "students' language and partial understandings as building blocks to shape the direction of classroom conversations" (p. 899).

Measurement experts might have more to contribute in helping teachers learn how to develop classroom *summative* tests, but here too we should ask where the center of gravity should be. If the goal is to represent valued learning goals as authentically and fully as possible, and to coherently link formative and summative assessment, then projects, portfolios, and performance assessments are at least as important as traditional test formats, if not more so. In addition, being able to create a supportive learning environment also requires that teachers have access to the research literature on motivation so as to develop an understanding about why using grades to motivate and control student behavior works against equitable and deep learning opportunities, and how it is that "extrinsic rewards drive out intrinsic motivation" (Shepard et al., 2018, p. 29; see also Deci, Koestner, & Ryan, 1999).

A Place for "Measurement" of Curricular Goals

To support the type of coherent curriculum, instruction, and assessment activity system envisioned here for classrooms (and elaborated in Shepard, 2019; Shepard et al., 2018), psychometricians and measurement specialists have an important role to play, but only *in those applications where rigorous quantifications are needed*. Examples might include end-of-course departmental exams or formally developed curriculum-embedded assessment systems such as learning progression-based assessments. In Shepard et al. (2018), we discussed the vertical coherence called for in *Knowing What Students Know* (NRC, 2001) connecting classroom-level assessments (formative and summative) with external, large-scale assessments. We argued that in the United States, because of local control of curriculum, *school districts are the more appropriate level of authority* to take on the conjoint development of curriculum, instructional repertoires, and assessments for both classroom-level and district-level purposes. Districts are the locus for teacher professional development and the level at which commitments and discourses about equity are held. At present, it is often the case that district-led teacher professional development in content domains—early literacy, implementation of Common Core State Standards, 3D science instruction, etc.—is carried out separately from assessment initiatives, such as interim test implementation, competency-based grading, or data-driven decision-making. When these initiatives are conceptually incongruent, none are implemented well, or, as is more often the case, accountability oriented practices win out, as is seen in the DDDM literature (Datnow et al., 2017; Garner, Thorne, & Horn, 2017).

Research–practice partnerships (RPPs) (Coburn, Penuel, & Geil, 2013) are one means of addressing the challenging development work entailed in creating integrated curriculum, instructional activities, assessment, and teacher professional learning communities faithful to visions of equitable and ambitious teaching. Measurement experts are urgently needed participants in such partnerships. RPPs involve district content specialists, teachers, and researchers (with both disciplinary and assessment expertise) in long-term collaborations addressing local problems of practice. The mutuality of RPPs, with practitioners and researchers on equal footing, and their long-term horizons make it more likely that necessary recursive cycles of development and adaptation will actually be possible. Although funding from the National Science Foundation and philanthropic foundations is important, especially to support the research component of such projects, similar projects are also possible when large districts or district consortia bring together their own content area and assessment experts and redirect resources presently allocated separately to textbooks, interim tests, and instructional technology.

As part of their RPP, Briggs and Furtak (this volume) describe how a learning progression—or some other model of learning—can serve as the organizing framework around which both instructional uses of performance-based tasks and district-level assessments can be organized, thus ensuring conceptual coherence between the two but with very different use profiles. Project researchers created an initial progression for modeling energy flows and sample tasks as "starting points," but then teachers developed their own assessment tasks that were more closely attuned to their specific disciplinary contexts. The project's commitment to teacher professional development can be seen in the recursive and adaptive nature of teacher meetings focused on analyzing student work, recognizing distinctions, and then advancing specific aspects of student thinking. For district-level comparative purposes, performance-based tasks (such as those used as part of instructional activities) could be combined with phenomenon-based item clusters and conceptually oriented multiple-choice items to meet aggregate-level requirements for standardization and reliability.

Measurement specialists will be most at home contributing to the aggregate, formal, monitoring side of assessment systems. But this should by no means be a call for business as usual. Rather, measurement and subject matter expertise is needed jointly to engage in *research and development efforts to better represent ambitious learning goals* and the intermediate steps toward those goals. Contemporary standards call for quite different curricula and instructional repertoires that have only begun to be developed in practice (e.g., for a comprehensive review of research on high-level learning goals in literature, science, and history, see Goldman et al., 2016). Changes in measurement representations of learning goals have typically lagged behind instructional reforms. Often traditional test item formats are relied upon that only nominally address intended learning targets. An alternative approach would be to start with instructional artifacts and evidence of student learning *in situ* and ask how such evidence could be lifted to the level of formal assessments (not for classroom uses, but for large-scale monitoring purposes). Briggs and Furtak (this volume) discuss the use of psychometric models to evaluate the validity of a learning progression "hypothesis," but more broadly it will be important to use an array of methodological tools, including clinical interviews, to study what students are learning, what interventions or teaching moves further that learning, and ultimately what summary indicators can best be used to capture that learning for comparative and monitoring purposes.

Conclusion

In this commentary, I have argued that quantification and measurement should not be at the center of teacher learning about classroom assessment. A review of the research on formative assessment and its efficacy in furthering student learning makes it clear that learning theory, subject matter knowledge, and pedagogical expertise required for ambitious teaching practices are much more critical for teacher professional development than knowledge of testing standards could ever be.

The model I present for creating a learning-focused classroom culture is based on socio-cultural theory and is intended to illustrate the importance of classroom practices that attend to students' cultural resources from home and community and then integrate, on an ongoing basis, development of students' identity-producing intrapersonal and interpersonal competencies along with discipline-specific cognitive development. To do this, learning goals and success criteria for formative and summative assessment practices must be conceptually coherent, and neither can be based on point systems or grading practices that result in normative comparisons, shaming, or other forms of commodification that undercut intrinsic motivation to learn. While I continue to endorse the call in *Knowing What Students Know* (NRC, 2001) for vertical coherence between classroom-level and large-scale assessments, I have more recently argued that for teacher learning purposes, formative assessment practices can be more deeply understood and enacted if they are developed as a strand within high-leverage, ambitious teaching practices.

There is a great deal of agreement in the learning and motivation literatures about the features of formative assessment that best explain its effectiveness (see also Black & Wiliam, 2009; Penuel & Shepard, 2016; Shepard et al., 2018). The model I offer is consistent with the framing provided by Alonzo (this volume) and by Wylie and Lyon (this volume). Alonzo, for example, considers the discourse practices by which disciplinary criteria are developed and internalized and also the relational aspects of classroom interactions that affect "effort, engagement, motivation, and self-efficacy" (McMillan, 2003, p. 37). Wylie and Lyon's study involved creation and research on a digital tool intended to support students' participation in self- and peer assessment. These practices have the potential to improve metacognition and self-regulation, but have been taken up less frequently than other more familiar aspects of formative assessment.

The negative stance in this commentary—against measurement specialists taking the lead in teaching teachers about assessment—is rooted in prior negative experiences. While interim tests can, of course, be used formatively, they do not reflect the kinds of ongoing instructional interactions called for in the formative assessment literature (Black & Wiliam, 1998; Shepard, 2008). Moreover, it is inconceivable that those products that use only multiple-choice formats could adequately measure disciplinary practices called for by contemporary standards (note that the only randomized study examining the effects of interim tests on achievement found no-difference results for grades 3–8 and negative effects for grades K–2; Konstantopoulos et al., 2016). The use of these and other achievement measures as a core focus of data-driven decision-making has been studied extensively but only in terms of teacher conversations, data use skills, and institutional supports, not the effects of DDDM on the quality of instruction or student learning. In fact, some recent studies show that convening teacher learning communities around accountability mandates and impoverished data sets may undermine rather than enhance equity goals (Bertrand & Marsh, 2015; Braaten et al., 2017; Garner et al., 2017).

204 • Lorrie A. Shepard

With the exception of many of the authors in this volume, most measurement specialists lack the teaching and learning and disciplinary expertise needed to lead ambitious teaching reform efforts. Thus, there is a connection between *who* should lead the effort and *what* the priorities are likely to be set for teacher learning. Focusing on the test standards, even if offered in teacher-friendly language, is likely to repeat many of the refrains from old "tests and measurements" courses that emphasized technical requirements, test formats, and the role of external tests. These should not be the main focus of teacher learning.

For new or veteran teachers, development of learning-focused "assessment cultural practices" (Shepard et al., 2018) makes the most sense when it is coherent with other professional development efforts—on new Common Core State Standards and Next Generation Science Standards and high-leverage instructional practices. Disciplinary expertise is clearly needed to lead such efforts. Instead of separate assessment or data literacy efforts, I have argued that measurement specialists have a more important role to play if they *partner with disciplinary experts* to address those particular assessment applications where rigorous quantification methods are required. These instances occur when formal learning models are developed linking classroom level and district or state assessments, as with the Briggs and Furtak (this volume) research–practice partnership. Because school districts have responsibility for curriculum, teacher professional development, and equity, districts could be the site for disciplinary and measurement experts coming together to develop much more thoroughly integrated curriculum, instruction, and assessment systems in support of deeper learning (Shepard et al., 2018).

References

Alonzo, A. C., & Steedle, J. T. (2009). Developing and assessing a force and motion learning progression. *Science Education*, 93(3), 389–421.

American Educational Research Association (AERA), American Psychological Association (APA), & National Council on Measurement in Education (NCME). (2014). *Standards for educational and psychological testing*. Washington, DC: American Educational Research Association, American Psychological Association, & National Council on Measurement in Education.

Ames, C. (1992). Classrooms: Goals, structures, and student motivation. *Journal of Educational Psychology*, 84(3), 261–271.

Ball, D. L., & Forzani, F. M. (2011). Building a common core for learning to teach and connecting professional learning to practice. *American Educator*, 35(2), 17–21, 38–39.

Bennett, R. E. (2011). Formative assessment: A critical review. *Assessment in Education: Principles, Policy & Practice*, 18(1), 5–25.

Bertrand, M., & Marsh, J. A. (2015). Teachers' sensemaking of data and implications for equity. *American Educational Research Journal*, 52(5), 861–893.

Black, P., & Wiliam, D. (1998). Assessment and classroom learning. *Assessment in Education: Principles, Policy & Practice*, 5(1), 7–74.

Black, P., & Wiliam, D. (2009). Developing a theory of formative assessment. *Educational Assessment, Evaluation and Accountability*, 21(1), 5–31.

Boerst, T., Sleep, L., Ball, D., & Bass, H. (2011). Preparing teachers to lead mathematics discussions. *Teachers College Record*, 113(12), 2844–2877.

Braaten, M., Bradford, C., Kirchgasler, K. L., & Barocas, S. F. (2017). How data use for accountability undermines equitable science education. *Journal of Educational Administration*, 55(4), 427–446.

Brookhart, S. M. (2018). Learning is the primary source of coherence in assessment. *Educational Measurement: Issues and Practice*, 37(1), 35–38.

Chappuis, J., Stiggins, R., Chappuis, S., & Arter, J. (2012). *Classroom assessment for student learning: Doing it right—using it well* (2nd ed.). Upper Saddle River, NJ: Pearson.

Coburn, C. E., Penuel, W. R., & Geil, K. (2013). *Research–practice partnerships at the district level: A new strategy for leveraging research for educational improvement*. New York: William T. Grant Foundation.

Coburn, C. E., & Turner, E. O. (2012). The practice of data use: An introduction. *American Journal of Education*, 118(2), 99–111.

Datnow, A., Greene, J. C., & Gannon-Slater, N. (2017). Guest editorial. *Journal of Educational Administration*, 55(4), 354–360.

Deci, E. L., Koestner, R., & Ryan, R. M. (1999). A meta-analytic review of experiments examining the effects of extrinsic rewards on intrinsic motivation. *Psychological Bulletin, 125*, 627–668.

Deming, W. E. (1986). *Out of the crisis.* Cambridge, MA: MIT Press.

Garner, B., Thorne, J. K., & Horn, I. S. (2017). Teachers interpreting data for instructional decisions: Where does equity come in? *Journal of Educational Administration, 55*(4), 407–426.

Goldman, S. R., Britt, M. A., Brown, W., Cribb, G., George, M., Greenleaf, C., Lee, C. D., Shanahan, C., & Project READI. (2016). Disciplinary literacies and learning to read for understanding: A conceptual framework for disciplinary literacy. *Educational Psychologist, 51*(2), 219–246.

Hattie, J., & Timperley, H. (2007). The power of feedback. *Review of Educational Research, 77*(1), 81–112.

Kahl, S. (2005, October 26). Where in the world are formative tests? Right under your nose! *Education Week, 25*, 38.

Kluger, A. N., & DeNisi, A. (1996). The effects of feedback interventions on performance: A historical review, a meta-analysis, and a preliminary feedback intervention theory. *Psychological Bulletin, 119*(2), 254–284.

Konstantopoulos, S., Miller, S. R., van der Ploeg, A., & Li, W. (2016). Effects of interim assessments on student achievement: Evidence from a large-scale experiment. *Journal of Research on Educational Effectiveness, 9*(1), 188–208.

Koyama, J. (2013). Global scare tactics and the call for US schools to be held accountable. *American Journal of Education, 120*(1), 77–99.

Lampert, M., & Graziani, F. (2009). Instructional activities as a tool for teachers' and teacher educators' learning in and for practice. *Elementary School Journal, 109*(5), 491–509.

Mandinach, E. B., & Gummer, E. (2015). *Teachers College Record, 117*(4).

Marsh, J. A., Farrell, C. C., & Bertrand, M. (2016). Trickle-down accountability: How middle school teachers engage students in data use. *Educational Policy, 30*(2), 243–280.

McManus, S. (2008). *Attributes of effective formative assessment.* Washington, DC: Council for Chief State School Officers.

McMillan, J. H. (2003). Understanding and improving teachers' classroom assessment decision making: Implications for theory and practice. *Educational Measurement: Issues and Practice, 22*(4), 34–43.

National Council of Teachers of Mathematics. (1989). *Curriculum and evaluation standards for school mathematics.* Reston, VA: National Council of Teachers of Mathematics.

National Research Council (NRC). (2001). *Knowing what students know: The science and design of educational assessment.* Committee on the Foundations of Assessment, J.W. Pellegrino, N. Chudowsky, & R. Glaser (Eds.). Board on Testing and Assessment, Center for Education. Division of Behavioral and Social Sciences and Education. Washington, DC: National Academies Press.

National Research Council (NRC). (2012). *Education for life and work: Developing transferable knowledge and skills in the 21st century.* Committee on Defining Deeper Learning and 21st Century Skills, J. W. Pellegrino & M. L. Hilton (Eds.). Board on Testing and Assessment and Board on Science Education, Division of Behavioral and Social Sciences in Education. Washington, DC: National Academies Press.

National Research Council (NRC). (2013). *Next Generation Science Standards: For states, by states.* Washington, DC: National Academies Press.

Penuel, W. R., & Shepard, L. A. (2016). Assessment and teaching. In D. H. Gitomer & C. A. Bell (Eds.), *Handbook of research on teaching* (5th ed., pp. 787–850). Washington, DC: American Educational Research Association.

Perie, M., Marion, S., & Gong, B. (2009). Moving toward a comprehensive assessment system: A framework for considering interim assessments. *Educational Measurement: Issues and Practice, 28*(3), 5–13.

Ryan, R. M., & Deci, E. L. (2000). Intrinsic and extrinsic motivations: Classic definitions and new directions. *Contemporary Educational Psychology, 25*(1), 54–67.

Senge, P. (1990). *The fifth discipline: The art and practice of the learning organization.* New York: Doubleday.

Shepard, L. A. (2000). The role of assessment in a learning culture. *Educational Researcher, 29*(4), 4–14.

Shepard, L. A. (2006). Classroom assessment. In R. L. Brennan (Ed.), *Educational measurement* (4th ed., pp. 623–646). Westport, CT: Greenwood Publishing Group.

Shepard, L. A. (2008). Formative assessment: Caveat emptor. In C. A. Dwyer (Ed.), *The future of assessment: Shaping teaching and learning* (pp. 279–303). New York: Lawrence Erlbaum.

Shepard, L. A. (2019). Classroom assessment to support teaching and learning. In A. Berman, M. J. Feuer, & J. W. Pellegrino (Eds.), *The ANNALS of the American Academy of Political and Social Science* (pp. 183–200). Thousand Oaks, CA: SAGE.

Shepard, L. A., Penuel, W. R., & Pellegrino, J. W. (2018). Using learning and motivation theories to coherently link formative assessment, grading practices, and large-scale assessment. *Educational Measurement: Issues and Practice, 37*(1), 21–34.

Shute, V. J. (2008). Focus on formative feedback. *Review of Educational Research, 78*(1), 153–189.

Strauss, V. (2014, February 14). How "data walls" in classrooms humiliate kids. *Washington Post.* Retrieved from www.washingtonpost.com/news/answer-sheet/wp/2014/02/14/how-data-walls-in-classrooms-can-humiliate-young-kids/?utm_term=.3577016bf4c0

Turner, E. O., & Coburn, C. E. (2012). Interventions to promote data use: An introduction. *Teachers College Record*, *114*(11), 1–13.

Van der Kleij, F. M., Feskens, R. C. W., & Eggen, T. J. H. M. (2015). Effects of feedback in computer-based learning environments on students' learning outcomes: A meta-analysis. *Review of Educational Research*, *85*(4), 475–511.

van Es, E. A., & Sherin, M. G. (2002). Learning to notice: Scaffolding new teachers' interpretations of classroom interactions. *Journal of Technology and Teacher Education*, *10*(4), 571–596.

Wiliam, D. (2018). *Embedded formative assessment* (2nd ed.). Bloomington, IN: Solution Tree Press.

Wiliam, D., & Thompson, M. (2007). Integrating assessment with instruction: What will it take to make it work? In C. A. Dwyer (Ed.), *The future of assessment: Shaping teaching and learning* (pp. 53–82). Mahwah, NJ: Erlbaum.

Windschitl, M., Thompson, J., Braaten, M., & Stroupe, D. (2012). Proposing a core set of instructional practices and tools for teachers of science. *Science Education*, *96*(5), 878–903.

Part III
Emerging Issues in Classroom Assessment

11

Towards Measures of Different and Useful Aspects of Schooling

Why Schools Need Both Teacher-Assigned Grades and Standardized Assessments

Alex J. Bowers

Introduction

Summative assessments in classrooms typically result in teacher-assigned grades. Grades are well known to be highly predictive of high school graduation, college enrollment, and college completion, but there has been little research that explains why. Additionally, in the psychometrics literature, there is a persistent perception that while standardized tests scores are objective measures of fundamental academic knowledge, grades are more subjective assessments that may vary school by school. This chapter examines the extent to which grades in high school include teacher perceptions of student effort, participation and behavior that is a different and useful measure for schools and school leadership beyond what can be provided by standardized test scores, and to what extent grades vary between schools. The chapter is organized into three related sections. To provide a discussion of these issues with grades, I first review the literature on the relationship of grades to standardized test scores, the construct validity argument that grades represent a valid measure by teachers of engaged participation, that engaged participation correlates with overall student life outcomes, and how some research has suggested that grades may be "fairer" than standardized tests as grades appear to vary less by student demographics and socioeconomic status (SES) than standardized test scores. Across this discussion, I also note how there has been a continual question in the literature about the extent that grades vary by schools, but that there is little evidence that has investigated this issue. Second, I then provide an example of testing these ideas using a hierarchical linear modeling strategy to analyze the large nationally U.S. generalizable sample, the Education Longitudinal Study of 2002 (ELS:2002), which includes almost 15,000 students across hundreds of high schools in the United States. In this example study, I look to apply the main findings and questions from the literature on grades to examine the relationship between grades and standardized tests, student background and SES, mathematics and English teachers' perception of student participation in class, and how individual student grades vary within and between schools, with a special focus on school-level context and demographics. In the third and final section, I relate the findings from the analysis to the application of the literature to the question of the utility of grades as valid classroom assessments in educational measurement, as the literature and the included study provide an argument that teacher-assigned grades are a multidimensional assessment of student work that is a different construct from academic knowledge, and that grades do not seem to be particularly dependent to a large extent on which school a student attends.

Historically, grades have been maligned by psychometricians for their "hodgepodge" nature (Brookhart, 1991), in which when asked what they assign a grade for, teachers respond that grades are assigned for a multitude of outcomes, such as academic knowledge, student participation, effort, and behavior (Cross & Frary, 1999; McMillan, 2001), known as "kitchen-sink" grading (Cizek, Fitzgerald, & Rachor, 1995–1996). Some scholars have interpreted this to mean that grades are subjective and unreliable measures of academic performance, and thus must be reformed to align much more to standardized test scores (Brookhart, 1991, 2011). As noted in this research domain, "student's grades often have little relation to their performance on state assessments" (Guskey & Jung, 2012, p. 23). But *should* grades have a relation to standardized test performance (Brookhart, 2015)? If test scores are assumed to be an accurate and reliable measure of fundamental academic knowledge, why would schools need another measure of this factor? The purposes of schooling in the United States are far from agreed upon (Labaree, 1997), and some have argued that test scores are a poor measure of what the many different stakeholders in schools are looking for schools to instill in their students (Brighouse, Ladd, Loeb, & Swift, 2018; Nichols & Berliner, 2007). Could grades measure different but important aspects of schooling?

Standardized test scores have historically lacked criterion validity to overall schooling outcomes (Atkinson & Geiser, 2009), to such an extent that many states throughout the United States, as well as countries globally, have begun to mandate exit and end-of-course exams (Allensworth, 2005a; Blazer, 2012; Nichols & Berliner, 2007; Warren, Jenkins, & Kulick, 2006) that artificially connect test scores to outcomes through retention, grade promotion, and graduation requirements (Maag Merki & Holmeier, 2015). By contrast, teacher-assigned grades are strong predictors of overall schooling outcomes, such as graduation or dropping out (Allensworth, 2005b; Barrington & Hendricks, 1989; Battin-Pearson et al., 2000; Bowers, 2010b; Bowers & Sprott, 2012; Bowers, Sprott, & Taff, 2013; Brookhart et al., 2016; Lloyd, 1978), as well as college attendance and graduation (Atkinson & Geiser, 2009; Cliffordson, 2008). In addition, grades are seen as being "fairer" assessments than standardized tests, since grades are not as strongly related to socioeconomic status (SES) (Atkinson & Geiser, 2009). As noted by Atkinson and Geiser (2009), "High school grades are sometimes viewed as a less reliable indicator than standardized tests because grading standards differ across schools. Yet although grading standards do vary by school, grades still outperform standardized tests in predicting college outcomes" (p. 665).

The focus that I aim to address in this chapter is to ask the question: Why? What is it about grades that make them a strong predictor of overall schooling outcomes that adds to the knowledge gained about student learning from standardized test scores? If schools have two measures of different and useful factors about different student outcomes from schooling, then schools should use both sets of measures to inform their practice and decision-making (Bowers, 2009, 2011; Brookhart et al., 2016; Farr, 2000).

Examining the Research on Grades in Relation to Standardized Tests

Across K-12 schooling assessment research over the past 100 years, a perennial issue has been the relationship between teacher-assigned grades and standardized assessment scores (Brookhart, 2015; Brookhart et al., 2016). As recently reviewed in their literature review of 100 years of research on grades, Brookhart et al. (2016) discuss the numerous studies that have demonstrated that across multiple contexts, as well as nationally, grades and standardized test scores continually correlate at about 0.5 (Bowers, 2011; Brennan, Kim, Wenz-Gross, & Siperstein, 2001;

Duckworth, Quinn, & Tsukayama, 2012; Linn, 1982, 2000; Welsh, D'Agostino, & Kaniskan, 2013). As noted by Brookhart et al. (2016):

> Although some variability exists across years and subjects, correlations have remained moderate but remarkably consistent in studies based on large, nationally representative data sets. Across 100 years of research, teacher-assigned grades typically correlate about .5 with standardized measures of achievement.
>
> (p. 882)

This suggests that about 25% of the variance shared between grades and what is assessed by standardized test scores is academic knowledge. (Bowers, 2011).

Grades are also well known to be strong predictors of overall schooling success (Brookhart et al., 2016). For example, low or failing grades are some of the most accurate predictors of students dropping out of high school (Bowers et al., 2013) in both single time point studies (Allensworth & Easton, 2005, 2007) as well as longitudinal research (Bowers, 2010a, 2010b; Bowers & Sprott, 2012). Additionally, grades are strong predictors of college enrollment and completion (Atkinson & Geiser, 2009; Attewell, Heil, & Reisel, 2011; Cliffordson, 2008), as well as years of schooling and long-term earnings (Jones & Jackson, 1990; Miller, 1998). For example, using the large nationally generalizable NCES High School and Beyond data set, Miller (1998) showed that for students who were in tenth grade in 1980, their high school grades significantly predicted their annual earnings in 1991, finding a strong independent effect of grades on earnings when controlling for a range of context variables, an effect in addition to years of schooling. Miller (1998) concludes that:

> One might question whether employers are really benefiting from higher grades or from the greater aptitude that is reflected in higher grades . . . [this] suggest[s] that it is the actual learning, not aptitude, that matters in predicting longterm productivity. Furthermore, the evidence presented here suggests that some part of the productivity gains might be coming from the soft skills that employers say they want and grades appear to contain. These soft skills of regular attendance, preparation, hard work, and lack of disciplinary problems that employers say they value are also valued by schools and reflected in grades.
>
> (pp. 306–307)

Thus, grades are predictive of overall schooling outcomes, yet only moderately correlate with standardized test scores. A persistent question has thus been: What does the other 75% of grades represent if it is not what is measured in standardized assessment tests (Bowers, 2011; Brookhart, 2015; Brookhart et al., 2016)? In the above quote, Miller (1998) alludes to the idea that perhaps grades are signals of "soft skills," what might be called non-cognitive skills in more recent research (Levin, 2013; West et al., 2016), which include skills that schools and employers highly value that are not included on standardized tests, such as "preparation, hard work, and lack of disciplinary problems."

This issue of what the majority of grades represent has also been a consistent issue in the grading research (Brookhart et al., 2016). As noted throughout this work, this is a question around the validity of grades (Brookhart, 2015). For example, over 70 years ago, Swineford (1947), in a study of teacher grades and marks for one elementary school, noted, "in any event, the data . . . clearly show that the marks assigned by teachers in this school are reliable measures of something, but there is apparently a lack of agreement on just what that something should be" (p. 517). Multiple surveys of teachers have shown that teachers award grades for a variety of student behaviors in addition to academic achievement (Brookhart, 1993,

1994; Cizek et al., 1995–1996; Cross & Frary, 1999; McMillan, 2001). For example, McMillan (2001) surveyed over 1,400 teachers in Virginia asking them about their grading practices, and, using factor analysis, identified that teachers award grades for a range of behaviors quite similar to those listed above by Miller (2008), behaviors that schools and employers prefer, including effort, ability, improvement, work habits, attention, and participation. Thus, rather than teacher grades being subjective and unreliable, as is intimated by the "hodgepodge" and "kitchen-sink" metaphors used in some of the research in this area noted above, it appears that teachers award grades for a variety of student behaviors that are important for overall life outcomes and are valued by students, parents, schools, and future employers (Bowers, 2009). However, much of the survey research asking teachers about their grading practices relies exclusively on teacher perception of their grading practices, rather than on the grades that they actually assign.

A growing set of research studies over the past two decades has focused on the grades that teachers assign. The research has postulated that grades are multidimensional (Bowers, 2011; Brookhart et al., 2016), assessing academic knowledge to a limited extent, but more importantly assessing what has been termed a "conative" factor (Willingham, Pollack, & Lewis, 2002), a "common grade dimension" (Klapp Lekholm, 2011; Klapp Lekholm & Cliffordson, 2008, 2009; Thorsen & Cliffordson, 2012), and a "success at school factor (SSF)" (Bowers, 2009, 2011). Across these studies, other than academic knowledge, grades appear to measure student engagement through measuring effort, participation, and behavior (Brookhart et al., 2016). As recently noted in research examining the relationship of high school grades to college readiness in the state of Alaska (Hodara & Cox, 2016), the authors note that:

> High school grade point average may be useful because it is not just a measure of cognitive ability; instead, it is a cumulative measure of academic achievement in multiple subjects across a student's high school career and thus may signal a broader range of skills related to college readiness, such as a student's academic tenacity and motivation.
>
> (p. i)

Recent research has confirmed that while grades reflect student self-perception, self-efficacy, and self-control across subjects (Klapp Lekholm & Cliffordson, 2009), these factors are mediated through teacher evaluations of student conduct and homework completion (Duckworth et al., 2012). Thus, these findings indicate that beyond assessment of the academic knowledge reflected in standardized test scores, what teachers assess with grades is student engagement, effort, participation, and behavior, which reflect measures of student self-control and self-efficacy. This research postulates that it is these factors that give grades their predictive validity with overall schooling outcomes, since if grades are a valid measure of how well a student can negotiate the non-academic components of the schooling process, then it is these factors that predict later student ability to conform to the institutional expectations that lead to completing high school as well as post-secondary schooling and employment (Bowers, 2011; Brookhart et al., 2016). This issue is exemplified by Kelly (2008), who analyzed data from over 1,500 students across 115 middle school English and language arts classrooms and their teachers in Wisconsin and New York. The study included grading data as well as surveys of students and observation and video data from the classroom, making Kelly (2008) one of the most comprehensive and rich data sets analyzed to date in the grading literature. Using a hierarchical linear modeling framework, the author found that grades were strongly related to student participation and engagement, and that higher grades appeared to be awarded for engaged participation, rather than "going through the motions." However, there were some differences by student background. As stated by Kelly (2008):

This study found that in addition to achievement, effort and participation in class are important predictors of the grades that students receive. The chances of an average student receiving a high mark increase dramatically when the student is engaged in class and completes his or her assignments. It is important to note, though, that not every form of participation is rewarded by high marks. Using detailed data on participation in classroom discourse, it is possible to distinguish between procedural engagement ("going through the motions") and substantive forms of engagement . . . I found that only substantive engagement leads to higher grades. This finding suggests that most teachers successfully use grades to reward achievement-oriented behavior and promote a widespread growth in achievement. However, the grading process is not entirely meritocratic. Boys, low-SES students, and Hispanic students all receive lower grades than do other students.

(p. 45)

In sum, across this research domain, grades have been shown to be a strong multidimensional assessment of both academic knowledge and student engaged participation in schooling, of which the latter is predictive of overall schooling outcomes (Brookhart et al., 2016). Assessment of engaged participation, then, is through teacher perception of student performance, which is subsequently incorporated into grades. Indeed, these findings from the grading literature align well with the broader research on teacher expectations of students. For example, using the Education Longitudinal Study of 2002 (ELS:2002), Gregory and Huang (2013) show that positive teacher expectations predict schooling outcomes, such as college-going, and are stronger predictors than many context and background variables (Gregory & Huang, 2013). As another example, in examining the difference between traditional "at-risk" predictors and teacher expectations from the NCES NELS:88 data set of a nationally generalizable sample of students in eighth grade in 1988, Soland (2013) showed that:

Generally, teachers were quite accurate at predicting student outcomes . . . This accuracy appears to have been driven largely by informational asymmetries, because teachers tend to rely on data related to student attitudes, behavior, and effort . . . Results concomitantly showed that teachers proved quite accurate in their predictions, often because they relied on academic tenacity data not easily captured in administrative datasets . . . Teachers naturally collect a huge amount of data, especially related to academic tenacity, simply by observing their students on a daily basis.

(pp. 246, 259)

Thus, rather than subjective measures of a hodgepodge of factors, this literature clearly demonstrates that grades assess student engaged participation, that grades are predictive of overall outcomes, and that it is important in this research to take teacher perceptions of student performance into account when examining the relationship between grades and test scores. Nevertheless, while this rich literature provides a strong argument for the validity of grades as a multidimensional assessment, one area that has not been explored in depth is the question of the variance in grades across schools. The between-school issue is an issue that relates directly to the reliability and validity of grades. For instance, if there is a strong between-school effect on grades, then which school a student attends would then largely determine that student's grades. Conversely, if the variance between schools in student grades is low, then the interpretation would be that the vast majority of schools grade students on similar scales and for similar reasons. One interpretation of a difference in grades at the school level could be the issue of grade inflation. Yet research that has used the multiple large-scale nationally generalizable NCES decadal surveys has found no grade inflation is evident in K-12 schooling in the

United States (Pattison, Grodsky, & Muller, 2013). Nevertheless, little of the research on grades has examined the between-school variance in grades to examine the relationship of student background, test scores, and teacher perception of student performance, while controlling for the nested dependent nature of students nested in schools. If a large amount of the variance in grades lies between schools, this could pose a strong validity threat to this literature on the multidimensional validity of grades as useful assessments in schools.

Testing the Claims and Questions from the Literature on Grades

In this section, I apply the literature discussed above to examine the extent to which teacher-assigned grades are a useful assessment of student engagement, using a large nationally generalizable sample of U.S. tenth grade high school students. This section examines three main aspects of this issue. First, to date, while the standardized grading practices literature claims that grades are unreliable and subjective measures that vary too much across schools to be useful, very little research has been done to examine the extent to which grades actually do vary within and between schools. Second, while critics of standardized assessments note that socioeconomic status and ethnicity are strongly associated with test scores, little work has been done to examine the extent to which grades, test scores, and SES are related, and to what extent grades may be a fairer or more "just" assessment that does not vary as strongly by SES or the demographic background of the student as do standardized assessments. Third, once these two main issues are addressed (within-/between-school variance and student SES/background variables) with control variables, the remaining variance in grades that is not explained by standardized test scores can be examined to show the extent that teacher evaluation of student effort (e.g., participation and behavior) is associated with the grades they assign, and whether this assessment is consistent across schools, and thus perhaps more reliable than previously inferred from the past psychometrics literature.

To examine these issues, I analyzed the restricted use Education Longitudinal Study of 2002 (ELS:2002) data set. ELS:2002 was originally collected by the National Center for Education Statistics (NCES), in which about 15,400 U.S. tenth grade students across 750 schools in 2002 were surveyed on a large array of items concerning their high school experience, as well as collecting demographic information, standardized assessments in mathematics and reading that were aligned to NAEP and PISA, and student report card grades and overall GPA (Ingles et al., 2007). In addition, NCES surveyed the student's English and mathematics teachers from the 2001/2002 academic year, asking the teachers about each student's performance in their courses. As noted in Table 11.1, for this analysis I included the non-cumulative grade point average across all courses for students in tenth grade, as well as tenth grade mathematics and reading standardized tests scores and a range of student and school background variables, as well as teacher ratings of student engagement. In addition, because ELS:2002 is not a simple random sample, but a probabilistic complex sample, I applied the sampling weights to allow for generalization to all 3 million students who were in tenth grade in the United States in 2002. Due to the restricted nature of the data, all sample sizes are rounded to the nearest 10.

For my variable selection, I drew on the literature in this domain reviewed above, particularly relying on previous research on teacher perception and grades using the ELS:2002 data set, such as Gregory and Huang (2013). At the student level, I included perceptions from both English teachers and mathematics teachers as the previous research in this area has shown that while these perception variables are moderately related at about a 0.5 correlation, they performed well independently in the previous research when loaded into the same equation (Gregory & Huang, 2013). At the school level, previous research has indicated that grades may be related to school-level factors, such as student demographics and school size (Roderick & Camburn, 1999). For the analysis, to examine the issues outlined above in grades across schools I used hierarchical linear

Table 11.1 Descriptive statistics from analyses of ELS data

	Mean	(SD)	Min	Max	ELS:2002 variable label and description
GPA for all tenth grade courses	2.67	0.87	0	4	F1GPA10: Non-cumulative grade 10 GPA all courses
Tenth grade mathematics	50.71	9.91	19.38	86.68	BYTXMSTD: Grade 10 mathematics stand. T-score
Tenth grade reading	50.53	9.89	22.57	78.76	BYTXRSTD: Grade 10 reading stand. T-score
SES	0.03	0.74	−2.12	1.87	F1SESR: Student socio-economic status
Female	0.50	0.50	0	1	BYSEX = 1 (male ref. group)
African American	0.17	0.38	0	1	BYRACE2 = 1
Student is Hispanic	0.15	0.35	0	1	BYS15 = 1
Asian	0.13	0.33	0	1	BYRACE3 = 1
Hawaiian/Pacific Islander	0.02	0.14	0	1	BYRACE4 = 1
Native American	0.04	0.21	0	1	BYRACE5 = 1
English is native language	0.83	0.38	0	1	BYSTLANG = 1
Nontraditional family	0.41	0.49	0	1	BYFCOMP > 1: Both birth parents not present in home
English teacher rating					
Student works hard for good grades	0.69	0.46	0	1	BYTE04: 0 = no, 1 = yes
How often student completes homework	3.01	1.01	0	4	BYTE13: 0 = never, 1 = rarely, 2 = some of the time, 3 = most of the time, 4 = all of the time
How often student is absent	1.16	0.72	0	4	BYTE14: (same as previous)
How often student is tardy	0.63	0.84	0	4	BYTE15: (same as previous)
How often student is attentive in class	2.95	0.88	0	4	BYTE16: (same as previous)
How often student is disruptive in class	0.59	0.87	0	4	BYTE17: (same as previous)
Mathematics teacher rating					
Student works hard for good grades	0.68	0.47	0	1	BYTM04: 0 = no, 1 = yes
How often student completes homework	2.99	1.02	0	4	BYTM13: 0 = never, 1 = rarely, 2 = some of the time, 3 = most of the time, 4 = all of the time
How often student is absent	1.15	0.70	0	4	BYTM14: (same as previous)
How often student is tardy	0.58	0.80	0	4	BYTM15: (same as previous)
How often student is attentive in class	2.96	0.89	0	4	BYTM16: (same as previous)
How often student is disruptive in class	0.55	0.84	0	4	BYTM17: (same as previous)
School-level variables					
Urban	0.34	0.47	0	1	URBAN = 1 (rural ref. group)
Suburban	0.34	0.47	0	1	URBAN = 2 (rural ref. group)
% Free lunch	24.51	19.13	0	96.2	CP02PLUN
% Minority students	34.36	31.20	0	100	CP02PMIN
Student–teacher ratio	16.62	4.25	4.39	40	CP02STRO
Enrollment (in thousands)	1.27	0.84	0.02	4.64	CP02STEN/1000

modeling (HLM) (Hox, 2010; Raudenbush & Bryk, 2002) in SPSS (Heck, Thomas, & Tabata, 2012) to examine two models with fixed effects. For both HLM analyses, the dependent variable is non-cumulative tenth grade GPA, which is the average of a student's grades across all subjects from only tenth grade. In each model, I control for student and school context and background variables, as well as student mathematics and reading achievement. In the second model, I add teacher perception of student performance using the variables outlined in Table 11.1.

The analysis resulted in three main findings. First, while the unconditional HLM indicated that there is a statistically significant amount of variance in grades between schools (Wald $Z = 13.390$, $p < 0.001$), the intraclass correlation coefficient (ICC) shows that only 16.52% of the variance in tenth grade GPA is between schools. This indicates that less than one-fifth of the variance in grades is between schools as indicated by the variables in the database. As noted in the literature review and framing above, if there is a large effect on grades depending on which school a student attends, the hypothesis would be that how teachers grade students is related to which school those teachers and students are in, which would throw into doubt the literature on the usefulness of grades as assessments of engaged participation in schooling since this difference would manifest through between-school variance. The ICC result suggests that there is a small amount of variance in grades between schools. This indicates that while there is some relationship between which school a student attends and the grades that the student receives, the vast majority of the variance for these data (83.48%) is at the student, rather than school, level.

Second, Table 11.2 presents the results of the two HLM analyses. For each coefficient for each model, I first present the coefficient for each variable (Coeff.), followed by the standardized coefficient (β), which can be interpreted as the effect size, followed by the standard error (SE). In Model A, only student mathematics and reading achievement, student background, and school-level background and context variables are included, which account for 36.83% of the variance at the student level and 45.54% of the variance at the school level. In Model B, English and mathematics teacher ratings of student effort, participation, and behavior explained an additional 33.17% of the variance in tenth grade GPA at the student level and an additional 13.49% at the school level (subtract Model B variance explained from Model A at each level). These results indicate that controlling for test scores, and background and demographic variables at the student and school level, teacher

Table 11.2 Hierarchical linear models explaining tenth grade GPA of ELS data

Parameter	Model A				Model B			
	Coeff.		β	SE	Coeff.		β	SE
Student-level variables								
Tenth grade mathematics	0.032	***	0.371	0.001	0.021	***	0.235	0.001
Tenth grade reading	0.015	***	0.168	0.001	0.009	***	0.103	0.001
SES	0.166	***	0.142	0.011	0.085	***	0.073	0.010
Female	0.303	***	0.175	0.013	0.108	***	0.062	0.012
African American	−0.066	**	−0.029	0.021	−0.013			0.020
Hispanic	−0.019			0.027	0.039			0.025
Asian	0.088	*	0.034	0.034	0.054			0.032
Hawaiian/Pacific Islander	−0.062			0.054	−0.054			0.057
Native American	−0.092	**	−0.022	0.030	−0.064	*	−0.015	0.027
English is native language	−0.147	***	−0.064	0.026	−0.015			0.025
Nontraditional family	−0.133	***	−0.076	0.014	−0.054	***	−0.031	0.012
English teacher rating								
Student works hard for good grades					0.208	***	0.111	0.018
How often student completes homework					0.153	***	0.179	0.009
How often student is absent					−0.088	***	−0.074	0.010
How often student is tardy					0.008			0.009
How often student is attentive in class					0.055	***	0.055	0.010
How often student is disruptive in class					−0.008			0.008

Mathematics teacher rating

Student works hard for good grades					0.163	***	0.088	0.018
How often student completes homework					0.144	***	0.169	0.009
How often student is absent					−0.077	***	−0.062	0.010
How often student is tardy					−0.028	**	−0.025	0.009
How often student is attentive in class					0.064	***	0.066	0.010
How often student is disruptive in class					0.030	**	0.029	0.008
School-level variables								
Urban	−0.076			0.046	−0.051			0.042
Suburban	−0.023			0.036	−0.006			0.032
% Free lunch	0.004	**	0.086	0.001	0.004	***	0.096	0.001
% Minority students	−0.002	*	−0.062	0.001	−0.002	**	−0.084	0.001
Student–teacher ratio	0.006			0.004	0.011	**	0.053	0.004
Enrollment in thousands	−0.099	***	−0.096	0.022	−0.081	***	−0.078	0.021
Intercept	0.325			0.083	−0.230	**		0.087
Percentage of variance explained								
At student level	36.83				70.00			
At school level	45.54				59.03			
BIC	22,000.13				9,211.69			

evaluations of student effort, participation, and behavior make up a significant portion of what grades represent.

Third, in examining the individual parameter estimates in the full final Model B in Table 11.2, the only significant ethnicity variable is Native American, and the standardized coefficient (beta) for SES is relatively small, in stark contrast to the literature on these variables as they relate to standardized test scores. In contrast to previous research (Kelly, 2008), I find no evidence that Hispanic students have significantly lower grades controlling for the other variables in Model A or Model B. The estimates of multiple other variables are of interest. As an example, in replication of multiple studies in the grading literature (DiPrete & Buchmann, 2013; Kelly, 2008; Lewis & Willingham, 1995; Thorsen & Cliffordson, 2012), females received higher grades on average than males (0.108 grade points) controlling for the other variables in the model. For teacher perceptions of student performance for both English and mathematics teachers, these variables confirm much of the literature on student engaged participation being strongly related to student grades. Strong positive predictors were "student works hard for good grades," "how often student completes homework," and "how often student is attentive in class." Interestingly, for English teachers, "how often student is tardy" and "how often student is disruptive in class" were not significantly related to grades, whereas both of these variables were significantly related to grades for mathematics teachers. Mathematics teacher perception of tardiness for mathematics classes was negatively related to student grades as expected; however, student disruptions were positively related with a small effect size.

While Model B explained 70% of the 83.5% of the variance at the student level, Model B also explained over half (59%) of the 16.5% of the variance at the school level. At the school level, context and demographics of the student body were significantly related to individual student grades. For negative relationships, students in schools with a higher percentage of minority students and larger enrollment schools receive lower grades. However, there were also two significant positive findings, with students in schools with higher percentages of free and reduced-price lunch students receiving higher grades, as well as students who attend schools with larger student teacher ratios. While the effect sizes are small, these two positive relationships perhaps indicate that teachers in poorer schools and schools with larger student–teacher ratios give slightly higher grades.

The Utility of Grades as Valid Classroom Assessments in Educational Measurement

As noted in the first section, throughout the literature and from the analysis discussed in this chapter, teacher assigned grades include assessment of student engaged participation as well as academic knowledge. However, also noted in the literature is a lack of attention to the question of the extent to which grades vary across schools (do your grades depend to a large part on which school you attend?), how grades may vary based on school context and demographics (do richer schools give higher grades?), how student demographics relate to grades (do grades vary by demographics such as test scores?), and finally how teacher perceptions of student classroom performance relate to grades (testing the engaged participation component of grades). Overall, across the literature and the analyses presented in this chapter (limited to variables in the ELS database), the evidence suggests that teacher-assigned grades are a useful and consistent measure of student engaged participation across schools. Since there is little variance between schools in grading, grades may perhaps represent a fairer distribution in relation to student demographics and SES than standardized tests. Clearly, teacher perceptions of engaged participation account for a large percentage of what grades assess. I consider each issue in turn throughout this final section of the chapter.

In considering the issue of the extent that grades vary between schools, while there is a statistically significant proportion of variance in grades at the school level, it is relatively small. As noted in the literature in the first section, an area that has lacked attention in the grading literature has been the issue of examining between-school variance. If a large amount of the variance in grades is between schools, then which school you attend determines to some extent student grades. I find that there is weak evidence at best for this hypothesis. It does not appear that which school a student attends determines to a large extent the student's grades. In comparison, the proportion of variance between schools for standardized test scores has long been reported to be around 25% (Borman & Dowling, 2010; Coleman, 1990; Rumberger & Palardy, 2005). This suggests that the vast majority of the variance in grades is at the student or classroom level. Indeed, I recommend further research in this area, as research in the grading literature has indicated variability at the classroom level. For instance, Kelly (2008) notes:

> I found a strong contextual effect of classroom achievement level on grades, where a student's chances of receiving a high grade improve if she or he is in a lower-achieving class. This frog-pond type effect of being high achieving compared to one's classmates is quite strong. For both high- and low-achieving students, being in a classroom where students are low achieving substantially increases the chances of receiving an A. A likely explanation for this phenomenon is that grading is a relativistic process; teachers' expectations of students' performance are conditioned by experiences in the classroom.
>
> (p. 45)

This quote is a strong indication that additional research is needed in this area, as perhaps a three-level model would provide additional information on this issue, nesting students in classrooms in schools. If there is a strong classroom effect, across multiple classrooms and averaged into a single GPA, this effect might wash out and not be detectable using a two-level model of students in schools as presented in the second section here, limited to the data that are available in ELS:2002.

Nevertheless, I do identify four variables at the school level that are weakly related to grades, with small effect sizes. In contrast to the individual-level parameters, which show that higher SES students receive somewhat higher grades, controlling for the other variables in the model, students who attend poorer schools (as defined by higher percentages of free and reduced-price lunch students) and students in schools with larger student–teacher ratios receive slightly higher grades on average. These results may be an indication of the "frog-pond" effect above, or perhaps are a weak indication of grade inflation for students attending under-resourced schools, or schools in historically disadvantaged contexts. I encourage future research in this domain.

At the student level, the analysis in the second section provides a good example of the effects noted in the literature. As with the previous literature discussed above (Brookhart et al., 2016), grades are a multidimensional assessment of both student academic achievement and engaged participation. In the analysis of the ELS data, both the mathematics and reading standardized assessment scores were significantly related to tenth grade GPA in the final model. Interestingly, for Model B, including teacher perception of student effort and participation, explained about as much of the variance in grades as did test scores and demographics combined. Teacher perception of how hard a student works for good grades and how often the student completes homework had comparable magnitude of effect sizes to the mathematics and reading standardized assessments, a core component of grades noted throughout the literature.

However, how tardiness and disruption relate to grades is discussed much less in the literature. Of note in the analyses reported here, for English teachers, perceptions of student tardiness and disruption to the classroom were not significantly related to student grades, while both of these variables were significantly related to grades for mathematics teachers. However, the disruptive to class variable for mathematics teachers was positive, which was unexpected. Perhaps when controlling for the variance explained by all of the other variables in Model B, disruption may have a positive effect uniquely in mathematics, as mathematics achievement, working hard, completing homework, absences, tardiness, and attentiveness are already controlled for. I encourage future research in this area.

Finally, I turn to the issue of how student demographics relate to grades, discussed in the literature and examined in Model B of the analyses presented in this chapter. First, for SES, the analyses replicate and agree with the previous research showing that teacher perceptions are stronger than SES when it comes to grading (Gregory & Huang, 2013), as the magnitude of the effect size for SES on grades is smaller than the teacher perception variables. However, there is a large reduction in the effect size for SES on grades depending on what variables are included in the analyses. For example, some of the variance in grades that is explained by SES in Model A is taken up within the teacher perception variables in Model B. A much more profound example of this is demonstrated with African American and Asian students. In Model A, the coefficient for African American students is negative, while it is positive for Asian students, controlling for other variables in the model. When controlling for teacher perception of student performance in Model B, these two variables are no longer significant. I interpret this in two ways. First, it may be that teacher perception is in effect an equalizer, making grades "fairer" than test scores, as test scores are strongly related to student demographics, even when controlling for internal school and teacher processes and perceptions (Rumberger & Palardy, 2005). Alternatively, a second explanation may be that the variance that was contributing to the negative coefficient for African American students on grades and the positive coefficient for Asian students in Model A can then be attributed to teacher perception in Model B. Indeed, there is a long-running debate in education research on teacher expectations and self-fulfilling prophecies (Madon, Jussim, & Eccles, 1997; Raudenbush, 1984). It may be that if there is a significant bias in teacher perceptions of students based on student ethnicity, then the results of this study may indicate that this bias perhaps acts through teacher perception of student hard work, homework completion, absences, tardiness, attentiveness, and disruption in class. I encourage future research in this area.

Conclusion and Implications

While some of the past literature has claimed that grading is "hodgepodge," in this chapter I have discussed the literature and an analysis framework that demonstrates that teacher-assigned grades include student engaged participation that does not vary extensively by school. Additionally, of the variance within and between schools, the variables nominated in the literature that I included in the analysis in this chapter explain the vast majority of the variance in grades, both at the student level and between schools. This leads me to three main implications. First, it appears that in comparison to standardized tests cores, less of the variance in grades is between schools (16.5% here) than it is for tests (usually reported to be around 25% in the literature). Thus, in comparison to standardized tests, for grades it matters even less which school a student attends. Overall, there does not appear to be strong evidence for "easy grading" or "hard grading" schools. However, as noted in both sections above, the classroom level may be a different story, as individual classes may have very skewed grading ranges (such as honors high school English). But overall, I interpret these findings to suggest that teachers are fairly consistent in how they grade in the aggregate across schools in the United States. This can be seen as an argument for the reliability of grades.

Second, teacher perception of student engaged participation makes up a large portion of grades. When I define engaged participation as the teacher's perception of how hard students work for good grades, homework completion, absence and tardiness, attentiveness, and class disruptions, these account for more than half of the variance explained in tenth grade GPA. These components of engaged participation mirror those that teachers note across the surveys discussed earlier in this chapter when teachers are surveyed about what they award grades for.

Together, these results mirror recent findings from over 100,000 students' grades in Chicago public schools (Allensworth & Luppescu, 2018), in which the authors looked primarily at the relationship of attendance (as a proxy for participation) and test scores to grades. As noted by Allensworth and Luppescu (2018):

> School-level variance is almost completely explained by observable factors. This suggests some degree of consistency in assigning grades among education professionals; the standards for grades across schools may not be as arbitrary as is often believed. Rather than finding large unexplained differences in grades based on which school a student attends, or which teacher they have, we find there are observable factors that systematically explain most of the differences in the grades that students receive in different types of schools, and with different teachers . . . the factors that are most strongly associated with differences in students' GPAs are their course attendance and tested skills.
>
> (p. 31)

Thus, given this literature and the analysis in this chapter, I argue for the usefulness of grades as accurate assessments of classroom engaged participation. In combination with standardized test scores, grades provide a valuable means to understand both student academic achievement as well as their levels of engaged participation in the schooling process. In the work of schools in helping to promote student success and transitions throughout primary, secondary, and post-secondary schooling, and into careers, ensuring that grades and test scores are included together in a balanced conversation about supporting student performance and success is vital to ensuring that schools promote a focus on both academic achievement and engaged participation.

References

Allensworth, E. M. (2005a). Dropout rates after high-stakes testing in elementary school: A study of the contradictory effects of Chicago's efforts to end social promotion. *Education Evaluation and Policy Analysis, 27*(4), 341–364. doi:10.3102/01623737027004341

Allensworth, E. M. (2005b). *Graduation and dropout trends in Chicago: A look at cohorts of students from 1991 through 2004.* Retrieved from www.consortium-chicago.org/publications/p75.html

Allensworth, E. M., & Easton, J. Q. (2005). *The on-track indicator as a predictor of high school graduation.* Retrieved from www.consortium-chicago.org/publications/p78.html

Allensworth, E. M., & Easton, J. Q. (2007). *What matters for staying on-track and graduating in Chicago public high schools: A close look at course grades, failures, and attendance in the freshman year.* Retrieved from www.consortium-chicago.org

Allensworth, E. M., & Luppescu, S. (2018). *Why do students get good grades, or bad ones? The influence of the teacher, class, school, and student.* Retrieved from https://consortium.uchicago.edu/sites/default/files/publications/Why%20Do%20Students%20Get-Apr2018-Consortium.pdf

Atkinson, R. C., & Geiser, S. (2009). Reflections on a century of college admissions tests. *Educational Researcher, 38*(9), 665–676. doi:10.3102/0013189x09351981

Attewell, P., Heil, S., & Reisel, L. (2011). Competing explanations of undergraduate noncompletion. *American Educational Research Journal, 48*(3), 536–559. doi:10.3102/0002831210392018

Barrington, B. L., & Hendricks, B. (1989). Differentiating characteristics of high school graduates, dropouts, and non-graduates. *Journal of Educational Research, 82*(6), 309–319.

Battin-Pearson, S., Abbott, R. D., Hill, K. G., Catalano, R. F., Hawkins, J. D., & Newcomb, M. D. (2000). Predictors of early high school dropout: A test of five theories. *Journal of Educational Psychology, 92*(3), 568–582. doi:10.1037/0022-0663.92.3.568

Blazer, C. (2012). *National trends in end-of-course assessment programs.* Retrieved from https://eric.ed.gov/?id=ED536522

Borman, G. D., & Dowling, M. (2010). Schools and inequality: A multilevel analysis of Coleman's equality of educational opportunity data. *Teachers College Record, 112*(5), 1201–1246.

Bowers, A. J. (2009). Reconsidering grades as data for decision making: More than just academic knowledge. *Journal of Educational Administration, 47*(5), 609–629. doi:10.1108/09578230910981080

Bowers, A. J. (2010a). Analyzing the longitudinal K-12 grading histories of entire cohorts of students: Grades, data driven decision making, dropping out and hierarchical cluster analysis. *Practical Assessment Research and Evaluation, 15*(7), 1–18.

Bowers, A. J. (2010b). Grades and graduation: A longitudinal risk perspective to identify student dropouts. *Journal of Educational Research, 103*(3), 191–207. doi:10.1080/00220670903382970

Bowers, A. J. (2011). What's in a grade? The multidimensional nature of what teacher-assigned grades assess in high school. *Educational Research and Evaluation, 17*(3), 141–159. doi:10.1080/13803611.2011.597112

Bowers, A. J., & Sprott, R. (2012). Examining the multiple trajectories associated with dropping out of high school: A growth mixture model analysis. *Journal of Educational Research, 105*(3), 176–195. doi:10.1080/00220671.2011.552075

Bowers, A. J., Sprott, R., & Taff, S. (2013). Do we know who will drop out? A review of the predictors of dropping out of high school: Precision, sensitivity and specificity. *The High School Journal, 96*(2), 77–100.

Brennan, R. T., Kim, J., Wenz-Gross, M., & Siperstein, G. N. (2001). The relative equitability of high-stakes testing versus teacher-assigned grades: An analysis of the Massachusetts Comprehensive Assessment System (MCAS). *Harvard Educational Review, 71*(2), 173–215.

Brighouse, H., Ladd, H., Loeb, S., & Swift, A. (2018). *Educational goods: Values, evidence, and decision-making.* Chicago, IL: University of Chicago Press.

Brookhart, S. M. (1991). Grading practices and validity. *Educational Measurement: Issues and Practice, 10*(1), 35–36.

Brookhart, S. M. (1993). Teachers' grading practices: Meaning and values. *Journal of Educational Measurement, 30*(2), 123–142. doi:10.1111/j.1745-3984.1993.tb01070.x

Brookhart, S. M. (1994). Teachers' grading: Practice and theory. *Applied Measurement in Education, 7*(4), 279–301. doi:10.1207/s15324818ame0704_2

Brookhart, S. M. (2011). *Grading and learning: Practices that support student achievement.* Bloomington, IN: Solution Tree Press.

Brookhart, S. M. (2015). Graded achievement, tested achievement, and validity. *Educational Assessment, 20*(4), 268–296. doi:10.1080/10627197.2015.1093928

Brookhart, S. M., Guskey, T. R., Bowers, A. J., McMillan, J. H., Smith, J. K., Smith, L. F., . . . Welsh, M. E. (2016). A century of grading research: Meaning and value in the most common educational measure. *Review of Educational Research, 86*(4), 803–848. doi:10.3102/0034654316672069

Cizek, G. J., Fitzgerald, S. M., & Rachor, R. E. (1995–1996). Teachers' assessment practices: Preparation, isolation and the kitchen sink. *Educational Assessment, 3*(2), 159–179.

Cliffordson, C. (2008). Differential prediction of study success across academic programs in the Swedish context: The validity of grades and tests as selection instruments for higher education. *Educational Assessment, 13*(1), 56–75. doi:10.1080/10627190801968240

Coleman, J. S. (1990). *Equality and achievement in education.* San Francisco, CA: Westview Press.

Cross, L. H., & Frary, R. B. (1999). Hodgepodge grading: Endorsed by students and teachers alike. *Applied Measurement in Education, 12*(1), 53–72.

DiPrete, T. A., & Buchmann, C. (2013). *The rise of women: The growing gender gap in education and what it means for American schools.* New York: Russell Sage Foundation.

Duckworth, A. L., Quinn, P. D., & Tsukayama, E. (2012). What *No Child Left Behind* leaves behind: The roles of IQ and self-control in predicting standardized achievement test scores and report card grades. *Journal of Educational Psychology, 104*(2), 439–451. doi:10.1037/a0026280

Farr, B. P. (2000). Grading practices: An overview of the issues. In E. Trumbull & B. Farr (Eds.), *Grading and reporting student progress in an age of standards* (pp. 1–22). Norwood, MA: Christopher-Gordon Publishers.

Gregory, A., & Huang, F. (2013). It takes a village: The effects of 10th grade college-going expectations of students, parents, and teachers four years later. *American Journal of Community Psychology, 52*(1–2), 41–55. doi:10.1007/s10464-013-9575-5

Guskey, T. R., & Jung, L. A. (2012). Four steps in grading reform. *Principal Leadership, 13*(4), 22–28.

Heck, R. H., Thomas, S. L., & Tabata, L. N. (2012). *Multilevel modeling of categorical outcomes using IBM SPSS.* New York: Routledge.

Hodara, M., & Cox, M. (2016). *Developmental education and college readiness at the University of Alaska.* Retrieved from http://ies.ed.gov/ncee/edlabs/projects/project.asp?projectID=393

Hox, J. (2010). *Multilevel analysis: Techniques and applications* (2nd ed.). New York: Routledge.

Ingles, S. J., Pratt, D. J., Wilson, D., Burns, L. J., Currivan, D., Rogers, J. E., & Hubbard-Bednasz, S. (2007). *Education longitudinal study of 2002: Base-year to second follow-up data file documentation.* Washington, DC: National Center for Education Statistics, Institute of Education Sciences, U.S. Department of Education.

Jones, E. B., & Jackson, J. D. (1990). College grades and labor market rewards. *The Journal of Human Resources, 25*(2), 253–266. doi:10.2307/145756

Kelly, S. (2008). What types of students' effort are rewarded with high marks? *Sociology of Education, 81*(1), 32–52. doi:10.1177/003804070808100102

Klapp Lekholm, A. (2011). Effects of school characteristics on grades in compulsory school. *Scandinavian Journal of Educational Research, 55*(6), 587–608. doi:10.1080/00313831.2011.555923

Klapp Lekholm, A., & Cliffordson, C. (2008). Discrepancies between school grades and test scores at individual and school level: Effects of gender and family background. *Educational Research and Evaluation, 14*(2), 181–199.

Klapp Lekholm, A., & Cliffordson, C. (2009). Effects of student characteristics on grades in compulsory school. *Educational Research and Evaluation, 15*(1), 1–23. doi:10.1080/13803610802470425

Labaree, D. F. (1997). Public goods, private goods: The American struggle over educational goals. *American Educational Research Journal, 34*(1), 39–81. doi:10.3102/00028312034001039

Levin, H. M. (2013). The utility and need for incorporating noncognitive skills into large-scale educational assessments. In M. von Davier, E. Gonzalez, I. Kirsch, & K. Yamamoto (Eds.), *The role of international large-scale assessments: Perspectives from technology, economy, and educational research* (pp. 67–86). New York: Springer.

Lewis, C., & Willingham, W. W. (1995). The effects of sample restriction on gender differences. *ETS Research Report Series, 1995*(1), 1–57. doi:10.1002/j.2333-8504.1995.tb01648.x

Linn, R. L. (1982). Ability testing: Individual differences, prediction, and differential prediction. In A. K. Wigdor & W. R. Garner (Eds.), *Ability testing: Uses, consequences, and controversies* (pp. 335–388). Washington, DC: National Academy Press.

Linn, R. L. (2000). Assessments and accountability. *Educational Researcher, 29*(2), 4–16.

Lloyd, D. N. (1978). Prediction of school failure from third-grade data. *Educational and Psychological Measurement, 38*(4), 1193–1200.

Maag Merki, K., & Holmeier, M. (2015). Comparability of semester and exit exam grades: Long-term effect of the implementation of state-wide exit exams. *School Effectiveness and School Improvement, 26*(1), 57–74. doi:10.1080/09243453.2013.861353

Madon, S., Jussim, L., & Eccles, J. (1997). In search of the powerful self-fulfilling prophecy. *Journal of Personality and Social Psychology, 74*(2), 791–809. doi:10.1037/0022-3514.72.4.791

McMillan, J. H. (2001). Secondary teachers' classroom assessment and grading practices. *Educational Measurement: Issues and Practice, 20*(1), 20–32.

Miller, S. R. (1998). Shortcut: High school grades as a signal of human capital. *Educational Evaluation and Policy Analysis, 20*(4), 299–311. doi:10.3102/01623737020004299

Nichols, S. L., & Berliner, D. C. (2007). *Collateral damage: How high stakes testing corrupts America's schools.* Cambridge, MA: Harvard Education Press.

Pattison, E., Grodsky, E., & Muller, C. (2013). Is the sky falling? Grade inflation and the signaling power of grades. *Educational Researcher, 42*(5), 259–265. doi:10.3102/0013189x13481382

Raudenbush, S. W. (1984). Magnitude of teacher expectancy effects on pupil IQ as a function of the credibility of expectancy induction: A synthesis of findings from 18 experiments. *Journal of Educational Psychology, 76*, 85–97.

Raudenbush, S. W., & Bryk, A. S. (2002). *Hierarchical linear models: Applications and data analysis methods* (2nd ed.). Thousand Oaks, CA: SAGE.

Roderick, M., & Camburn, E. (1999). Risk and recovery from course failure in the early years of high school. *American Educational Research Journal, 36*(2), 303–343. doi:10.3102/00028312036002303

Rumberger, R. W., & Palardy, G. J. (2005). Test scores, dropout rates, and transfer rates as alternative indicators of high school performance. *American Educational Research Journal, 42*(1), 3–42. doi:10.3102/00028312042001003

Soland, J. (2013). Predicting high school graduation and college enrollment: comparing early warning indicator data and teacher intuition. *Journal of Education for Students Placed at Risk (JESPAR), 18*(3–4), 233–262. doi:10.1080/10824669.2013.833047

Swineford, F. (1947). Examination of the purported unreliability of teachers' marks. *The Elementary School Journal, 47*(9), 516–521. doi:10.2307/3203007

Thorsen, C., & Cliffordson, C. (2012). Teachers' grade assignment and the predictive validity of criterion-referenced grades. *Educational Research and Evaluation, 18*(2), 153–172. doi:10.1080/13803611.2012.659929

Warren, J. R., Jenkins, K. N., & Kulick, R. B. (2006). High school exit examinations and state-level completion and GED rates, 1975 through 2002. *Educational Evaluation and Policy Analysis, 28*(2), 131–152. doi:10.3102/01623737028002131

Welsh, M. E., D'Agostino, J. V., & Kaniskan, B. (2013). Grading as a reform effort: Do standards-based grades converge with test scores? *Educational Measurement: Issues and Practice, 32*(2), 26–36. doi:10.1111/emip.12009

West, M. R., Kraft, M. A., Finn, A. S., Martin, R. E., Duckworth, A. L., Gabrieli, C. F. O., & Gabrieli, J. D. E. (2016). Promise and paradox. *Educational Evaluation and Policy Analysis, 38*(1), 148–170. doi:10.3102/0162373715597298

Willingham, W. W., Pollack, J. M., & Lewis, C. (2002). Grades and test scores: Accounting for observed differences. *Journal of Educational Measurement, 39*(1), 1–37.

12

Digital Technologies
Supporting and Advancing Assessment Practices in the Classroom

Michael Russell

Introduction

Over the past 20 years, digital technologies have been applied to teaching and learning in an increasing variety of ways. In some cases, they are used to support individual learners, particularly those with disabilities and special needs. In other cases, students employ digital tools to access content and produce work products. In still other cases, digital learning systems are employed to develop knowledge and understanding of all students (e.g., computer-based instruction, game-based learning, intelligent tutoring systems). As students interact with digital technologies, new opportunities arise to collect information about students' cognitive and non-cognitive development, and to communicate about this development to students and parents.

This chapter provides a survey of the current landscape of digitally based classroom assessment practices. The intent of the chapter is to expose readers at a high level to a variety of ways in which digital technologies can be applied to support assessment in the classroom. In some cases, the examples describe how large-scale summative applications of digital technologies can be applied to the classroom for either summative or formative assessment. In other cases, the applications are specific to formative assessment in the classroom. The survey of uses is organized into two broad categories: collecting evidence of understanding and digital enhancements to classroom assessment. Topics explored include approaches to collecting response information from students, new and emerging digital item and task types, identifying misconceptions and misunderstanding, assessing engagement and persistence, supporting evidence-based standards-based grading, and enhancing accessibility during assessment. Through this high-level survey, the chapter also identifies issues of equity and privacy that must be considered when applying technology to support classroom assessment. Before exploring these uses and issues, the manner in which the terms "classroom assessment" and "technology" are employed in this chapter are defined.

Classroom Assessment Defined

Assessment has long been defined as a process of collecting, analyzing, and interpreting information to inform a decision (Airasian, 1991). More recently, Mislevy's (Mislevy, Almond, & Lukas, 2003) evidence-centered design (ECD) approach to assessment development has shifted focus from assessment as information gathering to evidence gathering. From an ECD perspective, assessment is the process of collecting evidence to support a claim about a student or group of students. Kane's (1992) conception of assessment validation extends the use of evidence to support an argument regarding the strength of a claim about a student or group of students. These advances in assessment design and validation support redefinition of assessment as the process of purposeful evidence gathering to support claims and subsequent decisions about a student or a group of students.

In the classroom, teachers make a wide variety of decisions about individual students, groups of students, and the whole class of students. Many of these decisions focus on student learning or cognitive development. In some cases, as new content and concepts are about to be introduced, teachers make decisions about students' prior knowledge and whether that knowledge provides a sufficient foundation for the development of new knowledge or understanding. During instruction, educators continually make decisions about whether student understanding is developing as intended or whether there are specific aspects of a concept that require clarification or further development. Following instruction, educators often want to decide how much student understanding has developed and how much of the new knowledge developed during instruction has been retained or can be applied to new situations. Traditionally, these three phases of cognitive assessment have been termed pre-assessment or sizing up assessment, formative assessment or assessment during instruction, and summative assessment (Russell & Airasian, 2012).

In recent years, considerable attention has focused on formative assessment. In turn, the term formative assessment has taken on two meanings. In some contexts, the term formative assessment is used to refer to the process of assessment during instruction that is used to modify or shape the instructional or learning process. In other cases, formative assessment references a specific task employed to collect information about student learning, the intent of which is to be used to inform instruction. When used to reference a process, emphasis is often focused on the participants in the assessment process, reflection, and ultimately decision-making. When used to reference a specific task, the focus tends to be on specific characteristics of the task and the quality of information provided through the task. In this chapter, the examples of formative assessments take the form of specific tasks or products that are used to provide information about a student. The assumption is that the resulting information is then used as part of a larger process, but this process is not discussed.

While assessment of cognitive development is an important component of classroom assessment, there are many other assessment-based decisions educators make regularly. Some of these decisions focus on student engagement, effort, and motivation. Others focus on classroom management, pairing or grouping students, understanding the cause of unexpected behavior, identifying trigger topics for specific students, or determining whether to refer a student for further evaluation for a learning need. Despite the wide variety of social, emotional, psychological, behavioral, and cognitive decisions educators make routinely in the classroom, all classroom decisions are strengthened when informed by evidence.

For classroom assessment, the evidence used to inform instructional decisions ranges from more formal measures of student achievement to very informal observations made as teachers interact directly with students or as teachers passively monitor students' interactions during group activities. In addition, questions posed by students can serve as a source of evidence regarding points of confusion and/or concepts in need to further instruction. Thus, unlike large-scale summative assessment's reliance on well-structured measures of student knowledge, skill, and/or abilities, classroom assessment employs a much wider variety of types of evidence depending upon the decision under consideration.

This chapter explores at a high level a variety of ways in which technology can be employed to collect evidence to support both formal and informal assessment. In some cases, the evidence collected through a use of technology takes the form of structured indicators of student achievement. In other cases, the evidence does not yield a measure, but rather provides insight into student thinking, engagement, or persistence.

Technology Defined

Technology has been defined as a specialized set of procedures or methods for accomplishing a task (Ellul, 1964; Lowrance, 1986; Winner, 1977). In effect, any advance that introduces a new mechanism, product, or process that is used to support assessment is a new technology (Madaus, Russell, & Higgins, 2009). In this chapter, however, the focus is limited to technologies that affect the form and processes employed to gather and process evidence used to inform an instructional decision.

When considering the application of technology to testing, Bennett (1998) identified three stages of transition. The first stage focuses largely on transitioning paper-based practices to a digital format and establishing an infrastructure to support digitally based assessment. The second stage aims to increase efficiency and introduce new, but relatively minor, innovations, such as new item types. The third stage effectively reinvents the practice of testing. As described in the body of this chapter, the use of technology to support classroom assessment has entered the second stage. This is particularly true for uses of technology that aim to provide diagnostic information about student understanding, employ new item types and simulations, and meet student needs through accessibility supports.

Assessing Understanding in the Classroom

Evidence of students' current understanding is essential for tailoring instruction to meet students' current needs. During instruction, evidence gathering about current understanding occurs informally through the questions educators ask of students, observations made as students work on assigned tasks, and through cues provided through body language, facial expressions, and various behaviors. More formal evidence is also gathered through the analysis of assigned tasks such as in-class assignments, homework, projects, quizzes, or tests. Over the past two decades, several digital tools have become available to support formal collection of evidence of student understanding. Below, two categories of tools are presented, namely gathering responses from students and new item and task types. The utility of each is driven largely by the type of digital resources available in the classroom and/or outside of school.

Gathering Responses from Students

To assess student understanding during instruction, teachers often pose a question and call on a student or present a small set of problems for which individual students are asked to share their solutions. Evidence gathered from select individual students is then used to generalize to the class and inform decisions about whether to move forward with instruction or to continue exploring the topic at hand. While this approach is efficient, generalizing evidence gathered from select students to the entire class can result in misleading decisions about the current state of understanding of other students in the class.

Quizzes or small sets of questions asked of all students provide alternate approaches to collecting evidence that is more representative of the class. But analyzing this large body of responses in a timely manner is challenging. Digital technologies provide a vehicle for quickly collecting, analyzing, and summarizing student responses.

Student Response Systems

In the early 2000s, the availability of digital devices in classrooms varied widely, due in part to the high cost of desktop and laptop computers. At the time, student response systems were introduced as a low-cost alternative to full-functioning computers. Now used in many school systems, as well as college and university lecture halls, these response systems take the form of a small handheld device similar to a television remote control (Aljaloud, Gromik, Billingsley, & Kwan, 2015). Depending on the manufacture, the device limits student responses to a few response options (similar to selected-response options) or allows students to enter alphanumeric content. Each student is then provided a response controller that communicates with a receiver connected to the instructor's computer and communicates with software that allows the instructor to author items, administer the items, analyze student responses, and automatically generate displays summarizing student responses. Typically, response systems are used in conjunction with an LCD projector or large screen that is used to project the questions to the entire class and, depending on the instructor's practices, share summary statistics with students. Some systems also allow the instructor to select and project individual responses that can be the focus of discussion.

Student response systems are useful for gathering evidence of student understanding during the instructional process (Bojinova & Oigara, 2011). In most cases, an educator will purposefully develop questions or problems a priori that he or she anticipates presenting during instruction. But these systems also allow a question to either be developed and entered into to the system on the fly, or some systems allow a question to be stated orally or written on a white/blackboard, to which students then provide a response using their responders. While response systems are typically used to assess students' cognitive skills and understanding (Caldwell, 2007; Kay & LeSage, 2009; Mula & Kavanagh, 2009), the systems can also be used to collect information about students' beliefs and opinions (Beatty, 2004; Laxman, 2011). By systematically collecting and summarizing information about students' beliefs, a teacher can use this information as a springboard for further discussion or can make decisions about whether there is a sufficiently high interest level to continue a discussion or explore a topic (Aljaloud et al., 2015; Cubric & Jefferies, 2015).

Quizzing Software and Apps

Student response systems are useful in classrooms that have limited access to digital devices. In an increasing number of classrooms, however, students have access to mobile devices such as laptops, tablets, and/or cell phones. In such settings, these devices can be used to collect evidence of student understanding as instruction is occurring through the use of software and apps designed to support surveying and quizzing (Waite, 2007). In effect, these tools are similar to the student response systems with two important differences. First, instead of requiring questions to be projected to the entire class of students, the questions are transferred directly to each student's device. The student then responds directly on his or her device and the response is transferred back via a network communication to the educator. A second important difference is that because these systems present questions on a fully functioning digital device, a wider variety of evidence types can be collected by the educator. Depending on the software or app, these evidence types can range from traditional selected-response items or survey questions, open-ended alphanumeric responses, pictures, graphs or diagrams, or technology-enhanced items (see next section for examples). Depending on the decision being made, the evidence can take the form of responses to pre-constructed items or on-the-fly questions or points of confusion documented by students (e.g., "I am confused by . . ." or "I don't understand . . .").

In addition to assessing student understanding during instruction, quizzing software can also support assessment outside of the classroom, assuming students have access to digital devices and the Internet (McDaniel, Thomas, Agarwal, McDermott, & Roediger, 2013). In this way, quizzing software can be used to assign homework (e.g., questions about assigned reading or presentation of mathematics problem sets) that can be automatically scored and summarized for an educator prior to the next class meeting. For educators who employ formative assessment methods such as "exit tickets" or other techniques designed to encourage students to reflect on instruction and identify points in need of further clarification, quizzing systems can be used to gather this type of information at the end of a class session.

New Item and Task Types

With the increase in digitally based tests has come growing interest in expanding the types of items used to measure the knowledge, skills, and understanding that are the target of assessment (Bryant, 2017; Drasgow & Olson-Buchanan, 1999; Russell, 2006; Scalise & Gifford, 2006; Washington State, 2010). In particular, interest in new item types is motivated by a desire to measure cognitive constructs in more authentic ways (Russell, 2016). As an example, both the Smarter Balanced and PARCC assessment consortiums proposed to develop items that measure constructs in ways that are more authentic than traditional selected or text-based open-response items (Florida Department of Education, 2010; Washington State, 2010). In turn, this desire has led to the introduction of several types of technology-based items (Bryant, 2017; Scalise & Gifford, 2006; Sireci & Zenisky, 2006).

Technology-based items fall into two broad categories. The first category includes items that contain media, such as video, sound, animations, and simulations that cannot be presented on paper. The second category includes items that require test-takers to demonstrate knowledge, skills, and abilities using methods for producing a response that differs from selecting from a set of options or entering alphanumeric content. To distinguish the two types of technology-based items, the term *technology-enabled* refers to the first category and *technology-enhanced* labels the second category (Measured Progress/ETS Collaborative, 2012).

Technology-Enhanced Items

All items are composed of at least two parts: (a) a stimulus that establishes the problem a test-taker is to focus on; and (b) a response space in which a test-taker records an answer to the problem. For items delivered in a digital environment, the response space has been termed an *interaction space* (IMS Global Learning Consortium, 2002) since this is the area in which the test-taker interacts with the test delivery system to produce a response.

For a multiple-choice item, an interaction space is that part of an item that presents the student with answer options and allows one or more options to be selected. For an open-response item, an interaction space typically takes the form of a text box into which text-based content is entered. For a technology-enhanced item, the interaction space is that part of an item that presents response information to a student and allows the student to either produce or manipulate content to provide a response.

Sireci and Zenisky (2006) detail a wide and growing variety of interaction spaces employed by technology-enhanced items. For example, one type of interaction space presents words or objects that are classified into two or more categories by dragging and dropping them into their respective containers. This is often termed "drag and drop" and is used to measure a variety of knowledge and skills, including classifying geometric shapes (e.g., see Figure 12.1a, in which shapes are classified based on whether or not they contain parallel lines) or classifying organisms based on specific traits (e.g., mammals versus birds versus fish, single-cell versus multiple-cell organisms, chemical versus physical changes, etc.). This interaction space can also be used to present content that the student manipulates to arrange in a given order. As an example, a series of events that occur in a story may be rearranged to indicate the order in which they occurred. Similarly, a list of animals may be rearranged to indicate their hierarchy in a food chain.

Another type of interaction space requires students to create one or more lines to produce a response to a given prompt (see Figure 12.1b). For example, students may be presented with a

Classify each shape below based on whether it contains at least one pair of parallel sides.

At Least One Pair of Parallel Sides	No Parallel Sides

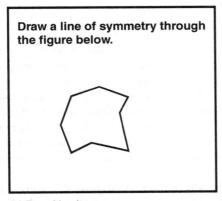

(a) Drag and Drop Item

Draw a line of symmetry through the figure below.

(b) Draw Line Item

Part B

Select two phrase from the paragraph that best support your answer in part A.

We hold these truths to be self evident, that all men are created equal, that they are endowed by their Creator with certain unalienable Rights, that among these are Life, Liberty and the pursuit of Happiness.—That to secure these rights, Governments are instituted among Men, deriving their powers from the consent of the governed,--That whenever any Form of Government becomes destructive of these ends, it is the Right of the People to alter or to abolish it, and to institute new Government, laying its foundation on such principles and organizing its powers in such form, as to them shall

(c) Select Text Item

Figure 12.1 Examples of interaction spaces: (a) drag and drop item; (b) draw line item; (c) select text item.

coordinate plane and asked to produce a line that represents a given linear function, a geometric shape upon which the test-taker is asked to produce a line of symmetry, or a list of historical events where the test-taker is to draw lines connecting each event to the date when it occurred.

A third type of interaction space requires students to highlight content to produce a response (see Figure 12.1c). For example, the student may be asked to highlight words that are misspelled in a given sentence, select sentences in a passage that support a given argument, or highlight elements in an image of a painting that demonstrate the use of a specific technique or imagery.

Although the use of technology-enhanced items was initiated by large-scale summative testing programs, they have high utility for providing evidence about many types of knowledge, skill, and ability developed during classroom instruction. Many educators (and test developers), however, believe the development of technology-enhanced items requires more time and a higher level of technical skill than is required to author multiple-choice questions. But this, in fact, is not the case. Tools such as TAO (see section below) provide templates that allow technology-enhanced items to be written as efficiently as multiple-choice items. These platforms are also able to score student responses to these items automatically. In this way, the time and technical expertise required to develop technology-enhanced items are essentially the same as that required for developing more traditional items.

Authentic Tasks

Despite advances in the types of interactions students may have as they work on test items, a shortcoming of many technology-enhanced items is the focus on a single discrete concept or skill that is often presented in an unauthentic manner. As an example, the item shown in Figure 12.1b focuses on the concept of symmetry and asks a student to produce a line of symmetry for a given shape. While this item is useful for measuring a student's discrete understanding of the concept of symmetry, rarely would a student encounter a situation in real life where they are presented with a figure and asked to produce a line of symmetry. Instead, the need to produce a line of symmetry is typically encountered when working on a more complex extended task that includes the integration of multiple skills and knowledge.

Interest in authentic assessment tasks rose rapidly in the 1990s in response to growing criticism of multiple-choice tests (Stecher, 2010). This movement led to the development of a variety of open-ended tasks in which students were provided supplies and asked to produce a product or a solution for a problem that might be encountered in the real world (Harmon et al., 1997; Mead, 1995) As an example, in science, students might be presented with a mixture along with various apparatus and be asked to separate and identify the components of the mixture. In mathematics, students might be given a balance scale and some known masses, along with a bag of rice, and be asked to produce smaller bags of rice with specific masses that are not equivalent to those provided.

These types of performance tasks were believed to provide more accurate information about student understanding because they required students to actively apply their knowledge in an integrated manner to solve a problem that authentically reflected the real world. Performance tasks, however, presented considerable challenges due to the need to provide materials for all students. In addition, these types of tasks required considerable preparation and cleanup time, and the types of problems presented were limited by safety—and the need to perform them in a typical classroom setting.

Digital technology, however, can be applied to address each of these shortcomings. As an example, the IMMEX project developed a large set of authentic assessment tasks that presented students with real-world problems. Students were also provided with digitally simulated tools they could use to explore the problem (Cox et al., 2008). As students worked through the problem, their actions were recorded. These process data were then used in conjunction with their final solution to categorize the students' level of knowledge and understanding. As an example, in one task students were presented with a scenario in which an earthquake has caused various chemicals to fall off a shelf. Like the performance task described above, students were also provided with a variety of tools they can use to examine the resulting mixture. But unlike the previous example, the variety of substances that the student must test is larger, and in some cases more dangerous.

Similarly, the Concord Consortium (2016) has developed several applications in which students must explore various scientific concepts. While many of these applications are designed as learning tools, they collect information about student understanding as students progress through the program—and then provide feedback to teachers about student learning. As an example, one application focuses on genetics and requires students to crossbreed creatures to produce offspring with specific genetic traits. As students work through the program, the complexity of the problems increase and mutations are introduced. While the creature a student works with is fictitious (a dragon), the scenario represents one that genetic biologists might encounter in the real world. Further, the ability to simulate reproduction allows the student to produce multiple generations in a relatively short period of time. This increases the amount of data and experimentation the student can access and perform, while also maintaining the student's engagement with the task.

Virtual Reality

Taking authentic tasks one step further, efforts have been made to develop virtual worlds in which students engage with a problem to demonstrate understanding. Perhaps the best example is work performed by Chris Dede and his colleagues (Code, Clarke-Midura, Zap, & Dede, 2012). This work focused on assessing students' scientific inquiry skills. To do so, a virtual world was created in which students control an avatar that is responsible for solving a given problem. In one example, the avatar is situated in a coastal area of Alaska in which the kelp population is rapidly declining. Students are asked to determine why this may be occurring. In the area, there is an energy plant, fishing piers, and a beachcomber.

The students also have access to scuba gear and instruments for collecting a variety of data. Through the avatar, the students are able to interact with other people in the environment to collect information from them, as well as collect other sources of data using the various instruments provided. The students can also maintain a lab book of notes and data. Periodically, the student is prompted to provide tentative hypotheses and asked to share their thinking behind those hypotheses. Ultimately, the students present their conclusions along with the evidence that supports their reasoning. Like IMMEX, process data as well as the students' final product are used to assess students' science inquiry skills.

While efforts to develop technology-enhanced items and digital performance tasks remain in the early stages, these efforts have great potential to increase student engagement. As noted above, they also hold potential to use process data in conjunction with outcome data to gain insights into students' current understanding.

Diagnosing Misconceptions and Misunderstanding

Traditionally, assessment of student understanding has focused on the products students produce in response to a given assessment activity. In effect, the focus of these assessments is on the outcome of the student's application of a knowledge, understanding, or skill. This focus on outcomes is useful for making decisions about whether or not a student can perform a given task or apply a given skill. For students who do not succeed, however, this outcome-based focus provides little insight into why a student may be struggling with a given concept or skill.

In effect, a fundamental shortcoming of achievement tests is that they fail to provide meaningful information about *why* students perform as they do.

To address this shortcoming of traditional summative tests, Leighton and her colleagues have advocated for the development of tests that capture information about the process students employ when developing solutions for a test item (Leighton, Gokiert, Cor, & Heffernan, 2010). One approach to collecting evidence regarding the cognitive process employed by a student is to design selected-response options such that they reflect the outcome of specific cognitive process, some of which represent accurate approaches to the problem and others that represent specific misunderstanding or misconceptions (Leighton & Gierl, 2007). This section presents two efforts to develop cognitively diagnostic assessments that provide information about why students may struggle with a given concept. The first focuses on mathematics and has developed diagnostic assessments for key concepts in algebra, geometry, and statistics. The second focuses on physics.

The Diagnostic Algebra Assessment

The Diagnostic Algebra Assessment (DAA) project set out to develop a comprehensive online assessment and instruction system that contains three key features. First, the system provides teachers access to a series of online quizzes, each of which focuses on a specific algebraic concept. For each quiz, items are designed to measure student understanding of the concept. For students who perform poorly, each item is also designed to examine whether the student holds a known misconception that is specific to the assessed concept. Thus, each quiz provides an indicator of student understanding of a given concept, and for low-performing students an estimate of the probability that a student holds a specific misconception that is interfering with his or her understanding.

A second feature of the system is the provision of immediate feedback to teachers. An initial report sorts students into three categories. The first category includes students who performed well on the test and appear to have a solid understanding of the assessed concept. The second category contains students who did not perform well and who appear to hold a specific misconception related to the tested concept. The third category contains students who also did not perform well but who do not appear to hold an associated misconception. By classifying students into three categories, teachers develop a better understanding of how well their students are performing and why some students are struggling with a given concept.

A third feature of the system is that it links teachers to lessons and activities designed to help students correct a given misconception. Students identified as having a given misconception are also connected to the relevant learning activities.

Research conducted to date provides evidence that this approach to diagnostic assessment is effective for improving student learning (Masters, 2014; Russell, O'Dwyer, & Miranda, 2009). In both cases, students who were identified with a misconception and were then provided instruction specific to that misconception corrected their understanding and performed adequately on subsequent assessments of the targeted concept.

Diagnoser

Findings for the DAA parallel those of Minstrell and his colleagues, who developed and examined the use of diagnostic assessments in physics (Thissen-Roe, Hunt, & Minstrell, 2004). Like the diagnostic mathematics assessments, Minstrell's Diagnoser provides teachers with access to a set of short tests, each of which focuses on a specific physics concept. The tests provide teachers with an estimate of the degree to which the students understand the concept and the extent to which a misconception specific to that concept may be interfering with understanding of the concept.

Research on Diagnoser suggests that the assessments built into it provide teachers with valuable information about student understanding and the presence of specific misconceptions (Thissen-Roe et al., 2004). Specifically, data indicated that the diagnostic information helped teachers recognize that some misconceptions believed to occur commonly were held by only a few students, while other misconceptions that were thought to be rare were in fact relatively common among students. Data also indicated that students whose teachers used Diagnoser performed higher than their peers whose teachers did not employ Diagnoser.

Efforts to develop embedded diagnostic tests that are designed to help inform instruction remains in an early state. Nonetheless, research suggests that these systems hold promise for providing teachers and students with immediate access to information designed to inform instructional practices. These initial efforts also provide sound examples of how teachers can capitalize on the widespread availability of computers in schools to develop and deliver tests that provide valuable diagnostic information that can be used to help improve student learning.

Enhancing Assessment Information

Each of the above applications of technology enhance classroom assessment by increasing efficiency and expanding the types of items and tasks from which assessment information is gathered. The type of information collected through these uses of technology, however, remains focused on student responses to discrete items and tasks collected in an on-demand context. In this section, enhancements that expand the type of response information that is collected from students, the communication of assessment information to students and parents, and improvements in the quality of assessment information are explored. Specifically, I explore uses of technology to collect process information as students engage in assessment tasks, a digitally based report card system designed to make student assessment more transparent and informative for parents, and recent advances in accessibility practices that aim to increase the validity of assessment information.

Assessing Engagement and Persistence

Engagement is requisite for learning (Greene & Miller, 1996). Recent research also indicates that persistence, or what is sometimes called grit, is also a factor that influences long-term learning outcomes (Duckworth, Peterson, Matthews, & Kelly, 2007). There are many informal sources of evidence that an educator can use to indicate students are engaged in and persist with a learning activity. Among these informal indicators are students' body language, active participation, questioning and contributions to discussions, formal requests for assistance, submissions of drafts for critical feedback, and extent of modifications to work based on feedback.

When students engage in learning activities in a digital format, opportunities arise to collect additional sources of evidence regarding engagement and persistence. Sometimes referred to as stealth assessment, learning systems, digital assessment instruments, and other digital learning resources can collect information based on mouse clicks and other actions that occur as students interact with a resource. These background actions can then be used to provide evidence about engagement and persistence.

As one example, many digital assessment delivery systems are able to track a student's actions as they engage with an assessment instrument. The types of information tracked can include the amount of time that a student displays a given assessment item on the screen, changes answers to questions, flags items for later review, revisits an item, and employs resources (e.g., a calculator, formula sheet, digital ruler) provided by the system while working on an item. Some of these data can then be used to provide insight into student engagement. As an example, students who spend little time on items and who do not consistently answer those items correctly can be inferred to have a low level of engagement with the assessment task. In contrast, students who invest adequate amounts of time displaying an item, make changes to answer choices, and revisit items can be inferred to be operating with a higher level of engagement.

When a system provides feedback to students, actions in response to that feedback can also be used to provide evidence of engagement and persistence. As an example, Lingo Jingo is a learning system designed to support development of a second language (e.g., English for students who speak a different primary language or students who are learning a modern language such as Spanish or French). A component of Lingo Jingo presents students with various word games. Upon completion, students receive a score indicating how well they performed on the game. Students are then able to replay the game multiple times to increase their score. Through replaying the game, students are repeatedly exposed to the learning content that is the focus of the game (e.g., vocabulary words, standard grammatical practices). For students who initially receive low scores, the frequency with which they replay the game until they receive a winning score can provide insight into both their engagement with the learning activity and their persistence in mastering the content of the game.

Google Docs can also be a source of evidence regarding both engagement and persistence specific to writing, as well as providing insight into a student's response to feedback. Through a shared document, an educator can view information about the amount of time spent working on a writing assignment, the time during which work was performed (e.g., days before the assignment is due or just moments before the due date), the number of times revisions were made, and even the specific revisions made. By examining these types of information prior to and following feedback, the educator can gain insight into how students respond to feedback and the extent to which they persist in the revision process to develop a final product. Clearly, this type of analysis can be informative for students who struggle with writing. But it can also provide insight on aspects of the writing process that can be focused on to help strong writers polish their writing to an even higher level.

Although it is possible to collect a large variety and amount of process data as students engage with digital tools, it is important to consider carefully the interpretations one makes based on process data. As an example, focusing on time spent working on test items without also considering the accuracy of responses might lead to a misimpression about the level of engagement made by a student for whom the content of the assessment is easy. Similarly, examining process data collected while students develop their writing using Google Docs may be misleading for students who perform much of their initial editing on paper before transcribing those edits into the final document. For such students, a poor inference about the level of engagement in the revision process might result simply because the system was not able to capture data from actions that occurred offline. Despite these potential shortcomings, process data hold potential to provide one source of evidence about student engagement and persistence.

Supporting Standards-Based Grading

The 1983 release of *A Nation at Risk* (Gardner, 1983) sparked a movement to establish content standards that define the knowledge, skills, and abilities (KSA) all students are expected to develop during each year of schooling. Since then, standards-based education has permeated classroom instruction. Many schools have realigned their curriculum to support the development of the KSAs defined by the content standards and define effective instruction as that which prepares students to meet performance standards associated with the content standards. In some cases, educators begin each lesson by identifying the standard(s) to be addressed during that class session. In other cases, the standards are employed to establish learning objectives for lessons.

To assist students in understanding the performance expectations they are expected to meet, many educators develop rubrics. In some cases, rubrics are assignment-specific. In other cases, they focus more generally on the aspects of products that indicate achievement of a given learning goal (e.g., communication, collaboration, problem-solving, etc.). When these more general rubrics are used to guide assessment of student work, the resulting scores or grades awarded to work products provide a source of information about students' progress toward achievement of the learning standards that are the focus of the rubric. In turn, marrying rubrics with exemplars that exemplify characteristics of work products at each performance level has potential to make explicit the level of performance expected of students. Collectively, rubrics, student products, performance ratings for the product, and exemplars combine to help students, and potentially parents, better understand what is expected of them and where they are in their development toward those expectations.

The reporting system developed by Knotion (2016) provides an example of an integrated approach to communicating expectations and each student's progress toward those expectations. The Knotion report card uses digital technologies to allow parents and students to explore information about student performance at various levels of detail. As an online curriculum and learning system being implemented in Mexican schools, there are three characteristics of Knotion that provide a powerful opportunity to deepen understanding of a student's academic development. First, the Knotion curriculum has been carefully designed to develop and assess student achievement of specific learning objectives associated with the adopted content standards. This adoption provides a framework for structuring student learning and makes clear what skills and knowledge are important for educators to assess. Second, for each learning objective, one or more assessment activities provides evidence of the student's achievement of that objective. While these assessment activities take many forms, including worksheets, quizzes, plays, performances, visual displays, etc., a common scoring rubric is employed for each open-ended work sample. In addition, exemplars for each performance level for a given assessment task are collected. Third, being a digital curriculum, a digital artifact of nearly all student work is collected and stored in the Knotion system.

Capitalizing on these three characteristics, the Knotion reporting system begins by grouping learning outcomes into a logical structure. For a given reporting period, the learning outcomes that were the target of instruction are highlighted. For each outcome, student performance on the associated assessment activities is summarized using the four-point scale employed by all scoring rubrics. Rather than provide an overall grade composed of several components, this approach makes clear which objectives students have achieved and which require further development. In the event that parents question a given score, the reporting interface can allow parents to view the products students produced for a given objective.

In addition, the scoring rubric and exemplars can be made available for parents to review. In this way, detailed information about student achievement is reported and the entire process is transparent. Over time, the display also serves as a progress map that shows which objectives have been addressed and what objectives must still be addressed, and the extent to which a student has achieved them. In addition, by providing access to scoring rubrics and exemplars, the report provides an opportunity to develop common expectations for student work. While this system is in the early stages of implementation, it provides an example of how digital technology can be used to report information about student achievement in a manner that deepens understanding both about what students can do and what they are expected to be able to do.

Enhancing Accessibility

Since the early 1970s, considerable concern has emerged about the accessibility of instructional and assessment materials. Initially, concerns about accessibility focused on students with physical and visual disabilities. Over time, the population of students for whom there are concerns expanded to include those with learning disabilities, language processing needs, attention and stimulus needs, auditory needs, and most recently students who are English language learners. Over the past decade, efforts to apply principles of universal design to the development and delivery of educational assessments have helped improve the quality with which access is provided to all students.

The concept of universal design focuses on "the design of products and environments to be usable by all people, to the greatest extent possible, without the need for adaptation or specialized design" (Center for Universal Design [CUD], 1997, p. 1). Rather than creating a single solution, universal design has come to embrace the concept of allowing users to select from among multiple alternatives. As Rose and Meyer (2002) emphasize:

> Universal Design does not imply "one sizes fits all" but rather acknowledges the need for alternatives to suit many different people's needs . . . the essence of [Universal Design] is flexibility and the inclusion of alternatives to adapt to the myriad variations in learner needs, styles, and preferences.
>
> (p. 4)

In the field of education, universal design for learning (UDL) applies these same design principles by considering the variety of accessibility and learning needs students may have when they encounter instructional materials. The three key principles of UDL (Rose & Meyer, 2002) focus on the provision of:

- alternative formats for presenting information;
- alternative means for action and expression; and
- alternative means for engagement.

When applied to student assessment, these three aspects of universal design for learning have important implications for: (a) the development of assessment content; (b) the interface used to deliver that content; and (c) the interaction between the examinee, the assessment content, and the delivery interface. Accessible test design provides a model that addresses these three elements to maximize the ability of assessment content to measure targeted knowledge or skills. The accessible test design model (see Figure 12.2) begins by defining the access needs of each individual student. These needs are then used to present specific representational forms of the content (e.g., text, Braille, sign, audio, alternate language, etc.) and to activate specific access tools embedded in a test delivery interface that align with the student's access needs. Through this interaction with assessment content and the delivery system, the administration of an assessment item or task is tailored to maximize the measurement of the intended construct and minimize the influence of unintended constructs.

Flexibly tailoring a student's experience with an assessment item depends on the access needs of each student and may require adaptations to the presentation of item content, the interaction with that content, the response mode, or the representational form in which content is communicated

As Mislevy et al. (2010) explain, several different representational forms can be used to present instructional or test content to a student. To enable a student to recognize and process content, the form used to present that content may need to be tailored based on the student's representational form need. As an example, a student who is blind cannot access content presented in print-based form. However, when that same content is presented in braille, the material becomes accessible for the student if the student is a Braille reader. Reading aloud content, presenting text-based content in sign language, Braille, tactile representations of

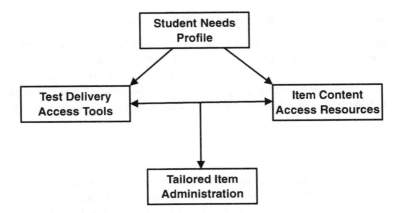

Figure 12.2 Accessible test design model.

graphical images, symbolic representations of text-based information, narrative representations of chemical compounds (e.g., "sodium chloride" instead of "NaCl") or mathematical formulas, and translating into a different language are all types of alternate representations.

For paper-based instructional and test materials, alternate representations often require the development of different versions or forms of the materials, or the use of translators or interpreters who present alternate representations to the student. In a digital environment, alternate representations of content can be built into item information and a digital test delivery system can then tailor the representational form presented to examinees based on their individual needs.

Today, universal design and accessible test design provide powerful opportunities to improve the accessibility of information collected from students. Large-scale assessment programs such as the Partnership for Assessment of Readiness for College and Careers (PARCC) and Smarter Balanced have applied these concepts and tools to develop items that contain multiple representations. They have also developed tools to document student accessibility needs. And they use test delivery systems that apply a student accessibility profile to tailor the delivery of test content to improve accessibility for each individual student. This has helped improve the accessibility of tests and in turn is improving the accuracy of information collected about student achievement.

These same functions have also been incorporated into an open-source platform that classroom teachers can use to develop and deliver their own assessment content. Specifically, the TAO assessment platform is a fully functional platform that allows educators to author their own quiz, test, or survey questions. Once created, educators can indicate different representational forms of the content. In some cases, such as American Sign Language, the educator must create this alternate content. But in other cases, such as audio, Braille, or alternate languages, this content can be automatically generated and then refined by the educator.

With TAO, educators can also create student accessibility profiles and assign assessment tasks to students. Once done, the assessment task is then tailored to meet the accessibility needs of each student based on their profile. While use of a platform such as TAO requires training and time to develop the facility to create alternate representations of assessment content, a tool such as TAO has great potential to improve the accessibility of classroom quizzes, tests, and surveys. And because student work is produced digitally, it can be analyzed and summarized automatically. In this way, a platform such as TAO can help support both accuracy and timeliness of assessment information.

Challenges to Technology-Based Assessment in the Classroom

As Bennett (1998) argues, technology can lend several advantages for assessment. Chief among them are increases in efficiency, collection of new sources of evidence, and tighter integration with learning. In addition, technology can be used to increase student access to assessment content and in turn improve the quality of evidence collected through assessment activities (Russell, 2011). With these advantages, however, come at least three challenges: equity, privacy, and accessibility options.

Equity

Access to technology in schools has increased greatly over the past 20 years. This increase is seen in at least three ways. First, the variety of digital technologies available in schools has expanded greatly. Whereas in the late 1990s digital technology took the form of desktop computers, today a variety of digital devices are used in schools, including desktop computers, laptops, Chromebooks, tablets, and cell phones. Second, the ratio of students to digital devices has also decreased dramatically. Whereas there was, on average, only one computer available for every 10 students in 1997 (Coley, Cradler, & Engel, 1997), today more than 50% of teachers report having 1:1 access to digital technology in their classroom (EdTech, 2017). Finally, access to high-speed Internet has also increased greatly over this time period such that the vast majority of schools now report having such access (Camera, 2015).

While this increased access allows many of today's educators to employ technology to support classroom assessment, access remains a challenge in some settings. Although the majority of teachers report 1:1 access in their classroom, a substantial percentage of teachers do not have such access. Without access to digital technology for each student, teachers must move students from the classroom to a computer lab, bring carts of devices into the classroom, or implement procedures in which they rotate students on and off of devices. Clearly, such solutions are disruptive to classroom instruction and present a barrier to equitable use of technology of assessment across classrooms.

Some advocates of technology use in the classroom view cell phones as a viable solution (Graham, 2017; Lynch, 2017). The argument here is that most students possess a cell phone that can be substituted for a school-provided digital device. While this may one day be the case, today there is still a substantial percentage of students who do not have a cell phone (Versel, 2018). In addition, many schools have policies that limit or prohibit use of cell phones in school (Raths, 2012). And in some cases, cell phone coverage and/or poor wireless access in classrooms limits use of cell phones for learning or assessment activities in the classroom.

Collectively, the presence of schools that lack digital devices for all students, students' lack of access to cell phones, and limited coverage for cell phones create inequities that negatively impact use of technology to support assessment.

Privacy

As discussed above, stealth assessment collects information about the actions students take as they work on a task. The type of information collected ranges from the revisions made to a piece of writing in a Google Doc to the time a student begins and ends a given task in software such as Lingo Jingo, or each mouse click and decision a student makes as they work through a game or an encounter in a virtual environment. This information has potential to provide insight into students' cognitive processes and habits of mind that in turn might be used by educators to focus instruction.

Digital technology can also make assessment practices more transparent to students and educators by regularly posting assessment information in a reporting system such as that under development by Knotion. Such systems can also post student work as well as exemplars that reflect the quality of work associated with specific performance levels.

Stealth assessment and real-time assessment reporting systems hold potential to expand the type of information employed for assessment purposes and improve communication of assessment information. However, such approaches also raise issues of privacy.

For stealth assessment, students may not realize that their actions are being recorded. As a result, students may engage in activities that they do not wish to be recorded and in the process reveal information about themselves that they otherwise would not. As an example, as a student is working on a Google Doc, they may jot down notes of a personal matter that are latter deleted. The Google Doc history, however, preserves these recordings and may make them visible to others who have access to the document. Similarly, depending on how mouse click recording is implemented, data may capture actions that a student takes that are not directly relevant to the task at hand, but which unintentionally reveal private information about the student (e.g., visiting a website for personal reasons, performing a search for personal interest).

Similarly, recording and sharing student work in an online forum can also make public information that the student did not intend to share publicly. Such online distribution of student work and performance information is also vulnerable to access from unauthorized users.

To protect against such invasions of privacy, students should be fully informed of the type of data collected as they interact with a system and the ways in which their work products may be shared with others. In addition, security measures should be in place to limit access to student information from unauthorized people.

Selecting Accessibility Options

Applications of universal design to assessment have greatly expanded the tools available to meet the access needs of students. In turn, the shift in thinking about accessibility as an accommodation to a universal feature of assessment has greatly expanded both the types of accessibility decisions teachers must make and the number of students for which such decisions must be made. This impact is most clearly reflected in the shift from accommodation policies to accessibility policies for large-scale assessments such as Smarter Balanced (2018). Whereas accommodations were once reserved for students with identified needs documented in individual education plans, modern accessibility policies now permit use of a variety of accessibility supports by all students, regardless of whether or not they have an individual education plan (Russell, 2018). It is too early to document the effect that this shift in policy for large-scale assessments has had on classroom assessment practices. Nonetheless, the presence of increased accessibility options in assessment software available in the classroom may create challenges for educators who must now help students decide which options are appropriate.

The expansion of accessibility to all students creates a decision-making challenge for educators and students. To assist in this decision-making process, some organizations have begun developing digital tools for students and educators. As an example, CAST developed the AEM Navigator (CAST, n.d.). This tool focuses primarily on accessibility features designed to support access to text-based content. The tool allows students to select different accessibility options and then collects information about students' ability to access and understand text-based content under the selected conditions. This information is then made available to educators who can work with the student to make informed decisions about the options that work best for the student.

While not as interactive as the AEM Navigator, Smarter Balanced has also developed resources to assist in selecting accessibility supports for all students. These resources were originally designed to support development of an Individual Student Assessment Accessibility Profile (ISAAP) for the Smarter Balanced summative test. The general approach to making informed decisions based on input from students, parents, and experience performing practice assessment tasks under different conditions can be applied to classroom assessment.

Whether using an interactive tool, such as the AEM Navigator, that purposefully modifies access supports to provide evidence of effect, or employing a reflective approach that collects information from students about what works best for them, the increase in variety of accessibility supports and the expansion of accessibility concerns from students with disabilities to all students creates a new set of assessment decisions for educators to address.

Looking to the Future

The examples presented in this chapter only scratch the surface of the many ways in which digital technology can be used to support classroom assessment. In some cases, digital tools have advanced to the point that they provide a relatively easy and efficient method for collecting and summarizing evidence about students and their learning. As an example, the many digital quizzing tools available today require only a short time to learn how to develop and administer assessment content. And after this initial learning period, the time required to develop new quizzes, tests, questionnaires, or assignments is identical to creating paper-based assignments using a word processor.

In other cases, the technology is in an earlier stage of maturation. As an example, the learning curve for using TAO to develop accessible assessment content is steep. And even when one becomes proficient, the process of creating and proofing alternate versions of assessment content remains time-consuming. Similarly, tools such as the Diagnostic Algebra Assessment System and Diagnoser are effective for identifying misconceptions for a limited number of algebra and physics concepts. However, the breadth of misconceptions that students may develop stretches well beyond these two subject areas and there is much work to do to more fully support assessment of misconceptions across domains.

Finally, the development of technology-enhanced items and more interactive assessment environments can help increase student engagement with assessment. But while engagement is important for quality assessment, a more critical issue is the collection of evidence that is aligned with the decisions an educator aims to make. It is essential that the "glitz" of these new assessment tools does not outshine the construct relevance of the evidence provided by these tools.

As the field continues to evolve, the use of technology to support classroom assessment will continue to expand. As this occurs, one aspect of technology-based assessment that will be interesting to observe is student analytics. Currently, there is great interest in advancing the types of information about student processes that is collected as students work on tasks, and the ways in which this information is used to understand student learning. This type of information holds potential to provide educators with new types of evidence to support their decision-making in the classroom. But as with all forms of technology-based assessment, it is essential that the collection, analysis, and use of evidence gathered about students be aligned with the decisions educators make about students. As student data analytics, development of new item and task types, and expansion of the types of assessment activities performed digitally continue to evolve, developers are encouraged to maintain a focus on the decisions they aim to support and to align the evidence gathered and analytic methods employed to those decisions. It is only through such alignment that sound classroom assessment will be supported by technology.

References

Airasian, P. W. (1991). *Classroom assessment*. New York: McGraw-Hill.

Aljaloud, A., Gromik, N., Billingsley, W., & Kwan, P. (2015). Research trends in student response systems: A literature review. *International Journal of Learning Technology, 10*(4), 313–325.

Beatty, I. (2004). *Transforming student learning with classroom communication systems.* EDUCAUSE Center for Analysis and Research (ECAR), no. 3, pp. 1–13.

Bennett, R. E. (1998). *Reinventing assessment: Speculations on the future of large-scale educational testing.* Princeton, NJ: Policy Information Center, Educational Testing Service.

Bojinova, E. D., & Oigara, J. N. (2011). Teaching and learning with clickers: Are clickers good for students? *Interdisciplinary Journal of E-Learning and Learning Objects, 7*(1),169–184.

Bryant, W. (2017). Developing a strategy for using technology-enhanced items in large-scale standardized tests. *Practical Assessment, Research & Evaluation, 22*(1). Retrieved from http://pareonline.net/getvn.asp?v=22&n=1

Caldwell, J. E. (2007). Clickers in the large classroom: Current research and best-practice tips. *Life Sciences Education, 6*(1), 9–20.

Camera, L. (2015, November 19). *More schools have access to high-speed broadband than ever.* Retrieved from www.usnews.com/news/articles/2015/11/19/more-schools-have-access-to-high-speed-broadband-than-ever

CAST. (n.d.). *AEM Navigator.* Retrieved from http://aem.cast.org/navigating/aem-navigator.html#.W7TCmpNKjow

Center for Universal Design (CUD). (1997). *About UD: Universal design principles.* Retrieved from www.design.ncsu.edu/cud/about_ud/udprincipleshtmlformat.html

Code, J., Clarke-Midura, J., Zap, N., & Dede, C. (2012). Virtual performance assessment in immersive virtual environments. In H. Wang (Ed.), *Interactivity in e-learning: Cases and frameworks.* New York: IGI Publishing.

Coley, R. J., Cradler, J., & Engel, P. K. (1997). *Computers and classrooms: The status of technology in U.S. schools.* Princeton, NJ: Educational Testing Service.

Concord Consortium. (2016). *Revolutionary digital learning for science, math, and engineering.* Retrieved from https://concord.org/projects

Cox, C. T., Cooper, M. M., Pease, R., Buchanan, K., Hernandez-Cruz, L., Stevens, R., Picione, J., & Holme, T. (2008). Advancements in curriculum and assessment by the use of IMMEX technology in the organic laboratory. *Chemistry Education Research and Practice, 9*(2), 163–168.

Cubric, M., & Jefferies, A. (2015). The benefits and challenges of large-scale deployment of electronic voting systems: University student views from across different subject groups. *Computers and Education, 87*, 98–111.

Drasgow, F., & Olson-Buchanan, J. B. (1999). *Innovations in computerized assessment.* Mahwah, NJ: Lawrence Earlbaum Associates.

Duckworth, A. L., Peterson, C., Matthews, M. D., & Kelly, D. R. (2007). Grit: Perseverance and passion for long-term goals. *Journal of Personality and Social Psychology, 92*(6), 1087–1101.

EdTech. (2017, February 1). *More than 50 percent of teachers report 1:1 computing.* Retrieved from https://edtechmagazine.com/k12/article/2017/02/more-50-percent-teachers-report-11-computing

Ellul, J. (1964). *The technological society.* New York: Vintage Books.

Florida Department of Education. (2010). *Race to the Top assessment program application for new grants.* Retrieved from www.smarterbalanced.org/wordpress/wp-content/uploads/2011/12/Smarter-Balanced-RttT-Application.pdf

Gardner, D. P. (1983). *A nation at risk.* Washington, DC: The National Commission on Excellence in Education, US Department of Education.

Graham, E. (2017). *Using smartphones in the classroom.* Washington, DC: National Education Association. Retrieved from www.nea.org/tools/56274.htm

Greene, B. A., & Miller, R. B. (1996). Influences on achievement: Goals, perceived ability, and cognitive engagement. *Contemporary Educational Psychology, 21*(2), 181–192.

Harmon, M., Smith, T. A., Martin, M. O., Kelly, D. L., Beaton, A. E., Mullis, I. V., . . . & Orpwood, G. (1997). *Performance assessment: IEA's third international mathematics and science study (TIMSS).* Chestnut Hill, MA: International Association for the Evaluation of Educational Achievement.

IMS Global Learning Consortium. (2002). *IMS question and test interoperability: An overview final specification version 1.2.* Retrieved from www.imsglobal.org/question/qtiv1p2/imsqti_oviewv1p2.html

Kane, M. T. (1992). An argument-based approach to validity. *Psychological Bulletin, 112*(3), 527–535.

Kay, R. H., & LeSage, A. (2009). Examining the benefits and challenges of using audience response systems: A review of the literature. *Computers and Education, 53*(3), 819–827.

Knotion. (2016). *Knowledge in action: Curricula Knotion.* Retrieved from http://knotion.com/curricula-knotion/

Laxman, K. (2011). A study on the adoption of clickers in higher education. *Australasian Journal of Educational Technology, 27*(8), 1291–1303.

Leighton, J. P., & Gierl, M. J. (2007). *Cognitive diagnostic assessment for education: Theory and applications.* Cambridge: Cambridge University Press.

Leighton, J. P., Gokiert, R. J., Cor, M. K., & Heffernan, C. (2010). Teacher beliefs about the cognitive diagnostic information of classroom- versus large-scale tests: Implications for assessment literacy. *Assessment in Education: Principles, Policy & Practice, 17*(1), 7–21.

Lowrance, W. W. (1986). *Modern science and human values.* New York: Oxford University Press.

Lynch, M. (2017, March 24). *How to manage cell phone use in your classroom.* Retrieved from www.thetechedvocate.org/how-to-manage-cell-phone-use-in-your-classroom/

Madaus, G., Russell, M., & Higgins, J. (2009). *The paradoxes of high stakes testing: How they affect students, their parents, teachers, principals, schools, and society.* Charlotte, NC: Information Age.

Masters, J. (2014, April). *The diagnostic geometry assessment system: Results from a randomized controlled trial.* Paper presented at the annual meeting of the American Educational Research Association, Philadelphia, PA.

McDaniel, M. A., Thomas, R. C., Agarwal, P. K., McDermott, K. B., & Roediger, H. L. (2013). Quizzing in middle-school science: Successful transfer performance on classroom exams. *Applied Cognitive Psychology, 27,* 360–372.

Mead, N. A. (1995). International assessment of educational progress. In *International comparative studies in education: Descriptions of selected large-scale assessments and case studies* (pp. 48–57). Washington, DC: National Academy of Sciences, National Research Council.

Measured Progress/ETS Collaborative. (2012). *Smarter Balanced Assessment Consortium: Technology-enhanced items.* Retrieved from www.measuredprogress.org/wp-content/uploads/2015/08/SBAC-Technology-Enhanced-Items-Guidelines.pdf

Mislevy, R. J., Almond, R. G., & Lukas, J. F. (2003). *A brief introduction to evidence-centered design.* Princeton, NJ: ETS Research Report Series.

Mislevy, R. J., Behrens, J. T., Bennett, R. E., Demark, S. F., Frezzo, D. C., Levy, R., Robinson, D. H., Rutstein, D. W., Shute, V. J., Stanley, K., & Winters, F. I. (2010). On the roles of external knowledge representations in assessment design. *Journal of Technology, Learning, and Assessment, 8*(2). Retrieved from www.jtla.org

Mula, J. M., & Kavanagh, M. (2009). Click go the students, click-click-click: The efficacy of a student response system for engaging students to improve feedback and performance. *E-Journal of Business Education and Scholarship of Teaching, 3*(1), 1–17.

Raths, D. (2012, March 28). *Revisiting cell phone bans in schools.* Retrieved from https://thejournal.com/articles/2012/03/28/revisiting-cell-phones-bans-in-schools.aspx

Rose, D. H., & Meyer, A. (2002). *Teaching every student in the digital age: Universal design for learning.* Alexandria, VA: Association for Supervision and Curriculum Development.

Russell, M. (2006). *Technology and assessment: The tale of two perspectives.* Greenwich, CT: Information Age.

Russell, M. (2011). Computerized tests sensitive to individual needs. In S. N. Elliott, R. J. Kettler, P. A. Beddow, & A. Kurz (Eds.), *Handbook of accessible achievement tests for all students* (pp. 255–273). New York: Springer International.

Russell, M. (2016). A framework for examining the utility of technology-enhanced items. *Journal of Applied Testing Technology, 17*(1), 20–32.

Russell, M. (2018). Recent advances in the accessibility of digitally delivered educational assessments. In S. N. Elliott, R. J. Kettler, P. A. Beddow, & A. Kurz (Eds.), *Handbook of accessible instruction and testing practices: Issues, innovations, and applications* (pp. 247–262). New York: Springer International.

Russell, M. K., & Airasian, P. W. (2012). *Classroom assessment: Concepts and applications.* New York: McGraw-Hill.

Russell, M., O'Dwyer, L., & Miranda, H. (2009). Diagnosing students' misconceptions in algebra: Results from an experimental pilot study. *Behavior Research Methods, 41*(2), 414–424.

Scalise, K., & Gifford, B. (2006). Computer-based assessment in e-learning: A framework for constructing "intermediate constraint" questions and tasks for technology platforms. *Journal of Technology, Learning, and Assessment, 4*(6). Retrieved from http://ejournals.bc.edu/ojs/index.php/jtla/article/view/1653/1495

Sireci, S. G., & Zenisky, A. L. (2006). Innovative item formats in computer-based testing: In pursuit of improved construct representation. In S. M. Downing & T. M. Haladyna (Eds.), *Handbook of test development.* New York: Routledge.

Smarter Balanced. (2018). *Usability, accessibility, and accommodations guidelines.* Retrieved from https://portal.smarterbalanced.org/library/en/usability-accessibility-and-accommodations-guidelines.pdf

Stecher, B. (2010). *Performance assessment in an era of standards-based educational accountability.* Stanford, CA: Stanford Center for Opportunity Policy in Education.

Thissen-Roe, A., Hunt, E., & Minstrell, J. (2004). The DIAGNOSER project: Combining assessment and learning. *Behavior Research Methods, Instruments, and Computers, 36*(2), 234–240.

Versel, L. (2018, October 3). *As cell phones proliferate in K-12, schools search for smart policies.* Retrieved from https://blogs.edweek.org/edweek/DigitalEducation/2018/02/smartphones_student_learning_classrooms_K12_education.html

Waite, J. (2007). Weekly quizzing really works: Online software makes it easy. *Tech Directions, 66*(7), 16–21.

Washington State. (2010). *Race to the Top assessment program application for new grants.* Retrieved from www.smarterbalanced.org/wordpress/wp-content/uploads/2011/12/Smarter-Balanced-RttT-Application.pdf

Winner, L. (1977). *Autonomous technology: Technic-out-of-control as a theme in political thought.* Cambridge, MA: MIT Press.

13

Fairness in Classroom Assessment

Joan Herman and Linda Cook

The diversity within today's classrooms demands classroom assessment practices that are equitable and inclusive of all students. Consider recent statistics on the demographic characteristics of the U.S. public school population: 20% of students live in poverty, 50% are ethnic minorities, 9.4% are English learners (ELs), 13% are students with disabilities (National Center for Education Statistics [NCES], 2017), and the proportions of students who are members of ethnic or cultural subgroups are growing, as are those who are classified as ELs. The public school population of California, for example, has more students classified as minority than majority, and ELs constitute more than 20% of the public school population (California Department of Education, 2017). But these simple statistics provide only a part of the picture and do not convey the complexity of diversity in today's classrooms; the numbers mask the substantial heterogeneity that exists within each of these demographic categories. For example, the EL group includes students with a wide range of home languages and cultures, English language proficiency, and prior educational histories. The students with disabilities group combines students with diverse types of disabilities, with diverse prior educational experiences, and requiring a variety of different accommodations. Adding to this heterogeneity, some students cross multiple groups (e.g., ELs with disabilities). Moreover, virtually every classroom exhibits a broad range of diversity in students' backgrounds and cultures, prior knowledge and skill levels, and prior instructional experiences. The reality of diversity in today's classrooms, coupled with persistent achievement gaps for diverse populations (e.g., see NCES, 2018), forms important context for classroom assessment and creates the imperative for equity and fairness in supporting all students' learning.

To address these imperatives, this chapter considers how the *Standards for Educational and Psychological Testing* (the *Test Standards*) (American Educational Research Association [AERA], American Psychological Association [APA], & National Council on Measurement in Education [NCME], 2014) can inform principles of fairness for classroom assessment to support all students achieving high standards. While acknowledging the literature and existing standards on classroom assessment (Brookhart, 2011; Camilli, 2013; Cowie, 2015; Klinger et al., 2015; McMillan, 2011; National Research Council [NRC], 2001a; Popham, 2017), we draw on the *Test Standards* for several reasons. First, existing criteria for classroom assessment—e.g., the *Classroom Assessment Standards* (Klinger et al., 2015)—tend to focus on assessment as a process and give relatively less attention to the quality of the assessment evidence, which is a hallmark of the *Test Standards*. Second, fairness issues may be threaded through existing standards for classroom assessment, but the 2014 edition of the *Test Standards* brings fairness to the fore as a core foundation for all measurement. It therefore seems timely to consider what foundation the "fairness in testing" standards (fairness standards) provide for classroom assessment. Finally, our intent is to serve as a bridge between the robust measurement theory embodied in the *Test Standards* and the practice of classroom assessment. We identify both points of congruence and areas beyond the purview of current measurement theory, areas that may be ripe for future exploration.

In the sections below, we start by sharing the *Test Standards* definition of fairness and making the connection between this terminology and the terminology of standards-based classroom instruction and assessment. Based on the *Test Standards*, we then outline important issues and obstacles in promoting fairness in assessment and share key messages for achieving fairness in classroom assessment. We then consider how these messages relate to broader views of fairness in assessment and conclude with implications for classroom practice and future directions for measurement.

What Is Fairness in Assessment?

The *Test Standards* acknowledge the societal debate over the meaning of "fairness" but limit its purview to issues that are legitimately under the control of measurement specialists and for which they may be held accountable. Fair assessment is defined as "assessment that is responsive to individual characteristics and testing contexts so that test scores will yield valid interpretations for intended uses" (AERA et al., 2014, p. 50). Scores from a test that is fair reflect the same construct and have the same meaning for all individuals for whom the test is intended and neither advantage nor disadvantage individuals because of characteristics that are irrelevant to the construct being measured. For example, a test of science that includes complex directions in English or that requires reading an extended scenario in English may be unfair to English learners or to struggling readers because the reading demands of the assessment may prevent these students from demonstrating their capacity in science. Similarly, the font size of a document students had to read for a test on the Civil War would pose an obstacle to a visually impaired student showing what he or she knows if the font used to display the document was too small for the individual to read. A third example might be a math question included on an international assessment of mathematics skills. Suppose students were asked to respond to a problem that uses terms such as dollars and quarters. The use of these terms would disadvantage students from backgrounds that do not use this terminology, and the test scores could not be fairly interpreted as providing an estimate of the students' mathematics skills.

Fairness, according to the *Test Standards*, thus is a fundamental validity issue: a fair test provides valid information for a given purpose for all students, regardless of their background characteristics; it gives all students an unobstructed opportunity to show what they know, unimpeded by characteristics unrelated to the construct being assessed. Although the *Test Standards* definition may be concerned with the validity of scores and score inferences that are derived from a test, we believe that it applies equally well to classroom assessment and the wide variety of evidence, including test scores, that classroom assessment entails.

Applying the Test Standards Definition in Classroom Assessment

As the introduction to the volume observes (p. 4), classroom assessment is a *process through which teachers and students gather, interpret, and use evidence of student learning for a variety of purposes.* These purposes range from more formative ones such as diagnosing student learning needs and monitoring student learning progress to inform immediate instruction, to more summative purposes such as determining how successful students have been in achieving learning goals, assigning students' grades, and reporting to parents, administrators, and others about students' progress and attainments.

This process may draw on evidence from a variety of formal and less formal methods, including classroom tests and quizzes, short- and longer-term performance assessments, observations, classroom discussion, dialogue with and among students, analysis of student work products, and student and peer assessment. Although the nature and grain size of the resultant evidence may vary with purpose, all of the methods share a common element with standardized tests, and that is the critical process of observing a sample of student responses or behaviors and transforming these observations into valid and usable information. In standardized testing, students respond to a systematic sample of items and/or tasks representing a specified construct(s), and these responses are converted into scores that yield inferences about students' standing on the construct(s) for a specific purpose. Similarly, each of the classroom assessment methods involves eliciting and transforming an appropriate sample of student behavior (what students say, do, write, build, etc. in the classroom) into evidence that yields valid inferences about student learning to support a specific classroom assessment purpose.

Accepting this parallelism, we can apply the *Test Standards* definition of fairness to the evidence used in classroom assessment: fairness means that the evidence fueling the classroom assessment process, be it from a formal test, from an observation of student behavior, or from an analysis of student interactions, should enable accurate inferences on all students' learning, *regardless of differences in students' characteristics*, while serving whatever formative and/or summative purpose may be intended.

Admittedly, the fairness or quality of the assessment is only one part of what is needed to support fairness in the process of teaching, learning, and assessment, but clearly it is a necessary one. Without valid evidence, the value of the classroom assessment *process* is stymied. And without valid evidence for all students—fairness—teaching and learning and instructional decision-making is compromised for some students, and with that the potential power of assessment to leverage more equitable outcomes, as we discuss further below.

The Teaching/Learning and Assessment Cycle

Testing uses the language of "construct" to identify its targets. For classroom assessment, the relevant constructs or targets of assessment are the goals of classroom teaching and learning. In today's standards-based learning world, these are the specific goals that collectively will enable students to achieve the college- and career-ready standards they need for future success, and assessment is viewed as integral to that success.

Transparency is an important hallmark of the process and critical to students' perceptions of the fairness of classroom assessment (Rasooli, Zandi, & DeLuca, 2018; Tierney & Koch, 2016). Teachers and students are supposed to be clear on and understand the learning goals and standards they need to accomplish and the criteria by which their success will be judged (e.g., see Brookhart, 2001; Camilli, 2006; Klinger et al., 2015; McMillan, 2011; Tierney, 2013).

The process, according to many theorists, starts not only with transparency in learning goals and success criteria, but also with grounding in an expected progression of learning that takes students from wherever they are in the progression to the accomplishment of rigorous standards or to whatever grade- or course-level goals have been established (e.g., see Heritage, 2008; Herman, 2016; Shepard, Penuel, & Pellegrino, 2018; Wilson, 2018). The progression reflects a developmental sequence of smaller lesson learning goals and performances that form the pathway to students' attainment of unit and/or other intermediate learning goals that in turn will coalesce in the broader, transferrable competencies represented by standards or other classroom learning expectations (see Figure 13.1).

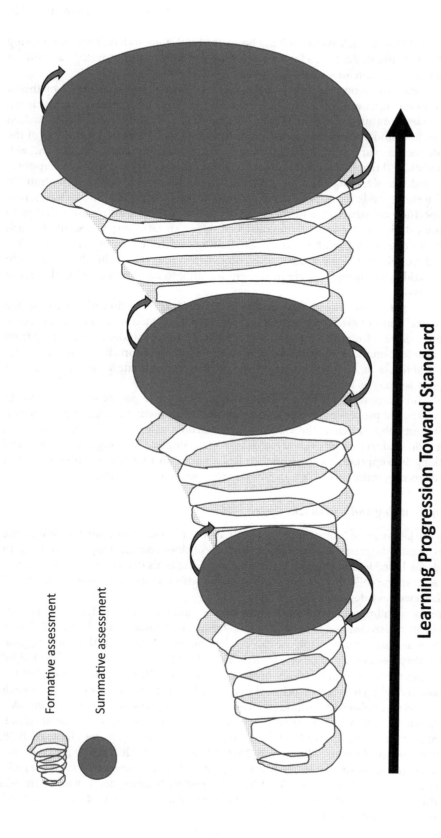

Formative assessment

Summative assessment

Learning Progression Toward Standard

Figure 13.1 Learning progression-based system of classroom assessment

Classroom assessment provides important feedback throughout the process about where students are in their learning and what action may be needed to enable students to meet the goal(s). Classroom summative assessment, whether it be formal tests, projects, research reports, or other culminating performances, embodies larger learning goals and establishes formal checks at key points along the learning progression to document what students have learned for reporting and grading purposes and potentially to identify student strengths and weaknesses for subsequent action. Formative assessment fuels student success on these more summative assessments by providing ongoing and continuous feedback on where students are in their lesson learning trajectories. Continuous evidence of and probing from classroom discourse, observation and analysis of students' in-process work and interactions, and formal checks afford the diagnostic information teachers and students need to take immediate steps to fill in any gaps and keep students on the pathway to success. The evidence gathering of formative assessment may utilize both formal and informal methods and be more dynamic, interactive, and individually oriented than that of summative assessment; however, the targets of formative assessment, in our view, still represent constructs to be measured.

Poor measurement of these constructs will produce faulty evidence that may detour learning and hamper student success. Further, if evidence is less valid—faultier and less fair in the language of the *Test Standards*—for some students or subgroups than others, then these students will likely be disadvantaged in their learning.

Core Themes in the Fairness Standards

Having made the case that the *Test Standards* definition of fairness is relevant for classroom assessment, we are not claiming that individual standards developed to evaluate standardized tests can be applied wholesale to classroom assessment evidence. Rather, we believe that the major perspectives that inform the fairness standards and the major ideas they embody are highly relevant and actionable for supporting fairness in classroom assessment, even as there are aspects of classroom assessment that are not well addressed by these standards.

The fairness standards incorporate four major interrelated ideas in assuring fairness in assessment. Sometimes these ideas push in different directions and need careful balancing, such as the tension between equality—treating all students the same—and equity—providing differential treatment or distribution of resources to give all students what they need for success (Cowie, 2015; Tierney & Koch, 2016). Although apparent in the *Test Standards*, as we discuss below, this tension perhaps surfaces more visibly in classroom assessment, where the charge is more directly to respond to individual differences. Similarly, the treatment of context varies substantially between the two. The *Test Standards* treat context largely as an exogenous threat to valid and fair inferences, a factor to be controlled. But in classroom assessment, modern sociocultural theories conceptualize context and its interactions as key elements and processes in assessment. Assessment evidence is situated in and involves the interaction of learners, their environment, and the resources within that environment (people, language, instruction resources), and cannot be cleanly separated from context (see Cowie, 2015; Shepard et al., 2018).

1. **Fairness in Treatment during the Assessment Process.**

   Fairness was and continues to be a fundamental justification for standardized testing. Standardized tests are intended to level the playing field. All aspects of the test administration and scoring process are standardized to try to assure that all students have the same opportunity to demonstrate their knowledge and skill and that differences in administration time, conditions, and/or scoring do not inadvertently affect some students' performance. Teachers, too, need to be available and guard against contextual differences that may inadvertently benefit some students over others, such as work done at home that may get parental help, differential access to and facility with technology, and scoring where individual biases creep in.

2. **Fairness as Reducing Measurement Bias.**

Here, the concern is with characteristics of the assessment itself or its use that may introduce construct-irrelevant challenges or advantage some students over others because of student characteristics (their culture, language, prior knowledge, disability status) that are not part of the construct being measured. Obvious examples are the obstacles English learners or struggling readers face in showing their knowledge of science or math constructs if the assessment uses unnecessarily complex or confusing language. Consideration of culture and prior experience further complicates the examination of potential measurement bias, as we discuss further below.

3. **Fairness as Access to the Construct Being Measured.**

While fairness in treatment and in reducing measurement bias focus on obstacles to valid inferences for *some* students, the 2014 *Test Standards* addition of accessibility as a key theme introduces a more proactive stance in assuring that assessments provide all students in an intended population a full opportunity to show what they know and can do. The *Test Standards* call for universal design, a staple of classroom practice guidance (see CAST, 2011), to assure that tests are as inclusive and accessible as possible to the widest range of students.

Accessibility means that assessments must be designed with all due attention to the diversity of the student population for whom they are intended by removing obstacles that otherwise would hinder students with a range of physical, cognitive, sensory, or linguistic challenges and providing them the opportunity to demonstrate their knowledge and skill (Beddow, Elliott, & Kettler, 2009; Ketterlin-Geller, 2008). In contrast with accommodations for special needs being an afterthought, the use of universal design means anticipating the background, language, culture, and other challenges and characteristics of the full range of students who will be assessed and planning the assessment accordingly.

Through universal design, the *Test Standards* advocate tests that will be accessible for the widest possible range of students, but also explicitly acknowledge the need for changes in standardized test procedures to enable some students to fully demonstrate their capacity. In contrast to the theme of fairness in equality of treatment (see above), the *Test Standards* here recognize that changes in an assessment are sometimes needed to get a valid picture of what students know and can do. Fairness as equality in treatment must be balanced with equity in enabling all to demonstrate their full capacity. Here, the fairness standards define two types of changes: accommodations, which maintain the construct being assessed, and modifications, which do not.

Although the *Test Standards* largely view accommodations relative to the special populations of those with disabilities and those with limited language proficiency, the same principles can be extended more broadly in classroom assessment to consider other differences among students. As Cowie (2015) notes, fairness demands that all students have access to the benefits of formative assessment, with equitable opportunities to be accurately assessed, and, based on that assessment, to get accurate and appropriate feedback on their learning. Such equity requires responsiveness to diverse individual backgrounds, cultures, prior experience, and modes of learning and interaction.

4. **Fairness as Opportunity to Learn.**

Fairness in opportunity to learn (OTL) is based on a straightforward precept: students should not be held accountable—summatively assessed on—learning outcomes that they have not had the opportunity to learn. Although less obvious an issue in classroom assessment than in large-scale testing, both research findings and observation protocols evaluating the quality of teaching suggest that OTL is relevant for teachers' practice as well. Teachers, in fact, vary in their ability to align learning goals, classroom instruction, and assessment (Clare-Matsumura & Pascal, 2003; Danielson, 2013; Stiggins, 2002). This means that the alignment of instruction with classroom assessment can be faulty, and with it the opportunity for students to have developed the knowledge and skills on which they are assessed. Moreover, research suggests that teacher expectations may lead to differential opportunities to learn within classrooms (Gipps & Stobart, 2009; Tierney, 2013).

The Fairness Standards

Based on these core perspectives on fairness, the fairness standards provide an overall directive:

> All steps in the testing process, including test design, validation, development, administration and scoring procedures should be designed in such a manner as to minimize construct-irrelevant variance and to promote valid score interpretations for the intended uses for all examinees in the intended population.
>
> (AERA et al., 2014, p. 63)

This overall standard is then subdivided into four clusters of more specific guidance:

1. Test design, development, administration, and scoring procedures that minimize barriers to valid score interpretations for the widest possible range of individuals and relevant subgroups.
2. Validity of test score interpretations for intended uses for the intended examinee population.
3. Accommodations to remove construct-irrelevant barriers and support valid interpretations of scores for intended purposes.
4. Safeguards against inappropriate score interpretations for intended uses.

As we mentioned earlier, we do not believe that the specific standards within each of these areas necessarily or fully apply to classroom assessment, but most of their driving concepts do, including the foundational principle that fairness is a fundamental driving consideration in the development and use of all classroom assessment. In the section that follows, we take each of the remaining clusters in turn, framed for classroom assessment. Our framing substitutes "classroom assessment" for "test," substitutes "implementation" for "administration," and uses the more general "evidence analysis" to encompass "scoring." Rather than referring to "intended population" of examinees, we refer to "students," and for "intended uses" simply refer to "formative and summative" uses.

To whom do these standards apply? We believe that for classroom assessment, the "test developer" role is most frequently fulfilled by classroom teachers and by the developers of curriculum materials or programs, which teachers commonly draw on for class and homework that can be the basis for formative assessment, and unit and other exams and applications that may be the basis for summative assessment.

Assessment Design, Development, Implementation, and Evidence Analysis That Minimize Construct-Irrelevant Barriers

This cluster starts with the key idea that all steps of the classroom assessment process, supported by principles of universal design, need to be designed to promote valid interpretations of assessment evidence for the full range of students—or as many as possible—in the classroom (standard 3.1). This means starting by knowing who students are and their individual characteristics that may influence their engagement with and responses to classroom assessment. It also means starting with being very clear on the construct(s) to be measured, which in classroom assessment means being very clear on immediate learning goals to be assessed and the learning progression that will take students from where they are to success on standards or other grade-level or course expectations. With these understandings in mind, assessment tasks and strategies can be designed or selected to be accessible to as many students as possible.

Traditional Sources of Bias

The *Test Standards* tend to take a rather deficit-oriented view (Bishop, Berryman, Cavanagh, & Teddy, 2009; Valencia, 1997) of student characteristics that might impede valid inferences, emphasizing characteristics that otherwise might provide obstacles to or confound students' ability to demonstrate their standing on the assessed construct(s). As the *Standards* advise, assessment developers are responsible for developing assessments that measure the intended construct and "minimize the potential interferences of construct-irrelevant characteristics . . . such as linguistic, communicative, cognitive, cultural, physical and other characteristics" (standard 3.2). From this perspective, the same basic techniques that are prevalent for reducing construct-irrelevant variation in standardized testing are appropriate for classroom assessment. Examples include assuring simple, intuitive, and clear directions and assessment procedures; minimizing construct-irrelevant reading and comprehension demands in the test as a whole and in individual items; and maximizing legibility and reducing aspects of tasks, items, and/or questions—and their contexts—that could advantage some students over others based on culture, prior experience, home background, or other factors (Abedi, 2010; Chang, Lozano, Neri, & Herman, 2017; Pitoniak et al., 2009; Solano-Flores, 2008; Thompson, Johnstone, & Thurlow, 2002).

The large body of research examining the characteristics of tests and test questions that influence the fairness of large-scale standardized assessments also has relevance here. For example, Willingham and Cole (1997) observe that all tests sample from a larger universe of content to be measured. Because choice of content is always a matter of judgment, fair assessment demands that those judgments be made with knowledge of how content interacts with subgroup characteristics.

Pitoniak et al. (2009) describe research-based strategies that can be used to reduce the impact of lack of English proficiency on fairness. They point out the importance of distinguishing between language that is construct-irrelevant and language that is part of the construct being tested when designing and developing tests for this population. Similarly, Zieky (2016) points out the importance of identifying and avoiding construct-irrelevant specialized knowledge, along with content that may lead to affective reactions that could bias test results. These are just a few points that can be drawn from a review of the literature on designing and developing fair and valid large-scale assessments.

Checklists available for reviews of large-scale assessment certainly could be adapted for classroom purposes (e.g., see Abedi, 2010; Beddow et al., 2009; Sato, 2011). For example, the TAMI test accessibility matrix (Beddow et al., 2009) directs users' attention to specific aspects of task passages or accompanying stimulus, item, or task stems, answer choices (if any), visuals, and layouts that might cause confusion or obstacles for some students. Similarly, Abedi (2011) offers a guide to reducing language load by reducing specific demands with features of vocabulary, grammar, style of discourse, and content-specific features.

Influence of Culture and Prior Experience

Deeper consideration of the effects of culture and prior experience opens up a broader set of concerns about construct-irrelevant biases. For example, consider the role of prior knowledge in assessing reading comprehension, a relationship that is long established and a central tenet of all modern theories of reading (Hirsch, 2003; Pearson, Hansen, & Gordon, 1979; Pressley et al., 1992). If students with more prior knowledge of a reading topic can more easily comprehend a reading text, then choice of text—whether in classroom assessment or more standardized testing—can inadvertently advantage or disadvantage some students' ability to show their comprehension skill. The literature on funds of knowledge similarly highlights the role that students' home and cultural experiences play in learning and assessment (Guitart & Moll, 2014; Moll, Amanti, Neff, & Gonazalez, 1992; Zipin, 2009) and demonstrates the subtleties of minimizing bias in assessment. For example, in some Native American cultures, students may be hesitant to demonstrate their skills publicly until they have achieved mastery (Pewewardy, 2002), so judging these students' learning based on a public presentation may inadvertently disadvantage their ability to show what they know. Sato (2010), for example, documents how culture and cultural diversity can manifest in meaning-making of presented information (e.g., through social orientation, epistemological beliefs, temporal perceptions, and cognitive patterns).

Sociocultural views of learning and assessment, however, encourage a wider lens and incorporate a more asset-oriented set of characteristics to meaningfully connect assessment and instruction to students' prior background, culture, motivation, and sense of self (Shepard et al., 2018). Just as in teaching and learning, tools and strategies that build on students' home and cultural experiences—their funds of knowledge—as well as their content knowledge can make assessment more relevant and meaningful for students (Chang et al., 2017; Moll, Soto-Santiago, & Schwartz, 2013). Rather than focusing on creating the same—or equal—opportunities for all students, the intent might be to create equitable assessment opportunities and engagements that stimulate individuals' maximum learning and performance. This is certainly the case in formative assessment, which explicitly seeks to respond to individual differences and necessarily adapts evidence gathering and action to individual needs.

Universal Design

Principles of universal design for learning (UDL), developed by the National Center on Universal Design in Learning (CAST, 2011), then, may offer deeper guidance for classroom assessment, both in designing summative classroom assessments that are appropriate for all students and for designing accommodations or variations that may be adapted to individual differences. The three principles that structure the specific guidance—(1) provide multiple means of representation; (2) provide multiple means of action; and (3) provide multiple means of engagement—provide general review categories for evaluating accessibility of classroom assessment. That is, are the modes of representation appropriate and accessible for all students? Are the required means of performance and action appropriate and accessible? What about means of engagement and participant structures? Or will some students need additional scaffolding or alternatives in one or more of these areas? While we treat the possible variations implied by the guidance to meet individual differences in the section below on accommodations, the message from these principles here resonates with a common measurement dictum: the importance of using multiple measures to make any important decision about students (see standards 3.18, 12.10; see also Brookhart, 2009; Camilli, 2013; McMillan, 2011). That is, the lesson for fair classroom assessment, formative or summative, is to select or develop assessment tools and strategies that address target construct(s) through multiple modes of representation and use a variety of formats and action to gauge student learning.

Other Standards in the Cluster

The standards in this cluster go on to call for comparable treatment of students during the assessment and scoring process (standard 3.4).[1] Although this dictum appears to be at odds with formative assessment processes, which are directly aimed at being adaptive and responsive to individual student needs, the guidance is particularly apt for fairness in summative assessment and its scoring. And in fact, studies indicate that students view this latter issue as an important issue in judging the fairness of classroom assessment (Rasooli et al., 2018). Toward this end, when scoring constructed-response assessments, teachers are commonly advised to use well-developed rubrics and to check their consistency by rescoring some early scored responses later in the process, and for school-wide assessments to engage in training and moderation processes (Black, Harrison, Hodgen, Marshall, & Serret, 2010; McMillan, 2011).

The final standard in this cluster (standard 3.5) advises assessment developers to document what they have done to avoid construct-irrelevant barriers for all their students. Although actual documentation would seem an unrealistic expectation for teachers, they can and should consider the question in a final review of their assessment plans and tools: What have I done to assure that all my students will be fairly assessed, will have full opportunities to demonstrate their learning, and that assessment evidence will be as free as possible from any extraneous influences? In conducting such a review, teachers would reconsider the possible influence of students' cultural, language, cognitive, communicative, physical, and other characteristics that are not part of the intended construct. Such reviews should also check for content that could be considered insensitive, offensive, or inappropriate for some students (see also standard 4.8), unless the presentation of such content serves an explicit instructional or assessment goal. Moving beyond the *Test Standards*, such a review might also consider student interests and motivation.

When teachers use assessments developed by commercial publishers or those that accompany curriculum materials, these too should be judged by these same standards of fairness. That is, developers of curriculum-embedded assessments and other commercial assessments should be expected to both follow these expectations for universal design and document the procedures they have used to support fairness.

The standards of the first cluster imply the need for sophisticated design in selecting or developing assessment tools and strategies that will be sensitive to the full range of individuals in the classroom and an intricate mapping between assessment tools and strategies and the full diversity of individual characteristics in the classroom: diversity in background knowledge, culture, and interests, and in cognitive, linguistic, communicative, sensory, and physical characteristics. In this regard, the *Test Standards* represent a paradigmatic shift: rather than planning for instruction and assessment for the "average" or typical students, teachers need to start by taking account of and understanding the characteristics of the full range of students in their classes.

Validity of Evidence Interpretations for Intended Uses for the Intended Student Population

The standards in this cluster recognize that subgroups often differ in their performance and that some subgroups, such as low SES students, English learners, students with disabilities, and underrepresented minorities, consistently score below others. Although these differences in performance in and of themselves are not evidence of unfairness or bias, they may raise questions about whether the assessment is fair and what the source of score differences might be.

Standard 3.6 essentially says this: When there are subgroup differences in scores,[2] examine the evidence supporting the validity of score interpretations for individuals in lower-performing subgroups. In other words, put extra effort into assuring that the results of summative assessments are not biased against some students. The technical validity analyses and follow-up studies expected in large-scale and standardized testing generally are not feasible for teachers' classroom assessment, but what might teachers and the developers of curriculum-embedded assessment do to assure the fairness of their assessment results? A first step is examining the results by classroom subgroup, where there are sufficient numbers (e.g., by ethnicity, culture, language status, disability). Where there are significant subgroup differences in scores, teachers can ask themselves at least two questions: First, what else do I know about the learning of the individuals within this group? Are these results consistent with other indicators of these individuals' learning? Second, how good was the assessment? Did the content well represent what was taught and what was learned? Did the assessment include items or tasks that advertently disadvantaged these students—for example, gaps in prerequisite knowledge, offensiveness in content, cultural biases or insensitivities, or absence of needed accommodations (see Gipps & Stobart, 2009; McMillan, 2011)? Or, to the extent the assessment involves constructed-response tasks, was the scoring consistent and free from the influence of stereotypes?

Standard 3.8[3] goes deeper into this latter issue and asks for special attention to the scoring of constructed responses, where there is danger of subjectivity and personal biases inadvertently entering the process. Here again, the first step is analyzing the data: Are there significant differences by classroom subgroups? If so, consider whether the scores of individuals in the low-scoring group are as expected, based on other classroom evidence, and reconsider the fairness of the assessment task, the rubric, and the assessment context (Camilli, 2013; Gipps & Stobart, 2009; McMillan, 2011). Did the task inadvertently disadvantage students in the low-performing subgroups because of construct-irrelevant language demands, culturally insensitive content, or construct-irrelevant content that was less familiar to these individuals? How well did the rubric address the targeted construct(s)? Did it include construct-irrelevant features that might disadvantage students in this subgroup? Did students understand the task? Were they clear on the assessment criteria? Might construct-irrelevant factors, personal biases, or stereotypes have influenced the scoring? What accommodations or scaffolds might have enabled students to better show their learning?

Accommodations to Remove Construct-Irrelevant Barriers and Support Valid Interpretations of Scores

Increasing the accessibility of assessment through general principles of universal design will help to combat some sources of construct-irrelevant barriers, but additional adaptations may be needed to assure fairness for all students. It is worth underscoring that fairness in the *Standards* means that the test scores have the same meaning regardless of individual background or characteristics. Accommodations are changes or variations in assessment that *do not* change the construct being measured. In contrast, assessments that modify the construct being measured (e.g., by simplifying tasks or reducing their rigor or cognitive demand) are called "modifications" in the language of the *Standards*.

Appropriate Accommodations

These distinctions are important for classroom assessment as well. If all students are being held to the same high expectations, then if changes in classroom assessments are needed to assure accessibility for some students, at least for summative assessment, those changes ought to be accommodations. The situation is different in formative assessment, where the whole nature of the process involves differentiation and responding to individual needs. Through probing, scaffolding, and other evidence gathering during the course of instruction, teachers (and the students themselves) may differentially query some students, at different points along a learning progression, to determine where they are in their learning. They may delve more deeply for some to understand gaps in learning and to take immediate action to fill in those gaps

Teachers as assessment developers or users are responsible for providing accommodations "when appropriate and feasible, to remove construct irrelevant barriers that otherwise would interfere with examinee's ability to demonstrate their standing on the target constructs" (AERA et al., 2014, p. 67). According to the *Test Standards*, an appropriate accommodation, as noted earlier, is one that responds to individual characteristics that otherwise would interfere with construct-irrelevant features of an assessment while still maintaining the construct—learning goal—being assessed (Almond et al., 2010; Dolan et al., 2013; Winter, Kopriva, Chen, & Emick, 2006). As with large-scale testing, classroom assessment also can provide alternative forms of representation that respond to specific individual characteristics (e.g., as an alternative to text-based content—where reading is not the primary construct): reading aloud, sign language, Braille, translating to a different language, or symbolic or graphic representations (Almond et al., 2010). Access to specialized dictionaries or dual-language glossaries that offer translations for non-construct-related language and terminology are other accommodations that have offered some benefit (Abedi, Hofstetter, & Lord, 2004). Presumably, these accommodations are used in instruction and should be carried over to assessment.

Because maintaining the same construct is key to what constitutes an acceptable accommodation, it is essential to be very clear on the construct to be measured (Almond et al., 2010; Thompson et al., 2002) so that that which is construct-related and that which is not can be cleanly differentiated. For example, the use of read-aloud options are appropriate when the constructs to be measured do not include reading comprehension (e.g., in assessment of history, science, or math), but may be inappropriate if they do; a calculator may be appropriate for assessing math constructs that focus on application and/or problem-solving goals, but may not for goals that include calculation. But even these decisions of construct relevancy can be more complicated than they appear at first glance (e.g., read-aloud may be appropriate for reading goals that do not involve the ability to decode), such as students' ability to analyze a theme or understand character development.

The key issue in classroom summative assessment, then, is offering alternatives that hold all students to the same high standard and do not change the construct being assessed or simplify and reduce the rigor of the learning goal. In attempting to respond to English learners, however, teachers may provide scaffolding that not only acts to reduce the language load of instructional and assessment tasks, an appropriate accommodation if language is construct-irrelevant, but also reduces their cognitive demand (see Chang et al., 2017). For example, rather than having ELs write or outline an explanation of the causes of a historical event, the teacher may give students a series of sentence starters to fill in that provide the explanation. This issue encapsulates the more formal concern of standard 3.11—that when tests are changed to improve access to some constructs, the developers and/or users are responsible for documenting the validity of the resultant scores.

Here, too, as in the first cluster, the demands and purposes of classroom assessment may require a broader lens to not only reduce barriers for English learners and students with disabilities, but to maximize all students' learning and ability to perform (e.g., for example by appealing to student agency, interests and motivation) (CAST, 2011; Shepard et al., 2018; Tierney & Koch, 2016). In contrast to typical standardized testing, classroom assessment may offer students options and choices to promote their engagement, such as in project-based learning, exhibitions, presentations, research or other reports, or other performances that may serve as culminating assessments. The trick, of course, is to hold the construct constant across different task variations, which underscores the necessity to be very clear on the expectations of classroom learning goals and what constitutes construct-relevant performance, which must remain conceptually consistent, and what constitutes construct-irrelevant aspects of performance, and thus can be allowed to vary.

Universal Design

The principles of UDL (CAST, 2011) also offer guidance for adapting both formative and summative assessment to meet individual needs. As mentioned earlier, the principles call for multiple modes of engagement, multiple modes of action or performance, and multiple forms of representation. Each principle is elaborated by a series of guidelines and more specific checkpoints for classroom practice. The guidelines and checkpoints related to multiple modes of engagement offer suggestions that may be useful for devising summative assessment options supporting student motivation and agency. For example, one guideline suggests optimizing relevance and authenticity "by varying activities and sources of information so that they are

- Personalized and contextualized to learners' lives
- Culturally relevant and responsive
- Socially relevant
- Age and ability appropriate
- Appropriate for different racial, cultural, ethnic, and gender groups.

(CAST, 2011)

The UDL guidelines and check points may also provide apt suggestions for formative assessment probes and scaffolds when gaps in understanding are in evidence. For example, the principle of "provide multiple means of representation" includes the guideline "provide options for comprehension." The checkpoints are:

- activate or supply background knowledge;
- highlight patterns, critical features, big ideas, and relationship;
- guide information processing, visualization, and manipulation; and
- maximize transfer and generalizability.

(CAST, 2011)

Each of these checkpoints, with its elaboration, offer potential sources of gaps in learning and suggest strategies for filling them.

Validity of Accommodations

Although the quantitative analyses encouraged by the *Test Standards* may not be feasible for classroom teachers, teachers' qualitative analysis of the validity of any assessment variations is feasible. Teachers should consider: Does the variation still measure the same learning goal and incorporate the same high expectations? Will student responses provide a good or equivalent indicator of how well students have accomplished the goal? Do any available scaffolds support non-construct-related aspects of the task or are they part of the learning goal?

The remaining standards in this cluster focus specifically on accommodations that might be needed for students whose home language is not English and who are not proficient in the language of the assessment. These standards speak to the difficulty of translating an assessment from one language to another (standard 3.12) and to the desirability of implementing assessment in the language that is most relevant and appropriate to the test purpose (standard 3.13). For classroom assessment, research suggests that the language of instruction, with appropriate language supports as needed, is the most appropriate language for assessment (Abedi, Lord, & Hofstetter, 1998; Liu, Anderson, Swierzbin, & Thurlow, 1999; Turkan & Oliveri, 2014).

The accommodations cluster in the fairness standards continues to underscore important themes for classroom assessment: clarity in the construct or learning to be measured and the need for deep knowledge of individual students' background, prior experience, and other characteristics that may influence their learning and performance. The *Test Standards* promote maximizing assessment accessibility by being attuned to the interaction between individual characteristics and assessment conditions and providing accommodations that will minimize construct-irrelevant barriers (Dolan, Rose, Burling, Harms, & Way, 2007; Ketterlin-Geller, 2008). The standards here open the door toward an equity perspective in fairness.

In the classroom assessment context, we not only want to reduce construct-irrelevant *barriers*, but potentially enable construct-appropriate options that respond to a fuller range of student characteristics and interests, and thereby enable students to maximize their performance. In a related vein, Mislevy et al. (2013) have noted that equivalent surface conditions in an assessment do not necessarily yield equivalent evidence about what different students know and can do, and have argued instead for flexibility in an assessment's surface characteristics, but not the underlying construct, so that examinees can better show their capability.

Safeguards against Inappropriate Evidence Interpretations for Intended Uses

Several of the standards in this section apply largely to publicly reported and/or high-stakes tests and seem less relevant for classroom assessment. Two, however, represent important principles for classroom assessment as well. First, as noted earlier, users should not use the results of one assessment as the sole indicator of a student's learning, attitudes, or dispositions; instead, multiple sources of information and the judgment of professionals should be brought to bear on decisions (standard 3.18; see also standard 12.10).

The issue of opportunity to learn, which is a frequent concern in broader discussions of fairness in assessment (Camilli, 2006; Gipps & Stobart, 2009; Tierney, 2013), also draws attention. The fairness standards advise that students should not suffer negative consequences—such as low grades—if they are assessed on content they have not had the opportunity to learn (standard 3.19; see also standard 12.8). There is wide agreement across communities on this issue, including students who perceive it as unfair when they are tested on content they have not had the opportunity to learn (Rasooli et al., 2018; Tierney, 2013).

Here, too, classroom assessment offers a broader lens for both viewing and supporting opportunity to learn and fairness in assessment. Classroom assessment precepts encourage teachers to communicate and discuss learning goals and success criteria with students, so that students will be clear on what they are expected to learn, a key to students' perceptions of fairness (Camilli, 2013; Rasooli et al., 2018), and can play a more active role in their own learning (e.g., see Bailey & Heritage, 2018; Gipps & Stobart, 2009; Tierney, 2013). Through classroom formative assessment, students may have more effective opportunities to learn and achieve classroom learning goals (e.g., see Black &Wiliam, 1998; Herman, 2013; Kingston & Nash, 2011).

Discussion and Conclusion

In this final section, we consider the *Test Standards* definition of fairness in light of broader perspectives on fairness in assessment, consider what we know about the current status of classroom practice relative to the fairness standards, and end with concluding thoughts on future directions.

Fairness in Classroom Assessment: The Test Standards in Relation to Broader Views

This article has summarized the *Test Standards* perspective on fairness in testing and applied it to classroom assessment. The perspective derives from the basic definition of fairness as assessment that is "responsive to individual characteristics and testing contexts so that test scores will yield valid interpretations for intended uses" (AERA et al., 2014, p. 50), and starts from the basic proposition that:

> All steps in the [assessment] process, including [assessment] design, validation, development, administration and scoring procedures should be designed in such a manner as to minimize construct-irrelevant variance and to promote valid score [evidence] interpretations for the intended uses for all examinees in the intended population.
>
> (p. 63)

In other words, fairness is an issue of validity and assuring that classroom assessment provides valid evidence for all students in a classroom, and not just the average student or the majority.

Although, as mentioned earlier, the *Test Standards* approach to fairness may seem narrow to some, it responds to issues that the *Standards* developers felt are under the control of test developers and users—rather than other stakeholders or the larger society. The approach also links intimately with broader views of assessment, which we now consider.

Broader Views of Fairness

At the most basic level, fairness means "Impartial and just treatment or behavior without favoritism or discrimination" (Fairness, n.d.). Few could disagree with such a concept, and the literature reveals that perceptions of fairness actually can influence students' learning, motivation, and satisfaction with teachers and teaching (Rasooli et al., 2018). But what constitutes "just" treatment is open to considerable debate.

Some have considered just treatment and fairness as a matter of equality of inputs, which, as we have seen, is a fundamental principle in standardized testing. Everyone gets the same or equivalent test, with the same directions, under the same conditions. Because the inputs are the same, it is thought that students' scores, the outputs, will be influenced as little as possible by administration circumstances, and all students thus will have an "equal" opportunity to demonstrate their knowledge. By emphasizing the control of construct-irrelevant variation and bias and the importance of equality of meaning, the *Test Standards* essentially seem to give heavy weight to this "equality" view of fairness.

Equal treatment and identical treatment, however, are not one and the same in other dominant views of fairness. As the international *Declaration of Principles of Equality* notes, "To realise full and effective equality it is necessary to treat people differently according to their different circumstances, to assert their equal worth and to enhance their capabilities to participate in society as equals" (Equal Rights Trust, 2008, p. 5). Both the *Test Standards'* attention to accessibility and accommodations and the whole idea of formative assessment clearly incorporate this view of fairness. That is, assessment tools and strategies need to be adapted to be sensitive to individual characteristics that otherwise could impede access and compromise the validity of evidence for some students. The whole notion of formative assessment, furthermore, speaks to the need to monitor students' ongoing learning, tap into individual sources of challenge, and adapt and differentiate assessment and instruction to meet individual needs, reflecting more of an equity perspective.

The *Declaration of Principles of Equality* goes on to stress that positive action is needed to combat prior disadvantage and to accelerate progress toward equality. Although the *Test Standards* definition of fairness definitely excludes this push toward equality of outcomes, it is the case that fair assessment can enable more effective action toward that goal. Subsequent action may be outside the scope of the *Test Standards* definition, but the potential for effective action, as previously noted, will likely be thwarted if it is not fueled by accurate evidence on all students' learning.

Fairness in Classroom Assessment: Status of Classroom Practice

Fairness in classroom assessment, based on the *Test Standards*, thus may not provide an all-encompassing view of fairness, but it does—at the very least—present the critical underpinning to such fairness. What may seem to be a fairly narrow, measurement-oriented view provides necessary but perhaps not fully sufficient conditions for fair assessment. Importantly, the *Test Standards* advance fairness as an overarching foundation and fundamental consideration for all assessment. How does current teaching and classroom practice comport with these perspectives? The answer, in brief, is that we know very little.

Certainly, as noted earlier, *Standards for Classroom Assessment* exist (Klinger et al., 2015), as do state standards for the teaching profession, which almost always incorporate standards related to teachers' assessment practices. However, these standards tend to emphasize the process of assessment rather than the quality of the assessment evidence.

For example, one of California's six *Standards for the Teaching Profession* (Commission on Teacher Credentialing, 2009) focuses on "assessing students for learning" and indicates that teachers should be able to:

- Apply knowledge of the purposes, characteristics, and uses of different types of assessments.
- Collect and analyze assessment data from a variety of sources and use those data to inform instruction.
- Review data, both individually and with colleagues, to monitor student learning.
- Use assessment data to establish learning goals and to plan, differentiate, and modify instruction.
- Involve all students in self-assessment, goal-setting, and monitoring progress.
- Use available technologies to assist in assessment, analysis, and communication of student learning.
- Use assessment information to share timely and comprehensible feedback with students and their families.

Issues of fairness (e.g., in using assessment to differentiate and modify instruction) are embedded within this long list of competencies.

Similarly, the Illinois teaching standards say, in regard to assessment, "The competent teacher understands various formal and informal assessment strategies and uses them to support the continuous development of all students" (Illinois State Board of Education [ISBE], 2010), and also lay out a substantial list of more specific competencies that emphasize knowledge and use of assessment, but not their quality. Again, issues of fairness are embedded within a long list of performance indicators (e.g., "Uses assessment strategies and devices which are nondiscriminatory and take into consideration the impact of disabilities, methods of communication, cultural background, and primary language on measuring knowledge and performance of students").

Perhaps one can assume that the quality of classroom assessment is implicit in these standards, but on what basis can we determine whether teachers are actually able to implement high-quality, fair assessment? The literature is largely absent direct measures of teacher practice.

Paucity of Relevant Assessments of Teachers or Practice

Traditional exams required for teacher credentialing tend not to go into great depth on assessment issues, much less fairness in assessment, and even more performance-oriented teacher assessments tend to blend attention to classroom assessment within broader issues of pedagogical practice and to embed even further issues related to fairness in classroom assessment.

For example, the National Board for Professional Teaching Standards (NBPTS) threads classroom assessment expectations through the three major components of its teaching task assessment: differentiation in instruction, teaching practice and learning environment, and reflective practitioner. Attention to fairness in assessment (as defined in this chapter), however, appears implicit in only the first component, differentiation of instruction, where expectations include having "a thorough knowledge of students as individual learners" and being "able to accurately and thoughtfully describe and analyze student work in ways that recognize student progress" (NBPTS, 2017, p. 21). The bottom line is that these exams can provide little explicit evidence of teachers' abilities to implement fair classroom assessment.

The same is true for commonly used observation protocols for evaluating teacher practice. For example, the Danielson Framework (Danielson, 2013) encompasses four major domains, and assessment issues explicitly surface in two of them: planning and preparation, and instruction. One of the six elements in the planning domain addresses designing and student assessment, which stresses the congruence between assessments and outcome expectations, a critical issue in opportunity to learn and the fairness of classroom assessment, and also includes attention to the availability of modified assessments for individual students who need them. Within the domain of instruction, using assessment in instruction is one of five aspects of performance, and the criteria here focus on process: being explicit on assessment criteria, continual monitoring, feedback to students, and involving students in self-assessment and monitoring of progress. This again leads to a major implication of this chapter's definition: we know little about the fairness of classroom assessment practices, and research is needed to clarify this critical area of classroom assessment practice and to consider the best ways to promote it.

It is interesting that although the Danielson Framework does not include assessment dimensions that map fully to the definitions here, its conceptualization of the "knowledge of students with the planning and preparation" domain encompasses critical aspects of knowledge, in addition to assessment knowledge, that teachers need to provide fair classroom assessment (i.e., knowledge of students' skills, knowledge, and language proficiency, of student interests and cultural heritage, and of students' special needs). That is, both to reduce construct-irrelevant barriers and to enable students to fully show what they know in classroom assessment, teachers must first know the characteristics of their students relative to language proficiency, cultural background, and prior experience that might otherwise compromise the validity of assessment. And then they must know how to adapt assessment to these characteristics.

Needed Knowledge and Skill

Teachers need sophisticated disciplinary and pedagogical knowledge, along with specialized assessment literacy, to engage in the kind of classroom assessment expected in today's standards-based classrooms (Chin & Teou, 2009; Heritage, 2018; Shepard, 2005; Tierney, 2013). In the simplest case, teachers need to be able to lay out an effective progression of disciplinary learning and to use assessment to probe, scaffold, engage, and propel diverse students, who are at different points along the way, to success on complex learning goals and to be able to gauge student progress and achievement with fair and valid assessment. Taking diversity seriously, teachers must bring to bear their knowledge about diverse students with that about assessment, an integration that is challenging for teachers (DeLuca & Lam, 2014). Teachers need to understand and customize classroom instruction and assessment to their students' prior experience, cultures, and other characteristics, as well as to incorporate, monitor, and support multiple goals simultaneously (e.g., instruction for English learners optimally will incorporate both disciplinary goals and those for English language development).

What limited data we have about teachers' capacities in this area raises cause for concern. For example, surveys of teachers' assessment literacy and practices continue to show gaps and struggles, and experts have called for professional development to build teachers' assessment capacity to support new standards (e.g., see Clare-Matsumura & Pascal, 2003; Coombs, DeLuca, LaPointe-McEwan, & Chalas, 2018; DeLuca & Klinger, 2010; DeLuca, Valiquette, Coombs, LaPointe-McEwan, & Luhanga, 2016; Maclellan, 2004; Mertler, 2009; NRC, 2001b, 2014; Popham, 2014; Stiggins, 2002). Adding to this challenge, the critical mandate for fairness for an increasingly diverse student population—and what this means for the knowledge teachers must possess about their students—makes the calculus even more demanding.

Thus, we need to know more about teachers' capacity to engage in fair assessment. Similarly, because teachers often rely on their curriculum materials for their assessment tools and strategies, so too do we need to understand the current status of curriculum-embedded classroom assessments (i.e., those that accompany text and other curriculum materials). We know these tend to be in wide use, so leveraging their greater attention to fairness could provide important supports for teaching and toward fairness assessment and equity in learning. For teachers and publishers alike, fairness in assessment cannot be an afterthought, but must be built in from the get-go.

Concluding Thoughts

Knowing more about the current status of fairness in classroom assessment practice is a first step in understanding and addressing any needs for improvement, and certainly this is a critical mandate given the growing diversity in today's classrooms. But through what lens should we view that practice? In applying the fairness standards to classroom assessment, this chapter makes the case that the validity and fairness of the classroom assessment evidence that teachers use—be it teacher-developed, or available through curriculum materials or other sources—need substantial attention. We also think that classroom assessment, like the *Test Standards*, would benefit from an overarching focus on fairness. That is, every step in the process through which teachers and students gather, interpret, and use evidence of student learning for a variety of purposes (p. 244) ought to be guided by attention to fairness.

We suspect that both classroom assessment and measurement theorists and specialists would easily agree at an abstract level with such a focus, but at the same time the chapter has identified areas of tension in the theorists' views of fairness and in their conceptions of the enterprise of interest. We summarize some of these tensions with the intent to build future bridges.

A first issue is the perspective on fairness itself and the tension between equality and equity. As we have seen, the *Test Standards* lean heavily toward standardization to support equality of score meaning, while still opening the door to equity with some flexibility in assessment to eliminate construct-irrelevant barriers to performance. However, the changes permitted by current accommodations not only maintain the construct, but stick closely to the original assessment items or tasks. Classroom assessment, in contrast, aims toward sensitivity to individual learning needs, across a range of characteristics, to support equity in all students' learning. Classroom assessment not only encompasses a wider range of assessment types (e.g., including extended projects, presentations, exhibitions, or other applications), but also may permit more varied and authenic options (e.g., by offering students a choice of topics and/or modes of representation for a culminating research or design project).

In responding to such variation, measurement specialists might question whether these variations maintain the intended construct and well represent target standards and/or learning goals and stress the need to do so in classroom assessment, as advised by the fairness standards. At the same time, the social-cultural perspectives informing modern classroom assessment

(Shepard et al., 2018) might suggest to measurement specialists that maintaining equality of meaning is more complex to accomplish than simply standardizing tasks and scoring. By better responding to student identity, culture, interests, and the interactive processes through which students develop capability, variations in the surface features of an assessment—such as holding students to the same criteria but permitting choice—may yield a better and fairer estimate of student capability. Might measurement specialists want to consider how they can extend their methodologies to deal with such surface variations in tasks that maintain the given goal(s) or construct(s) but enable all students to well demonstrate their knowledge and skill? As cited earlier, Mislevy et al.'s (2013) work on "conditional inference" moves us in this direction.

A second issue is that the conception of assessment similarly differs between the two, as we have repeatedly noted throughout the chapter. Although the fairness standards' focus on the quality of evidence is clearly a foundation for classroom assessment, it is only a part of what is involved in assuring the fairness of the classroom assessment *process*. In contrast to the *Test Standards*, where the fairness of score inferences are predicated on a particular use, the use of assessment for instructional decision-making is part and parcel of the classroom assessment process; and rather than seeking to be independent of specific contexts, the process of classroom assessment incorporates and is interactive with local context, as is most obviously the case in ongoing formative assessment. Currently, these latter issues are beyond the purview of measurement theory and the *Test Standards*. Should they continue to be? Or are there ways to extend and apply measurement concepts to the benefit of the classroom assessment process? How might measurement theory and the *Test Standards* benefit from the active consideration of broader fairness issues in classroom assessment?

We close by noting that the large-scale assessments that are currently the focus of the *Test Standards* certainly impact the quality of education for most schoolchildren. However, we could argue that this impact would be even greater if these standards could influence the quality and fairness of classroom assessment that touches every student daily and guides their ongoing learning. The experience of writing this chapter reminds us that there is much to be learned at the intersection of measurement theory and classroom assessment. Both areas can inform the other, and we hope to continue the dialog.

Notes

1 We have purposely skipped standard 3.3 because it deals with including relevant subgroups in psychometric studies of validity and reliability/precision, which seem unlikely for teachers' assessments.

2 Standard 3.6 adds the caveat that this should be done "when credible evidence indicates that test scores may differ in meaning for relevant subgroups in the examinee population," but in the world of education there is nearly always credible evidence, even if popular belief, that the scores are biased.

3 Standard 3.7 has not been included here because it deals with the differential prediction of a criterion and does not seem relevant to classroom assessment, and the sample sizes are insufficient to support such analyses.

References

Abedi, J. (2010). *Performance assessments for English language learners*. Stanford, CA: Stanford University, Stanford Center for Opportunity Policy in Education.

Abedi. J. (2011). *Language factors in the assessment of English learners: The theory and principles underlying the linguistic modification approach*. Washington, DC: LEP Partnership. Retrieved from https://ncela.ed.gov/files/uploads/11/abedi_sato.pdf

Abedi, J., Hofstetter, C., & Lord, C. (2004). Assessment accommodations for English language learners: Implications for policy-based empirical research. *Review of Educational Research, 74*(1), 1–28.

Abedi, J., Lord, C., & Hofstetter, C. H. (1998). *Impact of selected background variables on students' NAEP math performance*. CSE Technical Report No. 478. Los Angeles, CA: University of California, National Center for Research on Evaluation, Standards, and Student Testing. Retrieved from www.cse.ucla.edu/products/reports/TECH478.pdf

Almond, P., Winter, P., Cameto, R., Russell, M., Sato, E., Clarke-Midura, J., Torres, C., Haertel, G., Dolan, R., Beddow, P., & Lazarus, S. (2010). Technology-enabled and universally designed assessment: Considering access in measuring the achievement of students with disabilities—a foundation for research. *Journal of Technology, Learning, and Assessment, 10*(5), 4–49. Retrieved from www.jtla.org

American Educational Research Association (AERA), American Psychological Association (APA), & National Council on Measurement in Education (NCME). (2014). *Standards for educational and psychological testing.* Washington, DC: American Educational Research Association, American Psychological Association, & National Council on Measurement in Education.

Bailey, A., & Heritage, M. (2018). *Self regulation in learning: The role of language and formative assessment.* Boston, MA: Harvard Education Press.

Beddow, P. A., Elliott, S. N., & Kettler, R. J. (2009). *TAMI accessibility rating matrix.* Nashville, TN: Vanderbilt University. Retrieved from http://peabody.vanderbilt.edu/tami.xml.

Bishop, R., Berryman, M., Cavanagh, T., & Teddy, L. (2009). Te Kotahitanga: Addressing educations disparities facing Mallori students in New Zealand. *Teaching and Teacher Education, 25*(5), 734–742.

Black, P., Harrison, C., Hodgen, J., Marshall, B., & Serret, N. (2010). Validity in teachers' summative assessments. *Assessment in Education: Principles, Policy & Practice, 17*(2), 215–232.

Black, P., & Wiliam, D. (1998). Inside the black box: Raising standards through classroom assessment. *Phi Delta Kappan, 80*(2), 139–148.

Brookhart, S. (2001). Successful students' formative and summative uses of assessment information. *Assessment in Education, 8*(2), 153–169.

Brookhart, S. (2009). The many meanings of multiple measures. *Educational Leadership, 67*(3), 6–12.

Brookhart, S. M. (2011). Educational assessment knowledge and skills for teachers. *Educational Measurement: Issues and Practice, 30*(1), 3–12.

California Department of Education. (2017). *CalEdFacts.* Sacramento, CA: California Department of Education. Retrieved from www.cde.ca.gov/ds/sd/cb/cefelfacts.asp

Camilli, G. (2006). Test fairness. In R. Brennan (Ed.), *Educational measurement* (4th ed., pp. 221–256). Westport, CT: ACE/Praeger Series on Higher Education.

Camilli, G. (2013). Ongoing issues in test fairness. *Educational Research and Evaluation, 19*(2–3), 104–120.

CAST. (2011). *Universal design for learning guidelines version 2.0.* Wakefield, MA: CAST. Retrieved from www.udlcenter.org/research/researchevidence

Chang, S., Lozano, M., Neri, R., & Herman, J. (2017). *High leverage principles of effective instruction for English learners.* Los Angeles, CA: Center for Standards and Assessment Implementation. Retrieved from www.csai-online.org/resources/high-leverage-principles-effective-instruction-english-learners

Chin, C., & Teou, L. Y. (2009). Using concept cartoons in formative assessment: Scaffolding students' argumentation. *International Journal of Science Education, 31*(10), 1307–1332.

Clare-Matsumura, L., & Pascal, J. (2003). *Teachers' assignments and student work: Opening a window on classroom practice.* CSE Technical Report #602. Los Angeles, CA: CRESST.

Commission on Teacher Credentialing (2009). *California standards for the teaching profession.* Retrieved from www.ctc.ca.gov/docs/default-source/educator-prep/standards/cstp-2009.pdf

Coombs, A., DeLuca, C., LaPointe-McEwan, D., & Chalas, A. (2018). Changing approaches to classroom assessment: An empirical study across teacher career stages. *Teaching and Teacher Education, 71*, 134–144.

Cowie, B. (2015). Equity, ethics and engagement: Principles for quality formative assessment in primary science classrooms. In C. Milnes, K. Tobin, & D. Degennaro (Eds.), *Sociocultural studies and implications for science education: The experiential and the virtual* (pp. 117–133). Dordrecht: Springer.

Danielson, C. (2013). *Framework for teaching.* Retrieved from http://danielsonframeworkforteaching.weebly.com/domain-1.html

DeLuca, C., & Klinger, D. A. (2010). Assessment literacy development: Identifying gaps in teacher candidates' learning. *Assessment in Education: Principles, Policy & Practice, 17*, 419–438.

DeLuca, C., & Lam, C. (2014). Preparing teachers for assessment within diverse classrooms: An analysis of teacher candidates' readiness. *Teacher Education Quarterly, 41*(3), 3–24.

DeLuca, C., Valiquette, A., Coombs, A., LaPointe-McEwan, D., & Luhanga, U. (2016). Teachers' approaches to classroom assessment: A large-scale survey. *Assessment in Education: Principles, Policy & Practice, 25*(4), 355–375.

Dolan, R., Burling, K., Harms, M., Strain-Seymour, E., Way, W., & Rose, D. (2013). *A universal design for learning-based framework for design accessible technology-enhanced assessment.* Retrieved from http://images.pearsonclinical.com/images/tmrs/dolanudl-teaframework_final3.pdf

Dolan, R. P., Rose, D. H., Burling, K. S., Harms, M., & Way, W. (2007, April). *The universal design for computer-based testing framework: A structure for developing guidelines for constructing innovative computer-administered tests.* Paper presented at the National Council on Measurement in Education Annual Meeting, Chicago, IL.

Equal Rights Trust (2008). *Declaration of principles of equality.* Retrieved from www.equalrightstrust.org/ertdocumentbank/Pages%20from%20Declaration%20perfect%20principle.pdf

Fairness. (n.d.). In *Oxford English dictionary online*. Retrieved from www.oed.com

Gipps, C., & Stobart, G. (2009). Fairness in assessment. In C. Wyatt-Smith & J. Cumming (Eds.), *Educational assessment in the 21st century* (pp. 105–118). Dordrecht: Springer.

Guitart, M., & Moll, L. (2014). Funds of identify. *Culture and Psychology, 20*(1), 31–48.

Heritage, M. (2008). *Learning progressions: Supporting instruction and formative assessment*. Washington, DC: CCSSO. Retrieved from www.k12.wa.us/assessment/ClassroomAssessmentIntegration/pubdocs/FASTLearning Progressions.pdf

Heritage, M. (2018). Making assessment work for teachers. *Educational Measurement: Issues and Practice, 37*(1), 39–41.

Herman, J. (2013). *Formative assessment for Next Generation Science Standards*. Princeton, NJ: ETS. Retrieved from www.ets.org/Media/Research/pdf/herman.pdf

Herman, J. (2016). *Comprehensive standards-based assessment systems supporting learning*. Los Angeles, CA: Center for Standards and Assessment Implementation. Retrieved from www.csai-online.org/resources/comprehen sive-standards-based-assessment-systems-supporting-learning

Hirsch, E. D., Jr. (2003). Reading comprehension requires knowledge—of words and the world. *American Educator, 27*(1), 10–29.

Illinois State Board of Education (ISBE). (2010). *Standards for all teachers*. Retrieved from www.imacc.org/com moncore/illinois_teaching_standards.pdf

Ketterlin-Geller, L. (2008). Testing students with special needs: A model for understanding the interaction between assessment and student characteristics in a universally designed environment. *Educational Measurement: Issues and Practice, 27*(3), 3–16. http://dx.doi.org/10.1111/j.1745-3992.2008.00124.x

Kingston, N., & Nash, B. (2011). Formative assessment: A meta-analysis and a call for research. *Educational Measurement: Issues & Practice, 30*(4), 28–37.

Klinger, D., McDivitt, P., Howard, B., Rogers, T., Munoz, M., & Wylie, C. (2015). *Classroom assessment standards for preK-12 teachers*. Kalamazoo, MI: Joint Committee on Standards for Educational Evaluation.

Liu, K., Anderson, M., Swierzbin, B., & Thurlow, M. (1999). *Bilingual accommodations for limited English proficient students on statewide reading tests*. NCEO State Assessment Series, Minnesota Report No. 20. Minneapolis, MN: University of Minnesota, National Center on Educational Outcomes.

Maclellan, E. (2004). Initial knowledge states about assessment: Novice teachers' conceptualisations. *Teaching and Teacher Education, 20*(5), 523–535.

McMillan, J. H. (2011). *Classroom assessment: Principles and practice for effective standards-based instruction* (5th ed.). Boston, MA: Pearson Education.

Mertler, C. A. (2009). Teachers' assessment knowledge and their perceptions of the impact of classroom assessment professional development. *Improving Schools, 12*(2), 101–113.

Mislevy, R., Haertel, G., Cheng, B., Ructtinger, L., DeBarger, A., & Murray, E. (2013). A "conditional" sense of fairness in assessment. *Educational Research and Evaluation, 19*(2–3), 121–140.

Moll, L., Amanti, C., Neff, D., & Gonazalez, N. (1992). Funds of knowledge for teaching: Using a qualitative approach to connect homes and classrooms. *Theory into Practice, 31*(2), 132–141. Retrieved from www.jstor.org/stable/147639

Moll, L. C., Soto-Santiago, S., & Schwartz, L. (2013). Funds of knowledge in changing communities. In K. Hall, T. Cremin, B. Comber, & L. Moll (Eds.), *International handbook of research on children's literacy, learning and culture* (pp. 172–183). Chichester: Wiley-Blackwell.

National Board for Professional Teaching Standards (NBPTS). (2017). *Scoring guide: Understanding your scores*. Retrieved from www.nbpts.org/wp-content/uploads/NBPTS_Scoring_Guide.pdf

National Center for Education Statistics (NCES). (2017). *Condition of education*. Retrieved from https://nces.ed.gov/pubs2017/2017144.pdf

National Center for Education Statistics (NCES). (2018). *2017 NAEP mathematics & reading results*. Retrieved from www.nationsreportcard.gov/reading_math_2017_highlights/

National Research Council (NRC). (2001a). *Classroom assessment and the national science education standards*. Washington, DC: National Academies Press. https://doi.org/10.17226/18409

National Research Council (NRC). (2001b). *Knowing what students know: The science and design of educational assessment*. Washington, DC: National Academies Press. https://doi.org/10.17226/10019

National Research Council (NRC) (2014). *Developing assessments for the Next Generation Science Standards*. Washington, DC: National Academies Press. https://doi.org/10.17226/18409

Pewewardy, C. (2002). Learning styles of American Indian/Alaska Native students: A review of the literature and implications for practice. *Journal of American Indian Education, 40*(3), 22–56.

Pearson, P. D., Hansen, J., & Gordon, C. (1979). The effect of background knowledge on young children's comprehension of explicit and implicit information. *Journal of Reading Behavior, 11*(3), 201–209.

Pitoniak, M., Young, J., Martiniello, M., King, T., Buteux, A., & Ginsburgh, J. (2009). *Guidelines for the assessment of English learners*. Princeton, NJ: ETS.

Popham, W. J. (2014). *Classroom assessment: What teachers need to know* (5th ed.). Boston, MA: Pearson Education.

Popham, W. J. (2017). *Classroom assessment and what teachers need to know* (8th ed.). Upper Saddle River, NJ: Pearson.

Pressley, M., Wood, E., Woloshyn, V., Martin, V., King. A., & Menke, D. (1992). Encouraging mindful use of prior knowledge: Attempting to construct explanatory answers facilitates learning. *Educational Psychologist, 27*(1), 91–109. doi:10.1207/s15326985ep2701_7

Rasooli, A., Zandi, H., & DeLuca, C. (2018, March). Reconceptualizing classroom assessment fairness: A systematic meta-ethnography of assessment literature and beyond. *Studies in Educational Evaluation, 56,* 164–181.

Sato, E. (2010). Culture in fair assessment practices. In J. Hong & Robert Lissitz (Eds.), *Test fairness in a new generation of large scale assessments* (pp. 147–160). Charlotte, NC: Information Age.

Sato, E. (2011). *A guide to linguistic modification: Increasing English language learner access to academic content.* Washington, DC: LEP Partnership. Retrieved from https://ncela.ed.gov/files/uploads/11/abedi_sato.pdf

Shepard, L. (2005). Linking formative assessment to scaffolding. *Educational Leadership, 63*(3), 66–70.

Shepard, L., Penuel, W., & Pellegrino, J. (2018). Classroom assessment principles to support learning and avoid the harms of testing. *Educational Measurement: Issues and Practice, 37*(1), 52–57.

Solano-Flores, G. (2008). Who is given tests in what language by whom, when, and where? The need for probabilistic views of language in the testing of English language learners. *Educational Researcher, 37*(4), 189–199.

Stiggins, R. (2002). Assessment crisis: The absence of assessment *for* learning. *Phi Delta Kappan, 83*(10), 758–765.

Thompson, S., Johnstone C., & Thurlow, M. (2002). *Universal design applied to large scale assessments.* Synthesis Report 44. Minneapolis, MN: University of Minnesota, National Center on Educational Outcomes. Retrieved from http://education.umn.edu/NCEO/OnlinePubs/Synthesis44.html

Tierney, R. D. (2013). Fairness in classroom assessment. In J. H. McMillan (Ed.), *SAGE handbook of research on classroom assessment* (pp. 125–144). Thousand Oaks, CA: SAGE.

Tierney, R. D., & Koch, M. J. (2016). Privacy in classroom assessment. In G. T. L. Brown & L. R. Harris (Eds.), *Handbook of human and social conditions in assessment* (pp. 267–283). New York: Routledge.

Turkan, S., & Oliveri, M. (2014). *Considerations for providing test translations accommodations to English language learners on Common Core standards-based assessments.* Research Report ETS RR-14-05. Princeton, NJ: ETS.

Valencia, R. (Ed.). (1997). *The evolution of deficit thinking.* Washington, DC: Falmer.

Willingham, W. W., & Cole, N. S. (Eds.). (1997). *Gender and fair assessment.* Mahwah, NJ: Lawrence Erlbaum Associates.

Wilson, M. (2018). Making measurement important for education: The crucial role of classroom assessment. *Educational Measurement: Issues and Practice, 37*(1), 5–20.

Winter, P. C., Kopriva, R. J., Chen, C.-S., & Emick, J. E. (2006). Exploring individual and item factors that affect assessment validity for diverse learners: Results from a large-scale cognitive lab. *Learning and Individual Differences, 16,* 267–276.

Zieky, M. (2016). Developing fair tests. In S. Lane, M. Raymond, & T. Haladyna (Eds.), *Handbook of test development* (2nd ed., pp. 81–99). New York: Routledge.

Zipin, L. (2009). Dark funds of knowledge, deep funds of pedagogy: Exploring boundaries between lifeworlds and schools. *Discourse: Studies in the Cultural Politics of Education, 30*(3), 317–331. doi:10.1080/01596300903037044

14

Discussion of Part III
Emerging Issues in Classroom Assessment

Mark Wilson

In this chapter, I will first review the three chapters in the "Emerging Issues in Classroom Assessment" part of this volume, taking each on its own terms, and commenting on what I see as noteworthy and/or questionable in each. In the second part of the review, I then consider some themes that span the three chapters and add my own perspectives to discuss some issues that, at this point in time, I see as being important regarding the relationship between classroom assessment and measurement.

The Importance of Teacher Grades

The first chapter in this section is by Alex J. Bowers: "Towards Measures of Different and Useful Aspects of Schooling: Why Schools Need Both Teacher-Assigned Grades and Standardized Assessments." This title lays out a strong aim for the chapter, seeking to establish that there are important and distinct purposes for both grades and standardized tests in schools.

I will take a step back to try to understand why this question is so important. My own K-12 educational experience (in the Australian state of Victoria) was focused very heavily on school grades, with standardized tests making only one or two fleeting appearances. This was also the experience of U.S. students until the 1940s when the SAT and the ACT tests became more common, although, of course, these tests were only for those who reached the top end of high school—and then that was far fewer than today. Although sample-based testing was common in some states earlier on (e.g., the CAP program in California), it was not until the 1970s that standardized testing became common, and not until the 1990s that it became universal with the federal NCLB program. But in the ensuing years, standardized tests have grown enormously in importance in the educational context. This was accompanied by the establishment of state standards, which initially had the measurement purpose[1] of ensuring that tests reflected accurately what should be taught in the schools. But the reality in the classroom is that the tests are present in the classroom while the standards are on a website somewhere else, often unread, and hence the message being given to teachers is that they should teach whatever the tests test. Thus, the implication is that teachers' grades of their students should reflect what the tests test.

With this in mind, then, the import of the question about "grades versus tests" is that many policymakers in education act as though they believe that standardized tests indicate the true grades that students should get. My own view is much more in line with the sentiment expressed in the second half of Bowers' title: yes, schools do need *both* standardized tests and grades.

In his chapter, Bowers initially lays out a wide-ranging and convincing research literature base supporting the proposition that "grades in high school include teacher perceptions of student effort, participation and behavior that is a different and useful measure for schools and school leadership beyond what can be provided by standardized test scores" (Bowers, this volume, p. 209). I will not repeat his arguments in detail here, but do note a few of the salient points he brings to bear:

(i) Grades have consistently been found to correlate at about 0.5 with standardized test results[2] (Linn, 1982).

(ii) Grades are significant predictors of important life events and achievements, such as college enrollment (Atkinson & Geiser, 2009), college completion (Attewell, Heil, & Reisel, 2011), and annual earnings (Miller, 1998).

(iii) Teachers report that they give grades based on student characteristics that go beyond student test performance, several of which one would expect to be related to test performance, such as "effort, ability, improvement, work habits, attention and participation" (McMillan, 2001, reported in Bowers, this volume, p. 212).

(iv) Researchers have attempted to elucidate what it *is* that teacher grades are assessing, but there is no universal consensus on this. Some ideas put forward have been: a "conative" factor (Willingham, Pollack, & Lewis, 2002), engaged participation (Kelly, 2008), a "common grade dimension" (Klapp Lekholm & Cliffordson, 2008), and a "success at school factor" (Bowers, 2009). The latter two seem somewhat circular in their conceptualization. Bowers concludes the review, mainly based on the work of Kelly (2008), that "grades have been shown to be a strong multidimensional assessment of both academic knowledge and student engaged participation in schooling" (Bowers, this volume, p. 213).

(v) In his review, Bowers seeks to counter the notion that teacher grades have a "hodge-podge" and/or a "kitchen-sink" nature (Cizek, Fitzgerald, & Rachor, 1995–1996). He concludes that the review also "provides a strong argument for the validity of grades as a multidimensional assessment" (Bowers, this volume, p. 213).

Following this review, he describes a specific study he has carried out to illuminate the findings of the review. I will first comment on the review described above, and then proceed to describe and discuss the study.

First, considering (i) above, given the background I described above about the perceived importance of standardized tests in education, it seems surprising that teachers are still so resistant to fully align their grades with standardized test performances—they persist in maintaining only a 0.5 correlation with standardized tests. Bowers (this volume, p. 214) noted studies confirming this dating from 2001 to 2016. However, in my view, we should congratulate teachers for maintaining their practice of being sensitive to broader criteria than standardized tests. In historical terms, the policy "press" has been going the other way for a long time. I would interpret this to be associated with a foundational position of the teacher profession—*what is most important are the students*. Teachers are, in general, decidedly giving their best judgments of students through the grades they assign. These grades are related to students' performances on standardized tests (as they should be if the tests are "valid"), but where the tests fall short teachers are certainly prepared to go beyond the test results. The findings, noted in (ii) above, which show the relevance of grades for important life events after schooling, confirm that these efforts to go beyond test results are broadly successful.

Second, considering (iii) above, the content of what is contained in grades beyond tests becomes much clearer: "effort, ability, improvement, work habits, attention and participation" (McMillan, 2001, reported in Bowers, this volume, p. 212). I agree with Bowers (this volume) that this is a list of personal characteristics "that are important for overall life outcomes and are valued by students, parents, schools, and future employers" (p. 212). This is no doubt one reason why we see the findings in (ii). It certainly makes sense that all these characteristics would be associated with test performance, but it would be dubious indeed to expect that test performance would be a good summary of them all (although, indeed, these student characteristics may themselves have contributed to student achievement). Hence, it makes sense that one should value teachers' grades for summarizing more than what is conveyed by standardized tests. In fact, it is, in part, this logic that has led to the current focus on assessment of "twenty-first-century skills" and "socio-emotional skills" in K-12 education. Interestingly enough, there have not been calls to use grades as an indicator of these.

Third, considering (iv) above, although Bowers makes an argument for Kelly's work as providing sufficient evidence for the vision of "academic knowledge and student engaged participation" as being the underlying constructs behind teacher grades, his argument, in my view, does not give sufficient grounds to accept his conclusion. It is not clear, for instance, how "student engaged participation" matches McMillan's much broader set (*sans* achievement, of course): effort, improvement, work habits, attention, and participation. In particular, what would be needed here to establish his claim would be an account of how one would test such a hypothesis methodologically (e.g., one approach could be a confirmatory factor analysis or multidimensional IRT analysis), and this is lacking. I think the jury must still be out on this specific conclusion by Bowers.

Fourth, considering (v) above, the final conclusion of his review that he has provided "a strong argument for the *validity* of grades as a multidimensional assessment" (Bowers, this volume, p. 213, emphasis added), I am afraid this too is lacking. There is no comprehensive account of what is even meant by "validity" in his argument. There is a long history of the examination of validity in the educational measurement literature, and the accepted standards (American Educational Research Association [AERA], American Psychological Association [APA], & National Council on Measurement in Education [NCME], 2014) give a list of five important strands, and demand an argument that spans across them. There is no engagement with this standard of professional work, and hence I do not see "a strong argument for the validity of grades as a multidimensional assessment" (Bowers, this volume, p. 213) in this chapter.

Turning now to the final part of Bowers' chapter, he argues for "the usefulness of grades as accurate assessments of classroom engaged participation." Now, there are several ways that one could interpret this statement:

(a) Probably the most common choice that data analysts might make—how well can we predict student engagement from teacher grades?

(b) Perhaps a likely candidate in an NCME-sponsored volume—how well would student engagement be *measured* by teacher grades?

If we used the logic of the first approach, then we would set up a regression predicting student engagement from grades. If we used the second, then we would set up a measurement model for the latent variable of student engagement, and use observations of grades as indicators of that—we could report typical measurement results such as reliability indices, standard errors, etc. Examples of both such approaches are in the literature, and are reported by Bowers (this volume). However, Bowers' analysis proceeds in a different direction that I do not see as being useful for this purpose. I will not go into the details of the specific analyses, given the overarching problem, but will note that, in my view, several specific steps and calculations need careful re-examination, in particular the calculation and interpretation of proportion of variance accounted for in a multilevel situation, and the complexities of interpreting the predictions of grades using the *residuals* from the test results.

In summary, I see much to be applauded in Professor Bowers' summary of the literature establishing a unique and important role for teacher grades in the classroom and beyond. The delineation of multiple aspects of what goes into teacher grades, such as effort, ability, improvement, work habits, attention, and participation, is very valuable. And pointing to the evidence for how this explains the strength of teacher grades to predict later life outcomes (beyond that of achievement tests) is important. However, the connection of this literature to the specific study described in the chapter seems mis-designed to me. Alternative approaches would seem more direct and more interpretable, especially when "multidimensionality" is a central concept.

Technological Innovations in Classroom Assessment

The second chapter in this part is by Michael Russell: "Digital Technologies: Supporting and Advancing Assessment Practices in the Classroom," and the title very appropriately summarizes the aims of the chapter. Professor Russell's chapter surveys recent developments in the ways that technology has been entering into classrooms over the last decade or two.

He initially, and helpfully, provides wide-ranging definitions of both technology and assessment. "Assessment" he defines as "the process of purposeful evidence gathering to support claims and subsequent decisions about a student or a group of students" (Russell, this volume, p. 225), which helps move the common focus away from the aspect of assessment that is usually most prominent—the visible aspects, such as images of items, or (in the more informal case) the dialogue among teacher and students. Of course, in thinking about technology, one might substitute screenshots and "chat" on a website. In contrast, his definition is focused on the purpose of the assessment (the "subsequent decisions"), and the logic and evidence on which those decisions are to be based ("purposeful decisions"). This helps avoid simplistic thinking about assessment—it is not a matter of "WYSIWYG" (what you see is what you get), but rather that what you get (i.e., the decision) has a complex relationship to the visible aspects of the assessments (i.e., the item text, student responses, etc.). I will return to this issue later.

He also defines "technology": "a specialized set of procedures or methods for accomplishing a task" (Russell, this volume, p. 226). This too is helpful, as it frees our thinking about technology from its typical binding today to electronic devices. Indeed, in past ages, technology has been seen as residing "in" quite different materials. For example, the age of the sailing ship has been referred to as depending on a technology of wood, and rope (where knots are the "software of rope!") (De Decker, 2010). Even within education, other sorts of technology have been important, from the "blackboard and chalk" of the nineteenth century to the "SRA kits in boxes" so new and promising in the 1960s. Again, this helps us focus attention away from the visibles of edtech to the purpose of the technology—focusing the decisions to be made on the basis of the assessments. I will return to this issue later.

Following the setting of a broad background, Russell embarks upon the main body of his review. This consists of two different areas of innovation: (a) the assessment of understanding in the classroom; and (b) enhancement of assessment information.

In the first area, he begins by surveying new ways that classroom technology can enhance data gathering from students to improve assessment. One type is typified by "clickers," small handheld devices that allow every student's response to questions to be gathered and displayed in the classroom, thus avoiding the traditional reliance on a light sample from the most eager students to dominate. Typically, these devices are limited in their response range, but are nevertheless capable of modifying lecture-style classroom contexts to make them more interactive education environments. Where personal computers are available, the response range can be made much wider, and computer-based interactivity becomes available in the form of "quizzing software." The assessment items and their sequence can be pre-supplied by software vendors, or can be open for teachers to create their own tests. This development has the potential to be a very significant impact on classrooms, especially in combination with the next broad innovation.

The second innovation in data gathering involves new item and task types that become available with technology—again, he distinguishes two types. On the one hand, *technology-enhanced* items add new media and content to items that have not been available in traditional paper-and-pencil formats, such as video clips, sound-based material, cartoon animations, and various sorts of simulations. On the other hand, *technology-based* items allow students to respond in ways that are not available in traditional testing, such as following through on investigations in simulated environments that interact with the sequence of student actions.

The third innovation in data gathering involves the diagnosis of student misconceptions and misunderstandings. This aspect of innovation brings us much closer to the purpose of assessment and the technology, by allowing the storage and examination of evidence of a student's solution processes in solving a problem, not merely considering the correctness of the final outcome. He sees this as being "effective for improving student learning" (Russell, this volume, p. 232), but unfortunately provides only one example, and references a few others in a burgeoning field.

This third aspect of data gathering has close links to the second major area of innovation that he describes, the *enhancement of assessment information*. Under this designation, he identifies three major innovations: (a) the ability to use assessment information as an indicator of student engagement and persistence (mainly through the process data mentioned in the previous paragraph); (b) the addition of curriculum-based information to the interpretation of assessment results using the technology of "standards" that is now so common in K-12 education; and (c) the enhancement of accessibility that technology can offer beyond the traditional paper mode, using combinations of technology-enhanced and technology-based strategies to address the various challenges that many students face, culminating in the ideas of universal design.

Following these surveys of innovations, Russell rounds out his review by also discussing three *challenges* raised by these innovations. First, regarding equity, he points out that the advantages afforded by technology, as noted in this previous section, will tend to exacerbate gaps between well-off and poorer schools due to the relative abundance of technology in the former. Second, regarding privacy, he notes the potential for "assessment by stealth" to become common, where students are not aware about what aspects of their interactions with software are being recorded and used, and even not being aware of being assessed at all. Third, related to the broadening of accessibility delineated in the previous paragraph, he discusses how this may complicate the interpretation of student performance—although this seems much less problematic than what was previously the case—where they were, in the main, left out altogether.

Professor Russell concludes with an important observation: "It is essential that the 'glitz' of these new assessment tools does not outshine the construct relevance of the evidence provided by these tools," and I commend this thought to the reader. The coverage of content and issues in this chapter, is, in my view, very thorough and thoughtful, with many useful observations being made along the way. It provides a comprehensive overview for a newcomer to the field and orients them to the main thrusts and issues of the multitude of ways that technology is affecting assessment. That said, it is a bit out of date regarding the latest developments in the technology of assessment. Of course, it is hard to keep up, as this is a very rapidly developing field, as its impetus is driven not so much by research and development in educational assessment, but rather by the commercial possibilities that are seen by software development companies in the education sector of technology enterprises. Perhaps one way to keep up is to read the proceedings of the relevant conferences in this area. For example, one could read through the latest compilation of papers from the 2017 Technology Enhanced Assessment conference (Ras & Guerrero Roldan, 2018), or even better go along to this year's conference. For example, some more recent developments that could be included are the integration of assessment into computerized educational software (Scalise, 2018), the field of learning analytics (e.g., Wilson, Scalise, & Gochyyev, 2017), and the potential complexities of how technology interacts with the "gaps" that impede educational progress (Paul, 2014).

Fairness

The third chapter in this part is by Joan Herman and Linda Cook: "Fairness in Classroom Assessment." The authors quote the definition of fairness from the classic *Standards for Educational and Psychological Testing* text (AERA et al., 2014) as "assessment that is responsive to individual characteristics and testing contexts so that test scores will yield valid interpretations for intended uses," and note that this is "a fundamental validity issue" (Herman & Cook, this volume, p. 244). They see the need for fairness to be considered throughout the teaching/learning cycle, not just for the assessment part of that cycle. Further, they note that the *Standards* incorporate four aspects of fairness: fairness in treatment, fairness as reducing measurement bias, fairness as opportunity to learn, and fairness as access to the construct being measured. And they also quote the relevant overall standard (which I also quote here, as I think it is worth rereading):

> All steps in the testing process, including test design, validation, development, administration and scoring procedures should be designed in such a manner as to minimize construct-irrelevant variance and to promote valid score interpretations for the intended uses for all examinees in the intended population.
>
> (AERA et al., 2014, p. 63)

They expand upon this for the related fairness standards, and they invoke useful and important concepts as they survey the field, concepts, and distinctions, such as testing "accommodations" (where the construct does not change) and testing "adaptations" (where it does). The coverage and discussion of these topics is very comprehensive and nuanced, and strongly connected to relevant literature. The reader will benefit both from the completeness and depth of the discussion.

In their concluding sections, Herman and Cook take a more expansive view of fairness, going outside the usual sphere of educational testing, to discuss how the narrow professional view can be expanded by considering, for example, the larger perspectives offered by the Equal Rights Trust's *Declaration of Principles of Equality*. Here, they note that a deeper concept of fairness should entail concepts that relate to the broader society in which the assessment takes place. One such is the idea that identical treatment may not, in fact, be equal treatment (an idea already broached in the discussion of accommodations and adaptations). And they then go on to observe that certain aspects of fairness may require not just fairness in treatment, but also positive action to strive toward equality of outcomes. This, presumably, would be informed by assessment, but that is not usually included in the range of actions within assessment. One way to see how this perspective does indeed relate to fairness in assessment is to consider what it might mean if otherwise valid outcomes of assessment had been found to consistently have differential outcomes for different groups—in this circumstance, the fairness of the assessments themselves would be "nice," but surely that would be found to be very much lacking value in the face of the persistent problem of inequality. That this does indeed apply here is clear—given the ample evidence of maintained racial and ethnic inequalities in educational outcomes, even when conditioned on SES, and so on. This expanding view is then related to questions of what "just" treatment is, leading to a discussion of distributed justice, procedural justice, and interactional justice. The authors have made a strong case for the concept of fairness in classroom assessment being seen in a more expansive way in their chapter.

Herman and Cook conclude their chapter by focusing on the implications of their chapter for practice in classrooms, a very important contribution, and one that would have strengthened the previous two chapters. Here, they point out that, despite very detailed listings of what should be included in teacher classroom practices in state teacher standards, including references to fairness as one of the important characteristics, very little is known about the actual *quality* of teacher classroom practice regarding assessment, including, of course, the qualities regarding fairness. They cite the need for increased attention to the need for teacher professional development in this area (including, of course, attention at the pre-service level), and note that this has been the subject of advisories from the National Research Council (NRC, 2001, 2014).

Synthesis and Reactions

Looking across these three chapters, and considering their joint contributions, one can get a general impression that: (a) there are major changes on the way for classroom assessment; yet (b) little is known about what actually goes on in the classroom, specifically with respect to assessment (although assessment is only one area where such lacunae exist). This is due partly to the classic context of the classroom as a "closed-door" space where the teacher and his or her class are relatively isolated from the rest of the world, but also partly due to the very interactive and ephemeral nature of assessment within the classroom space. Much of what we might term as "assessment" occurs in talk between teacher and students, and among students, and even when there are written parts of the assessment, such as teacher quizzes and student written response, these tend to be quite idiosyncratic, hard to retrieve, and hard to interpret when they are examined. Of course, there has been very important research done in observing and working in classrooms, as is evident in the contents of the chapters of this volume, and also including significant work done in other countries such as the work of the Assessment Research Group in the UK (Association for Achievement and Improvement through Assessment [AAIA], 2017).

But the introduction of interactive digital technology into the classroom portends to change all of this dramatically. As informational hardware invades the classroom, in the shape of smartphones, iPads, and other web devices, laptops, and desk computers, and with the associated Internet connectivity, the gathering of both traditional and new forms of evidence will become (eventually) pervasive. This will open the classroom space as it has never been open before, making available data that could be used for assessment on a scale never known before. Moreover, the software and connectivity made available by that hardware also brings the possibility for very fast analysis of these data within the classroom (as well as at higher levels of aggregation, such as schools, districts, etc.). This is, in my view, the major event "on the horizon" for educational measurement at this point in time (for *much* more on this, see Wilson, 2018).

In my view, in this coming revolution, the main way that assessment-related technology will enter into the classroom is not in the form of classical "measurement," but rather as an integrated part of classroom software that will do much more than just measure. There will be: (a) apps that provide supplementary instructional tools to the teacher, such as homework apps, quizzing apps, and drilling apps; (b) apps that help the teacher be organized; (c) apps that take the place of teachers; and (d) tools that surveil the classroom in one way or another.

In this invasion of attention into the classroom, the role of assessment will be highlighted, and possibly the role of measurement diminished. Assessment will be highlighted because the way that all these apps will initially interact with teachers and students will be by gathering data from the classroom, making assessment a focus of much attention. The possible diminishment of measurement will occur because the designers and purveyors of these many apps that will be available in the edtech marketplace will likely not be well connected to the educational measurement profession or literature. In the main, they will be well connected to the parts of the I.T. business that are centered on the education domain, such as companies that develop and sell learning/teaching software, and to the domain of learning analytics. The connections between measurement and the edtech companies are, at best, idiosyncratic, depending on personal contacts and histories. The connection between measurement and the learning analytics are somewhat negative, as they can be seen as intellectual and professional competitors having overlapping domains—there are some efforts being made to span that space (Wilson, Scalise & Gochyyev, 2016, 2017), but such efforts are not something that is seen as "mainstream" at the current time.

Moreover, even if these connections were strong, it is not clear to me that the field of educational measurement is ready to cope with the demands of these developments. The heart of this goes back to the definition of assessment offered by Russell in Chapter 12, and already quoted above, but I will do so again, as I think it is worth paying attention to: assessment is "the process of purposeful evidence gathering to support claims and subsequent decisions about a student or a group of students" (Russell, this volume, p. 225). The point is that the provision of "scores" and "estimates," the usual products of educational measurement, even if accompanied by an indication of uncertainty, is less than what is needed to carry out this role. It may suffice in the context of the current focus of educational measurement on large-scale state and national testing where there are well-established forms and processes for interpretation. But it will not suffice in the classroom situation where the product needs to be information that can be tied very closely and readily to teacher interpretations and teacher decisions. This has not been a focus of educational measurement, which has seen it as a "user issue," and that has left educational measurement poorly prepared for this situation.

What would educational assessment need to look like if it were to fulfill this function of being integrated into a decision-making scenario? One thing it would need to do would be to have a means of articulation between the educational intents of the teacher and the outcomes from the assessments. This would have to relate the usual measurement outcomes (scores or estimates) to the sorts of decisions that the teacher needs to make, whether they were decisions about individual students or groups of students, and whether the decisions were in-the-moment actions or required for medium-term planning of instruction. Moreover, teachers' workloads must not be increased by this, so that the burden of development of the materials should not be borne by teachers while they are teaching—although, of course, teachers need to be involved in the development process.

One such approach has been developed by the Berkeley Evaluation and Assessment Research (BEAR) Center, called the BEAR Assessment System (Wilson, 2005; Wilson & Sloane, 2000), by combining the curriculum and standards ideas of learning progressions with statistical modeling using Rasch scales, and applying that combination to teacher-managed and classroom-based assessment of student performance. The BEAR Assessment System consists of interrelated components that are congruent with national assessment reform efforts (NRC, 2001, 2014) as well as the measurement *Standards* (AERA et al., 2014). The assessment system is based on the idea of measuring developmental trajectories of students as they progress through their education—these learning progressions are built up from construct maps that embody the curriculum intentions (Wilson, 2009). An implementation of the BEAR Assessment System is constructed using embedded assessments, which are based on the purposes and content of the instruction in which the assessments are embedded, and which produce student responses that can be mapped back to the levels of the initial construct maps (Black, Wilson, & Yao, 2011). Data are collected to allow these responses to be scaled, thus allowing the student estimates to be: (a) interpreted in terms of the levels of the construct maps; and (b) produced from differing sets of items under different circumstances (Wilson, 2005). In addition, direct judgments of student locations can also be integrated into the system, allowing a convergence of item-based and judgmental data. The BEAR Assessment System has been implemented within a range of educational contexts, including achievement settings such as early childhood (Choi, Park, Lee, Burmester, & Wilson, 2016), science education (Morell, Collier, Black, & Wilson, 2017), mathematics learning (Lehrer, Kim, Ayers, & Wilson, 2014), non-cognitive settings such as tolerance for diversity (Hermisson, Gochyyev, & Wilson, in press) and collaborative problem-solving (Zhang, Wilson, Alom, Awwal, & Griffin, 2018), and in teacher professional development (Duckor, Draney, & Wilson, 2017).

This is not the only such approach, however—a very general approach called evidence-centered design (ECD) has been developed by Mislevy, Almond, and colleagues (Mislevy, Steinberg, & Almond, 2003), and this approach is particularly useful in contexts where there are multiple purposes for the assessment. The main thrust of such approaches is to focus on the interpretation of the assessment outcomes for decision-making. The current state of measurement in education has been largely influenced by the traditional perspective, focused on the production of statistical estimates of group abilities in large-scale settings, where the interpretations were to be made for policy purposes. This has been rhetorically supported by also supplying individual-level estimates to parents and students, but the interpretations at this level have not been directed at specific decisions that the parents must make.

Taking the focus into the classroom offers a completely different perspective—one where the educational interpretations must be more focused on specific decisions and need to be actionable within the classroom. The possibility of making a positive contribution relies heavily on the ease of application, the swiftness of information return, and the usefulness of the information for classroom decision-making. With the help of information technology, the ease and swiftness can be achieved. But it will take assessment technology, such as the BEAR or ECD approaches, to channel measurements to be interpretable by teachers.

There are other important developments in store for classroom assessment, including the different perspectives offered here, but as I noted above the coming invasion of attention is, in my view, the most important. Sound measurement can have a positive influence on that inevitable invasion, but it will need to expand its range significantly beyond its current "testing industry" perspective.

Notes

1   Of course, these standards have an instructional purpose too—to direct what teachers should be teaching.
2   Bowers later notes that this translates to an approximate R^2 of 25%, and that "A persistent question has thus been: What does the other 75% of grades represent . . .?" (Bowers, this volume, p. 211). This is, of course, an exaggeration, as the 75% "unexplained variance" will include random errors of several kinds (sampling, measurement, etc.), and these will not be scientifically explicable, and hence cannot be said to "explain" anything.

References

American Educational Research Association (AERA), American Psychological Association (APA), & National Council on Measurement in Education (NCME). (2014). *Standards for educational and psychological testing*. Washington, DC: American Educational Research Association, American Psychological Association, & National Council on Measurement in Education.

Association for Achievement and Improvement through Assessment (AAIA). (2017). *Assessment reform group*. Retrieved from www.aaia.org.uk/blog/2010/06/16/assessment-reform-group/

Atkinson, R. C., & Geiser, S. (2009). Reflections on a century of college admissions tests. *Educational Researcher, 38*(9), 665–676. doi:10.3102/0013189x09351981

Attewell, P., Heil, S., & Reisel, L. (2011). Competing explanations of undergraduate noncompletion. *American Educational Research Journal, 48*(3), 536–559.

Black, P., Wilson, M., & Yao, S. (2011). Road maps for learning: A guide to the navigation of learning progressions. *Measurement: Interdisciplinary Research and Perspectives, 9*, 71–123.

Bowers, A. J. (2009). Reconsidering grades as data for decision making: More than just academic knowledge. *Journal of Educational Administration, 47*(5), 609–629. doi:10.1108/09578230910981080

Choi, I.-H., Park, S., Lee, H. K., Burmester, K., & Wilson, M. (2016, April). *Measurement of young children's development using the Desired Results Developmental Profile.* Paper presented at the American Educational Research Association annual conference, Washington, DC.

Cizek, G. J., Fitzgerald, S. M., & Rachor, R. E. (1995–1996). Teachers' assessment practices: Preparation, isolation and the kitchen sink. *Educational Assessment, 3*(2), 159–179.

De Decker, K. (2010). Lost knowledge: Ropes and knots. *Low-Tech Magazine.* Retrieved from www.lowtechmagazine.com/2010/06/lost-knowledge-ropes-and-knots.html

Duckor, B., Draney, K., & Wilson, M. (2017). Assessing assessment literacy: An item response modeling approach for teacher educators. *Pensamiento Educativo: Journal of Latin American Educational Research, 54*(2), 1–26.

Hermisson, S., Gochyyev, P., & Wilson, M. (in press). Assessing pupils' attitudes towards religious and worldview diversity: Development and validation of a nuanced measurement instrument. *British Journal of Religious Education.*

Kelly, S. (2008). What types of students' effort are rewarded with high marks? *Sociology of Education, 81*(1), 32–52. doi:10.1177/003804070808100102

Klapp Lekholm, A., & Cliffordson, C. (2008). Discrepancies between school grades and test scores at individual and school level: Effects of gender and family background. *Educational Research and Evaluation, 14*(2), 181–199.

Lehrer, R., Kim, M.-J., Ayers, E., & Wilson, M. (2014). Toward establishing a learning progression to support the development of statistical reasoning. In A. Maloney, J. Confrey, & K. Nguyen (Eds.), *Learning over Time: Learning Trajectories in Mathematics Education* (pp. 31–60). Charlotte, NC: Information Age.

Linn, R. L. (1982). Ability testing: Individual differences, prediction, and differential prediction. In A. K. Wigdor & W. R. Garner (Eds.), *Ability testing: Uses, consequences, and controversies* (pp. 335–388). Washington, DC: National Academy Press.

McMillan, J. H. (2001). Secondary teachers' classroom assessment and grading practices. *Educational Measurement: Issues and Practice, 20*(1), 20–32.

Miller, S. R. (1998). Shortcut: High school grades as a signal of human capital. *Educational Evaluation and Policy Analysis, 20*(4), 299–311. doi:10.3102/01623737020004299

Mislevy, R. J., Steinberg, L. S., & Almond, R. G. (2003). On the structure of educational assessment (with discussion). *Measurement: Interdisciplinary Research and Perspective, 1*(1), 3–62.

Morell, L., Collier, T., Black, P., & Wilson, M. (2017). A construct-modeling approach to develop a learning progression of how students understand the structure of matter. *Journal of Research in Science Teaching, 54*(8), 1024–1048. doi:10.1002/tea.21397.

National Research Council (NRC). (2001). *Knowing what students know: The science and design of educational assessment.* Washington, DC: National Academies Press. https://doi.org/10.17226/10019

National Research Council (NRC). (2014). *Developing assessments for the Next Generation Science Standards.* Washington, DC: National Academies Press. https://doi.org/10.17226/18409

Paul, A. M. (2014, June 25). *Educational technology isn't leveling the playing field: In fact, it's making achievement gaps even bigger.* Retrieved from https://slate.com/technology/2014/06/neuman-celano-library-study-educational-technology-worsens-achievement-gaps.html

Ras, E., & Guerrero Roldan, A. E. (Eds.). (2018). *Technology Enhanced Assessment: 20th International Conference, TEA 2017, Barcelona, Spain, October 5–6, 2017, Revised Selected Papers.* Heidelberg: Springer International.

Scalise, K. (2018). Next wave for integration of educational technology into the classroom: Collaborative technology integration planning practices. In P. Griffin, E. Care, & M. Wilson (Eds.), *Assessment and teaching of 21st century skills. Vol. 3: Research and applications* (pp. 239–276). Dordrecht: Springer.

Willingham, W. W., Pollack, J. M., & Lewis, C. (2002). Grades and test scores: Accounting for observed differences. *Journal of Educational Measurement, 39*(1), 1–37.

Wilson, M. (2005). *Constructing measures: An item response modeling approach.* Mahwah, NJ: Erlbaum.

Wilson, M. (2009). Measuring progressions: Assessment structures underlying a learning progression. *Journal for Research in Science Teaching, 46*(6), 716–730.

Wilson, M. (2018). Making measurement important for education: The crucial role of classroom assessment. *Educational Measurement: Issues and Practice, 37*(1), 5–20.

Wilson, M., Scalise, K., & Gochyyev, P. (2016). Assessment of learning in digital interactive social networks: A learning analytics approach. *Online Learning, 20*(2), 97–119. Retrieved from https://olj.onlinelearningconsortium.org/index.php/olj/article/view/799/205

Wilson, M., Scalise, K., & Gochyyev, P. (2017). Intersecting learning analytics and measurement science in the context of ICT literacy assessment. In P. Griffin, E. Care, & M. Wilson (Eds.), *Assessment and teaching of 21st century skills. Vol. 3: Research and applications* (pp. 211–223). Dordrecht: Springer.

Wilson, M., & Sloane, K. (2000). From principles to practice: An embedded assessment system. *Applied Measurement in Education, 13*(2), 181–208.

Zhang, Z., Wilson, M., Alom, M., Awwal, N., & Griffin, P. (2018). *Adopting a process perspective of collaborative problem solving.* Paper presented at the NCME annual meeting, New York.

Index

Abedi, J. 250
academic achievement: evidence of 225; grades 212, 218, 219, 220; language practices 46–47, 57; non-cognitive factors 31
accessibility: fairness 248, 250, 251, 253, 256, 257; technology 235–237, 239–240, 269
accommodations: fairness 248, 251, 253–256, 257; technology 239; test administration 102, 106–107, 114
accountability 60, 202, 203; accessibility 248; "accountability creep" 4, 100; culture of 198; large-scale assessments 48, 120; purpose of assessment 122–123; state accountability tests 99, 117; trustworthiness of classroom assessment 140–141
accuracy 7; functional perspective 19, 21, 25; measurement perspective 14–15, 16, 17, 22, 23, 24, 87; *Standards for Educational and Psychological Testing* 115
Achievement-Emotions Questionnaire (AEQ) 33
Adie, L. E. 170
adverse experiences 27
AEM Navigator 239, 240
AEQ *see* Achievement-Emotions Questionnaire
AERA *see* American Educational Research Association
AfL *see* assessment for learning
alignment 102, 105, 110–112
Allensworth, E. M. 220
Almond, R. G. 273
Alonzo, Alicia C. 3, 5, 83, 88–89, 120–145, 193, 194, 199, 203
ambitious teaching 194, 195, 203, 204
American Educational Research Association (AERA) 244, 254, 267
American Psychological Association (APA) 267
analytics 240, 270, 272
Anderson, R. 134
anxiety 38, 39, 40, 48
APA *see* American Psychological Association
apps 227–228, 271–272
argument-based approach 12–14, 132

arguments 49, 50–51
Arter, J. 100–101, 200
Aspire project 5
assessment: challenges to technology-based assessment 238–240; conceptions of 261; cultural practices 204; definition of 224–225, 272; embedded 146–147, 157–167, 200, 201, 252–253, 260, 272–273; for monitoring 162, 165; NGSS 157–158; perspectives on 14–16; sociocognitive 51–52, 54, 59, 60; technology-enhanced 176–188, 233–237, 240, 268–270, 271–272; *see also* classroom assessment; formative assessment; large-scale assessment; summative assessment
assessment for learning (AfL) 82, 100, 196
assets 53, 251
assignments 12, 17, 18, 22, 226
Atkinson, R. C. 210
attachment 34
authentic tasks 230–231
autonomy 172

Bailey, Alison L. 4, 6, 46–62, 81, 83–84, 86
Ball, D. 201
Balzer, W. K. 70, 71
Barajas-Lopez, F. 54
Bass, H. 201
Baxter, G. P. 66
BEAR Assessment System 272–273
behavior 210, 212, 216–217, 225, 245, 266
beliefs 136, 227
belonging 6, 29, 82, 194
benchmark assessments 4, 5, 99, 102, 246
Bennett, R. E. 122, 129, 167n1, 193, 196, 238
Berkeley Evaluation and Assessment Research (BEAR) Center 272–273
bias 7, 16, 49, 90; fairness 248, 250, 253; student ethnicity 219–220; teacher 53
biology 147, 148, 155–156, 158, 160, 161
Black, P. 123, 126, 133, 135–137, 176, 193
Blömeke, S. 133
Boerst, T. 201

Bonner, S. M. 88, 89
Boud, D. 176
Bourgeois, L. 175
Bowers, Alex J. 4, 6, 209–223, 265–268, 273n2
Braaten, M. 194
Braille 236, 237, 254
Briggs, Derek C. 3, 5, 146–169, 193, 194–196, 202, 204
Brookhart, Susan M. 1–7, 122, 129, 192; context of classroom assessment 84, 123; feedback 63–78, 80, 82, 85, 89; grades 210–211; reliability and validity 39–40; *Standards for Educational and Psychological Testing* 6, 97–119, 199
Brown, G. 172, 173
Bruning, R. 69
Buhagiar, M. A. 121
Bustos Gomez, M. C. 36
Butler, D. L. 69, 70, 72

Californian *Standards for the Teaching Profession* 258
Camp, G. 175
Carless, D. 134
Carstensen, C. 128
CASEL *see* Collaborative for Academic, Social, and Emotional Learning
CAST 239, 251
CCCs *see* crosscutting concepts
CCSS *see* Common Core State Standards
CCSSO *see* Chief Council of State School Officers
cell phones 238
challenge 86, 91–92
Chamorro-Premuzic, T. 31
Chappuis, J. 100–101, 200
Chappuis, S. 100–101, 200
CHAT *see* cultural historical activity theory
cheating 102, 109, 117, 173, 187
chemistry 147, 148, 155–156, 158, 160
Chief Council of State School Officers (CCSSO) 46, 121
Clark, D. B. 153
class performance 17, 18, 21, 24
classroom assessment 1–2, 6–7, 192, 271–273; assessment for monitoring distinction 162; context 79, 83–84, 92, 123–125, 134–135; definition of 3–5, 98–100, 224–225; digital technologies 224–242, 268–270, 271–272; fairness 243–264, 270–271; feedback 63–64; goals of 17–18, 21, 29–31, 66–67; importance of 63; language practices 47, 49, 51–60, 86; learning and motivation 79–83, 92; learning from large-scale assessments 48–49; personality traits 31–32; social-emotional factors 34, 35–43, 81, 84, 92; *Standards for Educational and Psychological Testing* 97, 102–118; student-centric focus 79, 85–87, 92; textbooks 200; trustworthiness 120–121, 127–142; types of 100–102; validity 11–26, 39–42, 88–92, 125–127; *see also* assessment;

formative assessment; grades; purpose of assessment; summative assessment
Classroom Assessment Standards 118, 243–244
Classroom Assessment Task Force 1, 2, 199, 200
"classroometric" measurement theory 125–126
"clickers" 177, 226–227, 268–269
co-regulation of learning 98
Coburn, C. E. 198
cognition 30, 31–32, 42
cognitive constructivism 34
cognitive development 30, 225
cognitive feedback 70–71, 72, 74, 75, 76
cognitive processes 102, 104–105, 111, 200
cognitive theory 79–80, 82, 89, 193; feedback 64–65, 66, 74; self-regulation 68–69
Cole, N. S. 250
Collaborative for Academic, Social, and Emotional Learning (CASEL) 30
collaborative learning 46, 49, 50, 195
commercial classroom assessment products 102, 103, 104–109, 252
Common Core State Standards (CCSS) 101, 111, 197, 201, 202, 204
communication 36
competencies 19, 194; functional perspective 20–21; language 46, 57, 59; learning culture 195, 203; measurement perspective 22, 23; self-awareness of 52, 58; *Standards for Educational and Psychological Testing* 103; teachers 135–136, 138, 139, 142; trustworthiness of classroom assessment 133, 136, 138
computer-based instruction 69–70
conceptual frameworks 20, 21–22
conceptually oriented multiple-choice items 161–162, 163–164, 165–166, 167, 202
Concord Consortium 231
connectedness 28, 29, 31, 36
consistency: fairness 252; high-stakes testing 12; reliability 25, 141–142; *Standards for Educational and Psychological Testing* 102, 108, 115–116
construct validity 18, 25, 209
constructivism 34, 79–80, 92; feedback 64–65, 66, 68, 74; learning culture 193
constructs 66, 67–68, 75, 81, 245; fairness in assessment 244, 248, 249–252, 253, 254, 256, 260, 270; formative assessment 49, 247; new item and task types 228; *Standards for Educational and Psychological Testing* 102, 105, 111–112; threats to validity 90
content learning 46–47, 48, 51, 57, 59
content-oriented evidence 102, 103–111
context 79, 83–84, 92, 98, 123–125, 132, 134–135, 247
Cook, Linda 4, 6, 243–264, 270–271
Cowie, B. 129, 130, 131, 137, 173, 248
Cox, M. 212
Crawford, M. 101
Crissman, S. 153

Cronbach, L. J. 11, 14, 15, 22, 25
crosscutting concepts (CCCs) 148, 150–152, 155–157, 160, 162, 166
cultural diversity 28, 29, 86, 251; *Classroom Assessment Standards* 118; language practices 47, 51, 53, 57, 59
cultural historical activity theory (CHAT) 51
cultural practices 135, 204
culture: fairness 248, 250–251, 252, 258, 259, 261; score interpretation validity 253; universal design 255
curriculum: BEAR Assessment System 272; curriculum-embedded assessment 146–147, 157–167, 201, 252–253, 260, 272–273; enacted 18; learning progressions 155–156; school districts 204; standards-based education 234, 269; summative assessment 101, 193; taught 5

DAA *see* Diagnostic Algebra Assessment
Danielson Framework 259
Darling-Hammond, L. 130
data collection: BEAR Assessment System 273; Californian *Standards for the Teaching Profession* 258; "data cycling" 148; digital technologies 224, 240, 272; formative assessment design cycle 163; GENIUs prototype 181; learning progressions 166; privacy issues 238–239; social-emotional factors 33–34; *see also* evidence gathering
data-driven decision-making (DDDM) 193, 198, 202, 203
data integrity 102, 109, 117
Davidson, K. L. 171
DCIs *see* disciplinary core ideas
DDDM *see* data-driven decision-making
DeBoer, G. E. 150, 153, 161
decision consistency 102, 108, 115–116
decision-making 4, 59, 268, 272, 273; "accountability creep" 100; data-driven 193, 198, 202, 203; fairness 245, 261; formative assessment 225; grades 210; technology 239, 240
Declaration of Principles of Equality 257, 270
Dede, Chris 231
deep learning 194, 201, 204
Deming, W. E. 198
DeNisi, A. 64, 197
Diagnoser 232–233, 240
diagnosis 29, 30, 41, 42, 43
Diagnostic Algebra Assessment (DAA) 232, 240
DiBello, L. V. 166
digital technologies 170, 176–188, 196, 224–242, 268–270, 271–272; *see also* technology
Dinsmore, D. L. 83
disabilities: accessibility 235–236; accommodations 248, 254; demographic statistics 243; Illinois teaching standards 258; score interpretation validity 252–253
disciplinary core ideas (DCIs) 148, 150–152, 155–157, 158–160, 162

disciplinary expertise 200–201, 204
disciplinary norms 129–130, 131, 132
discourse analysis 53, 59, 81
discourse practices 49, 51, 53–54, 193, 195, 201, 203; *see also* language practices
diversity 28, 29; accessibility 248; BEAR Assessment System 273; *Classroom Assessment Standards* 118; fairness 252, 259; language practices 47, 51, 53, 57, 59, 86; need for equitable classroom practices 243
Doherty, M. E. 70
Drost, B. 177
Duckworth, A. L. 33–34
Durán, Richard 4, 6, 46–62, 81, 83–84, 86

ECD *see* evidence-centered design
ecological systems view 28, 34, 40
Education Longitudinal Study (ELS:2002) 209, 213, 214, 218, 219
effort 210, 212–213, 216–217, 225, 266–268
Eggen, T. J. H. M. 197
Eisenkraft, A. 158–160
EL students *see* English learner students
ELA *see* English language arts
elaboration 69, 70
ELD/P *see* English language development of proficiency
Elementary and Secondary Education Act (ESSA) 81
elicitation: formative assessment 171; learning culture 195; trustworthiness of classroom assessment 121–122, 129, 131, 133, 135, 136, 139
ELS:2002 *see* Education Longitudinal Study
embedded assessments 147, 157–167, 200, 201, 252–253, 260, 272–273
emergent bilinguals 57–58, 60n3; *see also* English learner students
emotions 27–28, 29, 30, 32–34, 42–43; neuroscience 30–31; personality traits 32; self-regulation 31; student perceptions 85; teachers' messages 36
engagement: accommodations 254; *Classroom Assessment Standards* 118; digital assessment 233–234; educators' decisions 225; grades 212, 213, 214, 220, 267–268; relational aspects of classroom interactions 203; self-assessment 172; self-assessment and peer feedback 186; technology-enhanced assessment 240, 269; universal design 251, 255; *see also* participation
English language arts (ELA) 46, 54–55, 178, 179, 180, 201; *see also* reading
English language development of proficiency (ELD/P) 49–50, 60n2
English learner (EL) students 46–49, 52–54, 57–60, 83–84; accessibility of materials 235–236; accommodations 254, 255; demographic statistics 243; fairness in assessment 244, 248; Lingo Jingo 234; multiple goals 259; score interpretation validity 252; *see also* language practices

Enyedy, N. 54
Equal Rights Trust 257, 270
equality 247, 248, 257, 260–261, 270
equity 203, 243, 256; school districts 202, 204; sociocultural approaches 59; technology 238, 269; tension with equality 247, 248, 260; *see also* fairness
Erickson, F. 137
errors 7, 16, 81; academic 36–37, 38, 84; learning from mistakes 85, 87; single exemplar error 91; underestimation of 90
ethics 42, 117
ethnicity 214–217, 219–220, 243, 252–253, 255
evidence-centered design (ECD) 224–225, 273
evidence gathering 224–225, 226–233, 238, 240, 247, 268–269, 272; *see also* data collection; GENIUs prototype
exemplars 15, 91, 235, 239; self-assessment and peer feedback 174, 175, 177, 178, 179–180; video 187
expectations 19, 22, 87, 218; formative assessment 171; Knotion reporting system 235; learning progressions 245; NGSS 152, 156–157, 164; opportunity to learn 249; self-fulfilling prophecies 219; sociocultural theory 81; student learning objectives 101

fairness 6, 42, 49, 243–264, 270–271; accommodations 249, 253–256; broader views of 257; construct-irrelevant barriers 249–252, 254, 256, 259, 270; core themes 247–249; definition of 244–245; grades 209, 210, 214, 219; high-stakes testing 12; safeguards against inappropriate score interpretations 249, 256; status of classroom practice 258–260; student perceptions 131, 143n9, 245, 256; translation of *Standards for Educational and Psychological Testing* 102, 106–107, 113–114, 116; validity of score interpretation 249, 252–253; *see also* equity
feedback 63–78, 79, 82, 92, 122, 196, 247; academic errors 37; actionable 34–35, 37, 41, 42, 171; Californian *Standards for the Teaching Profession* 258; characteristics of 134; Danielson Framework 259; decision consistency 115; definition of 64–65; definition of classroom assessment 3, 4, 98; Diagnostic Algebra Assessment 232; digital technologies 234; embedded assessments 147; fairness 248; formative assessment design cycle 163; functional perspective 20; goals of assessment 17, 30; indications of persistence 233; information from 71–72, 73, 74, 76; language practices 47, 58; meaning 67–68, 76–77, 80, 84; measurement perspective 22; negative impact of 130, 197; Next Generation Science Standards 166; observations 101; personality traits 32; response to intervention 42; self-assessment 174; single exemplar error 91; social-emotional factors 28, 29, 39, 42, 84; student perceptions 85, 86, 91, 131; task difficulty 91; task focus 38; teacher-student relationships 137; teachers' interpretative frameworks 136; types of 68–71, 73, 74; validation 75–76, 77, 89, 132; *see also* peer assessment/feedback
Ferrara, Steve 3, 4, 6, 97–119, 192, 199
Feskens, R. C. W. 197
Feynman, Richard 149
fine granularity *see* granularity
flexibility of assessment 40–42, 43
fluidity 40, 42, 43, 80
formative assessment 4, 34–35, 84, 170–172, 192–193; accommodations 253; advantage of classroom assessment 59; commercial products 102, 103; context 98; "day-to-day" 48; definitions of 3, 99, 167n1; diagnostic data 30; evidence gathering 247; fairness 113, 248, 249, 251–252, 256, 257; feedback 64, 65, 67, 75–76; formative assessment design cycle 163–164, 167; frequent and flexible 40; functional perspective 20; informal 100, 129; item banks 102; language practices 47, 51, 52, 54–57; LEAFF model 35, 37; learning culture 195, 203; learning-oriented assessment 92; learning progressions 147, 155–156, 162, 165, 167, 246; meanings of 225; methods 101; moment-to-moment 82; motivation 83; as a process 143n7; purpose of assessment 121–122, 123, 244–245; quizzing systems 227–228; rubrics 73; self-efficacy 130; social-emotional factors 81; *Standards for Educational and Psychological Testing* 103, 106, 112–113, 116; student perceptions 85–86; summative assessment linked to 60, 196–197, 201; teaching practices 201; technology-enhanced 176–188, 224; test standards 200; textbooks 200; theoretical models 193–196; trustworthiness 131, 132–138, 139–140, 142; universal design 255; validity and reliability 126–127, 199
Frederiksen, J. 20
frequency of assessment 40–42, 43
"frog-pond" effect 218, 219
Fulmer, G. W. 83
functional perspective 11, 12, 14–17, 19–22, 25, 89; instructional and learning outcomes 84; learning-oriented assessment 92; self-assessment 87
funds of knowledge 195, 251
Furnham, A. 31
Furtak, Erin Marie 3, 5, 146–169, 193, 194–196, 202, 204

Gardner, H. 30
Gee, J. P. 53
Geiser, S. 210
gender differences 217
generalizability 19, 40, 112–113; evidence gathering 226; functional perspective 20, 21;

learning progressions 166; measurement perspective 15–16, 17, 22–24, 25; task reliability 127; trustworthiness of classroom assessment 132; universal design 255
GENIUs prototype 5, 178–187
genres 49, 54
Gipps, C. 70–71, 123
Glaser, R. 66
goals 17–18, 21, 29–31, 34, 54, 60n1; Californian *Standards for the Teaching Profession* 258; constructs 245; definition of learning goal 77n1; fairness in assessment 250, 256; feedback 67–68, 75, 76; formative assessment 171; GENIUs prototype 178, 179, 181; learning culture 195, 203; learning progressions 245; measurement of curricular 201–203; multiple 259; purpose of assessment 245; self-assessment 172, 173–174; setting 82, 83, 86, 163; small and large 66–67; summative assessment 247; teaching practices 201; unit-sized 113
Goldman, S. R. 166
Google Docs 234, 238, 239
grade point average (GPA) 212, 214–216, 218–219, 220
grades 4, 6, 101, 209–223, 265–268; definition of classroom assessment 3; digital tools 177; learning culture 195; motivation 201; multiple measures 143n8; post-tests 123; purpose of assessment 245; standards-based 235; *see also* summative assessment
granularity 40, 43, 66, 80, 110
Gregory, A. 213, 214
grouping 4, 102, 172
growth 123, 140, 146–147
growth mindset 36, 87
growth models of learning 47–48
Guo, Q. 32
Guskey, T. R. 210
Gustafsson, J.-E. 133

Haertel, E. 66
Hallgren, K. 122–123
Hammerness, K. 130
Harris, L. R. 172, 173
Hattie, J. 65, 67, 71, 72, 82
Hearn, J. 172
Heritage, M. 47, 54, 60n1, 134
Herman, Joan 4, 243–264, 270–271
Herrmann-Abell, C. F. 150, 153, 161
high-stakes testing 4, 11, 12, 115, 147–148, 192
history 130
Hodara, M. 212
Hogaboam-Gray, A. 173
"horizontal coherence" 171, 176
Huang, F. 213, 214

identity 6, 81, 82
Illinois teaching standards 258

IMMEX project 230, 231
immigrants 27
Individual Student Assessment Accessibility Profile (ISAAP) 239–240
inferences 17, 18, 88, 100–101, 245; formative assessment design cycle 163; functional perspective 20–21, 84; interpretation/use arguments 13; language practices 53, 54; learning progressions 165, 166; measurement perspective 23–24, 25; reliability of 102, 107–108; social-emotional factors 38; *Standards for Educational and Psychological Testing* 102, 103, 104–109, 112–113, 114–116; validation 75
information 2, 5, 18–19, 24, 29–30; consistency 115–116, 141–142; definitions of classroom assessment 98, 99; feedback 72, 73, 74, 76; functional and measurement perspectives 87; interpretation of 272, 273; for learning 71; from measurement 72–73; qualitative 123; student analytics 240; technological enhancements 233–237, 269; trustworthiness of classroom assessment 139; validity and reliability 126–127
instruction 68, 90–91; ambitious teaching 194, 195, 203, 204; context of classroom assessment 123; fairness 259; functional perspective 12; summative assessment 193
intelligence 36, 37
interaction spaces 228–230
interactions 12, 18, 19, 28, 203; context of classroom assessment 123–124; functional perspective 21; language practices 47, 49, 53, 54–57, 58, 59; measurement perspective 22, 23; social-motivational effects 130, 131; *see also* teacher-student relationships
interim assessments 5, 48, 99, 121, 142n2, 192, 197; "accountability creep" 4; commercial products 102; counterproductive effects of 193, 198, 203; data-driven decision-making 198; learning progressions 246; scholarly analysis 200
interpretation 41, 85, 122, 272; evidence-centered design 273; interpretation quality 133, 134, 135, 138, 139
interpretation/use arguments (IUAs) 13–14, 19, 20, 21, 22, 90
ISAAP *see* Individual Student Assessment Accessibility Profile
item banks 102
item difficulty 111–112
IUAs *see* interpretation/use arguments

James-Burdumy, S. 122–123
Järvelä, S. 29
Jung, L. A. 210

Kane, Michael T. 4, 5, 11–26, 84, 87, 88–91, 132, 166, 225
Kelly, S. 212–213, 218, 266, 267

Kluger, A. N. 64, 197
Knotion reporting system 235, 238–239
Knowing What Students Know (KWSK) 146, 193–194, 196, 201, 203
knowledge: Danielson Framework 259; funds of 195, 251; grades 212, 213, 266, 267; pedagogical content knowledge 18–19, 135–136
knowledge, skills and abilities (KSAs) 234
Konstantopoulos, S. 198
Koretz, D. 88
Kral, M. 175
Kuhn, D. 51
Kulhavy, R. W. 69

lab-based assessment 158–160, 165, 167
Lacy, S. 153, 155
language practices 46–62, 83–84, 86; accommodations 254, 255; fairness 250, 252, 258, 259; limitations of large-scale assessments 47–51; score interpretation validity 253; *see also* English learner students
large-scale assessment 1, 3, 7, 52, 66; accessibility of materials 237; accommodations 114; decontextualized 124–125; fairness 113, 250, 261; feedback 75; language and content learning 46–47, 48, 58; limitations of 47–51, 59; opportunity to learn 116; uses of 120; validity and reliability 39, 99, 126, 127, 142; *see also* standardized test scores; summative assessment
Law, N. 175
LEAFF *see* Learning Errors and Formative Feedback model
learning 2, 6, 79–82, 92; alignment of content and process outcomes 110, 112; co-regulation of 98; contextual complexity 83–84; deep 194, 201, 204; definitions of classroom assessment 3, 4, 99–100; digital technologies 224, 238; feedback 64–65, 67–68, 71–76, 80, 85; formative assessment 126, 170–172, 185; functional perspective 25; goals of classroom assessment 29–31; impact of classroom assessment on 128–132; information for 5, 71; Knotion reporting system 235; language practices 46–47, 54, 57, 58–59, 60; LEAFF model 35, 36, 37; learning culture 193, 194, 195, 203; opportunity to learn 116, 248–249, 256; self-assessment and peer feedback 185, 186–187; self-regulation 68–69; situative views of 72, 74; social-emotional factors 6, 27–30, 34, 38–39, 42–43, 81, 84; sociocognitive learning theory 52, 146, 166, 171, 194; student perceptions 114; summative assessment 122; test standards 200; theories of 146, 193–194, 200, 203; trait versus growth models of learning 47–48; trustworthiness of classroom assessment 142; universal design for 236, 251, 255; validity 12, 89; *see also* learning progressions
learning analytics 270, 272
learning disabilities 235–236

Learning Errors and Formative Feedback (LEAFF) model 35–39, 43, 87
learning-oriented assessment (LOA) 92
learning progressions 146–169, 171, 192, 194–196, 201, 245–246; BEAR Assessment System 272; functional perspective 21; research-practice partnerships 202; sociocognitive models 52; trustworthiness of classroom assessment 138–142
Lee, I. C. H. 83
Leighton, Jacqueline P. 4, 6, 27–45, 80–81, 83–84, 86–87, 89, 232
Li, M. 134
Li, W. 198
life outcomes 209, 211, 212, 266, 267, 268
Lingo Jingo 234, 238
linguistic diversity 28, 29, 86; *Classroom Assessment Standards* 118; language practices 47, 51, 53, 57, 59
Liu, X. 150, 161
LOA *see* learning-oriented assessment
local control 3–4, 5, 98, 99
Lorge, I. 65–66
Lu, J. 175
Luppescu, S. 220
Luxton-Reilly, A. 177
Lyon, Christine J. 4, 5, 86, 170–191, 193, 196, 203

Macfarlane-Dick, D. 175
Marsh, J. A. 197–198
Mason, B. J. 69
mastery orientation 197–198
mathematics 23, 67, 112, 201; accommodations 254; authentic tasks 230; BEAR Assessment System 273; Diagnostic Algebra Assessment 232, 240; fairness in assessment 244; GENIUs prototype 178, 180; grades 214–217, 219; interim assessments 198; language practices 46, 50; measurement 66
Maxey-Moore, Kristen 3, 4, 6, 97–119, 192, 199
McKeough, A. 150
McKown, C. 33, 34
McLuckie, J. 175, 177
McMillan, James H. 1–7, 79–94, 203; definition of classroom assessment 3, 98, 99; formative assessment 123; grades 212, 266, 267; self-assessment 172; social interactions 130; validity 5
McTighe, J. 100
meaning 67–68, 76–77, 80, 84
measurement 1–2, 6–7, 28–29, 63–78, 196–198; "classroometric" measurement theory 125–126; constructs 49, 90; curricular goals 201–203; definition of 64, 65–67; definition of classroom assessment 3; fairness 248, 260–261; impact of technology on 271–272; information from 72–73; interpretations 273; intrusion into the classroom 192, 193; meaning 67–68; measurement perspective 11, 14–17, 22–24, 25,

87, 89; role of 5–6; socio-emotional data 32–34, 38; *Standards for Educational and Psychological Testing* 97; *see also* psychometrics
Meehl, P. E. 25
Messick, S. 28, 32–33, 83
metacognition 31, 59, 136, 172, 186, 203
Meyer, A. 236
Miller, S. R. 198, 211, 212
Minstrell, Jim 134, 161–162, 232
misconceptions 23, 37, 38, 81, 87; formative assessment 171; self-assessment 173; technology to diagnose 231–233, 240, 269
Mislevy, R. J. 89, 224, 236, 256, 261, 273
mistakes 23, 36–37, 38, 84, 85, 87; *see also* errors
mobile devices 227, 238, 271
modifications 248, 253
Molloy, E. 176
Mosher, F. 47, 60n1
Moss, P. A. 20, 25, 124, 126, 143n6
motivation 5, 28, 31, 82–83, 200; definition of classroom assessment 3, 4; educators' decisions 225; feedback 134, 197; grades 201; informal surveys 38; mistakes 87; self-assessment and peer feedback 172, 186; social interactions 130, 203; sociocultural theory 79–80, 92, 194; student perceptions 114; task difficulty 91–92
multiple-choice items: conceptually oriented 161–162, 163–164, 165–166, 167, 202; interim assessments 197, 203; technology-enhanced items 228; trustworthiness of classroom assessment 136, 139
multiple modes of representation 236–237, 251, 254, 255

National Board for Professional Teaching Standards (NBPTS) 259
National Center for Education Statistics (NCES) 211, 213, 214
National Council on Measurement in Education (NCME) 1, 2, 63, 76, 77, 199, 267
National Research Council (NRC) 123, 146, 157–158, 162, 165, 166, 271
National Science Foundation (NSF) 147–148, 202
NBPTS *see* National Board for Professional Teaching Standards
NCES *see* National Center for Education Statistics
NCLB *see* No Child Left Behind
NCME *see* National Council on Measurement in Education
Neumann, K. 150
neuroscience 30–31
Newton, P. E. 88
Next Generation Science Standards (NGSS) 111, 148–152, 155–158, 163–164, 166–167, 194–196, 197, 204
Nicol, D. J. 175
No Child Left Behind (NCLB) 197, 265
Nolen, S. B. 129, 130, 143n8

nominal data 73
Nordine, J. 149
NRC *see* National Research Council
NSF *see* National Science Foundation

observations 12, 17, 18, 213, 245; classification of 73; definition of classroom assessment 3; errors 90; evidence gathering 226; feedback 101; formative assessment 121; informal 225; measurement perspective 23
O'Connor, R. 70
online learning 177, 232
openness to experience 32
opportunity to learn (OTL) 116, 248–249, 256
oral discussion 49, 50, 58
ordinal data 73
Ormrod, J. E. 125
Osborne, J. F. 51
OTL *see* opportunity to learn
outcome feedback 69–70, 74, 75, 76

Panadero, E. 173, 174, 175–176, 187
parents 39, 129, 131, 235, 273
Park, M. 150, 161
participation 209–210, 212–213, 216–218, 220, 266–268; *see also* engagement
Partnership for Assessment of Readiness for College and Careers (PARCC) 228, 237
Patterson, A. 51
PBICs *see* phenomenon-based item clusters
pedagogical content knowledge (PCK) 18–19, 135–136
pedagogy 193, 194
peer assessment/feedback 101, 171–172, 174–176, 196, 203, 245; GENIUs prototype 178, 180–187; language practices 55–57; learning culture 195; opportunities for 178; technology-enhanced 170, 177, 178
peer relationships 31, 36
Pekrun, R. 28, 30, 31, 33
Pellegrino, Jim W. 123, 166, 201
Penuel, William R. 52, 123, 171, 193–194, 201
Perez-Johnson, I. 122–123
performance assessments 6, 85–86, 101, 111, 200, 245
performance-based tasks 158–160, 161, 162, 163–164, 165, 167, 202
performance orientation 197–198
persistence 233–234, 269
personal feedback 71, 74
personality 28, 31–32, 33
phenomenon-based item clusters (PBICs) 160–161, 162, 163–164, 165–166, 167, 202
physics 147, 148–149, 155–156, 158, 160–162, 232, 240
Pianta, R. C. 28, 30
Pierson, A. E. 153
Pitoniak, M. 250
Plato 27

PLCs *see* professional learning communities
policy 4, 5, 83, 123, 131, 273
post-tests 121, 123, 131, 140, 141
poverty 27, 243
pre-assessment 225
pre-tests 121, 123, 131, 140, 141
predictions 18, 19, 20–21, 23, 90–91, 211, 213
prior experience 250–251, 255–256, 259
privacy 238–239, 269
professional development 163–164, 167, 198, 203;
    BEAR Assessment System 273; fairness 260,
    271; learning progressions 202; school districts
    202, 204
professional learning 176, 186–187, 188
professional learning communities (PLCs) 148,
    163, 167, 202
projects 12, 22, 226
psychologists 38, 39
psychometrics 24, 31, 88, 200; grades 209;
    "misfit" 134; reliability and validity 39–42, 120,
    121, 125–127, 139, 142; score precision 115;
    *Standards for Educational and Psychological
    Testing* 97, 102, 118; technology 4
purpose of assessment 12, 63, 79, 121–123,
    244–245; assumptions about 135; evidence-
    centered design 273; *Standards for Educational
    and Psychological Testing* 102, 108–109, 116–117;
    student perceptions 85; trustworthiness 120

qualitative data 73, 76, 80, 123
quantitative data 16, 73, 75, 76
questions 100–101, 201, 226, 227
quizzes 12, 17, 18, 21, 101, 240, 245, 271;
    Diagnostic Algebra Assessment 232; evidence
    gathering 226; item banks 102; Knotion
    reporting system 235; measurement perspective
    22; software and apps 227–228, 269; TAO
    assessment platform 237

Race to the Top (RTTT) 122–123, 198
reading 18, 19, 49; accommodations 254; fairness
    in assessment 250–251; grades 214–216, 219;
    interim assessments 198
reasoning 50; dialogic 55, 56
reinforcement 64, 71
relatedness 28–29, 30–31, 33, 36–38, 40, 42–43
reliability 6, 7, 25, 29, 125–127; aggregate-level
    requirements 202; assessment for monitoring
    162; *Classroom Assessment Standards* 118;
    commercial classroom assessment products
    102; consistency of information 141–142;
    grades 213, 220; guidelines for improving 97;
    large-scale assessment 99, 142; measurement
    perspective 15–16, 22, 23, 24; psychometric
    criteria of 120, 121, 139, 142; social-emotional
    assessment 33, 39–42, 43; *Standards for
    Educational and Psychological Testing* 102,
    107–108, 114–116; textbooks 200; traditional
    notions of 141, 143n9; *see also* trustworthiness

replications 102, 107–108, 114–115
report cards 235
research-practice partnerships (RPPs) 147–148,
    202, 204
responding to interpretations 122
response quality 133, 134, 135, 138
response to intervention 29, 37, 41, 42, 43, 52
rewards 71
rights 102, 108–109, 116–117
Rodriguez-Mojica, C. 57–58
Rolheiser, C. 173
Rose, D. H. 236
Ross, J. A. 173
RPPs *see* research-practice partnerships
RTTT *see* Race to the Top
rubrics 73, 80, 136, 235; digital tools 177; fairness
    252, 253; GENIUs prototype 178, 183–184, 185,
    187; peer assessment 175, 176
Ruiz-Primo, M. A. 70–71
Russell, Michael 3, 224–242, 268–270, 272
Rust, F. 130

Sadler, D. R. 67
Sato, E. 251
scaffolding 54, 55, 150, 164; accommodations
    253, 254; functional perspective 20; GENIUs
    prototype 179–180, 181, 182, 187; peer
    assessment 175, 176; performance-based tasks
    167; self-assessment 173, 174; universal design
    255
school districts 201–202, 204
Schwarz, C. V. 153
science 66, 130; authentic tasks 230, 231; language
    practices 46; learning progressions 147, 149–167;
    Next Generation Science Standards 111,
    148–152, 155–158, 163–164, 166–167, 194–196,
    197, 204; virtual reality 231
scientific and engineering practices (SEPs) 148,
    152, 155, 162
score interpretation validity 102, 103–113, 249,
    252–253, 256–257
security 102, 109, 117
self-assessment 92, 101, 172–174, 196, 203;
    Californian *Standards for the Teaching
    Profession* 258; Danielson Framework 259;
    GENIUs prototype 178, 180–187; learning
    culture 195; opportunities for 171, 178;
    student-centric focus 85, 86–87; student
    perceptions 91; technology-enhanced 170, 176,
    178
self-control 212
self-efficacy 5, 6, 82, 136, 142; formative
    assessment 130; grades 212; mistakes 87;
    relational aspects of classroom interactions 203;
    self-assessment 172
self-fulfilling prophecies 219
self-level feedback 71, 74
self-regulation 6, 31, 79, 82–83, 176, 193; feedback
    68–69, 70, 71, 74, 76, 82; GENIUs prototype

182; learning-oriented assessment 92; mastery orientation 197; mistakes 87; self-assessment 86, 172, 196, 203; sociocultural theory 194; student perceptions 91, 92; task difficulty 91
self-reports 33–34
Senge, P. 198
SEPs *see* scientific and engineering practices
SES *see* socioeconomic status
Shavelson, R. J. 133
Shaw, S. D. 88
Shepard, Lorrie A. 4, 80, 192–206; cultural practices 135; disciplinary content 130; feedback 71; "horizontal coherence" 171; interpretive arguments 166; measurement information 123; motivation 82; pre-tests 140; risk taking 137; sociocognitive models 52; sociocultural theory 51, 59; teachers' interpretive frameworks 136
Sherard, M. K. 153
short-cycle formative assessment 100
Shulman, L. S. 135
Shute, V. J. 65, 69, 70
Siegler, R. S. 40
single exemplar error 91
Sireci, S. G. 228
situative views of learning 72, 74
skills 211, 267
Sleep, L. 201
SLOs *see* student learning objectives
Smarter Balanced Assessment Consortium 50, 228, 237, 239
Smith, J. K. 116
social constructivism 34
social-emotional factors 6, 27–43, 81, 84, 86–87, 92
sociocognitive assessment 51–52, 53, 54, 59, 60
sociocognitive learning theory 52, 146, 166, 171, 194
sociocultural theory 79–80, 81–82, 92; context 247; dialogue and engagement 84; importance of 194; language practices 47, 51, 52–53, 54, 59; learning culture 193, 203; learning progressions 146; patterns of participation 129; prior background and culture 251; teaching practices 201; validity 89
socioeconomic status (SES) 209, 210, 213, 214–218, 219, 252
sociolinguistics 51, 52–53, 57, 59
"soft skills" 211
software 227–228, 269, 270, 271, 272
Soland, J. 213
speaking 49
standardization: aggregate-level requirements 202; assessment for monitoring 162; equality and equity 260; large-scale assessment 12, 120; measurement perspective 15, 22; review of standardized testing 199–200
standardized test scores 209, 210–212, 214, 218–220, 245, 247, 265–266
standards-based education 234–235, 269

Standards for Educational and Psychological Testing 6, 32, 48–49, 97–98, 102–118, 199; BEAR Assessment System 272; fairness 243–245, 247–257, 258, 260–261, 270–271; validity 89
states of emotion *see* emotions
stealth assessment 233, 239, 269
Steedle, J. T. 193
Steinberg, L. S. 273
Stevens, S. S. 73
Stiggins, R. J. 100–101, 200
Stobart, G. 132, 134
Stock, W. 69
Stone, M. H. 67
strengths and weaknesses: definition of classroom assessment 3, 4, 98; functional perspective 20–21, 25; goals of assessment 17–18; measurement perspective 22, 23, 24; task difficulty 91
Stroupe, D. 194
Struyf, E. 134
student analytics 240
student learning objectives (SLOs) 100, 101–103, 104–109, 192, 200
student perceptions 79, 85–86, 92, 114; fairness 131, 143n9, 245, 256; feedback 91, 131; GENIUs prototype 182; goals of assessment 18; of teachers 137
student response systems 177, 226–227, 268–269
student-teacher ratios 217–218, 219
student-work focus sessions 160, 164, 167
success criteria 172, 173, 186; GENIUs prototype 178, 179–181, 182, 187; language practices 51, 52; learning culture 203; *Standards for Educational and Psychological Testing* 109
summative assessment 4, 101, 193, 209, 225; accommodations 253, 254; advantage of classroom assessment 59; anticipatory effects 128–129, 131; assessment for monitoring 162; constructs 90; context 98; data 30; fairness 113, 249, 252; feedback 64, 75–76; formative assessment linked to 60, 196–197, 201; frequent and flexible 40; interim 48; item banks 102; language practices 49–50; large-scale assessment 120; LEAFF model 35, 37, 38; learning culture 195; learning goals 247; learning progressions 155–156, 162, 165, 167, 246; multiple measures 143n8; purpose of assessment 122, 123, 244–245; rubrics 73; shortcomings of 231–232; *Standards for Educational and Psychological Testing* 103, 106, 112–113, 116; technology-enhanced 224, 230; trustworthiness 131, 132; validity and reliability 11, 125–126; *see also* grades
Swineford, F. 211

Tan, K. H. K. 83
Tang, W. 32
TAO assessment platform 230, 237, 240
targets 3, 80, 90–91, 101, 113

task difficulty 19, 21, 22, 86, 91–92
task quality 133, 135, 138
task selection 21
Taylor, C. 129, 130, 143n8
teacher-assigned grades *see* grades
teacher evaluation 122–123
teacher-made assessments 39, 101, 103, 104–109, 111, 121, 123
teacher preparation 53, 118
teacher-student relationships: context of classroom assessment 123–124; social-emotional factors 28, 29, 30, 31, 36; student perceptions 131, 137; trustworthiness of classroom assessment 132, 137, 138
technology 4, 170, 176–188, 224–242, 268–270, 271–272; accessibility 235–237, 239–240, 269; assessment of engagement and persistence 233–234, 269; Californian *Standards for the Teaching Profession* 258; challenges to technology-based assessment 238–240, 269; definition of 226, 268; diagnosing misconceptions and misunderstandings 231–233, 269; gathering responses from students 226–228, 268–269; new item and task types 228–231, 269; standards-based education 234–235, 269
test administration accommodations 102, 106–107, 114
test preparation 102, 105–106, 112–113
test security 102, 109, 117
testing process 102, 106, 113–114
text 72
thinking skills 105, 110, 111, 112
Thompson, J. 194
Thorndike, E. L. 64
Timperley, H. 65, 67, 71, 72, 82
Tobin, R. G. 153
Topping, K. J. 175, 177
Toyama, Y. 54, 59–60
trait models of learning 47–48
transparency 245
trustworthiness 12, 89, 99, 115, 116, 120–121, 127–142
Tunstall, P. 70–71
Turner, E. O. 198

universal design 236–237, 239, 248, 251, 252, 253, 255, 269

validation 5, 11, 15, 132, 225; argument-based approach 12–14; construct 66; context 84; fairness 270; feedback 75–76, 77, 89; learning progressions 162

validity 5–6, 11–26, 29, 49, 99, 125–127, 199; accommodations 255–256; argument-based approach 12–14; *Classroom Assessment Standards* 118; commercial classroom assessment products 102; consequences 143n6; construct 18, 25, 209; fairness 244, 249, 252–253, 256–257, 259, 260; feedback 75–76; grades 211, 213–214, 267; guidelines for improving 97; language practices 59; large-scale assessment 99, 142; learning progressions 165–166, 167; perspectives on assessment 14–16, 87; psychometric criteria of 120, 121, 139, 142; social-emotional assessment 33, 39–42, 43; *Standards for Educational and Psychological Testing* 102, 103–113; textbooks 200; threats to 88–92; traditional notions of 141, 143n9; validity inquiries 132; *see also* trustworthiness
Van der Kleij, F. M. 69, 170, 197
van der Ploeg, A. 198
Van Lier, L. 51
van Popta, E. 175
verification 69, 70, 76
vertical coherence 201–202
virtual reality 231
visual impairment 236–237, 244

warrants 13, 20, 84
Weissberg, R. P. 30
well-being 38, 81
West, M. R. 33–34
Wiggins, G. 100
Wiliam, D. 98–100, 102–103, 123, 126, 133, 135–137, 176, 193, 200
Williams, E. 175
Willingham, W. W. 250
Willis, J. 170
Wilson, H. E. 83
Wilson, Mark 1, 3, 54, 59–60, 79, 128, 265–275
Windschitl, M. 194, 201
Winne, P. H. 69, 70, 72
Wiser, M. 153
Wools, Saskia 4, 5, 11–26, 84, 87, 88–91
working models 35, 37–38
Wright, B. D. 67
Wylie, E. Caroline 4, 5, 86, 170–191, 193, 196, 203

Yeager, D. S. 33–34

Zenisky, A. L. 228
Zieky, M. 250
Zimmerman, B. J. 68–69
Zwiers, J. 101

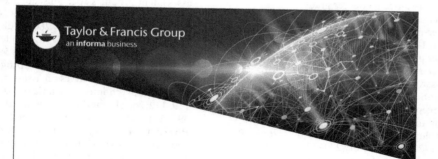